CULTURAL HISTORIES OF CINEMA

This new book series examines the relationship between cinema and culture. It will feature interdisciplinary scholarship that focuses on the national and transnational trajectories of cinema as a network of institutions, representations, practices and technologies. Of primary concern is analysing cinema's expansive role in the complex social, economic and political dynamics of the twentieth and twenty-first centuries.

SERIES EDITORS
Lee Grieveson and Haidee Wasson

FORTHCOMING
Subcinema: Mapping Informal Film Distribution, *Ramon Lobato*

Film and the End of Empire

Edited by **Lee Grieveson and Colin MacCabe**

•

A BFI book published by Palgrave Macmillan

© British Film Institute 2011
Editorial arrangement © Lee Grieveson and Colin MacCabe 2011
Individual essays © their respective authors 2011

First published in 2011 by
PALGRAVE MACMILLAN

on behalf of the

BRITISH FILM INSTITUTE
21 Stephen Street, London W1T 1LN
<www.bfi.org.uk>

There's more to discover about film and television through the BFI. Our world-
renowned archive, cinemas, festivals, films, publications and learning resources are
here to inspire you.

Palgrave Macmillan in the UK is an imprint of Macmillan Publishers Limited, registered
in England, company number 785998, of Houndmills, Basingstoke, Hampshire RG21
6XS. Palgrave Macmillan in the US is a division of St Martin's Press LLC, 175 Fifth
Avenue, New York, NY 10010. Palgrave Macmillan is the global academic imprint of the
above companies and has companies and representatives throughout the world.
Palgrave® and Macmillan® are registered trademarks in the United States, the United
Kingdom, Europe and other countries.

Cover design: keenan
Text design: couch
Images from The Future's in the Air, Strand Film Company; Women of India, Information
Films of India; School for Farmers, Films Division. Government of India; Amenu's Child,
Gold Coast Film Unit; The Knife, Malayan Film Unit; The Big Kitchen, Malayan Film Unit.

Set by Cambrian Typesetters, Camberley, Surrey
Printed in China

This book is printed on paper suitable for recycling and made from fully managed and
sustained forest sources. Logging, pulping and manufacturing processes are expected to
conform to the environmental regulations of the country of origin.

British Library Cataloguing-in-Publication Data
A catalogue record for this book is available from the British Library
A catalog record for this book is available from the Library of Congress
10 9 8 7 6 5 4 3 2 1
20 19 18 17 16 15 14 13 12 11

ISBN 978–1–84457–423–0 (pb)
ISBN 978–1–84457–424–7 (hb)

Contents

FILM/GOVERNMENT/DEVELOPMENT

PROJECTING AFRICA

AFTERTHOUGHTS ON COLONIAL FILM

Contributors

CHARLES AMBLER is Professor of History at the University of Texas at El Paso where he was formerly Dean of the Graduate School. He earned his PhD in African History from Yale University. He is the author or editor of two books and numerous chapters, articles and reviews on various aspects of modern African history, including most recently film and media. His article 'Popular Films and Colonial Audiences', appeared in the *American Historical Review* and has been reprinted in two film anthologies. In 2010 he served as President of the African Studies Association.

GARETH AUSTIN is Professor of International History at the Graduate Institute of International and Development Studies in Geneva. His past employers included the University of Ghana and the London School of Economics (Department of Economic History). His main interests are Ghanaian, West African, African, comparative and global economic history. A former editor of the *Journal of African History*, 2001–5, he is currently President of the European Network in Universal and Global History. Publications include *Labour, Land and Capital in Ghana: From Slavery to Free Labour in Asante, 1807–1956* (2005) and 'Resources, Techniques, and Strategies South of the Sahara: Revising the Factor Endowments Perspective on African Economic Development, 1500–2000', *Economic History Review* (2008). He is currently completing the writing of *Markets, Slaves and States in West Africa* and (with Kaoru Sugihara) and the editing of *Labour-Intensive Industrialization in Global History*.

ANTHONY BOGUES is Harmon Family Professor at Brown University where he is Professor of Africana Studies and Political Science, and an Affiliated Professor in the Department of Modern Culture and Media. He is an Honorary Professor at the University of Cape Town and an associate editor of the journal *Small Axe* and member of the editorial collective of the journal *Boundary 2*. His latest books are *Empire of Liberty: Power, Desire and Freedom* (2010) and *George Lamming and the Aesthetics of Decolonization* (2011).

FILIPA CÉSAR is an artist and film-maker whose work reflects on the porous nature of the relationship between the moving image and its public reception. Informed by her interests in exploring the fictional aspects of the documentary genre, and imbued with an urge to point out the politics behind moving images, works such as *F for Fake* (2005), *Rapport* (2007), *Le Passeur* (2008), *The Four Chambered Heart* (2009) and *Memograma* (2010) walk the thin line between storytelling, chronicling, documentary, and experimental film. César's installations suggest possible settings for an expanded production of moving images, which actively engage the spectator in his or her role as perceiver, and which are constituted by the presence of sociopolitical concerns. César has exhibited at, among other places, Istanbul Biennial, 2003; Kunsthalle, Vienna, 2004; Serralves Museum, 2005; Locarno International Film Festival, 2005; CAG-Contemporary Art Gallery, Vancouver, 2006; Tate Modern, 2007; St Gallen Museum, 2007; International Triennale of Contemporary Art, Prague, 2008; SF MOMA, San Francisco, 2009; 12th Architecture Biennial, Venice, 2010; and the 29th São Paulo Biennial, 2010.

PAUL GILROY teaches at the London School of Economics and Political Science. Before that he worked at Yale and Goldsmiths. Among his publications are *Small Acts* (1993) and *Darker Than Blue* (2010).

FRANCIS GOODING is a writer and researcher whose research interests include colonial history, art history and music. His publications include a book on modernist painting, *Black Light*, and he has written widely on art and music. He worked as a member of the postdoctoral research team on the 'Colonial Film: Moving Images of the British Empire' project, and he teaches at Birkbeck College and the London Consortium.

LEE GRIEVESON is Reader in Film Studies and Director of the Graduate Programme in Film Studies at University College London. He is author of *Policing Cinema: Movies and Censorship in Early-Twentieth-century America* (2004), and co-editor of various volumes, including *The Silent Cinema Reader* (2004), with Peter Krämer, and *Inventing Film Studies* (2008), with Haidee Wasson. Grieveson was co-principal investigator, with Colin MacCabe, of the 'Colonial Cinema: Moving Images of the British Empire' project, which aimed to digitally archive British colonial cinema spanning the twentieth century and to organise scholarly gatherings to investigate these materials. The project's website is <www.colonialfilm.org.uk>.

ISAAC JULIEN founded Sankofa Film and Video Collective (1983–92), and was a founding member of Normal Films in 1991. Julien was nominated for the Turner Prize in 2001 for his films *The Long Road to Mazatlán* (1999), made in collaboration with Javier de Frutos and *Vagabondia* (2000), choreographed by Javier de Frutos. Earlier works include *Frantz Fanon: Black Skin, White Mask* (1996), *Young Soul Rebels* (1991), which was awarded the Semaine de la Critique prize at the Cannes Film Festival the same year, and the acclaimed poetic documentary *Looking for Langston* (1989). Julien was the recipient of both the prestigious MIT Eugene McDermott Award in the Arts (2001) and the Frameline Lifetime Achievement Award (2002). His work *Paradise Omeros* was presented as part of Documenta XI in Kassel (2002). In 2003 he won the Grand Jury Prize at the Kunstfilm Biennale in Cologne for his single screen version of *Baltimore* and the Aurora Award in 2005. Most recently, he has had solo shows at the Pompidou Centre in Paris (2005), MoCA Miami (2005) and the Kerstner Gesellschaft, Hanover (2006). Julien is represented in the Tate Modern, the Pompidou Centre, the Guggenheim and Hirshhorn Collections.

COLIN MacCABE is Distinguished Professor of English and Film at the University of Pittsburgh, PA, and Associate Director of the London Consortium. He has taught at Cambridge, Strathclyde, Exeter and Birkbeck College, University of London. Between 1985 and 1998 he worked for the British Film Institute. His publications include *James Joyce and the Revolution of the Word*, *Godard: A Portrait of the Artist at 70*, *T. S. Eliot*, *The Butcher Boy* and the co-edited *True to the Spirit: Film Adaptation and the Question of Fidelity*.

LAURA MULVEY is Professor of Film and Media Studies at Birkbeck College, University of London. She is the author of *Visual and Other Pleasures* (1989; second edition, 2009), *Fetishism and Curiosity* (1996), *Citizen Kane* (in the BFI Film Classics series, 1996) and *Death Twenty-four Times a Second: Stillness and the Moving Image* (2006). She has made six films in collaboration with Peter Wollen including *Riddles of the Sphinx* (1978) and *Frida Kahlo and Tina Modotti* (1980) and with artist/film-maker Mark Lewis, *Disgraced Monuments* (1994).

HASSAN ABDUL MUTHALIB has been actively involved in the Malaysian film industry for over forty-five years variously as a graphic artist, animator, writer, director and sometimes actor. He has made public-service films, animated shorts, commercials, documentaries, created animation titling for feature films and directed Malaysia's first animated feature film. He lectures part-time at design, animation and film colleges and has also been invited to run training sessions in Singapore, Norway, Sudan, Brunei, India and the Philippines. His film and animation papers appear in international publications such as *Cahiers du Cinéma*, *Cinemaya*, *Southeast Asia Research*, *The International Film Index*, and in the books, *Being & Becoming – The Cinemas of Asia* and *The Little Black Book: Movies*. His book on Malaysian animation history will be published in 2011 by Universiti Teknologi MARA Malaysia, where he is a Senior Artist-in-Residence at the Faculty of Artistic and Creative Technology, researching early Malaysian cinema. He is currently working on two books, one on the history of the Malayan Film Unit and one on Malay opera and shadowplay as the proto-cinema of the Malays.

RICHARD OSBORNE was employed as a Research Fellow on the project 'Colonial Film: Moving Images of the British Empire'. His writing has appeared in the journals *Critical Quarterly*, *Popular Music History* and *Réseaux*, as well as in the collection *Mark E. Smith and the Fall: Art, Music and Politics*. He is currently employed as programme leader for the Popular Music undergraduate and postgraduate courses at Middlesex University.

ARJUNA PARAKRAMA is Professor in the Department of English at the University of Peradeniya. He is the author of *De-Hegemonising Language Standards: Learning from (Post)colonial Englishes about 'English'* (1995) and *Too Much Birdshit in the Gardens* (2002). He was a Fulbright New Century Scholar in 2007–8 and held Senior Fellow-ships at the US Institute of Peace (1999–2000) and the Carnegie Council on Ethics and International Affairs (2000–1). He is currently working on two books: one on the relationship between sexuality and protracted violent conflict, and the other a collection of essays that explores recurrent master tropes and concept metaphors within disciplinary and geographical space that belie antagonisms between past and present.

TOM RICE is a Lecturer in Film Studies at the University of St Andrews. Prior to this appointment, he was the senior researcher for three years on the 'Colonial Film' project. As part of this work, he wrote more than 200 historical essays, focused primarily on Africa and the Caribbean, which are published online at <www. colonialfilm.org.uk>. He has also written on Malaya and on Indian newsreels, and has undertaken extensive research on the colonial film units. His dissertation at UCL was on the racial politics of silent cinema, and he is currently developing this as a manuscript.

ROSALEEN SMYTH is a Professor in the Faculty of Arts at the Divine Word University in Madang, Papua New Guinea. She has previously lectured at universities in Tanzania, Australia, Zambia, Fiji, Dubai and Taiwan; and been the senior legislative research specialist in Aboriginal Affairs and Media Policy with the Social Policy Research Unit in the Parliamentary Library, Parliament House, Canberra. Among her publications featuring British colonial film are articles in the *Historical Journal of Film, Radio and Television*, the *Journal of African History*, *African Affairs*, the *Journal of Imperial and Commonwealth History* and *Social Policy Administration*.

FRANKLYN ST. JUSTE has been engaged in the production of motion pictures for nearly forty years, his experience including scripting, directing, photography, editing and sound. He has worked as Director of Photography on the films *The Harder They Come* (1972) and *Children of Babylon* (1980). He is currently a Lecturer at the Caribbean Institute for Media and Communication, University of the West Indies, in the areas of Television Production, Broadcast Media Management, Advertising and Social Marketing. St. Juste is the recipient of several Jamaican national honours, including the Order of Distinction (OD) and the Silver Musgrave Medal for achievement in Cinematic Arts and the Life Achievement Award for the Caribbean Tales Film Festival, as well as other awards, international and Jamaican.

MARTIN STOLLERY lectures part-time for the Open University. He is the author of *Alternative Empires: European Modernist Cinemas and Cultures of Imperialism* (2000) and co-author of *British Film Editors* (2004). He is currently researching a book about the British editor, scriptwriter and producer Ian Dalrymple, and co-editing a forthcoming special issue of the *Journal of British Cinema and Television* on post-war British documentary.

RAVI VASUDEVAN works at the Centre for the Study of Developing Societies, Delhi, and co-initiated Sarai, the centre's research programme on media experience and urban history. He is on the editorial advisory board of *Screen* and has edited *Making Meaning in Indian Cinema* (2000). He is one of the founder editors of the new journal *Bioscope: South Asian Screen Studies*, and author of *The Melodramatic Public: Film Form and Spectatorship in Indian Cinema* (2010–11).

VRON WARE is a Research Fellow based at the Centre for Socio-Cultural Change (CRESC) and the Centre for Citizenship, Identities and Governance (CCIG) at the Open University. Her books include *Beyond the Pale: White Women, Racism and History* (1992), *Out of Whiteness: Color, Politics and Culture* (2002, with Les Back) and *Who Cares about Britishness? A Global View of the National Identity Debate* (2007). She is currently working on a new project about the politics of racism and national identity in the contemporary British Army.

WENDY WEBSTER has published widely on questions of migration, ethnicity, gender, imperialism and national identity, including *Imagining Home: Gender, Race and National Identity* (1998), *Englishness and Empire, 1939–1965* (2005) and (with Louise Ryan) *Gendering Migration: Masculinity, Femininity and Ethnicity in Post-war Britain* (2008). *Englishness and Empire* won the prize for the best work in the field of media and history from the International Association for Media and History in 2006. Her current projects on Englishness and Europe 1939–72 and ethnicity in World War II Britain have been supported by a Leverhulme Fellowship and a Visiting Fellowship at Australian National University. She is Professor Emeritus of Contemporary British History at the University of Central Lancashire.

PHILIP S. ZACHERNUK is Associate Professor of History at Dalhousie University. His *Colonial Subjects: An African Intelligentsia and Atlantic Ideas* (2000) explores the history of southern Nigerian intellectuals in the context of changing ideas about race and progress over the century before 1960. His current work concerns how West Africans abroad during the colonial era engaged with ideas of Africa produced in Britain and North America, and worked to generate their own accounts and images of Africa's place in the world.

Acknowledgments

Film and the End of Empire grows like its companion volume *Empire and Film* out of an Arts and Humanities Research Council Major Resource Enhancement research project entitled 'Colonial Film: Moving Images of the British Empire', which ran from October 2007 to September 2010. The project produced a catalogue for the 6,200 films representing British colonies housed in the British Film Institute (BFI), the Imperial War Museum (IWM) and the British Empire and Commonwealth Museum. That catalogue, with over thirty hours of digitised films and various writings about the films and other institutions, can be visited at <www.colonialfilm.org.uk>.

The initial idea for the project came from Heather Stewart at the BFI, who asked Colin MacCabe, then at the University of Exeter, to lead the bid. While Colin MacCabe was preparing this initial bid with Patrick Russell, Senior Curator of Non-fiction at the BFI National Archive, and Kay Gladstone of the IWM, Emma Sandon of Birkbeck College alerted him to a complementary bid being prepared by Anna Maria Motrescu of the British Empire and Commonwealth Museum and she joined the team, which submitted a bid that also included the Bill Douglas Centre at the University of Exeter. This bid was turned down in 2006. A new bid was submitted later that year, which was prepared by Colin MacCabe, now based at Birkbeck, and Lee Grieveson of University College London (UCL), who became Co-director. The project was led by MacCabe and Grieveson, with a research team including Russell, Gladstone, Sandon and Nigel Algar, Senior Curator of Fiction at the BFI National Archive.

The research team started work in October 2007 with Tom Rice and Anna Maria Motrescu as postdoctoral researchers. Anna Maria left the project to work in Cambridge in 2009 and was replaced by Francis Gooding. Before that, with funds provided by the London Consortium, Richard Osborne had been recruited as a third researcher. In May 2009 Filipa César joined the team to prepare her film and installation *Black Balance*. The team held regular seminars throughout the three years: thanks to Stuart Hall, Paul Gilroy, Priya Jaikumar, Tom Gunning, Stephen Frears, Laura Mulvey, Patrick Manning and David Trotter. The seminars led to two conferences, one held in London in July 2010 and one held in Pittsburgh, PA, in September 2010.

The project was administered through Birkbeck College with particular efficiency by Liz Francis. We benefited greatly from support from both the London Consortium and the University of Pittsburgh. The London Consortium contributed considerable financial support and two of the postdoctoral researchers. The Director of the London Consortium, Steve Connor, was particularly helpful in ensuring that the project had a real multidisciplinary base. The conference in London was supported with help from the Faculty of Arts and Humanities at UCL (special thanks to Henry Woudhuysen), and the Department of English and Humanities at Birkbeck (special thanks to Sue Wiseman). In Pittsburgh, John Cooper, Dean of Arts and Sciences, and Lucy Fischer, Director of Film Studies, pledged very considerable financial support to the project from the start and their funds were supplemented by the Program in Global Studies (special thanks to Pat Manning and Nancy Condee), the Faculty Research Support Program (special thanks to Nicole Constable), the Humanities Center (special thanks to Jonathan Arac), the Department of English (special thanks to Johnny Twyning) and the Program in Cultural Studies (special thanks to Giuseppina Mecchia). Neepa Majundrar and Shalini Puri helped to plan the Pittsburgh conference with administrative support from Carol Myselwiec. Sarah Joshi organised both conferences with exemplary efficiency. We would like to thank also Lora Brill, Lauren and Riley Martin-Grieveson, Rebecca Barden and Sophia Contento at BFI Publishing, and our contributors to these two books.

Lee Grieveson and Colin MacCabe, London and Pittsburgh, March 2011

Introduction: Film and the End of Empire

Lee Grieveson

War marked, in many ways, the apotheosis of empire for Britain. The global conflict of 1939–45 was sustained by the material and economic resources gathered through extractive empire; by a mass imperial fighting force that automatically assumed belligerent status when Britain declared war; and by the control of territory and naval bases and consequently, the global circulation of materials and peoples.[1] All of this was accompanied by a newly urgent rhetoric of unity in a proliferation of official and popular stories that portrayed the wartime empire pulling together across differences of race and ethnicity in a transnational and global anti-fascist conflict.[2] Yet at the same time the flawed logic of this conception of the conflict and of empire 'unity' was apparent to many, not least to those colonised populations fighting fascism for the liberal rights of democracy, self-determination and freedom that were for them merely fictions. The biopolitical atrocities of fascism directed attention toward racism.[3] And the disconnect between the rhetoric of unity and freedom and the reality of colonial governance grew ever more visible, as violence – and its threat – sustained imperial dominance (in, for example, the suppression of the 1942 Indian uprising, and the mass imprisonment of members of the Indian National Congress (INC); the occupations of Iraq, Syria and Iran; and the shooting by police and military of strikers in the economically essential region of the Northern Rhodesian Copper Belt in 1940). In August 1941 the widely publicised 'Atlantic Charter' affirmed the 'rights of all peoples to choose the form of government under which they will live', prompting the American Under-Secretary of State to declare that 'the age of imperialism is dead'.[4] Not quite. Liberalism had, after all, long lived with the contradictions between declarations of human rights and democratic rule and the realities of slavery and colonial expansion and exploitation.[5] Even so, military losses in Asia in 1942 – including the loss of the crucial naval base at Singapore – undercut the fiction of racial supremacy upon which colonial governance relied.[6] The certainty, and longevity, of colonial rule and the global colonial order was put into doubt, amid uncomfortable questions about the connections between liberalism, colonialism and fascism.

Alternative fictions were pressed into service to prop up the seemingly ailing age of imperialism and its distinctive formation of racialised governance and ordering of space and power. The rhetoric of unity was urgently supplemented with ideas of 'development' and 'Commonwealth', as the British colonial state accelerated trends visible in the interwar period to emphasise its benevolent trusteeship and its role in establishing economic self-sufficiency. In 1940 the Colonial Development and Welfare

Act set in place structures of welfarism that were designed to forestall radical social and political action, preceding the establishment of the welfare state in the metropole in the post-war period.[7] Education policies were developed to better integrate colonial subjects into a market economy.[8] Alongside economic 'development', the colonial state began preparation for divesting governmental control, albeit haltingly and with no immediate end in sight. India, for example, was 'offered' Dominion status in 1942 (it is when leading members of the INC refused, and formed the Quit India movement, that they were imprisoned).[9] In July 1943 the Secretary of State for the Colonies, Oliver Stanley, told Parliament that the British government was 'pledged to guide Colonial people along the road to self-government within the framework of the British Empire'.[10] Any such road would, it was imagined, be connected back to Britain, sustaining economic ties in the aptly named 'Commonwealth' and the objectives of geopolitical 'security'.

At stake was the transition of colonial dominance to economic imperialism, guided in part by the model provided by the United States and indeed provoked also partly by the opposition of that country to colonial rule. This opposition was motivated in part by the British state's earlier erection of a structure of economic protectionism that attempted to place the materials and markets of colonial states beyond the reach of American capital. US policy, particularly in the post-war settlement, would require that these barriers be removed (that this was fundamentally an economic question, and not a question of liberal ethics, was apparent in the US policy to help prop up the British empire when it served US Cold War agendas).[11] At the end of the war, deeply in debt to the US and unable to re-establish the old balance of power, Britain was clearly a fading geopolitical force. The revelation of Britain's financial and military weakness in the 1956 Suez Crisis made this clearer.[12] At the same time, the rise of colonial nationalism – demanding the logical freedoms of liberalism – led to wars of decolonisation in Africa and Southeast Asia, and to what Paul Gilroy describes in his essay in this volume as the 'slow, fractious, blood-soaked decomposition of the British empire'.[13] Under pressure from subaltern populations, nationalist movements and newly established American global hegemony, Britain's empire began to crumble: India became independent in 1947, followed later by rapid bursts of decolonisation in West Africa and Southeast Asia in 1956–7, and Western and Eastern Africa between 1960–5.[14] The number of people living under British rule in the two decades after 1945 was cut from 700 million to 5 million; the largest and probably the most ambitious imperial venture in human history was reduced, as Francis Gooding reminds us in his contribution here, 'to a mere rump, a far-flung global archipelago'.[15]

What roles did film play across the period 1939–65, in the face of these rapidly changing geopolitical strategies and realities? What were the varied ways in which film registered, and projected, colonial discourse? What do these films now reveal about the fantasies and realities of colonial rule? The essays in this collection offer varied answers to these questions, in dialogue with the materials assembled by the 'Colonial Film' project.[16] At their broadest, the essays address the enmeshing of cultural representation and political and economic control. They examine the ways in which state and non-state actors harnessed film to instructional and pedagogical functions, putting media to work to shape the attitudes and conduct of populations to sustain colonial governmental order. The considerable investment in 'colonial film' by the

British – the most sustained and extensive use of film for governmental purposes by a liberal state – was predicated on ideas both about film as a symbol of technological modernity that embodied and projected colonial authority and, relatedly, about its persuasive power over 'unsophisticated' populations. The specific work of film to supplement colonial governance in this period began, contributors here teach us, with efforts to generate loyalty to the colonial power and its geopolitical strategies; moved through the attempted elaboration of an 'imagined community' that transcended the nation-state and was properly transnational;[17] and was cathected to the efforts to establish new economic relationships, to 'develop' the colonies in ways that supplemented the British economy and to educate colonial subjects about, principally, the market and its demands in the coming era of self-governance. These essays suggest new ways of conceptualising British cinema as a cinema of imperialism; and in turn propose new models for mapping the circulation of what we might call the visual regimes of geopolitics. Together, they urge us to resist the marginality of colonial history, and to more fully engage with the colonial ordering of the world and its articulation through the medium of cinema.

Various forms of film facilitated and visualised colonial rule and its mutation into 'Commonwealth partnership'. Governments, educationalists, entrepreneurs, missionaries and the film industry all made films, and so inscribed in varying ways colonial discourse onto, and as, film. The essays here address the newsreels that were produced in different languages; state-produced 'documentaries'; corporate-financed non-fiction films about economic relationships; and narrative fiction films telling stories about the history and present moment of imperialism and its ostensible dissolution (encompassing long-established fantasies of conquest and domination but also new rhetorics of 'progress' and development). Across these differing filmic forms, there emerged a set of related formal practices and tropes, belying any simple separation of the real and the imaginary. Time and time again in these films we see white characters central to the frame educating and guiding the marginal colonial subjects in learning about and using modern technology. Frequently the sound of an English upper-class voice embodies authority and directs our attention. Cruelty, hierarchy, domination are displayed, naturalised and justified. A common format shows the right and wrong way to accomplish various tasks, a 'Mr Wise and Mr Foolish' format that embodies a pedagogical and paternalistic logic. Trusteeship, benevolence even, is central to the colonial relationship, these films often propose. Yet other films offer a more unfiltered record of what Laura Mulvey calls 'the gaze of the regime'.[18] Amateur films made by military personnel and other colonial officials occasionally reveal truths about colonial attitudes and events suppressed in official films. Violence, rarely seen in the official record of empire, is glimpsed in the margins of these films, as, for example, in the films made by Major William Rhodes James discussed by Vron Ware, which show the British military clearing Chinese villagers away from their homes and into new camps during the Malayan Emergency.

Along the way, specific institutions were formed to foster colonial film, most notably the Colonial Film Unit (CFU), set up in 1939 under the auspices of the Ministry of Information (MOI) initially to mobilise colonial support for the war but remade in the post-war period to better reflect new projects of education and economic development. Local units were established in the Gold Coast, Nigeria, Central Africa,

Jamaica and Malaya. The advent of filmic independence mirrored, and crossed over with, that of political independence – both fraught with similar complexities for the British state, and new independent states, in charting change and continuity.

The establishment of institutions to foster the production of didactic film was supplemented also by the elaboration and intensification of novel methods of distribution and theatrical and non-theatrical exhibition. Legislation at times ensured short didactic films would be shown in cinemas before fictional features. Elsewhere, mobile cinema vans were constructed, and equipped with projection equipment, and these circulated widely in remote areas, presenting films and so 'projecting the State', as Charles Ambler shows here, to largely illiterate audiences who probably confronted colonial propaganda for the first time lit up on screens in the night sky. Film itself as 'shock and awe', perhaps. The development of such a system was pioneered in the interwar years, but reached a wider audience in the post-war period when these new pathways of film distribution and exhibition facilitated the mobile economic relations that were so central to post-war colonial strategies.[19] Across this period there developed infrastructures to deploy film as a medium of information and communication, accompanied by considerable discussion of the best ways to manage and orchestrate this.

All these efforts were predicated on ideas about the utility of cinema for engineering consent and managing the conduct of diverse populations. Often these proto-film theoretical arguments proposed that structures of 'identification' in film texts functioned to draw audiences into sharing the beliefs embodied in the films. The ideas about audiences and the effects of film embodied colonial logic, for it was based on the belief that colonial subjects would be more easily and profoundly influenced by media than Western subjects. Likewise, the efforts to harness film to the project of colonialism were predicated also on beliefs about the necessity and efficacy of 'fictions' to sustain colonial rule (even better when those fictions claim truth status, as, for example, documentaries and newsreels do). Film could supplement colonial rule carried out a distance. At the core of the elaboration of colonial film, and its infrastructures, were ideas about the efficacy of film and fiction for (colonial) government.

●

Film and the End of Empire begins with Paul Gilroy's essay 'Great Games: Film, History and Working-through Britain's Colonial Legacy'. Gilroy's widely, and justly, influential work has argued that the British empire is the crucial repression within contemporary national memory, and that the failure to think through the process by which Britain dominated one-quarter of the globe for the better part of two centuries significantly contributes to current traumas around race and religion.[20] The film material assembled for the 'Colonial Film' project offers, Gilroy argues here, the possibility of re-engaging with that past, confronting the realities of the divisions and differences that have been so central to the British state. Working-through the ways cinema was deployed to elaborate an imperial mythography – as the cultural mandate, Gilroy argues, of white supremacy – is a crucial and urgent project to consolidate a liveable, convivial, multiculture. Gilroy argues that the social, political and economic upheavals that attended the end of European empires are epochal developments, heralding our post- and neocolonial world. The urge to understand those, and their refraction through the prism of cinema, is central to Gilroy's project – and indeed to the essays gathered together here.

Gilroy reminds us also that colonialism is always war, and so requires, constantly, propaganda; that information, culture, power and government were, from the early twentieth century onwards, complexly intertwined. War frequently makes propaganda imperative, though this was, for a colonial power ostensibly fighting for democracy, certainly a complex process. The essays in the first section of this book address this period and this complexity. In 'The Last Roll of the Dice: *Morning, Noon and Night*, Empire and the Historiography of the Crown Film Unit', Martin Stollery traces out the production history of a film that was ultimately never completed and suggests that this failure reveals something of the instability in colonial order towards the end of the war. The film was started in 1942 by the Crown Film Unit, operating under the auspices of the Ministry of Information. Crown produced such canonical wartime documentaries as *Target for Tonight* (1941), *Listen to Britain* (1942) and *Fires Were Started* (1943). It was intended though that *Morning, Noon and Night*, as it was provisionally called, would focus not on Britain or on frontline fighting by colonial troops, as other wartime propaganda had, but on the infrastructure which supported the British empire's war effort: food production; the manufacture of military equipment; medical and welfare services; training, and so on. The story of the empire pulling together in this fashion would, it was thought, help enact the unity the film imagined and also contribute to the ongoing effort to persuade the US of the benign nature of British imperialism. To tell its story of a united empire, the producers planned to edit together film from across the empire, literally uniting materials and images and presenting them as a coherent whole – as film, uniting pieces of celluloid, and in turn sound with vision, and so mimicking the 'unity' of the empire itself. It was, though, never finished. Unity was hard to fabricate. The difficulty and ultimately the impossibility of mixing footage from across the empire and embodying a global vision makes apparent, because it is caused by, the broader political divergences of the moment.

Representation failed to hold together difference, to imagine a global community or stitch together rhetoric with reality. The complex jarring of image and reality, and film and geopolitics, is also central to Richard Osborne's account of film made in India between 1939, the outset of the war, and 1947, the moment of Independence. Osborne traces out the production of film by the MOI, by the Government of India and by the American newsreel company March of Time. The films enact differing visions of India, caught up in the throes of radical transformation, and fractured across the differing political imperatives of the British, Indian and (to some extent) American state. The British films are mostly silent about the political situation, and the Quit India movement, and this is characteristic of the evasions, lacunae, of the official filmed record. Yet the political situation was described in more detail in the American newsreels, which were initially supported by the MOI again in the hope that they would portray enlightened British governance. At the end of the war, immediately prior to the granting of Independence, the Central Office of Information (COI, the peacetime successor to the MOI) made the film *Indian Background* (1946), telling the wearily familiar colonial story about 'primitive' cultures necessarily confronting industrial modernity. Osborne shows how the film was a composite print, shot silently with sound added later because this enabled the commentary to be dubbed into various languages and so transformed according to the political valences of its audiences. It was composite also in that it was made up of previously used footage, a kind of compilation film holding together, in its very form, the past and present as it imagined the future. These formal practices strove to offer a comforting fiction of coherence, of unity – the suturing of sound and vision, of past and present – that bore little relation to the radical transition and indeed Partition that was becoming visible outside the frame and the cinema theatre.

Towards the end of his essay on government and amateur film-making in India, Ravi Vasudevan also ponders the way film functions as both a medium of disaggregation and recombination. Addressing amateur films made by colonial officials in India, Vasudevan shows how they combine forms and functions, stretching from domestic scenes, to scenes of 'Orientalist curiosity', to public events and to the celebration of what he calls 'developmental vistas'. The amateur film-maker in this colonial context stitches together diverse events, often by the simple expedient of editing in the camera: scenes and events tumble together, allowing a glimpse into the varied movement of colonial officials, as the camera captures the physicality of people and objects and material life in the colonial world. Vasudevan is interested in how the disaggregative logics of film enable recombination for informational and rhetorical purposes. It is these purposes that sustained the elaboration of state policies in India, particularly in the 1940s, for the production, circulation and exhibition of films. Vasudevan maps out the establishment of state production practices and media infrastructures in the first part of his essay, showing how these emerged to better facilitate the dissemination of information to diverse Indian populations and so supplement the complex and unstable governmental rationality of the late colonial moment.

Vron Ware also examines film across the official/amateur divide to address the intersection of film and the establishment of a multiethnic fighting force that was deployed widely in the war and in later wars of decolonisation. Amateur and official films show us now how widely this colonial force was deployed across Europe, North Africa, Burma, Malaya and elsewhere to sustain the colonial order. The films supplement, and at times reorientate, the standard historical accounts of the empire at war and the policing of the crumbling empire in the post-war period. Ware demonstrates also how film was used to construct a racialised military imaginary, drawing on colonial constructions of ethnic difference that derived from the history of military Orientalism. Gurkhas, for example, were portrayed as a martial race, capable of great feats of military prowess, in a way that was entirely consistent with colonial discourse. The visual trope of the *kukri*, the knife used by Gurkha forces, appears across a number of films, emphasising and making material this conception of a colonial primitivism that was harnessed now to the sustenance of colonial order. The nature of that order is glimpsed outside the official film record. Ware shows us how amateur film shot by a Gurkha soldier during the Malayan Emergency, moving Chinese villagers to a British detention camp, makes visible, uncomfortably so, the realities of a multiethnic military order enforcing imperial rule.

The failure of film to stitch together difference in coherent visions of colonial unity, and transact the shift from colonial rule to post-war partnership and development in the shadow of the Atlantic Charter, is addressed by historian Philip Zachernuk in his essay on the production and reception of the fiction film *Men of Two Worlds* (1946). The Colonial Office began production of the film in 1942, with the aim of visualising new ideas about partnership developed during the war and accelerated in the post-war period, when the film was released. At vast expense – costing more than the budget of the Colonial Development and Welfare Act – the film told the story of an educated African, Kisenga (Robert Adams), returning to Africa with a white District Commissioner to help persuade Africans to move away from areas infested by the tsetse fly. Kisenga is a celebrated musician in England; but on his return to Africa, is cursed by a witch doctor and falls ill, lost between two worlds – Europe and Africa, the civilised and the savage – and unable, momentarily, to overcome what he describes as 'ten thousand years of Africa in my blood'. At his lowest, Kisenga is saved by the District Commissioner, who plays him his own musical composition – European-influenced, and distinct from threatening African drums. Zachernuk traces out the complex production history of the film, using various archival resources, and shows how the film sought to balance longstanding conceptions of primitivism, as embodied in the figure of the witch doctor, with new imperatives to imagine educated African elites as partners in the post-war future. The difficulties of this were apparent during the arduous production process, and again upon the film's release. African intellectuals in England, particularly the West African Students' Union (WASU), argued that the figure of the witch doctor was not only unrealistic but also a pernicious and racist conception of African backwardness and difference. WASU writers argued also that this was compounded by Kisenga's breakdown, with its intimation of essentialist ideas about race. These resistant reading practices eloquently discerned the colonialist logic underpinning the film's narrative of 'development', and made apparent the broader and more fundamental problematic of visualising and enacting a new post-war and, perhaps, postcolonial order.

What changed in the immediate post-war period? What were the ways that films were used to negotiate and manage these changes? The essays in the section 'Film/Government/Development' address these questions, probing the establishment of new filmic policies and practices in light of emergent post-war conceptions of partnership and development and showing how film was complexly implicated in the effort to preserve and protect colonial order. The transformation in the functioning of the Colonial Film Unit is emblematic of this. It was set up during the war years to foster the loyalty of colonial subjects. As war ended though, as Tom Rice shows us in his essay 'From the Inside: The Colonial Film Unit and the Beginning of the End', the CFU made a number of films about colonial subjects in England, seeking to make visual an ostensibly new paradigm of interconnection and partnership. Later the so-called Home Unit was disbanded, and local training schools and film units were established initially in the Gold Coast and Nigeria and shortly thereafter in Jamaica (Franklyn St. Juste considers some aspects of the history of the Jamaican Film Unit in his contribution here). The establishment of local film units seemed to mark a shift in both film and colonial policy. Rice probes this shift, showing us how the local film units operated, and how centralised and metropolitan authority continued behind the fictions of decentralised partnership. The films produced by the local units themselves frequently registered this uncertainty and ambiguity, Rice shows us, for though they engaged with a local specificity, the key production roles and decisions were taken by British film-makers and officials. This was frequently embodied in the familiar English voice of authority that accompanies the images and directs attention. As Rice demonstrates, the halting and partial move toward a decentralised film policy and practice mirrors the broader complex and stuttering shift toward decolonisation that gathered pace in the post-war years.

The transformation of the CFU into local units was accompanied by a newly urgent rhetoric of 'development' that sought to reorientate conceptions of colonial rule toward a more benign sense of trusteeship and partnership. Film played a central part in this transaction as Rosaleen Smyth conveys in her essay 'Images of Empires on Shifting Sands: The Colonial Film Unit in West Africa in the Post-war Period'. It did so both as an effort to legitimise and prolong colonial rule, and as part of a global public-relations exercise by a British state still seeking to differentiate its authority from that of fascist states and to appease American resistance to imperialism. Along the way, film came to be integrated with new educational practices around public health and agriculture in particular, as a central part of the colonial state's efforts to generate and 'develop' the economic utility of subaltern populations and colonial states. Later still, when political decolonisation became inevitable, film was used, Smyth argues, to try to maintain close economic and political ties between Britain and newly independent states in the transnational 'Commonwealth'.

Wars of decolonisation punctured the fiction of partnership and development. In Malaya, for example, the Malayan National Liberation Army (MNLA), the military wing of the Malayan Communist Party, began a guerrilla war against British forces in 1948. The British response to what they called the 'Emergency' centred on the massive relocation of Malayan and Chinese populations to new villages.[21] As the Emergency intensified, the government increasingly utilised propaganda to portray these villages as idyllic spaces, the MNLA as a barbarous force, and the British and Malayan populations as working together to develop Malaya and, from the mid-1950s, to establish the parameters of a new independent state that would be closely connected to Britain. Hassan Abdul Muthalib accounts for this history in his essay 'The End of Empire: The Films of the Malayan Film Unit in 1950s British Malaya'. As Muthalib shows, the propaganda policies of the British state were predicated on the estab-lishment of a mobile cinema network in Malaya to position the films of the Malayan Film Unit (MFU) in front of what was still then a largely illiterate audience. As such, film texts, and media infrastructures, dovetailed with brutal state policies, collectively designed to maintain, in particular, the economically crucial resources of Malayan tin and rubber.

Africa too became economically crucial for the British state in the post-war period, particularly in light of the loss of large parts of its empire in South Asia (India, centrally, but also Burma and Ceylon). The essays in the following section, 'Projecting Africa', address different aspects of that importance in the period leading up to the decolonisation of Western and Eastern African states in the mid-1960s. The innovation of new media infrastructures as a part of the information policies of the colonial power is addressed further by Charles Ambler in his essay 'Projecting the Modern Colonial State: The Mobile Cinema in Kenya'. Ambler focuses on the mobile exhibition of films in Kenya in the 1940s and 1950s, and the establishment of an exhibition circuit that connected with broader policies of mass education and that sought to compete with the increasingly aggressive anti-colonialism that erupted in particular in 1952 with the Mau Mau rebellion. Exhibition functioned, he proposes, as a performance of modern colonial power, a kind of ritual of state power that started with film itself as the embodiment of the technological modernity that colonial power claimed for itself and included other patriotic activities – addresses about the royal family, for example, or the raising of the Union Jack – and also the enactment of forms of order and rule in terms of the marshalling of audience behaviour, responses and in the organisation of seating hierarchies. Rituals and fantasies of colonial order and its continuation ignored, of course, the anti-colonial violence that erupted in the country. Colonial cinema is most frequently a cinema of evasion. Yet the policing of colonial rule at the cinema was not without its difficulties: at one screening in 1947, for example, the political leader Paul Ngei seized the microphone to advertise his cause; at others, audiences talked among themselves, ignoring the film's and the screening's attempted embodiment of colonial power.

In his essay on films made in the Gold Coast (later Ghana), historian Gareth Austin traces out a shift from interwar certainty about the longevity of colonial order to a new rhetoric of partnership that emerged during the war – he notices, for example, that the word 'native' shifts to 'African' – and that became more fully elaborated in the post-war period. These later films tell stories about the function of government, in, for example, films about taxation, seeking to model new practices of 'good citizenship' for the soon-to-be-independent African subjects/citizens. At the same time, the films show the centrality of capital-intensive technology for 'development', so ensuring the longevity of British industry and finance capital in neocolonial orders (a subject that Francis Gooding tackles in his contribution). Austin addresses the filmed record as a historian, tracing out what these films confirm for historians about this period and how they also propose some revisions to the historical record. Toward the end of his essay, he observes that the films give evidence about the extent of malnutrition and poverty in parts of Ghana: the indexicality of the image registering the materiality of the suffering body, and so acknowledging, if without comment, the failures of colonial rule.

Fiction films in this period also anxiously reflect on failure and loss as the colonial project careers towards its end. Wendy Webster considers aspects of this in her essay 'Mumbo-jumbo, Magic and Modernity: Africa in British Cinema, 1946–65'. Africa, she shows, was frequently associated with primitivism, its diversity homogenised and represented through repetitive tropes (notably of sound – chanting and drumming – and through the spectacle of rural and jungle spaces). Webster looks closely at a series of mostly fiction films from the mid-1940s through to the mid-1960s, tracing out how the films reflect and refract the complex shifts in the British imagination of Africa. The realities of colonial war in Kenya are largely avoided in fiction, aside from indirect references to a frightening atavism; later, in the early 1960s, new conceptions of an almost-modern Africa emerge, but only haltingly, always intertwined with ingrained colonial ways of thinking. Travelogues and newsreels showed ceremonies of independence, attended by members of the royal family and so celebrated the continued relevance of Britain even beyond the colonial moment. Yet at the end of this period, the fiction film *Guns at Batasi* (1964) can only imagine British impotence: in response to an African coup, British soldiers stay in their barracks, confined and mostly powerless.

Laura Mulvey addresses the dissolution of imperial certainties in the final essay in this section. Looking closely at two colonial compilation films, Vincent Monnikendam's *Mother Dao, The Turtle-like* (1995) and Filipa César's *Black Balance* (2010), Mulvey unpacks the complicated temporality of these films, which reuse archival film but interrogate the intertwined aesthetic and political logics encoded therein.[22] The initial films celebrated colonial power, and its enactment of processes of modernity: they carry the impression of empire, Mulvey remarks, like a stamp. Yet when reassembled now the certainty of imperial power and oppression dissolves, and what remains are visible signs and traces of the unequal relation between the coloniser and colonised. While the original films celebrate one story, they unwittingly record another, of domination and exploitation. For Mulvey, these images, these celluloid footprints and ghosts, carry from the past something of a promise that may, perhaps, be redeemed in the future. In this way, we return to the beginning – back to the future as it were – to Paul Gilroy's injunction that we use these films and the histories and fictions embedded in them to transform the present and future.

The complicated imbrication of temporalities, of the necessity of thinking together past, present and future, also animates our final section, 'Afterthoughts on Colonial Film'. Film-makers Filipa César, Isaac Julien and Franklyn St. Juste reflect on the film record of colonialism – its aesthetic and political powers, the possibility of resistance and the place of these films in continuing efforts to preserve and honour the struggles of the past. Anthony Bogues starts by noting the conjuncture of cinema and colonial technologies of rule to account for the way these films contain spectres, or traces, that continue to haunt the present and shape contemporary discourse. Arjuna Parakrama likewise probes the place of film in establishing complicities between late colonialist discourse and practice and ostensibly postcolonial nationalist practices in Sri Lanka. Francis Gooding similarly ponders the continuation of colonial orders. *Giant in the Sun* (1959), a film from Nigeria, speaks of the coming era of independence but contains within it, Gooding shows us, a brief sequence that reveals the continuation of the presence of British technology and finance capital. The switch to neocolonial order is almost invisible, accomplished in the blink of an eye.

At the end, it is perhaps this question of the 'end' in our title that comes to the fore. Certainly, as the dream of empire died, the British state still reflexively held on to imperial ambitions: the Suez Crisis of 1956 was caused by Britain seeking to hold on to the territorial, and so also economic, advantage of the canal. Its unilateral actions brought a rift with the US, which had tolerated the British empire in part because it frequently provided a bulwark against Communism. It had limited utility in the Cold War; but it was, ultimately, a break on the circulation of goods and capital – a walled-off zone, that must be broken down to facilitate the global circulation of capital guarded and guided now by the US, and no longer by London. The dissolution of the British Empire would facilitate the hegemonic ambitions of the US, which modelled an economic imperialism divorced from geographical rule.[23] Its neocolonial ordering of the world would be supported by a shamefully acquiescent British state, beholden to what its leaders – from Churchill onwards – imagine, absurdly, as a 'special relationship'.[24] As one empire subsided into shadows, glimpsed now in the scratched and grainy images from the archive, another emerged for its day in the sun – helped in part by the bright lights of Hollywood.

NOTES

1. Keith Jeffery, 'The Second World War', in Judith M. Brown and Wm. Roger Louis (eds), *The Oxford History of the British Empire, Volume IV: The Twentieth Century* (Oxford: Oxford University Press, 1999), pp. 306–28; Ashley Jackson, *The British Empire and the Second World War* (London: Hambledon Continuum, 2006). At the end of the war the Colonial Office estimated that 374,000 Africans had been recruited into the armed forces; and by 1945 there were about 2.25 million Indians serving in the forces. Jeffery, 'The Second World War', pp. 311–12.
2. Wendy Webster, *Englishness and Empire, 1939–1965* (Oxford: Oxford University Press, 2005), in particular pp. 19–54.
3. Hannah Arendt, *The Origins of Totalitarianism*, 1951 (New York: Schocken, 2004); and see also Paul Gilroy, *After Empire: Melancholia or Convivial Culture?* (London: Routledge, 2004), in particular pp. 13–21.
4. Sumner Welles, cited in J. M. Lee and Martin Peter, *The Colonial Office, War and Development Policy: Organization and Planning of a Metropolitan Initiative, 1939–45* (London: Institute of Commonwealth Studies, 1982), p. 122. The Atlantic Charter was a statement agreed between Britain and America, and meant as a blueprint for the post-war world. For an account of the agreement and its impact, see Wm. Roger Louis, *Imperialism at Bay 1941–1945: The United States and the Decolonization of the British Empire* (Oxford: Clarendon Press, 1987), in particular pp. 121–33.
5. The constitutive connections between liberalism and imperialism are explored in Bernard Semmel, *The Liberal Ideal and the Demons of Empire: Theories of Imperialism from Adam Smith to Lenin* (Baltimore, MD: Johns Hopkins University Press, 1993); and Uday Singh Metha, *Liberalism and Empire: A Study in Nineteenth-Century British Liberal Thought* (Chicago, IL: University of Chicago Press, 1999).
6. Christopher Bayly and Tim Harper, *Forgotten Armies: The Fall of British Asia, 1941–1945* (London: Penguin, 2004); Louis, *Imperialism at Bay*.
7. Stephen Constantine, *The Making of British Colonial Development Policy, 1914–1940* (London: Frank Cass, 1984).
8. See, for example, Colonial Office Advisory Committee on Education in the Colonies, *Mass Education in African Society*, Colonial no. 186, 1944; and J. A. Mangan (ed.), *'Benefits Bestowed'?: Education and British Imperialism* (Manchester: Manchester University Press, 1988).
9. Judith M. Brown, 'India', in Brown and Louis, *The Oxford History of the British Empire, Volume IV*, pp. 435–7.
10. 13 July 1943, *Parliamentary Debates*, CCCXCI (Commons), col. 48, cited in Jeffery, 'The Second World War', p. 321.
11. Wm. Roger Louis and Ronald Robison, 'The Imperialism of Decolonization', *Journal of Imperial and Commonwealth History* vol. 22 no. 3 (1994), pp. 462–511. See also Giovanni Arrighi, *The Long Twentieth Century: Money, Power, and the Origins of Our Times* (London: Verso, 1994), in particular pp. 58–73; Neil Smith, *The Endgame of Globalization* (London: Routledge, 2005), in particular pp. 53–121.

12. The Suez Canal had long been important to the British state because it provided a shorter sea route to its empire and to the oilfields of the Persian Gulf. When the canal was nationalised by Egypt in 1956, an Israeli–Anglo–French force attacked Egypt but was halted by the United Nations, acting under particular pressure from the United States. Anglo–American relations were strained; and the crisis starkly illuminated Britain's declining influence. W. Scott Lucas, *Divided We Stand: Britain, the US and the Suez Crisis* (London: Hodder & Stoughton, 1991).

13. Paul Gilroy, 'Great Games: Film, History and Working-through Britain's Colonial Legacy', this volume.

14. Wm. Roger Louis, 'The Dissolution of the British Empire', in Brown and Louis, *The Oxford History of the British Empire, Volume IV*, pp. 329–56; John Darwin, *Britain and Decolonization: The Retreat from Empire in the Post-war World* (London: Palgrave Macmillan, 1988).

15. Louis, 'The Dissolution of the British Empire', p. 330; Francis Gooding, 'Missing the End: Falsehood and Fantasy in Late Colonial Cinema', this volume.

16. The 'Colonial Film' project was an Arts and Humanities Research Council-funded project to examine British colonial cinema. The genesis and organisation of this project is discussed in Colin MacCabe, '"To take ship to India to see a naked man spearing fish in blue water": Watching Films to Mourn the End of Empire', in Lee Grieveson and Colin MacCabe (eds), *Empire and Film* (London: BFI, 2011). The project's website at <www.colonialfilm.org.uk> houses digitised films, a combined catalogue and writing about films and production units.

17. I reference here Benedict Anderson's influential argument about the place of news and imaginative media in the formation of national communities. Anderson, *Imagined Communities: Reflections on the Origins and Spread of Nationalism* (London: Verso, 1983).

18. Laura Mulvey, 'Dislocations: Some Reflections on the Colonial Compilation Film', this volume.

19. See here also Brian Larkin's important work on media infrastructures in colonial Nigeria in Larkin, *Signal and Noise: Media, Infrastructure, and Urban Culture in Nigeria* (Durham, NC: Duke University Press, 2008).

20. Paul Gilroy, *There Ain't No Black in the Union Jack* (London: Routledge, 1987); and *After Empire*.

21. The Emergency was the term used by the colonial government; the MNLA described it as an Anti-British National Liberation War.

22. Filipa César's *Black Balance* was produced as part of our project on colonial film. It is available online at <www.colonialfilm.org.uk/workinprogress>.

23. See David Harvey, *The New Imperialism* (Oxford: Oxford University Press, 2003).

24. Winston Churchill used these words in a widely publicised speech in the US in 1946. The 'special relationship between the British Commonwealth and Empire and the United States' would, he argued, form the basis of post-war peace. Churchill, cited in Webster, *Englishness and Empire*, p. 57.

2

Great Games: Film, History and Working-through Britain's Colonial Legacy

Paul Gilroy

This unique historical collection of British colonial cinema is important for many reasons.[1] Above all, its precious contents offer an opportunity to break with the seemingly intractable patterns of contemporary Britain's melancholic relationship with the imperial past. That difficult rupture is now necessary and urgent. If it could be accomplished, it would help to consolidate the country's liveable multiculture in a context where unruly plurality and insubordinate diversity thrive in spite of the fact that multiculturalism is said by successive governments to have failed.[2]

Taken together, these films contribute an implicit challenge to a position that remains popular and influential in Britain. It dictates that the nation's failure to adjust to its reduced postcolonial circumstances requires restorative cultural and psychological therapy. Those remedies can be discovered in a newly mystified, revisionist account of imperial power and prestige. Engineered from on high by government, this redemptive intervention will also be aimed at promoting national sameness and social cohesion.[3] How the history of empire and its unhappy endings should be revised has become a significant part of discussion over a divided, post-colonial country's response to involvement in what looks and feels like endless neocolonial warfare.

In that context, this film archive presents a number of opportunities. It can help to construct a new, ventilating flow between on the one side, the narrowing professional concerns of largely descriptive historical studies of film and on the other, the sclerotic procedures of imperial history. Outside higher education, it can furnish schools and colleges with the most vivid and compelling historical resources available. We should not underestimate that reckoning with the uncomfortable material that has been assembled here demands new interpretative approaches and a novel variety of social, cultural and historical enquiry that is consciously angled toward the contest over national identity. This reflexive turn will have to be assertively postcolonial. It should be cosmopolitan in its methods and adept at managing complex transitions between geographies, technologies and political dispositions that are by no means exclusively national. The difficult work involved will be most rewarding when it is undertaken in cosmopolitan company and in a dialogic spirit that brings both postcolonial parties: former colonisers and formerly colonised, into consciousness of a common predicament. Britain gains an opportunity to dispense with the layers of disabling common sense that have weighed upon discussions of race and empire, culture and representation conducted closer to home.[4] Its former colonies acquire a chance to enrich their understanding of the colonial phase and to see how to avoid repetition of the colonial mistakes and crimes perpetrated by the institutions they have inherited.

As it shifts beyond the narrow confines of exclusively literary analysis, postcolonial theory articulated from Europe must be prepared to work to overcome the limits of ingrained racial nationalism and regionalism. Britain's history of imperial dominion cannot be held as if it was property and it does not belong to Britain alone. Working-through it turns attention toward the agenda of difficulties that emerges from studying the relationship between imperial culture – particularly in its more popular forms – and the political and psychological events which comprised the slow, fractious, blood-soaked decomposition of the British empire. That process developed closely in step with the break-up of Britain but is not reducible to it. Britain's culture of empire involved geopolitical as well as parochial matters and this archive helps to chart both dimensions and to grasp their interrelation which must now be subjected to careful historical periodisation.

As the interpretative dialogue around this material becomes more extensive, we should appreciate that, though the pressure to maintain the fortifications around scholastic disciplines is particularly strong at the moment, it will not be possible to pursue the urgent obligation of working-through if we remain comfortably inside those academic boundaries. This material requires a systematic and substantive multidisciplinarity that we should be prepared to explain and defend.

COLONIAL FILM AND THE OVERCOMING OF MELANCHOLIA?

Economic and political power is currently being recentred far away from the Atlantic world. In future, it will be concentrated in torrid locations which are still being identified, according to the outworn logic of raciology, as backward and unmodern. Prodigious technological and economic achievements are overshadowed by old assumptions about Oriental despotism and Asiatic stagnation. The critical and cosmopolitan kind of postcolonial theory which can repudiate that style of thought must depart from a firm conviction that Britain's historic greatness has gone. Its prestige cannot be recovered, even through the everyday militarisation of initiatives like 'Help for Heroes' and other more cerebral investments in resurgent military Orientalism.[5] We may now represent the past while our former colonies stand for the future.

President Obama was recently described as something of a crypto-Fanonian anti-colonial. His fervently anti-Western view of contemporary geopolitical arrangements has been said to derive from an unhealthy obsession with his paternal grandfather's unjust treatment at the hands of the British during the Kenyan emergency.[6] At the risk of endorsing that kind of caricature, we have to appreciate that the latest wars do need to be seen in a long imperial sequence. Conflicts over decolonisation have not merely been captured obliquely in the wealth of propaganda that comprises the core of this archive. Because colonialism is always war, they have, in a profound sense, *created* the potent body of fantasies, myths and mystifications that we can access through this portal. The historic problem of Britain's decline should therefore be placed in the context provided by recognising that, against the grain of contemporary debate about globalisation, the end of empires and colonies was a *primary political question* of the twentieth century. It remains important now as the settlements involved in postcolonial independence come unglued under the impact of poverty, climate change, neo-imperialist commerce in scarce resources and various kinds of conflict in which the objectives of development become impossible to distinguish from those of security.[7] If these observations bring to mind George Orwell's disturbing remark that we have now reached such a depth that stating the obvious has become the first duty of intelligent people, then so be it.[8]

The strategic significance of this critical intervention in postcolonial Britain's cultural history is confirmed by the fact that a multinational constituency has been mobilised by the moral and political obligation to work-through the consequences of empire. By bringing together some of the different varieties of film that have registered and projected colonial history, this initiative lends credibility to the still contentious prospect of recognising Britain's culture as a postcolonial phenomenon. In a political era that can be characterised by culture's 'weaponisation'[9] and low-intensity warfare's identification of its 'human terrain',[10] the great importance of this historical material is farther than ever from being a narrowly scholastic affair. Contemporary problems remain pending in these timeworn representations of the British Empire and its endings. The empire's meaning is, for example, still being determined. That process continues, not merely among its immediate inheritors and beneficiaries who – disoriented and alienated by the speed of its disappearance – envy the unwavering certainties that derived previously from colonialism's 'manichaeism delirium'.[11] Their world is no longer entirely populated by the absolutely different: black and white, settler and native, cross and crescent. It is an uneven, complex environment where exotic difference has been mainstreamed and corporate multiculturalism has discovered unanticipated value in the management of ethnic enclaves and markets. How, or indeed whether the bloody sequence of decolonisation can be made to represent a smooth teleological movement from a Ukanian Greece to a US Rome remains to be seen. Certainly, the meaning of the empire to Britain does not coincide with its significance for the US, for the rest of Europe or for the no-longer colonised who may still look back at it with a measure of ambivalence.[12]

Despite Niall Ferguson's insistence to the contrary, there is significant resistance to the idea that the relationship between the US and the UK should be recognised as a pivotal feature of Britain's imperial phase. The economic dimensions of that linkage must be acknowledged but they are not always decisive. That connection is a funda-mental and inescapable aspect of the raciality reproduced in the contents of this archive, but if we are to explain why and how it came about, a longer detour through the history of race-thinking than these remarks can accommodate will be required.[13] Ideas about power, sovereignty and the geopolitical fate of different races, which were directly derived from the exigencies of US conquest and colonisation, contributed to the juridical, moral and military history of Europe's empires long before the diplomatic and military representatives of the United States sat down at the Berlin conference to allocate spheres of influence.[14] The complexity of long, philosophical and scientific interaction across a dynamic network of centres and margins makes it hard to generalise but a constitutive relationship does emerge to underpin distinctively racialised conceptions of progress and to endorse the political ontologies characteristic of imperial rule.[15] The racialised history and destiny of the West were configured according to the habits of white supremacy and the cultural mandate of absolute ethnicity.[16] The resulting imperial mythography acquired a great reach not least through the agency of the cinema. It shaped the grand projects of Cecil Rhodes, T. E. Lawrence and Winston Churchill and influenced the transatlantic lives of imperial intellectuals like Lord Curzon and Rudyard Kipling whose 'Wee Willie Winkie' would enjoy a hemispheric appeal.

The contemporary tribulations of the Obama presidency are but one sign that these racial formations and the diminished mode of politics they promote, have endured, albeit in a residual condition. They have been sustained and even augmented by a culture of colonial domination that can be traced through the contents of this archive and the transnational institutions that gave rise to them. A worldly genealogy of racism can be deduced from this history. It can contextualise and provincialise the US-centred views of the world's racial nature which are still being widely exported.

MOURNING AND THE CULTURE OF EMPIRE

I have argued for some time that, as far as Britain is concerned, a long-overdue process of working-through the post-imperial legacy remains obstructed by a disabling societal melancholia and neurosis. That pathological blockage affords its bewildered adherents a powerful filter to be deployed against the things that make them uncomfortable as well as a way to defend the guilty pleasures they derive from their imagined victimhood.[17] Though it can be defined by indifference, guilt and self-loathing, this melancholia encompasses positive moments. One of the most important rests upon an invented memory of World War II that is as partial as it is tendentious. This colonial and imperial archive has therefore acquired a strategic as well as an historical importance. As we interpret its contents, we are invited to consider the ways in which the different wars that have assembled Britain's imagined communities of race and nation, have been articulated together.

Critical interpretation can widen the discrepancies between the ideal colony and its profane realities. A film like *The Knife* (1952) can be used to unsettle the myths of imperial progress and native uplift that it re-enacts in the service of anti-Communism. An additional opportunity arises with acquisition of valuable points of entry into the difficult process of unmaking melancholia's distinctive, psychosocial projections. The mechanisms can be revealed and explored that screen out and reshape conflicts over decolonisation so that attention can dwell instead upon wounded Britain's triumphant anti-Nazi sacrifices. This pattern of responses cannot, of course, be separated from the politics of racial difference. First, because postcolonial immigration to Britain has so often been presented as an invasion that continues and completes Hitler's wartime assault, and second, because the dubious instrumental morality of empire was bolstered wherever it coincided with the empire-cum-Commonwealth's anti-Nazi efforts presented so artfully in *Hillmen Go to War* and *West Indies Calling*, both from 1944.

It should be no surprise that the overarching, iconic figure of Winston Churchill provides historic ballast for this political and social-psychological operation. Even in the depths of the country's greatest wartime emergency, his monumental presence was happy to concede that he found the word 'Commonwealth' difficult to articulate: 'Some people like the word Commonwealth, but others, and I am one of them, are not at all ashamed of the word "Empire". But why should we not have both?'[18] Some years later, in her famous declaration that society did not exist, Margaret Thatcher asserted that it was time to supersede the sociality associated with Britain's welfare state, and endorsed by its histories of class injury and militancy. The redundancy of that subjectivity and solidarity was confirmed by the installation of self-disciplining, self-reliant individuals who would be as homogenous culturally and racially as they were compliant and docile in the face of her aggressive exercises in regressive modernisation. Significantly for our purposes, the forms of community which could counterbalance the loss of sociality and history were explicitly identified in the dynamic and exhilarating possibility of the nation, effectively recomposed by its experience of being at war, in this case, with Argentina.

> Today we meet in the aftermath of the Falklands Battle. Our country has won a great victory and we are entitled to be proud. This nation had the resolution to do what it knew had to be done – to do what it knew was right … . Now that it is all over, things cannot be the same again for we have learned something about ourselves – a lesson which we desperately needed to learn … . When we started out, there were the waverers and the fainthearts. The people who thought that Britain could no longer seize the initiative for herself. The people who thought we could no longer do the great things which we once did. Those who believed that our decline was irreversible – that we could never again be what we were.
>
> There were those who would not admit it – even perhaps some here today – people who would have strenuously denied the suggestion but – in their heart of hearts – they too had their secret fears that it was true: that Britain was no longer the nation that had built an Empire and ruled a quarter of the world.[19]

It is relevant, though it need not detain us, that this martial, populist perspective provides an important key to the far more belligerent career of Thatcher's successor, Tony Blair. He strove to repeat her triumph by mimicking its telltale blend of nationalist themes. Since then, a variety of complicated subnational, regional and ethnic factors have intervened to alter Britain's geobody[20] and produce an uneven pattern of national identification as well as what might be called an identity-deficit among the English.[21] Liverpool's football fans still sing 'we are not English we are Scouse' and their insistence privileges locality over nationality irrespective of any ethnic dimensions. This treacherous sentiment looks toward Ireland and conveys something of the political geography involved in the continuing break-up of the United Kingdom. The fans' disaffiliation from that political community can be used to introduce the larger problem of how anchored or grounded collective identities are now being acquired and held on to, often as a means to offset the destabilising consequences of negative globalisation. A systemic precariousness preys upon atomised, hyper-individuated people desperate to recapture a measure of solidarity and collectivity in an inhospitable environment characterised by loneliness and anxiety, selfishness and privatisation. This difficulty has hit the non-metropolitan English with a greater force than Britain's other national and regional groups. In this context, identity has emerged as a political theme and become a fundamental concern. Ultranationalist organisations like the British National Party, the UK Independence Party and the English Defence League invoke its jeopardy and lack with an unerring regularity that betrays their grasp of its political effectiveness. That power is coveted by the mainstream groups.

Anxiety over who Britons are as a nation has been formed in these unstable conditions. The resulting cultural symptoms distort and diminish British political life, impacting destructively upon understanding of the country's place in the world and obstructing its ability to act justly and reasonably in governing political and economic problems that arise from inequality and are complicated further by immigration and multiculture as well as by an insecurity that is simultaneously personal, communal and national as well as economic, experiential and psychological. We are doomed by the fatal aspiration to sit at the world's top table and punch above our weight.

These anxieties now condition popular responses to wars that require sacralisation but can only be made intelligible through an increased familiarity with an imperial past that has largely faded from domestic consciousness. Their pre-history is neither taught in British schools nor recalled directly by the country's political elites. The difficulties arising from the inability and the disinclination to remember that past are multiplied by a radically unbalanced distribution of information. The peoples that Britons fought and killed, supposedly in order to educate, reform and democratise, now know and act upon British imperial history because they have understood that it is also their own. The long memory of previous wars retained by some rural Afghans has, for example, proved baffling to the most recently deployed troops. However, inside the carapace of a bewildered and neurotic national community, Britain's confused subjects are increasingly confounded by developments that they have lived through without acquiring any sense of how they might be interpreted in historical terms. Circulated as cheap common sense, today's aggressive civilisationism actually summons and produces the menacing, Manichaean geometry of power that its North American originators – Samuel Huntington, Bernard Lewis *et al.* – spent so much time fantasising about.

Disoriented by the chronic stress of apparently endless warfare, Britain's anxious public seeks a path back toward psychological and emotional comfort and increased ethical stability. The fact that their country nobly fights a righteous cause supplies the only justification for the horrors of the never-ending conflict. The warm, restorative and justificatory feelings that result from making the nation at war into a special object of affection and identification may be fleetingly felt on the packed streets of Wooton Bassett as flag-draped coffins brought home from Afghanistan roll steadily by. The same, heavily theatrical righteousness was also evident on the silent streets of London as Spitfires and Hurricanes, bent on commemorating the Battle of Britain, rumbled and buzzed overhead while the actor Robert Hardy intoned Churchill's finest words far more reverently than their statesman-author ever could have done.[22]

The melancholic affect can be discovered in the testing ambiguities of this colonial archive where the means of disrupting it can also be located. Both possibilities coexist there not just because the archive contains propaganda – though it certainly does – but because its sacred, foundational scripts repeat the essential statement of Britain's imperial liturgy sanctified in 1905 by another aristocratic English colonialist with extensive family connections in the US. Its esteemed author, Lord Curzon of Kedleston was, among his many other accomplishments, the notorious, governmental agent of Britain's 'imperial half century' (1871–1921). His deadly tenure as Viceroy of India has been estimated by the *Lancet* to have featured some 19 million deaths from avoidable famine and related problems of public health. The purpose of the empire, he explained, is:

> ... To fight for the right, to abhor the imperfect, the unjust or the mean, to swerve neither to the right hand nor to the left, to care nothing for flattery, for applause or odium or abuse ... but to remember that the Almighty has placed your hand upon the greatest of His ploughs, in whose furrow the nations of the future are germinating and taking shape, to drive the blade a little forward in your time, and to feel that somewhere among those millions you have left a little justice or happiness and prosperity, a sense of manliness or moral dignity, a spring of patriotism, a dawn of intellectual enlightenment, or a stirring of duty, where it did not before exist. That is enough. That is the Englishman's justification in India.[23]

Churchill's name has rightly been bestowed upon the core formation in twentieth-century Britain's nationalist politics. There should be no surprise that his over-inflated, celebrity profile can now provide postcolonial critique with an invaluable interpretative device capable of revealing how race, nation, war and culture can become connected and the special political power of the volatile mixture that results. When Prime Minister Thatcher identified the revitalising effect of her Falklands victory upon Britain's national character, she was mobilising what Anthony Barnett calls the 'Churchillist' discourse.[24] Though in Barnett's perspective, 'Churchillism' has seldom been primarily and explicitly concerned with overseas affairs, we should not forget that the veteran of small wars had been Britain's Colonial Secretary in 1922 or that three decades later he would still be urging his reluctant Conservative cabinet colleagues to fight a general election under the slogan 'Keep Britain White'. The great man was a consistent proponent of both Anglo-Saxon exceptionalism and racial hierarchy whose whiggish sense of the empire's progressive momentum and sharp appreciation of the order of rank to be found inside the white race should not make us hesitate in pronouncing him a racist. He was unabashed about his dislike of 'people with slit eyes and pigtails'. He condemned Hindus as a foul race 'protected by their mere pullulation from the doom that is their due' and advocated the 'punitive devastation' of Afghanistan.[25] In Iraq, which might, as Christopher Catherwood suggests, have been better named 'Churchill's Folly', the great leader urged the use of poison gas against 'uncivilised tribes', while in Ireland he supported the machine-gunning of Sinn Fein meetings from the sky. His stewardship of the Colonial Office coincided with the period in which Marcus Garvey's transnational Universal Negro Improvement Association (UNIA) endorsed the militant movement for Indian independence and despite sharing in the idea that a well-liveried steamship line might afford the only worthwhile index of the movement's proper national stature, provoked great concern among Whitehall's imperial administrators fearful of democratic contagion.[26]

This was not only the era of festive colonial expositions[27] and of the post-World War I surge in anthropological exploration and colonial domination by means of air power. It was also the period in which the political technology of modern propaganda was being drawn up and systematised after its uneven use between 1914 and 1918. As the institutional shape of the emergent, interwar world order solidified, new communicative techniques were employed to resell the idea of a colonial mission to war-weary and economically depressed European populations for whom the idea of imperial ascendancy provided scant compensation for their suffering.[28] Colonial propaganda was also unleashed to revive the martial spirit of people for whom war had been stripped of all glamour and romance by its recent catastrophic industrialisation. A colonial mission was offered to traumatised, poor and working-class people whom their blue-blooded rulers deemed scarcely less vulnerable to the seductions of Bolshevism than the disgruntled legions of Gandhi and Garvey.

As we now know, specific versions of this political material were tailored for the colonies where the task of maintaining an intimate connection with Britain could not be left to take care of itself. These two strands of government activity – the cultural diplomacy of imperial rule and the public-relations campaigns for domestic consumption – are ripe for the kind of braided, contrapuntal reading initiated by the pathbreaking historian Wendy Webster.[29] It is still far more usual to find those topics falsely divided and assigned to separate, sovereign specialisms. The frame of colonial governance needs to be made to contain the door of domestic antagonisms. The contents of this archive require us to identify and appreciate the hinges – their convergences and interconnections.

BEYOND CHURCHILLISM

A precious and little understood chance of change is signalled by the faint hope that Britain might recover from its imperial hangover and begin to assist other European nations with comparable problems to do the same thing. That remote possibility speaks to far-reaching geopolitical concerns, particularly those that bear upon the prosecution of the continuing wars and on the many other conflicts still erupting in postcolonial locations. The decision to conclude this research initiative with the formal declarations of national independence by Britain's ex-colonies forces the issue of why, half a century later, the country is still militarily involved in those very same places? That question can be connected to a second line of enquiry that bears upon the history of decolonisation, its periodisation and the way it has been registered at home. Why are the most successful films of the early 1960s, the central moment of official decolonisation, *Zulu* (1964), *Lawrence of Arabia* (1962) and so on, even now, repeatedly being screened on British television? Perhaps Britain is still seeking its own independence?

James Baldwin's characteristically insightful commentary on David Lean's epic portrayal of Lawrence provided some important clues to that film's longevity and enduring appeal:

> ... the weary melancholy underlying Lawrence of Arabia stems from the stupefying apprehension that, whereas England may have been doomed to civilize the world, no power under heaven can civilize England ... the principle illustrates the dilemma of all civilizing, or colonizing powers, particularly now, as their power begins to be, at once more tenuous and

more brutal, and their vaunted identities revealed as being dubious indeed. The greater their public power, the greater the private, inadmissible despair, the greater the danger to all human life.[30]

Suez was still freshly in mind when Baldwin made these astute observations. His central point remains powerful even though he retreats from the different interpretative agenda that might have been set by a greater appreciation of the emergence of Britain's postimperial nostalgia in the new context created by the Cuban Missile Crisis and the global rise of US-focused, popular and youth cultures for which the unprecedented careers of rhythm-and-blues-loving groups like The Animals, The Beatles and The Rolling Stones provide the best example. The meaning of empire and in particular, the significance of its military aspect, had been transformed by the end of national service in 1960. The rising generation which had evaded conscription's net, found new opportunities to voice its scepticism and its disenchantment in the corridors of the country's art schools.

Delicate political operations are a continuing factor in managing widespread opposition to contemporary conflicts, which need to be understood not through the simplifying lenses of Manichaean thinking (racial or civilisational) but as part of a sequence of colonial conflict which stretches back, in the first instance, to the 1857 uprising in India. If today's anatomists of Britain's imperial culture are committed to the interpretative power of the humanities and human sciences, they must develop a critical apparatus that can be deployed to explain the decolonising conflict that is still unfolding around us. The contemporary setting for postcolonial enquiry into these issues is being shaped not only by the immediate effects of war but also by the fact that the Iraq conflict drained Churchillism of much of its historic appeal. Support for the military action that showed the world and reminded ourselves how great we should be, has now been tainted (if not undone completely) by the results of going to war against the wishes of a popular majority. That fracture has not healed and the resulting split has decisively altered the ways in which Britain's sense of itself as a postcolonial entity is now being formed and lived.

Analysis of these films will hopefully contribute a deeper history to the ambivalence about today's wars and the battles over the meaning of being British and English, civilised and Western to which they give rise. National identity can be secured through the interlaced political languages of racism, and Islamophobia. Meanwhile, the ontological and psychological security they offer, mediates the privatisation, selfishness and ignorance that derive from a 'neoliberal' revolution which has not been affectively compelling and has often been invested with xenophobic magic in order to make it attractive. The haemorrhaging of solidarity so evident in the recent course of British culture has been intensified by the impact of digital technologies and economic crisis on conceptions of self and community: sameness, solidarity and subjectivity.

A POSTCOLONIAL REVISION?

I have defined the principal task of postcolonial scholarship in Britain heuristically as a difficult, multilayered and multidisciplinary project. It arose from the need to discuss, reinterpret and process the country's shameful, glorious colonial dominion. In practice, this means working to liberate ourselves and our plurality by disarticulating Britain's past from the realm of pathological fantasy so that it can be recognised ordinarily as history. This archive comprises a valuable mnemonic aid. Those of us based in education should not reduce that complex intervention to the more limited goals of making the empire *relevant* where it has been repressed and recognisable where it has been ignored. Those basic steps are necessary but they are insufficient. They have to be supplemented by ensuring that any re-theorisation of the era of 'European universalism' and of the partial, race-friendly conceptions of humanity on which it rested, remains a critical, urgent enterprise.[31] The negative labour involved is part of creating a shared present common to formerly colonised and formerly colonising peoples and powers. That precious opportunity defies the ways that racism and civilisationism assemble contrasting forms of life hierarchically, value them in relation to one another and distribute them along a linear, temporal scale so that being absolutely different becomes being either ahead or behind. That pattern is produced by war and we can examine its reproductive cycles in the contents of this archive. Breaking them is a far more difficult task than it sounds. However, the act of formally placing certain events, patterns and perspectives in the past can contribute integrity to what might be called a process of reparative resynchronisation. Transforming Britain's social and psychological relationships with alterity is a delicate operation. It should be distinguished from the voguish political appetite for what Prime Minister Blair used to call, in the easy jargon of management consultancy, 'drawing a line and moving on'.

Analysis of these extraordinary films can contribute to this supremely difficult task. It can highlight the discrepancies between what Britain did, what Britain thought it was and what it is no longer – a complicated multidimensional gesture that accumulates elemental force in a culture which appears increasingly to be bereft not only of its history but of any sociality that is not technologically mediated. Examining these films can be a painful and shocking experience, particularly for those of us who are not seeing their shadowy cast of characters for the first time but rather renewing our acquaintance with old friends and enemies, as well as with past, guilty pleasures and shame-inducing feelings of complicity. Viewers are disturbed, unsettled, not because we foolishly and immorally project today's 'politically correct' judgments back into a past they cannot fit. We are rightly disturbed because, in watching material like *A New Life* (1951) we can avoid neither the raw violence nor the sheer complexity of imperial and colonial history. We must be able to respond to the matter-of-fact, perlocutionary quality of colonial common sense: the numbing obviousness through which hierarchy, domination and cruelty are naturalised, routinised and justified. The wrongs and crimes are simplified, sometimes encoded, rendered inappropriately as comic or banal, but as history seen on film, the meaning they gave to colonial rule can be endowed with the power to dispel the myths of Britain's civilising mission and puncture the comforting fantasy in which tropical natives contentedly volunteered themselves into subservience to the Crown.

Analysis of colonial and imperial film cannot avoid the issues of race and racism which are usually dismissed as social and political objects that do not merit serious scholarly attention. If it escapes being defined as an incoherent concept that is unworthy of sustained investigation, racism gets consigned prematurely to the past.

It is either over or historically so remote that it has become inaccessible. Race on the other hand, is admitted to the present but approached almost exclusively as a problem of political ontology rather than as a social relationship involving a whole constellation of interlinked problems: scientific and military, epistemological and governmental.[32]

The racism in these films is rarely overt. It accumulates from episodic, patterned misrecognition and is consolidated by the repetition of fragments that are today as likely to appear paternalistic and stupid as they do malicious or hostile. Its familiar chains of meaning are built up incrementally and inferentially. Considered critically, the resulting genealogy of colonial race-thinking can lead us through the epicentres of Atlantic and imperial modernity. Even today, a non-immanent critique of race-thinking contains the promise of undoing the philosophical and juridical foundations of those fading colonial formations. Nonetheless, much still remains to be said about how the concepts race and racism have been employed in different locations and how their mutual articulation has been resolved in discrepant political idioms that doggedly resist translation.

I'm certain that many people – even those indiscreet enough to declare themselves sympathetic to the struggle against racialised injustice – not only find it impossible to imagine a world without racial difference but also feel that the attempt to do so is a reckless if not irresponsible exercise in utopianism or liberal colourblindness.[33] Making sense of this archive necessitates a more thoroughgoing anti-racist commitment than the rehearsal of those campus formulae will permit. We cannot avoid a direct confrontation with racism and the order of difference it created via the machinations of empire's necropolitical states and transnational governments. Without that instructive encounter, we would be unable to redefine and expand the scale of postcolonial thought in the cosmopolitical way I have suggested. Only after it, will the historical – not the natural – problems of racial hierarchy be graspable as a causal dynamic rather than some flimsy ideological embellishment gilding the machinery of exploitation.

The dregs of the academic left reveal a squeamishness with regard to anti-racism that often masquerades as political and theoretical sophistication. In that vapid form, it is connected to a second problem which resides in a great – and sometimes, a worthy – distaste for instrumentalist approaches to the study of political systems, ideologies and ideas. A principled turn away from reductionism accompanied the falling into disrepute of structurally oriented and functionalist analyses derived from or allied with Marxism. However, the generally healthy reluctance to tie ideas and representations to fixed and easily identifiable class actors has had another unhappy byproduct. It has hindered understanding of the phenomenon of propaganda or, as it rapidly came to be known during the twentieth century: 'public relations'. Just as we sink deeper into the morass of our infowar, raising the history and theory of propaganda appears to be a second vulgar and unserious act that compounds any indelicate interest in the study of race and racism.

In his determinedly analogue environment, W. E. B. DuBois took a different view. He is notorious for a provocatively crude specification of the authentic criteria of negro art. We should remember that his observations were articulated just a short time after he had sat close to Freud's nephew, Eddie Bernays (and indeed the mighty Lord Curzon) at the peace conference in Versailles. Bernays, who memorably set out his own influential view of political propaganda in a pithy, practical 1928 volume,[34] assisted James Weldon Johnson's National Association for the Advancement of Colored People (NAACP) during the 20s while also working for the cause of Arab nationalism in conjunction with T. E. Lawrence among others. All of these men, like Churchill and indeed like Britain's tradition-inventing, globetrotting, cigarette-smoking, radiophile, king-to-be, the 'princely link of empire', were thinking about the changing relationship of information to power and government in the third decade of the twentieth century.[35] Here is DuBois:

> ... all art is propaganda and ever must be, despite the wailing of the purists. I stand in utter shamelessness and say that whatever art I have for writing has been used always for propaganda for gaining the right of black folk to love and enjoy. I do not care a damn for any art that is not used for propaganda. But I do care when propaganda is confined to one side while the other is stripped and silent.[36]

These lines are usually interpreted as a statement about art's militant mission in a historical moment dominated by the new technologies of film and radio and marked by an imaginative proximity to the prospect of social and political revolution. However, there are other ways to read DuBois and we should begin by inverting his observation so that the possibility of propaganda as a cinematographic art emerges with greater clarity. His view of that art becoming politically significant in a new way was characterised by a sense of how the course of imperial power was being redirected as the colonial phase began to come to an end. Let me emphasise that any governmental instrumentality in that process is difficult to disentangle from the accelerated technological changes with which it was associated – think for example of Britain's technological sublime enacted and displayed during colonial festivities held at Wembley in 1924. My point is less about the centrality of imperial propaganda to the development of radio, phonography and film; and more about its dual significance as a governmental tool for simultaneously 'engineering' the consent of domestic forces while maintaining the colonial order and perhaps re-enchanting it for its primary victims overseas.

All of us who seek a critical course through this historical material are indebted to Hannah Arendt's eccentric account of totalitarianism's development from imperial and colonial systems of thought and rule. She presented a complex, rich and sometimes frustrating argument about the relationship of imperial governance to the new varieties and techniques of power that had also drawn DuBois's eye. I'm sure her arguments are familiar: imperial rule invested a particular significance in secrecy – dividing means from ends and promoting a new type of government that disassociated the immediate from the strategic, undermining both accountability and law while fostering indifference and enforcing the calculus of expediency. That quality was combined with special commitments to the power of spectacle at home and abroad designed, above all, to engage the psychological needs and politico-aesthetic appetites of the mob.

> When the European mob discovered what a 'lovely virtue' a white skin would be in Africa, when the English conqueror in India became an administrator who did not even believe in the

universal validity of his own law, but rather in his innate capacity to rule and when the dragon-slayers turned into either 'whitemen' of 'higher breeds' or into bureaucrats and spies, playing the Great Game of endless ulterior motives in an endless movement; when the British Intelligence Services (especially since the First World War) began to attract England's best sons who preferred to serve mysterious forces all over the world before serving the commonweal of their country, the stage seemed to be set for all possible horrors. Lying before anybody's nose were many of the elements which gathered together could create a totalitarian government on the basis of racism.[37]

Exactly as later figures like Fanon would have anticipated, the militaristic, spectacular culture of empire and colony is dominated by violence. The inevitable questions of sovereignty and deep statecraft aside, the backdrop of warfare was essential in highlighting the moral legitimacy of imperial rule and in specifying the desired national relationship between plucky individuals and the forbearing collective. It was, again to paraphrase Anthony Barnett's insights into the cultural and political complex that connects Churchill and Thatcher, only when the British nation went to war that it could discover what 'turned it on'. However, the small, colonial and counter-insurgency wars that populate the post-1945 sections of this archive are particular varieties of conflict. They were conducted through uniquely dishonourable procedures that blurred the simpler binary architecture of civilised against savage.

Hannah Arendt's argument for the sequencing of imperialism, racism and totalitarianism was particularly engaged by the romantic figure of T. E. Lawrence – 'the silent sentinel of the sand'. Our national pantheon of warriors requires that he should be positioned very carefully in relation to the figure of Churchill to whom he provided great inspiration. Arendt considered Lawrence in relation to the legacies of Rhodes, Cromer, Curzon and above all Kipling, whom she identified as the author of England's foundational imperial legend. That myth determined a distinctive imperial character, embodied in Lawrence, whose devious work also served to illuminate what she saw as the pivotal decivilising and depoliticising roles of the bureaucrat on the one hand and the secret agent on the other.[38] From this angle, Lawrence would create the initial template for an extra-legal operative like James Bond. It is no surprise then that his brand of military Orientalism has, like Kipling's, lately acquired a second or perhaps a third life.[39]

If we are to make this archive work for us, we should be less concerned about Lawrence's own activities than with the gap that separates them from David Lean's sumptuous film of his life which was reissued symptomatically to great critical acclaim in 1988. Although their politics may have overlapped, Lawrence and Churchill have been made to represent different tendencies in British national life and now afford contrasting examples that illuminate the difficulties involved in working-through. In different ways, Arendt and Baldwin both demand that we enquire into how Lawrence can still generate points of identification in Britain's popular engagements with Islam, Arabs, the Orient and, of course, with masculinity itself. How, to put it another way, has he been projected in popular culture as an enduring cipher of the country's inability to mourn?[40]

The cult of Churchill has a different historical contour and is anchored in his bold anti-Nazi leadership but these monumental Englishmen can be made to converge on the cinema screen. The punitive expedition on the North West Frontier that opens the Churchill biopic *Young Winston* (1972) with cries of 'Allah-u-akbar' and precedes its Lean-esque desert campaign of slaughter in Darfur, provides an example of that intersection. It underlines that we must be prepared to negotiate the impact of past and present wars and to address the distinctive juridical, moral and technological features of colonial warfare in particular. Notwithstanding Churchill's anachronistic cavalry charge and the melancholic argument to the contrary found in another popular film, *Zulu*; on those torrid and sandy battlefields, only one party was ever really vulnerable. This asymmetrical military activity was not really war in the conventional sense but rather something legally akin to torture that anticipated the vantage point of today's dishonourable drone operators, sitting, invulnerable at the screen of adapted games consoles in Colorado or Florida while dealing out death and collateral damage in Sangin to ensure security on the distant streets of London and Washington.

MOURNING, HEALING, WORKING-THROUGH

Contemporary Britain's political and media class has worked hard to ridicule and dispatch the local 'multiculturalism' that stubbornly refuses to expire. Sustaining the beleaguered, unruly initiatives for which that over-burdened term supplies an inadequate shorthand, necessitates cultivating the means to present the country historically and geopolitically in a postcolonial light. That change of perspective promises a liberation in which it might be possible to recover and re-narrate Britain's history and identity in a manner that is both more worldly and more modest than the outworn imperial specifications allow. The basic idea is that counter-narratives – accessed through a critical popular pedagogy that can only be refined in the interpretation of difficult material like these films – might therefore become an aid not only to social mourning and working-through but also to healing and reparation.

From a theoretical point of view, in contrast to the slow, private labours of the analytic hour, the collective work involved in societal mourning has been distinctly under-specified. There has been a lively debate around the concept of melancholia between those who, as I do, want the concept to remain pathological just as it was for Freud and others who would rather make it part of a general account of how identity is constituted via identification and of how political action is enabled by militant iterations of loss. Mourning, on the other hand, is less easily defined. Can or should it involve healing? Assuming mourning could succeed, what lies on the other side of its procedures? Where exactly might the social work of mourning stand in relation to the practice of national historiography and the ritualised commemorative stances that it promotes and institutionalises? How will we know when the mourning process is completed? What relation, if any, does working-through bear to the drama of apologies and reconciliations? We need to consider whether the task of mourning can specify an endpoint that we may use to orient ourselves. Speaking parochially, if Britain could consider those questions, it might become free from the corrosive expectation that the country will be able to shape the coming world militarily and economically as extensively as it did during the nineteenth century.

Demonstrating the extent of historical interdependency between here and there, then and now, are hardly popular pursuits. The notion of Britain as a postcolonial state is not widespread and where it has become an academic matter, the conversation so far has been dominated by sophistry largely based in US institutions that have generated a trickle of anodyne monographs directed towards the more ambivalent relationships between England and the Indian subcontinent. The storehouses of colonial film should not provide the fuel for the next exercises in circulating postcolonialism lite.

Proceeding towards more worthwhile alternatives, we must recall that the twentieth century began with many of the world's peoples firmly under the yoke of imperial and colonial governments. The social, political and economic upheavals that attended the end of European empires are seldom appreciated as an epochal development which heralds our post- and neocolonial world. The theories of globalisation currently in circulation downplay the significance of that change. If non-literary, postcolonial theory is to be credible, it is obliged to approach global history from several angles and to understand the overthrow of colonial orders as a profound change that unleashed new social forces and, both directly and indirectly, shaped contemporary arrangements. In other words, theories of globalisation should themselves be recognised as artefacts of postcolonial society and recomposed so that empire, colonisation, conquest and decolonisation become central to accounts of the formation and the decline of national states: territorial and networked.

The change of perspective and priorities advocated here proceeds most prod-uctively when it is articulated in conjunction with a critique of what Ulrich Beck calls 'methodological nationalism'.[41] That too needs a careful twentieth-century periodisation to which research in this archive (and its overlooked, embarrassing equivalents in many other European countries) will undoubtedly contribute.

That the representation of empire has weighed so heavily upon making the journey out of Britain's imperial pre-eminence both bearable and liveable, is an important cultural, political and historical question in its own right. It is certainly the case that accounting for the habitual patterns of representation found in this material will contribute to the elaboration of an alternative approach, perhaps by moving the apex of imperial power away from where literary analysis might locate it: in the configuration of new reading publics and educational institutions, and instead, seeing both the impact of cinema and the middle decades of the twentieth century as more important in the contest over what empire might have contributed to Britishness and might now mean in accounts of its development over time.

Churchillism has ebbed but the figure of Churchill remains integral to marking those boundaries.The Hollywood Mau Mau film, *Something of Value* (1957) was released during the course of the Kenyan emergency before the news of systematic brutality at Hola Camp had come to light. It included scenes of torture by the British and made a serious attempt to portray a balanced view of the conflict. The narrative uses a seemingly trifling slap to impel the radicalisation of Sidney Poitier's Kimani and thereby to detonate his previously brotherly connection to Rock Hudson. Today, it is interesting for the way it demonstrates how a liberal politics (in the US sense of being configured by a Civil Rights agenda) could, after Suez, be reconciled with a critical but essentially sympathetic view of Britain's colonial war. This timely concoction was going to be prefaced by a gobbet of Churchill's personal wisdom which assisted in the mapping of North America's domestic racial woes directly on to those of decolonising Kenya. However, his contribution was deemed unacceptable by the film's distributors. The film's trailer had announced that it had been produced like its predecessors *Simba* (1954) and *Safari* (1955) under military protection during the emergency – an important disclosure that reminds us – just as Leni Riefenstahl's enthusiastic employment of slave labour had done earlier – that the world created by a film could be connected to the history it represents in a number of complex ways that defy any simple separation of real and imaginary.

Britain's postimperial neuroses are easier to read in the comforting victim/victor couplet of 1964's *Zulu* where Welsh 'ethnicity' emerged as the symbolic equivalent to Zuluness mediated by the resurgent theory of martial races, but that is too easy a target. Alexander Mackendrick's overlooked *Sammy Going South* (1963), chosen for the previous year's Royal Command Performance, offers an especially compelling insight into postimperial melancholia's unfolding during that pivotal phase. Sammy (Fergus McClelland) is a young lad orphaned by an air raid on Port Said in 1956. Traumatised by that life-changing folly, he sets out to trudge the length of Africa to find his aunt who is comfortably lodged on the Indian Ocean shore of Apartheid South Africa. His charmless, picaresque tale cannot be recounted in detail here. Let us fasten instead upon its representation of the lost postcolonial nation in the form of an enterprising and bold but deeply disturbed child who measures himself and his British particularity against the yardsticks of alterity provided by a sequence of swarthy southern Europeans, lascivious Arabs, gentle Muslims, tropical animals, inhospitable environments and various North Americans led by a fatherly Edward G. Robinson.

It is striking that this plucky boy appears unconcerned by the death of his parents and eventually finds both comfort and an early manhood in the welcoming arms of his relative who has been advised by Robinson's ageing diamond smuggler how to support and encourage Sammy's self-reliance. The boy's blank suffering and ethnic steel are more Harry Potter than either Kim or Pip. His vagrant homelessness is telling, as is the cosmic injustice conveyed by the child's sudden reduction to the bestial floor of human existence from which the 4,500-mile southward journey sees him gradually ascend. The premise of this scenario licenses and perhaps fosters a melancholic response to the historical forces that collapse onto the allegorical scale of interpersonal conduct. Though it is not shown, Sammy's grief at becoming an orphan is compensated by his being able to navigate a postcolonial path to the security of kith and kin through the inhospitable core of the Dark Continent. The boy child's mastery of both nature and history is intact, absolute and unspoken. It is also, as his destination suggests, incontrovertibly racial.

Freud wrote of melancholia as a condition that precluded shame. He had struggled to reconcile its clinical combination of indifference, self-loathing and withdrawal from the world with the outbursts of manic elation that punctuated them among his patients. The politics of that pathological laughter frames what might at first seem to be an unlikely final gesture towards the complexities of working-through. Talbot Rothwell, the scriptwriter of *Carry on up the Khyber* (1968) had refined his own appreciation of innuendo and *double entendre* during time spent as a prisoner of war. The film's justly famous penultimate scene summons a crazed, liberating laughter which distinguishes itself with its capacity to violate popular culture's implication within postcolonial melancholia. That laughter suggested that British guilt and self-hatred will not be momentarily conjured away through the traditional mechanisms of banter and 'having a laugh'. The disbelieving, oppositional laughter invoked as the natives destroy the governor's mansion while he remains unperturbed at the dining table, appears altogether mad. Yet it draws on the carnivalising energy of English popular culture in order to interrupt that manic elation. In the hands of Sir Sidney (Sid James) and Lady Ruff-Diamond (Joan Sims) and their native foe, Kenneth Williams's Khazi, this intervention generates a pointed laughter carefully orchestrated so as to deploy the weapon of ridicule against the imperial varieties of power and injustice that still unexpectedly fetter the present. In an archive where any substantive comedy is at a premium, that very laughter may be our best critical and, indeed, political weapon.

The continuing struggle over which aspects of the history of empire are fit to be laughed at represents a final fold in the narrative of Britain's melancholia. It counterpoints the development of critical postcolonial perspectives and helps to historicise the nation's failed adjustment in a sequence descending from *Khyber*'s 1968 alternative to the siren call of Enoch Powell, through Alf Garnett and Jim Davidson, Freddie Starr and *It Ain't Half Hot Mum* (1974–81), to the not-very-satirical contemporary antics of Al Murray (the Pub Landlord) who began by adapting Ali G's poses to more conventional targets before eventually becoming their celebrant and their hostage.[42] The space of comedy has expanded the opportunities for pointed reflection upon the conceits of empire that emerged from the quiet cultural nationalism of intellectual art-school rockers who had missed out on conscription – a project that terminated in the proud treason of Britain's punks. I hope it does not sound far-fetched to suggest that postcolonial theory has something to learn from these struggles and their evolving tactics in the politics of affect. We should even try to use the anachronism and absurdity of some of this material to illuminate the deeper absurdities of the colonial order itself.

NOTES

1. See <www.colonialfilm.org.uk>.
2. See for example Prime Minister David Cameron's speech on this topic given on 5 February 2011, <www.number10.gov.uk/news/speeches-and-transcripts/2011/02/pms-speech-at-munich-security-conference-60293>.
3. Niall Ferguson, *Empire: The Rise and Demise of the British World Order and the Lessons for Global Power* (New York: Basic Books, 2002). See also <www.guardian.co.uk/politics/2010/may/30/niall-ferguson-school-curriculum-role>.
4. Stuart Hall, 'The Whites of Their Eyes: Racist Ideologies and the Media', in George Bridges and Ros Brunt (eds), *Silver Linings* (London: Lawrence and Wishart, 1981).
5. Rory Stewart, *The Places in Between* (London: Picador, 2004).
6. Dinesh D'Souza, 'How Obama Thinks', *Forbes*, 9 September 2010:

   ... to his son, the elder Obama represented a great and noble cause, the cause of anticolonialism. Obama Sr. grew up during Africa's struggle to be free of European rule, and he was one of the early generation of Africans chosen to study in America and then to shape his country's future.

I know a great deal about anticolonialism, because I am a native of Mumbai, India. I am part of the first Indian generation to be born after my country's independence from the British. Anticolonialism was the rallying cry of Third World politics for much of the second half of the 20th century. To most Americans, however, anticolonialism is an unfamiliar idea, so let me explain it. Anticolonialism is the doctrine that rich countries of the West got rich by invading, occupying and looting poor countries of Asia, Africa and South America. As one of Obama's acknowledged intellectual influences, Frantz Fanon, wrote in *The Wretched of the Earth*, 'The well-being and progress of Europe have been built up with the sweat and the dead bodies of Negroes, Arabs, Indians and the yellow races.'

See <www.forbes.com/forbes/2010/0927/politics-socialism-capitalism-private-enterprises-obama-business-problem_print.html> and <http://www.nationalreview.com/corner/246302/gingrich-obama-s-kenyan-anti-colonial-worldview-robert-costa>.

7. Mark Duffield and Vernon Hewitt (eds), *Empire Development & Colonialism* (Rochester, NY: James Currey, 2009).

8. See his January 1939 review of Bertrand Russell's *Power: A New Social Analysis* in the magazine *Adelphi*, <www.lehman.edu/deanhum/philosophy/BRSQ/06may/orwell.htm>.

9. See the debates recently conducted in the American Anthropological Association, <www.aaanet.org/issues/policy-advocacy/upload/Minerva-Letter.pdf> and <www.aaanet.org/issues/policy-advocacy/Anthropology-and-the-Military.cfm>.

10. See <humanterrainsystem.army.mil/>.

11. This important concept appears in the passages of *Black Skin, White Masks* where Fanon is adapting Dide and Guiraud's theory of 'hebephrenic schizophrenia' to the study of racial schemata. See footnote 48 of the chapter on 'The Negro and Psychopathology', p. 141 of the Pluto edition of Markmann's 1967 translation.

12. Jacob Dlamini, *Native Nostalgia* (Auckland Park, South Africa: Jacana Media 2009).

13. Ivan Hannaford, *Race: The History of an Idea in the West* (Baltimore, MD: Johns Hopkins University Press, 1996).

14. Tzvetan Todorov, *The Conquest of America: The Question of the Other* (New York: Harper and Row, 1984).

15. Enrique Dussel, *The Invention of the Americas: The Eclipse of "the Other" and the Myth of Modernity*, trans. Michael D. Barber (New York: Continuum, 1995).

16. Robert Young, *The Idea of English Ethnicity* (London: Blackwell, 2008); Silvia Federici (ed.), *Enduring Western Civilization* (London: Praeger, 1995); Alastair Bonnett, *The Idea of the West* (London: Palgrave, 2004).

17. A. and M. Mitscherlich, *The Inability to Mourn: Principles of Collective Behaviour*, trans. Beverley R. Placzek (London: Random House, 1975).

18. *War Speeches* (London: Cassell, 1946), pp. 162–4.

19. See <www.margaretthatcher.org/speeches/displaydocument.asp?docid=104989>.

20. This term derives from the work of Thongchai Winichakul. See his *Siam Mapped: A History of the Geo-body of a Nation* (Honolulu: University of Hawaii Press, 1994).

21. The Devonian folk duo 'Show of Hands' articulated this with precision on their nationalist anthem 'Roots', <www.youtube.com/watch?v=P5h4PFBuzvw>.

22. See <www.telegraph.co.uk/news/newsvideo/7957063/Robert-Hardy-reading-marks-anniversary-of-Winston-Churchill-Battle-of-Britain-speech.html>.

23. Curzon speech at the Byculla Club Bombay, 16 November 1905. In the microfilm collection, 'Curzon, India and Empire: The Papers of Lord Curzon (1859–1925)', the Oriental and India Collections at the British Library, London.

24. Anthony Barnett, *Iron Britannia* (London: Allison and Busby, 1982). See *New Left Review* vol. 1 no. 134, July–August 1982.

25. Richard Toye, *Churchill's Empire* (London: Macmillan, 2010); Madhusree Mukerjee, *Churchill's Secret War: The British Empire and the Ravaging of India during World War II* (New York: Basic Books, 2010); A. W. Brian Simpson, *Human Rights and the End of Empire* (Oxford: Oxford University Press, 2001).

26. Robert G. Weisbord, 'Marcus Garvey, Pan-Negroist: The View from Whitehall', *Race* vol. 6 no. 4, 1970, pp. 419–29.

> In March 1922 Garvey, in his capacity as Provisional President of Africa, pledged the support of four hundred million Negroes to Mahatma Gandhi, 'one of the noblest characters of the day', in the cause of a free India. Speaking to a massive audience at his Liberty Hall headquarters in New York, Garvey commented that it was customary for the British to suppress liberty and typical of them to imprison and execute the leaders of libertarian causes everywhere. In a cable to Lloyd George, then Prime Minister, Garvey asserted: 'We are for the freedom of India and the complete liberation of African colonies, including the Nigerias, Sierra Leone, Gold Coast and Southwest and East Africa. We wish your nation all that is good, but not at the expense of the darker and weaker peoples of the earth.' Of course, many of the darker and weaker peoples Garvey had in mind were under British rule in Africa. Also in March of 1922 a mammoth Garveyite assemblage unanimously and enthusiastically protested the 'brutal manner' in which the British Government had treated the indigenous population of Kenya: 'You have shot down a defenseless people in their own native land for exercising their rights.'

> See F.O. 371/7286: Copy of Press Release from UNIA, 13 March 1922.

27. See <www.britishpathe.com/record.php?id=75167>, notable for slow-motion footage of the Wembley athletics over elephants.

28. John MacKenzie, *Propaganda and Empire: The Manipulation of British Public Opinion, 1880–1960* (Manchester: Manchester University Press, 1984).

29. Wendy Webster, *Englishness and Empire 1939–1965* (Oxford: Oxford University Press, 2005).

30. James Baldwin, *The Devil Finds Work* (London: Michael Joseph, 1976), pp. 81–2.

31. Immanuel Wallerstein, *European Universalism: The Rhetoric of Power* (New York: New Press, 2006).

32. George Mosse, *Toward the Final Solution: A History of European Racism* (Madison: University of Wisconsin Press, 1978).

33. Patricia Williams, *Seeing a Color-Blind Future: The Paradox of Race* (Reith Lectures 1997) (New York: Farrar, Straus and Giroux 1998).

34. Edward Bernays, *Propaganda* (1928) (Brooklyn, NY: IG Publishing, 2004).

35. Eric Hobsbawm and Terence Ranger (eds), *The Invention of Tradition* (Cambridge: Cambridge University Press, 1983).

36. 'Criteria of Negro Art', *The Crisis* vol. 32, October 1926, pp. 290–9.
37. Hannah Arendt, *The Origins of Totalitarianism* (London: Allen & Unwin, 1967).
38. Lawrence was seduced into becoming a secret agent in Arabia because of his strong desire to leave the world of dull respectability whose continuity had simply become meaningless, because of his disgust with the world as well as with himself. What attracted him most in the Arab civilisation was its 'gospel of bareness … [which] involves a sort of moral bareness too', 'which has refined itself clear of household gods'. What he tried to avoid most of all after he came back to English civilisation was to avoid living a life of his own, so that he ended with an apparently incomprehensible position as a private in the British Army, which obviously was the only institution in which a man's honour could be identified with a loss of his individual personality. Arendt, *The Origins of Totalitarianism*, p. 218.
39. Kaja Silverman, 'White Skin, Brown Masks: The Double Mimesis, or, With Lawrence in Arabia', *Differences* no. 1, 1989, pp. 3–54.
40. Remember that Lean's 1962 film commences with Lawrence's death. Empire is celebrated, sacralised in what is a protracted act of grieving. That history returns after its loss, remains present in spectral form and cannot be renounced. See also Sigmund Freud 'Mourning and Melancholia':

    The distinguishing mental features of melancholia are a profoundly painful dejection, cessation of interest in the outside world, loss of the capacity to love, inhibition of all activity, and a lowering of the self-regarding feelings to a degree that finds utterance in self-reproaches and self-revilings and culminates in a delusional expectation of punishment. *The Standard Edition of the Complete Psychological Works of Sigmund Freud*, vol. 14 (London: Hogarth Press, 1953–74), p. 244.

41. Ulrich Beck, *The Cosmopolitan Vision* (London: Polity Press, 2006): <www.re-public.gr/en/?p=157>.
42. See Paul Gilroy, *After Empire: Melancholia or Convivial Culture?*, 1953–74 (London: Routledge, 2004).

EMPIRE AT WAR

•

3

The Last Roll of the Dice: *Morning, Noon and Night*, Empire and the Historiography of the Crown Film Unit

Martin Stollery

Morning, Noon and Night, an unfinished Crown Film Unit feature-length documentary about the empire war effort, went into production during 1942–3. The film was intended to focus not on frontline fighting by colonial troops, but on the infra-structure which supported the British empire's war effort: food production; the manufacture of military equipment; medical and welfare services; training, and so on. There is a useful basic distinction to be made between British documentary films that deal with specific parts of the empire, and those that deal with the 'idea of empire' more generally. Films belonging to the latter category include *One Family* (Walter Creighton, 1930), the first Empire Marketing Board (EMB) film project, and the films for Imperial Airways which Paul Rotha produced or directed during the 1930s, which I discuss in more detail elsewhere.[1] *Morning, Noon and Night* would have extended this tradition into World War II by including Canada, New Zealand, Australia, South Africa, Southern Rhodesia, India and Britain. *Morning, Noon and Night* was the last major film project sponsored by the British state, prior to the end of empire, which attempted to define a British imperial sphere of influence distinct from American conceptions of how the world should be organised. In this respect it can be seen as the last roll of the dice in a history that began with *One Family* and the EMB Film Unit. British state-sponsored film-making emerged and developed partly in response to widespread establishment concerns about American trade, values and ideas penetrating Britain and the British empire, undermining imperial sentiment, and contributing to a fundamental reconfiguration of the world order.

 Morning, Noon and Night also offers a route into rethinking the dominant narrative of British documentary during World War II in relation to what Paul Gilroy describes as Britain's 'buried and disavowed colonial history'.[2] Gilroy argues that 'the life of the nation has been dominated by an inability even to face, never mind actually mourn, the profound change in circumstances and moods that followed the end of the empire and consequent loss of imperial prestige'.[3] In Gilroy's analysis, the necessary working-through of these changed circumstances and moods has been deflected by the 'overarching figuration of Britain at war against the Nazis, under attack, yet stalwart and ultimately triumphant. That image ... has underpinned the country's unstable post-1945 settlement.'[4] As far as film history is concerned, the *locus classicus* of that defiant, stalwart image of Britain is the body of films produced by Crown during World War II. The Crown Film Unit was, however, involved in a wider range of film-making than this would suggest. The film-makers who worked on *Morning, Noon and Night* attempted to expand the framework of Crown films such as *Listen to Britain* (Humphrey Jennings and Stewart McAllister, 1942) and *Fires Were Started* (Humphrey Jennings, 1943). Their aim was for *Morning, Noon and Night* to represent not just the People's War confined to Britain as an island nation, but rather the People's War extended across what Wendy Webster has described as the 'People's Empire', whose future viability would be secured through progressive modernisation.[5] This involved some very particular challenges.

Dan North in his recent work on unfinished British films argues that 'the study of only those films which made it to the screen and found an audience gives an inaccurate picture of the ideas and concerns in circulation amongst Britain's film-making communities'.[6] This is true enough, but we need to further distinguish between unfinished projects that amount to little more than a speculative glint in a film-maker's eye, and those to which significant production resources had been devoted. Both have their place within the study of film history. Projects belonging to the latter category are, however, likely to indicate not only 'ideas and concerns in circulation', but more precisely ideas and concerns considered to have fairly immediate relevance and appeal to audiences. *Morning, Noon and Night* belongs to this category.

The film-makers involved in *Morning, Noon and Night* set themselves a number of substantial challenges. They wanted to produce a major new documentary film, with newly shot rather than archival footage, and new perspectives on its subject matter, that would restore faith in the British empire at a time when certain parts of it were under direct threat from enemy forces. One aspect of the project, echoing *One Family*'s and indeed *Listen to Britain*'s treatment of royalty, was the initial idea that material should be shot on or as near as possible to King George VI's birthday, 14 December 1942. The aim was to represent an ordinary yet symbolically resonant day in the life of the empire united under the monarch. More immediately, the film-makers wanted to engage with a range of doubts about and criticisms of empire circulating among sections of the British, American and empire audiences *Morning, Noon and Night* was primarily intended to address. The project was so ambitious in scope that it is not altogether fanciful to suggest that in some respects *Morning, Noon and Night* is the urtext of official British wartime documentary. The aim was to incorporate new footage from film units across the empire, from the Crown and service film units, from independent documentary units and from some commercial film units within Britain, to produce a film of truly global reach. *Morning, Noon and Night* would have included some of the type of material already associated with Crown. For example Humphrey Jennings was assigned to obtain footage of allotments, air-raid wardens and Liverpool Street station. Harry Watt, who had recently moved from Crown to Ealing Studios, was assigned women working in an iron-and-steel works. But *Morning, Noon and Night* would have situated the type of iconic images we now associate with Crown within a wider imperial framework.

Primary sources at the National Archives in London show that a considerable amount of time was spent planning and discussing *Morning, Noon and Night* during late 1942 and throughout much of 1943. Shot lists and references in these documents to material received from various film units throughout the empire suggest that a large amount of footage was shot and sent to London. Unfortunately, it appears that most of this no longer exists. The only rushes that have been identified as definitely belonging to this project represent Auxiliary Territorial Service (ATS) women, filmed in the Orkneys by the Army Film Unit, on the prescribed date of 14 December 1942. The most striking image from this material, in keeping with the emphasis upon modernity rather than tradition in *Morning, Noon and Night*, is a shot of an ATS operator standing behind and seemingly physically integrated with some range-finder equipment. This image bears some resemblance to the iconic close-up of a female worker's head super-imposed on an industrial bobbin in the Soviet montage film, *Man with a Movie Camera* (Dziga Vertov, 1929).

The status accorded to *Morning, Noon and Night* is indicated by the personal involvement of Jack Beddington, head of the Films Division at the Ministry of Information (MOI), of which Crown was part, during the early stages of the project. The film's status was also emphasised by the BBC announcer who introduced the talk Ian Dalrymple, head of the Crown Film Unit, gave about the film for an African Service broadcast on 18 January 1943. The announcer said Dalrymple was asked

> to tell you what his Unit will have to offer in the line of documentary films in 1943. He didn't think this was possible in a ten-minute talk, but instead he is going to tell you something about what he considers will be *the most interesting* documentary film of 1943.[7]

Admittedly, Dalrymple may have selected another Crown film as the most interesting of the year if the audience for this broadcast had been British rather than South African. Nevertheless, his surprising choice clearly highlights how the Crown Film Unit has been written into film history almost exclusively in terms of its production of films about Britain rather than its empire, and in relation to the British rather than the wider imperial war effort.

A slight shift in perspective is all that is needed to reconsider this assessment. If we expand the time frame slightly, the focus changes significantly. The Colonial Office was a major commissioner of Crown's services in the immediate post-war period, resulting in films such as *The Story of Omolo* (Basil Wright, 1946) and the award-winning *Daybreak in Udi* (Terry Bishop, 1950). The standard version of Crown's history, however, posits the first few war years under Dalrymple as its zenith, and the later war and post-war years as a gradual decline. Canonical Crown productions include the RAF bombing-raid film *Target for Tonight* (Harry Watt, 1941), the lyrical portrait of Britain at war, *Listen to Britain* and the narrative documentary about London firemen during the Blitz, *Fires Were Started*. Yet even if we provisionally accept the value judgments and historical narrative that identifies 1941–3 as the peak period of Crown's achievement, *Morning, Noon and Night* was one of the unit's most important projects during this supposed high point. It was a major production, estimated at approximately 7,000 feet, intended to equal the prestige of films such as *Target for Tonight* and *Fires Were Started*.

There were a number of reasons for *Morning, Noon and Night*'s emergence during 1942–3. As Lisa Lowe has argued, 'social events and circumstances other than the relationship between Europe and the non-European world are implicated in literature about the Orient, and ... the relative importance of these other conditions differs over time and by culture'.[8] 'Other conditions' were certainly important in this case. The project was initiated at a particular point in the war: after the US and the Soviet

Union had entered the conflict, and after the fall of Singapore, with the Japanese threatening to invade India. Each of these factors had a bearing on *Morning, Noon and Night*. As Arthur Calder-Marshall, the writer most involved with the project, stated later in 1943, German propaganda had been targeting a potential area of tension between Britain and its former colony: 'Americans are told … that Britain is fighting only for the *status quo*; that American boys are giving their lives so that British imperialists can exploit India.'[9] *Morning, Noon and Night* went into production during a period in which different interpretations of the Atlantic Charter, the joint declaration in August 1941 by President Roosevelt and Prime Minister Winston Churchill, were being contested. The charter's declaration on 'the right of all peoples to choose the form of government under which they will live' was later clarified by Churchill in a September 1941 speech as not applying to the British empire. Roosevelt, on the other hand, took the view that the charter was universally applicable. As Auriol Weigold has shown, the MOI was closely involved in trying to promote the perception in America that the British had made every reasonable effort to accommodate Indian nationalist leaders, and that British rule was a complex issue and on balance a positive thing.[10] There was a need, therefore, to reassert the unity, resolution and strength of the British empire while at the same time implicitly rebutting American concerns about fighting the war to rescue outmoded British imperialism. As Thomas Hajkowski has argued in relation to BBC wartime empire coverage, this international context, along with a perceived need to address British socialist opinion, led to attempts to represent a more progressive, forward-looking empire.[11]

These factors explain what now seems another odd rhetorical move in Dalrymple's radio broadcast about *Morning, Noon and Night*. Dalrymple directly linked this British film project to the recently completed Soviet documentary *One Day of War* (I. Soluyanov, 1942). This Soviet film ranged across various constituent nations of the USSR to cover, as Evelyn Russell put it in her *Monthly Film Bulletin* review, 'every possible corner of the "total war" front'.[12] Dalrymple emphasised in his radio broadcast about *Morning, Noon and Night* that the idea for the film 'came from the Russians'. He elaborated:

> it seemed highly desirable in these days, when not only our enemies but some of our friends are so assiduously pointing out the faults and futility of the British Commonwealth of Nations, that a similar film should be made to show something of our united states of free peoples, living together under one flag. Like the Russians, we have the same bewildering variety of lands and peoples to present: and we can certainly show overwhelming evidence of the same energy, the same courage and the same devotion to a single cause.[13]

The Battle of Stalingrad was being fought at this time and there was widespread admiration for the Soviet war effort. The MOI realised that this had to be acknowledged. Within a month of Dalrymple's broadcast, for example, the MOI arranged a meeting at the Albert Hall to celebrate the twenty-fifth anniversary of the Red Army, with a massed choir, readings by Laurence Olivier and John Gielgud, and politicians of all parties in attendance.[14] Dalrymple used the wartime alliance with Russia and the alleged similarity to *One Day of War* to pre-empt possible criticism of *Morning, Noon and Night* from the left and from listeners sympathetic to the Soviet war effort. As Ian McLaine has argued, one of the MOI's main propaganda tactics was to 'steal the thunder of the Left'.[15]

At the same time, Dalrymple's reference to 'our united states of free peoples' implicitly posits an equivalence between the British empire and the US, its other superpower ally.[16] Dalrymple's statements were partly an attempt to stake out a supportive reception context for this important film, but they also indicate the realignment of forces during the war that necessitated a genuinely different approach to the documentary representation of the British empire. *Morning, Noon and Night*'s production documents suggest that key figures who initially worked on the project were committed to projecting a more progressive, forward-looking representation of empire than in previous British documentary movement films.

As far as film style and structure is concerned, the currently accepted view is that Dalrymple's major contribution to the aesthetic development of Crown films during the war was, as James Chapman phrases it, to 'embrace' and 'develop to its fullest extent' an established trend towards 'reconstructed narrative-documentary'.[17] The primary evidence for this is the production during his tenure of films such as *Target for Tonight*, *Fires Were Started* and *Western Approaches* (Pat Jackson, 1944). This was certainly a major trend within Crown film production, but Dalrymple's support for *Morning, Noon and Night* demonstrates his openness to other modes of documentary as well.[18] Taking a longer view, beyond the political expediency of claiming an affinity between *Morning, Noon and Night* and *One Day of War*, both films can be placed within the history of European avant-garde and documentary films that eschewed narrative structures focused around individuals or small groups of people. These films took a different approach in an attempt to produce a more global vision that often transcends national boundaries. Films that could be included within this broad category include the Soviet *One Sixth of the Earth* (Dziga Vertov, 1926), the German *World Melody* (Walter Ruttmann, 1929) and British documentaries for Imperial Airways in the 1930s, such as *Contact* (Paul Rotha, 1933) and *The Future's in the Air* (Alexander Shaw, 1937). A final peacetime example, cited by Dalrymple in his radio broadcast as the precursor to *One Day of War*, was *A Day in Soviet Russia* (Mikhail Slutsky, Roman Karmen, 1940), described in the *Monthly Film Bulletin* as ranging from 'the Baltic to the Pacific, from the Atlantic to Turkestan'.[19]

For *Morning, Noon and Night* the initial plan was to produce a film in thirteen thematic sections. Within each section, activities from Britain, Canada, Australia, New Zealand, India, Southern Rhodesia and South Africa, and possibly other areas as well, would be represented. The directive telegraphed to the Dominions' and High Commissioners' offices at the beginning of December 1942 to give them a broad outline of the type of footage needed, summarised its overall structure. The primary borrowing from the antecedent Soviet films was the 'day in the life of wide-ranging territories' structure:

> Structure of film as follows stop sequence one battlefronts early morning ... sequence two peoples of commonwealth going to work stop thereafter rough direction of film is figuratively from out of earth into cannon's mouth stop sequence three mining sequence four transport of raw materials sequence five return to battlefronts at midday sequence six production of munitions sequence seven training for services and industrial army sequence eight defence

services sequence nine medical health and welfare sequence ten food production sequence eleven transport of munitions sequence twelve the day ends but war effort continues night shifts and population on guard sequence thirteen battlefronts night assessment of day's progress and night actions stop ... main object of film to show all varied types of peoples of commonwealth working to one common end stop ... .[20]

No single director was assigned to head up *Morning, Noon and Night*. Instead, a planning committee was assembled to steer the project. In the absence of any firm evidence confirming exactly why this approach was adopted, one can only assume *Morning, Noon and Night* was deemed too wide-ranging and ambitious for any one person to control. Again, Dalrymple had previous experience of more collective approaches to film production. Part of the planning committee's role was to deal with logistical issues. New footage was required from numerous different production units and several different continents. The initial aim was to have a completed cutting copy to show at the MOI by the end of April 1943, a trade show in mid-May 1943 and the premiere on 3 June 1943. Organisationally, 'one officer each of the planning committee [was] appointed to contact the independent documentary and shorts companies and units, the home newsreels, the home commercial producers [and] the Commonwealth official and independent newsreels'.[21] Ironically, it was suggested that in the absence of any British or empire film-makers in the Caribbean, American military or newsreel cinematographers could shoot material in this region.[22] Even within *Morning, Noon and Night* itself, cinematic representation of this region was partly ceded to the US.

The planning committee set up a subsidiary script committee to produce a detailed initial treatment from which the directive quoted earlier was derived. Arthur Calder-Marshall wrote the initial treatment. Calder-Marshall was well suited to this project. Influenced by the American novelist John Dos Passos, he had begun his career with a determined attempt to move away from what he considered bourgeois individualism in writing. Calder-Marshall's early novels such as *About Levy* (1933) and *Pie in the Sky* (1937) consist of multiple narrative strands, involving a diverse range of characters, which build up composite representations of institutions and social relationships. He adapted this approach to the structure of *Morning, Noon and Night*. Positioning himself to the left of John Grierson and his colleagues during the 1930s, Calder-Marshall published a critique of the British documentary movement's political limitations in his 1937 survey of contemporary culture, *The Changing Scene*.[23]

Although Calder-Marshall had previously been a trenchant critic of the British documentary movement, the pragmatic demands and political realignments of the war years saw him working on projects commissioned by the MOI Films Division. He scripted documentaries such as *White Battle Front* (Hans Nieter, 1940) and *Night Shift* (J. D. Chambers, 1942). Of Calder-Marshall's previous work, the most relevant to *Morning, Noon and Night* was, however, *Glory Dead*, a book about Trinidad published in 1939. Calder-Marshall made it clear at the book's outset that some of its analysis was applicable to other imperial contexts:

> Trinidad itself is a small island. In world affairs it is not of great importance. But the problems which arise in Trinidad arise everywhere in the world where there is white domination of subject races. It is the problem of Great Britain in the West Indies, in Africa and India.[24]

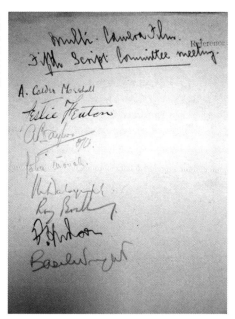

Calder-Marshall recounted lectures he had
given to Trinidadian trade unions where he
postulated 'the ultimate aims of unionism as
the establishment of socialism ... and finally the
sinking of colour distinction between white,
negro or East Indian and the realignment of
peoples according to class lines'.[25] Nevertheless,
with one eye on the coming war with Germany,
he also wrote about how the Trinidadian
population was '95 per cent solid in opposition to Fascism and Nazism'.[26] Calder-
Marshall's view was that 'the loyalty of the West Indian is not finally alienated', and
'can be won back, but only by a fundamental change of policy all round'.[27] This
developed into the determined attempt to fashion a progressive representation of
empire in his initial treatment for *Morning, Noon and Night*.

Calder-Marshall was committed to moving beyond some established ways of seeing
war and empire in *Morning, Noon and Night*. He argued at an early script committee
meeting that, by late 1942, audiences were already tired of certain clichéd documentary
representations of the war. In his previous work Calder-Marshall had opposed the lure of
exoticism; he stated at the beginning of *Glory Dead* that, despite the temptation, he was
determined to avoid a touristic account of Trinidad. Calder-Marshall was also dissatisfied
with previous documentary perspectives on empire. In *The Changing Scene*, he cited
Imperial Airways as one of the sponsors whose requirements shaped and constrained
what 1930s British documentary could represent. As I have argued elsewhere, the British
documentary films sponsored by this company in the 1930s lauded the potential for
progress and development within the empire. They nevertheless also intermittently
imply that colonial subjects would not achieve full accession to industrial, technological
and cultural modernity until some indefinite point in the future.[28]

The initial structure Calder-Marshall and the script committee worked out for
Morning, Noon and Night adopted a different stance on the relationship between
colonial subjects and industrialisation. Wartime propaganda objectives temporarily
dictated that, whatever the actual situation, emphasis should fall on how imperial
industrial productivity was outstripping the Axis across the board, especially in terms
of armaments. Dalrymple therefore described *Morning, Noon and Night*'s structure in
the following terms in his radio broadcast:

For the first time we will have the whole Commonwealth represented together within a single film: we shall pass from the mines of Wales to those of the Witwatersrand; from the sheep runs of Australia to the dairy farms of New Zealand to the paddy fields of India; from the tank, vehicle and aircraft factories of the English Midlands to those of Canada, Australia, India and South Africa.[29]

There was little indication here, unlike the Imperial Airways documentaries in the 1930s, of any developmental gaps impeding access to industrial modernity. Of course, absolute breaks with the past traditions of representation are rarely possible, especially in major films such as *Morning, Noon and Night*, designed to appeal to the widest possible audience that a wartime documentary might hope to attract. Some picturesque, 'touristic' details such as sheep runs and paddy fields are retained in Dalrymple's description, as they were in the directive telegraphed to the Dominions' and High Commissioners' offices at the beginning of December 1942, which asked contributors to include footage of 'characteristic scenery' and 'your unique, your unusual activities'.[30] Fundamentally, however, Dalrymple's description and the December 1942 directives placed the Dominions on a par with the imperial centre, and made no distinction between settler colonial societies and the Raj as far as the vital production of modern machinery to win the war was concerned. The empire was therefore represented in the initial *Morning, Noon and Night* treatment as an integrated, non-hierarchical whole. All of its constituent parts contribute raw materials, food and manufactured products on an equal and interchangeable basis, in a comity of nations that somehow transcended any established patterns of economic underdevelopment. Mindful, perhaps, of the need to tread carefully as far as Indian nationalist sentiment was concerned, Calder-Marshall explicitly recommended that *Morning, Noon and Night* should 'avoid giving the false impression that raw materials always go abroad either for processing or for manufacture'.[31]

With the Japanese in Burma threatening to advance further, India had become a pressing military as well as political issue by late 1942. It could not therefore be avoided in a major wartime documentary film about empire. Yet as Prem Chowdhry has shown, there was by the end of the 1930s a well-established tradition of Indian protests against anything in British films perceived as imperial propaganda or negative stereotyping. Indian protests against the Alexander Korda production *The Drum* (Zoltan Korda, 1938) made British feature-film producers wary of representing India during the war.[32] *Morning, Noon and Night* was a different category of film, where the footage was to be shot by Indian documentary film-makers working for the Indian Film Unit (IFU) rather than a visiting British crew. Nevertheless, the Indian film-makers within the IFU were criticised by some commentators within India for co-operating with the Government of India, and some of their films were also attacked for being politically compromised. One example is *The Voice of Youth* (1942), a filmed record of the All-India Students' Conference at Delhi released a few months before work began on *Morning, Noon and Night*. The journal *Filmindia* described it in August 1942 as 'a lop-sided denunciation of fascism', which did not 'include a denunciation of [British] imperialism which is felt by India's youth'.[33]

These issues formed the backdrop to the unenviable task facing the *Morning, Noon and Night* script committee in London. Calder-Marshall's notes in one version of the treatment referred to the difficulty of trying to work out how best to represent India:

So we go to India, where an Indian voice says, 'And we too, whatever the differences, agree the common enemy is the tyranny, which is Nazism and Fascism and the imperialism of Japan. They are turning them away from the recruiting stations, for lack of weapons to arm them with, and the factories are working night and day.' Here of course we are on ticklish ground, but there are many Indians who will say this and the IFU can surely find the visual material.[34]

The film-makers working on *Morning, Noon and Night* had to think carefully about how to forestall potential anti-colonial criticisms of their film. The phrase, 'whatever the differences', allows these differences between Indian nationalists and the British and Indian governments to be large or small, depending upon the listener, so long as they are not considered more significant than the war against Germany and Japan. It is also pertinent that Calder-Marshall proposed an Indian voice for this section of commentary. Some previous IFU films had been criticised within India on the grounds that their white, British middle-class male tones sounded alien to Indian ears.

For Calder-Marshall the positive counterweight to tentatively engaging with opposition to empire was the integration of black and Asian subjects into positions they had not previously occupied. To take one instance, the initial treatment for *Morning, Noon and Night* elaborated the relationship between colonial subjects and air power somewhat differently to the way it had been handled in the 1930s documentaries produced for Imperial Airways. A typical sequence in the earlier documentaries involved shots of a plane's shadow passing over the ground, colonised people looking up, straining to see a plane passing overhead, contrasted with the panoramic views afforded from the plane itself.[35] In his critique in *The Changing Scene* of British documentary films sponsored by Imperial Airways, Calder-Marshall challenged their universal humanist claims. He concluded by suggesting that this particular shot sequence, when viewed critically, carried connotations of domination and subordination:

> That epic sense of Man's conquest of earth, and sky and sea wouldn't sound so like stage thunder, if one could feel more certain 'what man?' What man has conquered the air for example? The man who designed the aeroplane; the men who built it but will never fly it; the professional pilot who is paid as much as a lorry-driver; the people who can afford to travel in it; the people who derive their incomes from aviation stock; or the man who looks up, shading his eyes with his hand, and takes a rest from his work till it disappears behind a cloud.[36]

Calder-Marshall's analysis anticipates Patrick Deer's general argument that in interwar British culture 'the mystique of imperial air power depended on relegating the "savage" colonized target to an "other" time and space', for example in re-enactments of the bombing of 'native' villages at Hendon air shows in the early 1930s.[37] This airborne racial hierarchy was also evident, for example, in juvenile fiction such as Captain W. E. Johns's popular *Biggles* books, published from 1932 onwards. Although the targets changed during World War II, the process of relegation to which Deer refers has nevertheless continued in a modified form since then. As Martin Francis has commented, in a specific example of Gilroy's general point about Britain's 'buried and disavowed colonial history', especially as far as the World War II is concerned, 'non-white aircrew have been largely erased from the dominant cultural memory of the wartime RAF'.[38]

Production still from *The Future's in the Air* (1937)

British representations of the RAF produced during the conflict itself were actually more varied and complex than the post-war dominant cultural memory of World War II which superseded them. The war broadened the terms of engagement established in the interwar period: British populations were bombed; British fighters engaged German ones; British bombers attacked European targets. The short British propaganda film *An Airman's Letter to His Mother* (Michael Powell, 1941) epitomises some aspects of the changing structure of feeling around the issue of air power during World War II, as well as some continuities with the interwar period. *An Airman's Letter to His Mother* was based upon an actual letter, written by a British airman for his mother in the event of his death, which provoked such interest after its initial reproduction in *The Times* that an estimated 500,000 copies were printed. In the film, opening and closing landscape shots frame the closer interior shots of the airman's mother reading the letter in his room. These images, and the language in the letter, read by John Gielgud, call up the idea of a 'Deep England', the nation's largely rural heartland, entwined with a primal appeal to protecting one's home and family. At the same time, the airman's letter links back to earlier representations of British air power by invoking the importance of personal sacrifice throughout history resulting in 'the British Empire where there is a measure of peace, justice and freedom for all, and where a higher standard of civilisation has evolved, and is still evolving, than anywhere else'.[39] Photographs of the dead airman confirm what might seem obvious to the point of invisibility, that these sentiments are expressed by a white man.

Calder-Marshall said of *Morning, Noon and Night* that 'we wish to show the fraternisation of all the imperial forces, care being taken to omit no opportunity of stressing the acceptance of coloured troops'.[40] By late 1942 the figure of the World War II airman was already so resonant that it was perhaps inevitable that *Morning, Noon and Night* would stage the 'acceptance' of a non-white representative from the empire into this mythical fraternity. The British media at this time made some tentative efforts to exploit the propaganda potential of non-white airmen. For example, a BBC *Postscript* broadcast in May 1943 featured airmen from Fiji and Nigeria.[41] Pilot officer Peter Thomas, the Nigerian airman, who became a celebrity among African audiences, also appeared in Colonial Film Unit productions.[42] *Morning, Noon and Night*'s production file demonstrates how carefully scripted such appearances were. For the seventh section of the film, in advance of any material being shot, Calder-Marshall envisaged a sequence involving pilots from across the empire being trained in a Canadian aerodrome. The airman picked out as a potential interviewee 'is a Canadian Chinese … . He wants to bomb Tokyo. But he has joined the RCAF [Royal Canadian Air Force] because the more you bomb Germany and Italy now, the sooner and harder you bomb Japan later.'[43] Chinese Canadian airmen were topical because they had only recently been permitted to enlist in the RCAF.[44] This particular one has different priorities, presumably motivated by his Chinese heritage, to the hero of *An Airman's Letter to His Mother*. The dialogue scripted for the Chinese Canadian airman in *Morning, Noon and Night* acknowledges that Commonwealth forces might have a range of reasons for participating in the war effort. A straight comparison with the different values expressed by the absent protagonist of *An Airman's Letter to His Mother* might suggest that the British pilot's reasons are also culturally and historically specific rather than universally valid. The two representations are not however entirely comparable in every respect.

Although significant efforts were made in Calder-Marshall's *Morning, Noon and Night* treatment to represent the 'acceptance of coloured troops', it still conforms to a general trend in wartime empire propaganda identified by Wendy Webster. Webster argues that most wartime British propaganda promoting an expanded 'People's Empire' version of the 'People's War' maintained 'boundaries between empire and metropolis where "home" was shown as white'.[45] Ethnic diversity within the United Kingdom was rarely acknowledged within this context. *Morning, Noon and Night* conforms to this pattern, insofar as diversity within the different countries of the Commonwealth remains external to Britain. In addition to the Chinese Canadian airman, the directive sent to New Zealand House suggested the representation of Maoris, but there is no evidence of any attempt to represent anything other than white inhabitants of Britain. Even the black servicemen who were temporarily present in large numbers during the war are absent from Calder-Marshall's treatment. Despite the committed attempt to encompass 'the whole Commonwealth represented together', as Dalrymple put it, the boundaries identified by Webster remained intact.

As far as the Chinese Canadian airman is concerned, certain aspects of his representation place him in a secondary and separate position to the prototypical white hero in *An Airman's Letter to His Mother*. Although the airman who wrote the actual letter was a bomber pilot, this is not mentioned in the text, and he is very much represented in similar terms to the fighter pilots who defended home, nation and empire during the Battle of Britain. Part of the Chinese Canadian airman's difference in *Morning, Noon and Night* is that he is more explicitly and unapologetically identified with the savage business of bombing civilians. Bombers were regarded more ambivalently than fighter pilots in World War II British culture. Bombing campaigns did not attain legendary status as quickly as the Battle of Britain did. *Target for Tonight*, dealing with a bomber raid, belonged to a particular moment early in the war when there was a perceived need to represent Britain hitting back as well as taking it. Successive films, such as the feature *The First of the Few* (Leslie Howard, 1942), and the Crown documentary *The Day That Saved the World* (J. D. Chambers, 1942), focused on RAF fighters during the Battle of Britain. The legendary status of this event began to be commemorated as early as its second anniversary on 15 September 1942, which was declared Battle of Britain Day.[46] *Morning, Noon and Night*'s egalitarianism does not extend as far as affording the Chinese Canadian airman this kind of status.

●

Tim Boon has proposed analysing some British documentary films of the 1930s and 1940s in relation to 'alliances of interests' that include but also extend beyond those immediately involved in their production. Boon discusses, for example, how *World of Plenty* (1943), a film commissioned by the Ministry of Food, a project in which Calder-Marshall was also involved, was 'made possible by sufficient agreement existing between the participants in its production. But its detailed form was also affected by the interests of separate powerful groups.'[47] The 'alliance-of-interests' model is well suited to *Morning, Noon and Night*, a state-sponsored film developed by two committees in liaison with numerous other production units.

Morning, Noon and Night's production process fell short of what the film was intended to promote: the ideal of a united and harmoniously functioning British empire. The discrepancy between this ideal and the differing values and interests that somehow had to be negotiated was acknowledged from the outset. The plan was to send every imperial territory involved in the film a directive and a copy of the initial treatment, for guidance on what to shoot. Yet a document in the *Morning, Noon and Night* production files dated 16 November 1942, entitled 'Suggestions for Further Procedure by the Script Planning Committee', asked:

> whether we should make different versions of the treatment for different territories. For example, I imagine that the anti-colour bar tone of the present version would be fine for New Zealand and dynamite for South Africa. This should be unofficial. But it should be done, if we are not going to arouse all sorts of unconscious, or at any rate unexpected resistances.[48]

There appear to have been a number of interrelated reasons why *Morning, Noon and Night* was never completed. Logistical problems arose, perhaps inevitably, in a project that involved the collation of so much newly filmed material from so many different sources. Some of the material conformed to the general directive but differed significantly from the initial treatment. Divergent perspectives emerged on how imperial wartime unity and particular contributions to it should be represented. Wider historical and political changes during its extended production schedule also posed serious challenges to key aspects of the propagandistic and progressive aspirations expressed in the initial treatment.

The surviving *Morning, Noon and Night* documents show a production schedule gradually slipping, as Dai Vaughan puts it, 'via optimism into fantasy'.[49] In a producer's report, dated 29 April 1943, Dalrymple noted that he and his colleagues were still awaiting material from Australia, Canada, South Africa and Rhodesia. Material from Australia, apparently despatched in December 1942, was presumed lost in transit.[50] A later producer's report, dated 30 June 1943, confirmed that all the material had arrived, but a subsequent one, dated 5 August 1943, indicated that the Canadian material was considered poor-quality, old footage shot in 1940 and 1941. John Grierson's film-makers at the National Film Board of Canada had apparently not shot new material, as requested, specifically for *Morning, Noon and Night*.[51] In addition, the brief summary commentary provided with the Canadian material was challenged for aggrandising Canada's role in the war. A note passed to *Morning, Noon and Night*'s editor, Stewart McAllister, dated 28 July 1943, read: 'The figure of 75% is not correct and the following one should be substituted: "More than 50% of the mechanised transport used by the British Eighth Army in North Africa was manufactured by Canada."'[52]

The material received from Southern Rhodesia would have required more thorough revision.[53] The shot list suggests some editing had taken place before this material was despatched. The shot list was accompanied by a detailed guide commentary with a very different tone from Calder-Marshall's initial treatment. Nothing in Calder-Marshall's version of *Morning, Noon and Night* reflected back upon the history of empire. Past conflicts were overlooked in order to focus upon the present and the future. The Southern Rhodesian commentary manifested a more conservative approach, secure in the conviction that imperial conquest was justified. It also traded in ambivalent colonial stereotyping, reassuring white listeners that the natives were docile, yet harnessing for the war effort the savagery that lingered just below the surface:

> Before the Pioneers came to Rhodesia just over fifty years ago the natives fought among themselves, and for a short time they fought the white man also. When they were conquered they settled down to lives of peaceful security. But when the drums of war sound they are eager to fight again, especially when the enemy is that hated German whose brutality in South-West Africa and Tanganyika they know well.[54]

Calder-Marshall had recommended particular types of shot that would furnish *Morning, Noon and Night* with a style appropriate to the united, modernised empire he wanted to represent. He was in favour of 'shots from behind guns and inside tanks [which give a] greater impression of attack'. He also recommended for the fourth section on transport of raw materials that a moving camera should attain a speed apparently greater than that of the train it was filming. *Morning, Noon and Night* was to be about the achievements of ordinary people across the empire setting their sights on the future rather than remaining beholden to the past. It was therefore agreed at the first meeting of the script committee that politicians and pious memorials were to be avoided: 'Ministers [are] not encouraged, and foundation stones prohibited.'[55] This dynamic, mobile empire was far removed from the Southern Rhodesian material. The relatively self-contained footage from Southern Rhodesia ends with a sequence in which, in contrast to Calder-Marshall's carefully selected Chinese Canadian interviewee, a group of exclusively white airmen from across Europe and the empire is fully incorporated into the nineteenth-century imperialist past. This is achieved through editing and commentary, which construct a seamless continuity between these latest arrivals and memorials of white conquest. The final shots in the sequence are:

63 CU Airmen
64 CU Grave of Rhodes
65 CU Shangani memorial
66 CU Airmen saluting
67 Inscription on memorial
68 Memorial against sky

The accompanying guide commentary says: 'The Rhodesians of today are convinced that if [Cecil] Rhodes could see the stream of young men pouring into the land he founded he would heartily approve.'[56]

Given time, documentary footage can be re-edited, and guide commentary can be discarded or rewritten. However, the 'alliance of interests' which had temporarily sustained Morning, Noon and Night started to fragment as the project began to run behind schedule. Crown acquired a board of management which first met on 25 March 1943. Dalrymple, who had operated successfully without this intermediate layer of management since he joined the Crown Film Unit on 12 August 1940, resigned at that meeting. The reasons he later gave for his resignation included not being permitted to address the implications of the wide-ranging welfare reforms proposed in the recently published Beveridge Report. The board meeting on 27 May 1943 warned that commercial exhibitors would be reluctant to screen Morning, Noon and Night unless it stressed the traditional virtues of 'gusto, strenuousness, and a victorious atmosphere'.[57] Dai Vaughan places this statement within the context of the parliamentary debate on the Beveridge Report in February 1943.[58] Churchill did not agree that implementing the report in its entirety when hostilities ended should be one of Britain's war aims. It therefore became a little more difficult for Crown, as an official body, to proceed with Calder-Marshall's initial conception of Morning, Noon and Night as a testament to a modernised, reformist empire, with its ninth section devoted to medical, health and welfare services.

Finally, if Morning, Noon and Night had proceeded along the lines of Calder-Marshall's initial treatment, one crucial propaganda point in it would have been increasingly undermined by reports reaching Britain through official channels and the news media. For section ten, on food production, Calder-Marshall noted that 'the Commonwealth has food and to spare ... food for itself and for countries starved under the Axis'.[59] This point was reiterated in the discussion of the script committee on 9 November 1942: 'For the food sequence – emphasise comparatively large rations.'[60] In one version of the treatment, Calder-Marshall waxed lyrical about the symbolism and sensuous appeal of the food that could be represented in *Morning, Noon and Night*:

> Food is the raw material of human life as minerals etc. are the raw material of production. The Empire is as rich in food as in minerals. We show not only the basic crops, but we show also the fruit which has to many parts of the world become the symbol of peace, oranges, bananas, grapefruit, pineapples. These are there, the visuals will promise, when the war is over. These luxuries will appeal to the audience in this country.[61]

As *Morning, Noon and Night* was delayed, however, reports of food shortages in Bengal accumulated in the British news media, to the point where the term 'famine' was being routinely used in British newspapers by September 1943.[62] Although these reports did not generally qualify as frontpage news, the film-makers working on *Morning, Noon and Night*, who were aware of facts about the empire such as the lifting of the RCAF colour bar on Chinese Canadians, and the source of the mechanised transport supplied to the British Eighth Army in North Africa, would have known about them. One would hope the enormity of the Bengal Famine gave them pause for thought.

The material received from Southern Rhodesia implicitly denied the idealism that sought to represent an increasingly egalitarian, modernised empire. *Morning, Noon and Night* production reports from the middle of 1943 onwards gradually conceded that it was proving difficult to hold the empire together even at the level of representation, and that separate short films about its constituent parts were more immediately realisable than the grand, overarching project that had initially been planned. On 30 June 1943, the minutes of the board of management meeting noted that 'it has been found possible to start work on a series of special shorts from the material sent in from the Dominions and Colonies. The first of these is to be on the subject of South Africa.'[63] This appears to have eventually surfaced as the fourteen-minute film *South Africa* (Terry Trench, 1944). The latest document in the National Archives relating to *Morning, Noon and Night* while it was still an active project is J. D. Holmes's producer's report to the board of management on 5 August 1943. By this time the view was, that although the main project was still being pursued, the material received 'covers so much ground and is so well shot that it will provide a very valuable library for future Empire films'.[64]

The precise reasons for abandoning *Morning, Noon and Night*, and when exactly this happened, are not clear. Individuals involved in the project went on to work on related films. Calder-Marshall scripted the documentary *Today and Tomorrow* (Robert Carruthers, 1945), which dealt with international co-operation to avert famine in the Middle East, and *The World Is Rich* (1947), the second film directed by Paul Rotha about global food distribution. *The World Is Rich* and its predecessor *World of Plenty* (1943) were largely compilation films, which interspersed archive footage with Otto Neurath's animated Isotype diagrams and newly filmed interviews with nutrition experts such as John Boyd Orr. This circumvented some of the logistical problems *Morning, Noon and Night* engendered. Dalrymple's close friend Humphrey Jennings, who was briefly involved in *Morning, Noon and Night*, also worked in the late 1940s on documentary film projects on Burma and the decline and fall of the British empire. These were also never completed.[65]

Paul Gilroy's analysis of the suppression within post-war British culture of imperial legacies in favour of an idealised image of World War II holds true when applied to film history. As Wendy Webster has pointed out, British films of the 1950s dealing with World War II, regardless of how they have been evaluated, have enjoyed a central place within discussions of British film history. British 1950s films dealing with the more difficult issue of empire have, on the other hand, been largely forgotten. A similar argument can be made in relation to the 1940s. Even if more unfinished British documentary films about empire, such as *Morning, Noon and Night*, or Jennings's decline-and-fall project, had been completed during this decade, there is no reason to believe the selective process of writing film history would have produced a significantly different narrative, given the larger cultural factors at play. Even completed films such as *World of Plenty*, *The World Is Rich* and *World without End* (Basil Wright, Paul Rotha, 1953), which relate to the immediate post-war 'UNESCO moment' Gilroy urges us to revisit, have been largely overlooked by contemporary film historians.[66] But some of the ground rules of British non-fiction and documentary film historiography may now be changing.

NOTES

I would like to thank Douglas Dalrymple for letting me have a copy of the text of his father's radio broadcast about *Morning, Noon and Night*. I am also grateful to Tom Rice and James Burns for their prompt responses to requests for information, and Scott Anthony and Dai Vaughan for their thoughtful reading of the finished essay. Dai's pioneering work convinced me *Morning, Noon and Night* was worth exploring in more detail. I am indebted to Toby Haggith at the Imperial War Museum for arranging for me to view the surviving footage, and to various participants at the 'Colonial Film: Moving Images of the British Empire' conference in July 2010 for their helpful comments.

1. Martin Stollery, *Alternative Empires: European Modernist Cinemas and Cultures of Imperialism* (Exeter: University of Exeter Press, 2000).
2. Paul Gilroy, *Postcolonial Melancholia* (New York: Columbia University Press, 2005), p. xii.
3. Ibid., p. 100.
4. Ibid., p. 99.
5. Wendy Webster, *Englishness and Empire, 1939–1965* (Oxford: Oxford University Press, 2005).
6. Dan North, *Sights Unseen: Unfinished British Films* (Newcastle: Cambridge Scholars, 2008), p. 1.
7. Ian Dalrymple, 'Calling South Africa: An Idea for 1943', BBC African Service broadcast, 18 January 1943, 16.50–17.00 GMT. Censored by J. Grenfell Williams. Emphasis in original.
8. Lisa Lowe, *Critical Terrains: French and British Orientalisms* (Ithaca, NY: Cornell University Press, 1991), p. 8.
9. Arthur Calder-Marshall, 'Are We United Nations?', *Army Bureau of Current Affairs (ABCA) Series – Current Affairs* no. 55, 6 November 1943, p. 12.

10. Auriol Weigold, *Churchill, Roosevelt, and India: Propaganda during World War II* (New York: Routledge, 2008).
11. Thomas Hajkowski, 'The BBC, the Empire, and the Second World War, 1939–1945', *Historical Journal of Film, Radio and Television* vol. 22 no. 2, 2002.
12. Evelyn Russell, '*One Day of War*', *Monthly Film Bulletin* vol. 10 nos 109–20, 1943, p. 18.
13. Dalrymple, 'Calling South Africa'.
14. Ian McLaine, *Ministry of Morale* (London and Boston, MA: Allen & Unwin, 1979), p. 203.
15. Ibid.
16. An initial suggestion for *Morning, Noon and Night*'s working title was *550,000,000 People*. This echoes the title of the recent anti-fascist pro-China solidarity film, *The 400 Million* (Joris Ivens, 1939), thereby aligning the project with both leftist politics and China's struggle against Japan.
17. James Chapman, *The British at War: Cinema, State and Propaganda, 1939–1945* (London: I. B. Tauris, 1998), pp. 128–9.
18. For a discussion of Dalrymple's early exposure to a range of different modes of film-making, see Martin Stollery, 'Technicians of the Unknown Cinema: British Critical Discourse and the Analysis of Collaboration in Film Production', *Film History* vol. 21 no. 4, 2009.
19. M. M., '*A Day in Soviet Russia*', *Monthly Film Bulletin* vol. 8 nos 85–96, 1941, p. 122.
20. Leach to Thapar, 1 December 1942, NA INF5/95.
21. Ian Dalrymple, Derek Twist and Alex Bryce, 'Preliminary Recommendation', 28 October 1942, NA INF5/97.
22. 'Suggestions for Further Procedure by the Script Planning Committee', NA INF5/96.
23. Arthur Calder-Marshall, *The Changing Scene* (London: Chapman and Hall, 1937). Calder-Marshall's comments in *The Changing Scene* are still quoted by some latterday critics of the British documentary movement. See, for example, Brian Winston, *Claiming the Real II: Grierson and Beyond* (London: BFI/Palgrave Macmillan, 2008), p. 65.
24. Arthur Calder-Marshall, *Glory Dead* (London: Michael Joseph, 1939), p. 12.
25. Ibid., p. 219.
26. Ibid., p. 255.
27. Ibid., pp. 254–5.
28. Stollery, *Alternative Empires*.
29. Dalrymple, 'Calling South Africa'.
30. Leach to Thapar, 1 December 1942, NA INF5/95.
31. Arthur Calder-Marshall, 'Summary and First Outline Treatment', 9 November 1942, NA INF5/97. The production file contains copies of two versions of the treatment, this one longer than the other, and with some minor differences of detail within the same overall structure. Both copies of the treatment appear to have been produced around the same date, so it is not possible to be absolutely certain which came first or whether one was considered definitive. Given the general similarity of both copies and the proximity in dates, I have not distinguished between them in the main body of this essay.
32. Prem Chowdhry, *Colonial India and the Making of Empire Cinema: Image, Ideology, and Identity* (New Delhi: Vistaar Publications, 2001).
33. Cited in Philip Woods, 'From Shaw to Shantaram: The Film Advisory Board and the Making of British Propaganda Films in India, 1940–1943', *Historical Journal of Film, Radio and Television* vol. 21 no. 34, 2001, p. 302.
34. Arthur Calder-Marshall, 'Treatment', 8–9 November 1942, NA INF5/97.

35. For further discussion of these films, see Stollery, *Alternative Empires*.

36. Calder-Marshall, *The Changing Scene*, pp. 38–9.

37. Patrick Deer, *Culture in Camouflage: War, Empire, and Modern British Literature* (Oxford: Oxford University Press, 2009), p. 65.

38. Martin Francis, *The Flyer: British Culture and the Royal Air Force, 1939–1945* (Oxford: Oxford University Press, 2008), p. 58.

39. Tony Williams, '*An Airman's Letter to His Mother*', *Senses of Cinema* no. 36, July–September 2005, <archive.sensesofcinema.com/contents/cteq/05/36/airmans_letter.html> (accessed 24 June 2010), points out that the film version eliminates some parts of the letter to emphasise 'the universal nature of self-sacrifice and the personal quality of the last communication that mother and son share'. Tellingly, however, the reference to empire is not eliminated.

40. Calder-Marshall, 'Summary and First Outline Treatment'.

41. 'Empire Today', *Scotsman*, 24 May 1943, p. 2.

42. Tom Rice, '*Africa's Fighting Men*', 'Colonial Film: Moving Images of the British Empire' website, <www.colonialfilm.org.uk/node/180>.

43. Calder-Marshall, 'Summary and First Outline Treatment'.

44. Marjorie Wong, *The Dragon and the Maple Leaf: Chinese Canadians in World War II* (London, Ontario: Pirie Publisher, 1994), p. 19.

45. Webster, *Englishness and Empire*, p. 41. Webster identifies the short film *West Indies Calling* (John Page, 1944), which represents Caribbean airmen and other forces personnel socialising in London, as an unusual exception to this trend.

46. For further discussion, see S. P. Mackenzie, *The Battle of Britain on Screen: 'The Few' in British Film and Television Drama* (Edinburgh: Edinburgh University Press, 2007).

47. Timothy Boon, 'Agreement and Disagreement in the Making of *World of Plenty*', in David F. Smith (ed.), *Nutrition in Britain: Science, Scientists, and Politics in the Twentieth Century* (London: Routledge, 1997), p. 186.

48. 'Suggestions for Further Procedure by the Script Planning Committee'.

49. Dai Vaughan, *Portrait of an Invisible Man: The Working Life of Stewart McAllister, Film Editor* (London: BFI, 1983), p. 120.

50. Ian Dalrymple, 'Producer's Report Submitted for the Second Board of Management Meeting', 29 April 1943, NA INF1/58.

51. J. B. Holmes, 'Producer's Report', 30 June 1943, NA INF1/58; J. B. Holmes, 'Producer's Report', 5 August 1943, NA INF1/58.

52. Miss Honstatt to Miss Illseley[?], memo, 28 July 1943, NA INF5/92.

53. Unfortunately, there is no evidence in the *Morning, Noon and Night* production documents confirming which unit shot the Southern Rhodesian material.

54. 'Commentary for Rhodesian Sequences', NA INF5/94. This document bears a handwritten note, 'copy with Pinewood April 30 1943'.

55. 'Minutes of the First Meeting of the Scripting Subcommittee', 2 November 1943, NA INF5/96.

56. 'Commentary for Rhodesian Sequences'.

57. 'Minutes of the Board of Management Meeting', 27 May 1943, NA INF1/58.

58. Vaughan, *Portrait of an Invisible Man*, p. 122.

59. Calder-Marshall, 'Summary and First Outline Treatment'.

60. 'Minutes of the Third Meeting of the Scripting Subcommittee', 9 November 1942, NA INF5/96.

61. Arthur Calder-Marshall, document entitled 'Handed in at Script Meeting', 14 November 1943, NA INF5/96.
62. See for example 'Famine Relief in Bengal', *The Times*, 8 September 1943, p. 3; 'Bengal Famine Deaths', *Manchester Guardian*, 21 September 1943, p. 6.
63. 'Minutes of the Board of Management Meeting', 30 June 1943, NA INF1/58.
64. Holmes, 'Producer's Report', 5 August 1943.
65. For further discussion of these projects see Kevin Jackson, *Humphrey Jennings* (London: Picador, 2004), pp. 320–8, 339–43.
66. Some recent exceptions are Timothy Boon, *Films of Fact: A History of Science in Documentary Films and Television* (London: Wallflower Press, 2008); Richard Farmer, 'Exploiting a Universal Nostalgia for Steak and Onions: The Ministry of Information and the Promotion of *World of Plenty* (1943)', *Historical Journal of Film, Radio and Television* vol. 30 no. 2, 2010; Richard Macdonald, *Film Appreciation and the Postwar Film Society Movement*, PhD thesis, Goldsmiths College (University of London), 2010.

4

India on Film, 1939–47

Richard Osborne

The names adopted by the opposing forces at the beginning of World War II have specific emphases. While Germany, Italy and Japan saw themselves as an *Axis* around which lesser countries would revolve, their opponents called themselves *Allies*, a name that had been used in some of the common defence pacts and military alliances signed by these countries before the war. Ideology was present in nomenclature, with the Allies selecting a group name that spoke of commonality and the collaborative nature of their enterprise. And yet the situation was not as straightforward as this terminology would have us believe. While sharing the ultimate goal of defeating the Axis powers, the Allies were not unified in their beliefs or in their levels of enthusiasm for the campaign. Moreover, in a war that marked 'the greatest and the ultimate "revival" of the British Empire', the Allies were far from unified in their beliefs about the benefits of British imperialism.[1] The campaign actually had the effect of highlighting differences among the countries. The Allies fought under the banners of 'freedom' and 'democracy', ideals that clashed with the realities of British imperial rule.[2]

In January 1942, shortly after America entered the war, President Franklin D. Roosevelt made his first use of the term 'United Nations' to describe the partners who were fighting the fascist countries, a name that again stressed the mutuality of the Allied response. The new alliance with the United States affected the relationship between Britain and its empire. On the one hand, it could be argued that it helped to make this relationship more harmonious. Aware of anti-imperial feeling within the US, Britain became more mindful of the way in which its involvement with its colonies was represented, and thus promoted the ideal of co-operative advancement.[3] On the other hand, the wartime alliance with America helped to destabilise Britain's imperial authority. The war effort engendered greater US military and economic involvement with many of the countries of the British empire.[4] This involvement redoubled the United States' interest in colonial policy; it also affected the balance of power in the countries with whom they were engaged.

It is in relation to India that the complexities of the wartime alliance are most evident. During the first half of the twentieth century, India had become the most advanced of the empire countries in terms of self-government and it had also been the most vocal in terms of opposition to British power. Despite this, the country had little choice regarding its wartime alliance with Britain. In September 1939, Lord Linlithgow, the Viceroy of India, had declared that because Britain was at war, India was at war, a stance that was adopted without consulting any Indian politicians.[5] Consequently, the leading Indian political party, the Indian National Congress (INC), decided to resign from government rather than support the war cause. Many Americans, including President Roosevelt, were sympathetic toward nationalist aspirations in India, thus deepening the need for Britain to resolve this situation.[6] In 1942, Sir Stafford Cripps, a member of the British war cabinet, was dispatched to India, where he made the promise of Dominion status for the country on the basis that the INC provide support for the Allied campaign. The INC rejected his offer and instead embarked on the open rebellion of the 'Quit India' movement, demanding full independence from Britain. Mahatma Gandhi, who had aligned himself with the INC in 1936, was arrested, as was the entire INC working committee. Gandhi was not released until 1944, and then only due to his ill health. The majority of the INC's leadership remained imprisoned throughout the war.[7] There was, nevertheless, also support for the war within India. Indians volunteered at the rate of 50,000 a month (there was no conscription in the country). The Indian Army grew from about 200,000 men in 1939, to 900,000 men by the end of 1941, and peaked at 2,600,000 men in 1945.[8] India was also transformed economically. The country produced more wartime supplies than Australia, New Zealand and South Africa combined.[9]

Film policy was a subset of this complex and shifting political situation. Government institutions were formed to generate film propaganda. The political perspectives that they promoted were often 'allied', but they also differed. In Britain, the Ministry of Information (MOI) was formed as the department responsible for publicity and propaganda.[10] Among its duties, the MOI sponsored wartime propaganda films, as well as monitoring the output of Britain's privately owned newsreel companies and military film production units.[11] Also part of the MOI's remit were filmic representations of the British Empire. In most empire countries, the MOI assumed responsibility for the factual films that were destined for overseas audiences, but in India a more complicated situation evolved.[12] Here, the outbreak of war led to the introduction of the Film Advisory Board (FAB), which was later replaced by Information Films of India (IFI). These organisations were affiliated to the Government of India, and were responsible for producing films aimed at both domestic and overseas audiences. The MOI was closely involved, however: it part-funded some of the films and was responsible for their distribution in other Allied countries.

The Colonial Film Database houses a diverse range of films about India, which provide evidence of the differing Allied perspectives during World War II. In the following, I devote separate sections to films made about the subcontinent by Indian and British companies, and a further section examines the ways in which the commercial American film company March of Time (MOT) addressed the history and current practices of British policy in India. While these films sometimes address issues directly, often it is the absence of particular issues that indicates the divergent nature of the Allies' beliefs. On other occasions, there are unexpected emphases: praise is given where it would not normally expected to be due.

With the cessation of hostilities, relations between India and Britain were once again altered. In the final section of this chapter, I turn to two films that were made about India during the period between the end of the war and the arrival of

Independence in 1947. These films reflect the new attitudes of this time, and they shed further light on the films made during the war. In one instance, quite literally so: the film reuses footage from earlier wartime productions to tell a story that has a new political aim. The reuse of film materials was a common practice throughout this period. Footage would be recombined and provided with new commentaries. In the same way that there was only an apparent unity between the Allied partners, there is only an apparent unity between the sound and vision of film. The United Nations had differing ideals of freedom, and they reused their film materials to promote these differing ideals.

THE WAR: INDIAN FILMS ABOUT INDIA

The Government of India wished to control wartime propaganda relating to the sub-continent. It realised that films aimed at an internal audience could be used to 'recruit and sustain the largest volunteer army in the world whilst simultaneously maintaining political stability in India'.[13] It also 'knew from experience that films about India shown in the rest of the world could also spark serious controversy in India'.[14] While the Government of India's priority was domestic propaganda, the British government's Ministry of Information wished to assume control of the representation of India abroad. In the early months of the war, it had planned to send a 'highly skilled unit' to the country in order to produce films that countered 'the concentrated, and to some extent successful, propaganda by Germany against British Imperial rule in India'.[15] These would be shown to the 'less well-informed sections of the community' in Britain, as well as in 'foreign countries, notably the United States'.[16] Philip Woods argues that the MOI realised the value of film in portraying 'British India to the Americans, in particular, to best advantage'.[17] Nevertheless, it was the Government of India which eventually assumed responsibility for films about India, albeit that it was reliant on funding from the MOI to help finance its productions. As a result, according to Woods, the two parties operated in 'constant tension'.[18]

The person initially placed in charge of factual Indian wartime films was Desmond Young, who was employed by the Government of India as its chief press advisor at the outbreak of war. Despite being a film novice, Young was enthusiastic about his task, believing that film was the ideal medium to encourage the extension of Indian military recruitment 'beyond the so-called "martial classes"'.[19] Young first turned to British advertising agencies operating in India to make his propaganda films; these agencies nevertheless turned to established Indian film studios for help with their productions.

In early 1940 Young showed his first batch of films to the MOI. Among them were *He's in the Navy* (1940, Wadia Movietone) and *Planes of Hindustan* (1940, Wadia Movietone). These films were made quickly and they are rudimentary in the extreme. Young conceded that 'Since there has been no demand for documentary shorts in this country in the past, direction is somewhat amateurish.'[20] There are, however, some important differences between the two films. *He's in the Navy* is indicative of the hierarchical nature of British rule. It shows British officers firmly in command of naive Indian naval recruits. *Planes of Hindustan* meanwhile is reflective of the special status enjoyed by the Indian Air Force, which the commentary informs us is the 'only armed unit of the Crown entirely officered by Indians'. In this film, Indian personnel are shown as being capable and mature, and the senior officers are shown sharing the same facilities as British staff. The MOI found these films 'interesting', but not of sufficient quality for distribution abroad.[21]

Young also had difficulty gaining cinematic distribution for his films in India.[22] It was this situation that led to the creation of the Film Advisory Board, formed 4 July 1940. Between them, the FAB's members controlled 'all the principal circuits in India'.[23] It was the FAB's remit to put before the Indian public 'films of interesting war subjects and others of informatory value'.[24] Several of the FAB's members, including its first chairman, J. B. H. Wadia, were nationalists, but they were willing to make films that supported British war aims. Srirupa Roy has called this a 'tactical manoeuvre', arguing that these members believed their support would help 'the long-term goal of national independence to be secured'.[25]

To help improve the quality of the FAB's films, Young requested an experienced film-maker to head production.[26] The MOI endorsed the appointment of the noted British documentary producer and director Alexander Shaw, who assumed his post in India in the winter of 1940.[27] During his period in charge, Shaw employed some talented Indian film-makers in his film unit, including the future head of Information Films of India, Ezra Mir. He had hoped to make films that addressed political subjects, but was refused permission by the Government of India.[28] Instead the thirteen short documentary films that Shaw produced are predominantly devoted to military matters.

Shaw had to reconcile a number of conflicting demands. While he had wished to introduce a more subtle form of propaganda to his films, J. B. H. Wadia insisted that the films be made simple in order to address the illiterate among the Indian audience.[29] Shaw also had to consider a variety of audiences abroad. In the period that he headed the film unit, the funding and the choice of subject matter of the FAB productions were split jointly between the Government of India and the MOI.[30] The MOI, bearing American audiences in mind, had laid ground rules for films that documented India. It stated that it was 'undesirable that the films should attempt a direct defence or advertisement of British rule'.[31] Consequently, in a film such as *The Handymen* (1941), which outlines the work of the Royal Bombay Sappers and Miners, there is no footage showing the British officers in command; instead Indian soldiers are depicted operating in a self-contained unit. However, there remained films such as *Defenders of India* (1941), which clearly depicts British officers in positions of seniority. This film documents the contribution of Indian soldiers to the Libyan campaign, and one of its aims was to reassure soldiers in Britain and the Commonwealth of the loyalty of Indian personnel.

While several of Shaw's films were shown in Britain and distributed to other empire countries, they were less readily accepted in America. R. R. Ford, the film officer for the British Library of Information of New York, noted that *Defenders of India* and *The Handymen* represented a 'great advance' on earlier films, but he felt that they were only suitable for non-theatrical distribution.[32] He claimed that 'The fundamental problem is the unfortunate fact that very little, if anything, that a British person says about Indian affairs is believed here'.[33] In accordance with Ford's instructions that there needed to be 'an emphasis on whatever social equality existed between Indians and Britons', and that British officers should be 'kept out of the picture', footage of Sir Claude Auchinleck, Commander-in-Chief of India, was excised from *Defenders of India* for its American release.[34]

There was a further problem. Shaw arrived in India at a time of nationalist civil disobedience. He later noted that the fact that his film unit was set up 'by the British to help create a favourable climate of opinion at a time when the Indian mind was entirely set on independence made it not only frivolous but also irrelevant'.[35] He resigned from his post on 21 October 1941, two months before the expiry of his contract. A telegram from the Department of Information & Broadcasting, Government of India, sent to the Secretary of State for India, states that Shaw

> rightly felt that he was not getting all the co-operation he expected from members of Film Advisory Board that the Producer being an Englishman was resented and that his having been specially drafted from England to teach them production of documentaries aroused professional jealousy.[36]

The Department of Information & Broadcasting thought it 'desirable to get an Indian Director in Shaw's place'. It selected V. Shantaram, a director working for the Prabhat Film Company, hoping his appointment would 'mollify Indian public opinion and secure hearty co-operation of Producers'.[37] Shantaram's period in charge coincided with the Quit India movement. During this period most of the FAB's films were produced for non-theatrical distribution in India. The Government of India felt 'compelled owing to the political situation to give preference to producing films for local display'.[38] These films do not address this political situation; instead the primary focus continues to be military matters. Censors within the Government of India ensured that any films destined for an Indian audience were devoid of references to the INC, Mahatma Gandhi, or even Independence.[39] Shantaram was a supporter of the nationalists' aims and, as such, eventually found his position untenable. He resigned after only a few months in his post.[40]

As the political situation within India intensified and the threat of a Japanese attack became more real, the Indian government took increased control of film propaganda. Its first step was to disband the FAB, and to put in its place a 'production and distribution manager appointed by Government'.[41] The disgruntled members of the FAB board tendered their resignations on 18 January 1943, and two months later the government launched the replacement organisation, Information Films of India. The Indian government then introduced specific legislation for the industry. On 15 May 1943, it issued an order under Rule 44A of the Defence of India Act, making it mandatory for every exhibitor in India to include in each programme one or more films approved by the government, this material providing a minimum running time of twenty minutes. This order became effective on 14 September 1943. The government justified this measure on the grounds that only about a third of Indian cinemas had been showing its official films.[42] A further measure was taken on 17 July 1943, when the government introduced a licensing system, which placed an embargo on the production of any unauthorised film.[43]

Ezra Mir, a stalwart of FAB productions, was chosen to head IFI. Rule 44A had been specific that official films should develop 'the right kind of war-mindedness'.[44] Mir responded by creating films such as *Hillmen Go to War* (1944), which details the enlistment of the men from Himachal Pradesh in northwest India (and does so without depicting any British or European military officers). Mir also wished to make films about India's history, trades and culture. Consequently, IFI produced films such as *Musical Instruments of India* (1944) and *In Rural Maharashtra* (1944), which, although dealing with military recruitment, is largely concerned with farming practices. According to B. D. Garga, Mir 'realized that the future of Indian documentary could be made secure not on war propaganda, which was transitory, but with films that dealt with the socio-economic and cultural life of the people'.[45] While the British government had wished to use films of India in order to show the 'progress that has been achieved under British rule, both economically and politically', IFI had different concerns.[46] For IFI, reaching out to foreign audiences was to be undertaken with the aim of raising 'the social status of Indians in their eyes', hoping to 'induce them to take a more sympathetic view of Indian interests abroad'.[47] Ezra Mir also brought more Indian personnel into the organisation. Winifred Holmes, who worked for IFI, noted that by 1945 'all but three of the production and administrative staff were Indian'.[48]

The Government of India supported Mir's aims. In March 1944, the Hon. Sir Syed Sultan Ahmed stated that 'I believe this is the right line and this is why people are beginning to look forward to our films instead of groaning when the title is screened.'[49] The Indian press had previously been hostile to the films of FAB and IFI, but toward the end of the war began to give them some qualified praise. The editor of the *Talkie Herald* wrote that 'Recent public appreciation of some of the short films produced by the Information Films of India has struck me as something rather unusual and creditable.'[50] The films also received interest from abroad. *Tree of Wealth* (1944), about the variety of uses for the coconut tree, drew praise from Walt Disney and was nominated for an Academy Award.[51] The Indian audience nevertheless remained the main focus for these films: by 1944 a few of IFI's films were being distributed non-theatrically in Britain, but none were receiving a commercial release.[52]

THE WAR: BRITISH FILMS ABOUT INDIA

Although there were only moderate provisions for military and government film propaganda in Britain at the outbreak of war, by the war's end the various armed-forces film units and the MOI were making extensive use of film to tell their side of the story of the global conflict.[53] Operations in India and the activities of Indian troops were filmed extensively, receiving outlets in newsreels, longer documentaries, government propaganda films and films made exclusively for the military. The Colonial Film Database contains around 300 wartime films that address India, many of which were produced by British companies. Yet despite this large output, the domestic or political matters of India are largely absent from these films, which instead mainly concern military activities.

Various explanations can be given. In order to counter the impression that India was not supportive of the Allied cause, there was a need to portray the country's wartime effort in a positive light, both to the domestic audience in Britain and to the multinational troops that Indian personnel would be serving alongside. Consequently, the stress in many of the films was upon the loyalty and hard-working nature of Indian volunteers, matched by the invigorated wartime production of India's factories. Another explanation is that it would have been hard for a British company to make a credible film about India. Bearing in mind R. R. Ford's warning that 'little, if anything, that a British person says about Indian affairs' would be believed in America, India is somewhat sidestepped in films that aim to show empire countries in a positive light. During the war, the MOI promoted the ideas of 'partnership' and 'development' in the colonies, a propaganda drive that aimed to enlist colonial support for the war cause, as well as to mollify Britain's American allies. One of the MOI's aims was to show that the people of the empire were 'loyal and happy under our rule and helping us to the limit of their resources'.[54] The complex situation in India made this objective difficult; thus other countries, in particular those of Africa, were better suited to this propaganda drive. A final reason for the lack of British-produced films about domestic Indian matters was the arrangement that had been made between the Government of India and the Ministry of Information. The FAB and IFI assumed primary responsibility for filmic representations of India during the war.[55]

Nevertheless, audiences in Britain and other Allied countries did receive a limited number of British films that addressed the political situation in India, particularly during the period of the Cripps Offer and the Quit India movement. One such film is *The Battle for Freedom*, made in 1942 by the Strand Film Company for the MOI. This film outlines the contribution of various empire countries to the war. Although India is only given a brief proportion of screen time, the film's commentary, written by Dylan Thomas, is unusually explicit. As India is introduced, there is an immediate reference to the 'refusal of the Cripps proposals'. The film nevertheless argues that the people of India are determined to fight for the Allied cause: they 'know that a successful Japanese invasion would mean slavery, would mean that the certainty of the British promise of India's independence would vanish like smoke'. The film does not show any Indian political leaders, but instead backs up its commentary with images of loyal Indian troops on the march. It documents the British empire's 'weapons of science', which have been used to 'fight against disease and suffering', and contrasts them with the rule of 'bayonet and gas bomb' that an Axis empire would usher in. It is notable that none of the images of hospitals, schools or agricultural development that can be seen in this film is situated in India: instead Africa provides the means by which the British film-makers represent the advances and advantages of empire.

Britain's newsreel companies also addressed the political situation at this time. During the war, the MOI allowed the five major newsreel companies (Movietone, Gaumont-British, Paramount, Pathé and Universal) to continue making films. Their films were nevertheless closely monitored, and the MOI also sponsored the companies to make specific productions.[56] In October 1942, Universal News devoted half of one of its editions to a story that focuses upon the Maharajah of Nawanagar, who is shown in the film addressing the Baroda Squadron of the RAF. This edition reverses the normal hierarchy of British films: it shows an Indian prince at an air base in Britain, where he assumes a position of authority and addresses an attentive British squadron (and, by extension, an attentive British audience in the cinema). Placing the Maharajah centre stage helps these British film-makers to make a credible film about Indian issues. The prince's story is nevertheless a familiar one. He tells the British personnel that Indian servicemen are their 'brothers in arms' and that 'two millions of them have volunteered and they will die for the same cause as yourselves'. He also imagines his audience's reaction when they see Indians in action: 'you will say that all brown boys are doing their job and doing it very well'. As always, this stress on Indian support is a tacit acknowledgment that not all Indians were allied to the cause. What is more, the prince does not always remain tacit. At one point he says: 'you may have read in the paper all sort of nonsense – that's not the real India', before adding that the 'real' India is 'your brothers in arms'.

The MOI also entered into the production of newsreels. *War Pictorial News* was a series compiled by the Cairo Office of the MOI, which was exhibited to Allied troops serving in the Middle East and the Mediterranean, as well as to local civilian audiences. Most of its footage was assembled from material provided by the British newsreel companies, which would be furnished with a new commentary, with versions being issued in English, French and Arabic as deemed appropriate. Released in April 1942, the fifty-first edition of the newsreel is wholly devoted to India. It displays a trait common to British films about the empire in that it barely mentions the political events that have occasioned its production. This film provides one of the most enthusiastic accounts of India's contribution to the war. It combines footage of Indian military personnel alongside footage of the country's wartime production. An argument is made that the war has helped to move the country forwards, industrialis-ing both its trades and its people. The film portrays a united India and a united empire: troops of various Indian faiths are shown working towards a common cause, and Indian personnel are seen marching alongside British forces. It is only at the end of the film that the commentary acknowledges the political situation in India. In a conclusion that is both confident and evasive, it speaks of an alliance: 'from the first days of the war, India has overwhelmingly demonstrated that her future is linked with that of the British Empire; her co-operation has been wholeheartedly given'. The commentary then briefly mentions political events in the subcontinent ('the inability of Indian leaders to accept Britain's recent proposals is purely a political issue') before making the positive statement that 'between the war purposes of the British government and the Indian people there are no differences: both are determined to defeat Japanese aggression and to achieve ultimate victory'.

THE WAR: AMERICAN FILMS ABOUT INDIA

In American films about India some of the differences between the Allied partners are made more apparent. During the war, the American company March of Time made three films that focused upon India: *India in Crisis* and *India at War* (both 1942), and *British Imperialism* (1944). These films are more open about Indian politics than contemporary Indian and British film productions. They also reveal some of the complexities in the relationship between Britain and America. While the US could be critical of imperialism, it could also structure its propaganda so that it provided support for its wartime ally. While welcomed by British authorities, the production of these films caused them some concern, both in terms of how British rule would be represented, and in relation to the commercial reach of March of Time, then the most successful newsreel company in the world. By 1938, March of Time's newsreels were being distributed to around 11,000 cinemas worldwide.[57]

India in Crisis and *India at War* were filmed and released back-to-back. This project was initiated in 1940, and was thus one of the first attempts to make films in India during the war. It was monitored closely by the MOI, which considered it to constitute a possible alternative to setting up an Indian film unit of its own. In May 1940, F. Burton Leach of the MOI wrote that

> it is hoped that the Government of India are giving the March of Time people assistance and encouraging them to produce films which will have some propaganda value, at least indirect propaganda, in showing modern developments in India as well as the purely picturesque side of the country. If so, the films might make it unnecessary to go to the expense of sending out a party to make films, as was proposed.[58]

The British government endorsed the March of Time project, believing that it would afford an 'opportunity to put across their idea of the benevolence of British rule in India to a global audience'.[59] While this statement confirms the commercial reach of March of Time, it also hints at the fact that an American-made film about British imperialism would be more credible than one made by a British company. The British government took the 'calculated risk' of allowing March of Time to ship its footage back to America uncensored.[60]

March of Time was originally interested in covering Gandhi's means of resistance to colonial rule; however, by the time of the films' completion in 1942, its remit had been expanded to take into account contemporary events. *India in Crisis* represents a filmic equivalent of the Cripps Offer: it acknowledges Indian demands for Independence, but at the same time wishes to enlist the country's support for the war cause. One of the film's arguments is that divisions within India have rendered the country susceptible to 'easy conquest' by the Japanese. Despite its war aims, the film provides a more supportive view of Indian political ambitions than can be witnessed in British-sponsored films of the same period. It believes that any large colonised populace should have the 'strength to throw off their conquerors and stand alone as a nation'. Indian leaders are accorded a significant amount of screen time, and there is no use of disparaging language when describing their actions. The 'sainted' Mahatma Gandhi is described as being the 'personification of the only unity India has ever known'. By closing with footage of Gandhi at his ashram, the film indicates that the future of the country lies with him.

India in Crisis also has praise for the British empire. Although the film is against imperialism *per se*, it is more directly positive about British rule than any British film aimed at an American audience would dare to be. The film argues that the British have 'served to the betterment of millions of Indians', and that they have 'brought material progress'. It is even suggested that it is enlightened British rule, and not British repression, that has given birth to the nationalist movement in India: the introduction of democratic ideals has led Indians to demand 'their share of freedom', and nationalist leaders have benefited from British-sponsored education.

Curiously, out of the two 1942 productions, it is *India at War*, rather than the political documentary *India in Crisis*, that is most overt in supporting India's desire for

Independence. This film is nevertheless also critical of the INC. It condemns the party's stance of non-co-operation in the war, and makes the counter-argument that

> today a majority of the Indian people know that the one way of getting the independence they have so long sought is by giving fullest support to the United Nations in their fight against the enemies of freedom and all free men.

In conclusion the film states that Indians

> are confident that as partners of the world's free people, sharing all the burdens and hardships of the war for survival, they will gain at last what they have so long been denied: the right to live as free men in a united and independent India.

These comments about freedom and democracy upset officials in London. Alec Joyce, Information Officer at the India Office, argued that the film's summary 'does not do justice to the facts', and suggested in vain that March of Time should alter phrases such as 'so long sought' and 'so long been denied'.[61] If the film can be regarded as being anti-British, it can also be viewed as being pro-American, or at least pro- the American way of life. The commentary denigrates 'distant' British rule and the fact that power 'has never been entrusted to the Indian people', statements that are backed up with images of an elaborate state ceremony, which takes place in a cavernous hall. The film then argues for 'full US co-operation in organising and developing India's own reserves of manpower and Industry', and in this sense marks the interests of the US in breaking up the empire to facilitate American trade and capital. Throughout, India's move towards Independence is coupled with the idea of the country becoming an industrial establishment.

In 1944, March of Time proposed *British Imperialism*, a compilation film about the British Empire that would feature India prominently. British authorities were wary of what would result. Lord Halifax, the British ambassador in Washington, telegraphed Sir Frederick Puckle, Director General of Public Information in the Government of India, 'We are anxious that film should avoid giving impression that India is governed from London and shall be grateful if you will do whatever you can to keep it on the right lines.'[62] Despite the fact that he unsuccessfully campaigned to get some 'offending passages' in *British Imperialism* changed or omitted, on seeing the film, Lord Halifax wrote of the 'good relations with MOT that we are building up'.[63] To a certain extent these good relations are mirrored in the film's portrayal of the wartime alliance between Britain and the United States. At the film's outset the commentary argues that the two countries 'have been growing together into an ever closer wartime partnership'. This alliance is also in evidence in the film's conclusion. The commentator states that 'Britons can proudly boast the widest system of organised freedom which has ever existed in history', a phrase that was seized upon by reviewers of the film.[64] However, in what Puckle described as 'an astonishingly uneven work', this conclusion is arrived at circuitously.[65] The empire is first described as being 'bound together by indefinable ideas and traditions', and the film states that its 500 million people live 'in varying degrees of freedom'. Moreover, the reviewers tended to ignore the first half of the film's conclusion, which states that 'and though their Empire was not built without wrongs and injustices ...'.

Britain's stewardship of the empire is first shown in its most abstract manner, via footage of the Colonial Office and the Dominions Office in London, where the empire countries are reduced to names on boxes within a filing system. The film then explores the Dominion countries before closing with India, 'which for over two centuries has been a British problem'. *British Imperialism* gives a different representation of the subcontinent than is seen in official British wartime films. On the one hand, the film displays some hostility to British rule, noting that, 'in defiance of a policy favouring greater equality and more independence', the Raj 'sought to keep the Indians in an inferior social and economic status' (this statement is accompanied by footage of upper-class couples playing golf among Mughal ruins, escorted by Indian caddies). On the other hand, the film is more critical of Indians than a British documentary of the same period would be; it also serves up a more disturbing representation of the subcontinent. The film talks of British plans for advancement and then places the blame for their failure on the Hindu religion, which perpetuates 'superstition, ignorance and poverty' (here the film shows an image of a crippled beggar). In addition, the film is more open about the political situation in India than contemporary British documentaries.

The British movie journal *Documentary News Letter* was critical of the visual material in this film, arguing that it was constructed 'from the cut-outs of itinerant cameramen with a quicker eye for a pretty picture than a plain fact'.[66] This is unfair on several levels. The film often depicts harsh truths, including what Lord Halifax termed 'a quite unnecessary shot of the police dispersing a crowd'.[67] It also depicts the leading political figures in India, whose images are largely absent from British and Indian films of the same period. The *Documentary News Letter* wished that the film material would be 'more relevant' to the newsreel's positive conclusion, arguing that the ambiguous array of images 'proves neither the existence of freedom nor of its opposite'.[68] However, this may have been precisely the balance that the March of Time team was trying to achieve. It is certainly reflective of the US government's ambiguous relationship with Britain during World War II. The countries fought together in the cause of freedom, but Britain's imperialist ambitions could not be squared with the way the US felt that freedom should be achieved.

TOWARDS INDEPENDENCE

Although the March of Time films are more open about the situation in India than British or Indian productions, they are still constrained by the wartime Alliance between Britain and the US. After the war's conclusion, and with the coming of Independence in India, we can witness new forms of representation of the subcontinent. This change is in evidence in a British-produced film about India, *Indian Background* (1946), which was sponsored by the Central Office of Information (COI, the peacetime successor to the MOI), and in a film made by IFI, *Bassien: An Indian Fishing Village* (1946).

While *Indian Background* is indicative of new attitudes towards India, it uses previously existing film material to make its case. One of the significant aspects of documentary films of this period is that most of them are composite prints: their visual component is usually shot silently, with the soundtrack added afterwards. This had various consequences. On the one hand, it helped to facilitate the international movement of these films, which could be dubbed into various languages. On the other hand, the film material could easily be edited and recombined into new forms. It is this latter aspect that is in evidence in *Indian Background*. To make its case, the film uses material sourced from a number of wartime government-sponsored films, among them the military newsreel *War Pictorial News No. 51*, and IFI's *Hillmen Go to War* and *In Rural Maharashtra*. The film was released in Britain in late 1946, receiving short descriptive notices in the *Monthly Film Bulletin* and *The Cinema*.[69]

By 1946 it was generally assumed that India would gain Independence from Britain. Judith Brown argues that it was only after the war that the British conceded that 'withdrawal was essential – and not for India but for British national and Imperial interests'.[70] She argues that India was becoming an economic liability rather than an asset to Britain; that the country was of less strategic importance geographically; and that it was becoming ungovernable. As such the British 'calculated that alliance with a free India within the Commonwealth was preferable to continued dominion'.[71] The pace and scale of change had yet to be determined. Although the Lahore Resolution of 1940 had posited the idea of a separate state of Pakistan, Partition was not a certainty.[72] Moreover, the current Viceroy, Lord Wavell, was proposing a staged withdrawal from power.[73]

Indian Background reflects this tumult. The film begins with sequences showing large Indian crowds, which are intercut with footage of the leading political figures of the day – Mahatma Gandhi, Muhammad Ali Jinnah and Jawaharlal Nehru – figures seldom seen in British wartime films. The commentary tells a story about India being a land of contrasts – rich and poor, old and new, Hindu and Muslim – contrasts that were downplayed during the war. It states that it is among these contradictions that 'a nation is being born'.

The film then provides its 'Indian background'. It first posits a belief that is familiar from pre-war British documentaries – that 'the life of India is in the villages' – and it uses materials from wartime rural films to underline this point. The tone and the reuse of materials are startling. The film pours almost vindictive scorn on the backwardness of farming communities, where tools have 'not altered in a thousand years' and where 'to live is an achievement of which there is little to be remembered'. It condemns both child and adult labour. A sequence from *Hillmen Go to War*, originally used to illustrate the increased productivity and wealth of the villages, is now accompanied by the information that 'much work, little food and the long summer's brutal heat age the peasants before their time'. Footage from *In Rural Maharashtra*, showing the villagers' crops on their way to market, is now accompanied by talk of global exploitation: 'the peasant is the producer, but most of his product goes from him, a journey that takes it into another world'. Both of the earlier films feature traditional village celebrations, where life is praised for its 'harmony' and the festivities are termed 'exciting'. Reused here, the commentator states that 'tradition is an invisible tyranny that binds the villager to his heritage of poverty, dirt, ignorance and disease'. The commentary does not entirely subvert the original use of the film material, however. The camerawork of the earlier films is commonly their most sympathetic aspect in terms of highlighting the dignity of the people. Now accompanied by a wholly partisan commentary, the images and the rhetoric are often at odds.

It is with mechanised India that *Indian Background* throws in its lot. The film cuts abruptly from footage of rural trades to scenes of a large factory. 'Now that's more like it', the commentator says. The commentary turns away from the trope of depicting the subcontinent by means of its village life, stating that 'this is happening in India too'. Footage from *War Pictorial News No. 51*, originally employed to illustrate the contribution of India's factories and factory workers to the war cause, is now enlisted to highlight general Indian mechanisation. The commentator instructs us that 'it's no use sentimentalising about machines destroying old crafts and old ways of living', these are 'changes for the better'.

In conclusion, the film returns to the contradictions of India. Footage of traditional celebrations is cut sharply into an image of urban nightlife. Next the film shows several shots of scientific buildings, among them a college of agriculture (these are possibly taken from the FAB film, *The Changing Face of India*, 1942). It asks 'How are these able to flourish in the same land and century as the villages rooted in the past?' (Here an image of a woman working a handloom is perhaps used to link this Gandhi-inspired practice with a backwards-looking India.) The film calls for 'changes in men's minds'. It argues for an India of technical progress, and it makes it clear from where this progress will be derived. The images of scientific endeavour are accompanied by Western music, and the commentary states that the future 'will inevitably be shaped by western methods'. Nevertheless, the parade of contradictory images has rendered the film-makers uncertain. This surprisingly complex, ambivalent, even confused film reflects the current situation in India. There is none of the (forced) certainty of the wartime documentaries: 'it's hard to understand what all this adds up to', the commentator states. An admission by British authorities that they do not understand India would have only been possible once Independence seemed inevitable. At the same time, *Indian Background* serves as a reminder of the British empire's power to reappropriate and channel the culture and products of India.

Information Films of India did not last until Independence. In March 1946 the Indian legislative assembly cut the organisation's grant, leading to its abolishment on 1 May 1946. IFI had been viewed with suspicion by many Indian nationalists, and had been accused of 'try[ing] to dragoon an unwilling nation into the war'.[74] And yet, in the final years of its existence, IFI made some of its most effective films.

In 1946, Indian and British film-makers at IFI produced *Bassien: An Indian Fishing Village*. This film is concerned with the daily lives of a fishing community, and would thus seem to correspond with *Indian Background*'s belief that 'the life of India is in the villages'. Like *Indian Background*, it explores themes that would not have been permissible during World War II. It is a significantly different film, however. Whereas *Indian Background* is confused and jarring, *Bassien: An Indian Fishing Village* is measured and philosophical.

The film makes subtle use of the fact that Bassien is a Catholic community, situated in an area of India that was first colonised by the Portuguese in the fifteenth century. At one point it shows the women of the village collecting water from a well in an abandoned fort. The commentary informs us that the Portuguese 'grew rich and powerful' through trading with Indians. The film then depicts the ruined fort and talks of the fact that as Portuguese 'power waned [...] their buildings were left to decay in India's encroaching jungle'. We next see an image of a Portuguese grave, which the commentary regards as 'a monument to past glories'; the shadow of one of the Indians falls across it. The commentary and symbolism in this film tell a different story to *Indian Background*: here it is the old crafts and the old ways of living that are reclaiming the colonised land. The film does not make any direct reference to the end of British rule. Instead, we are merely informed that 'the wells remained' and that, by implication, life went on. Later in the film, there is a scene of young children playing with toy boats, another image that speaks of continuing traditions. This film admits that some of these traditions have been inherited from colonial rule. We learn that the Portuguese legacy was their Catholicism, at which point there is a depiction of a doting wife praying at her altar for her husband's safe return.

CONCLUSION

The crusade for 'freedom' and 'democracy' was proclaimed regularly in wartime documentaries made by the Allies, and yet these concepts are sometimes absent from the films. In the films sponsored by the British and Indian governments these ideals are seldom mentioned in relation to India's political progress, and nor are they in evidence in the behind-the-scenes production of the films. Instead we witness a forced alliance of beliefs. The production of wartime documentaries by the commercial American company March of Time could be argued to be more democratic; however, here too, we see that the film-makers were constrained by the need to present a united front with their Allies. In the final two documentaries, made when India's freedom and democracy were imminent, things begin to change. Here the British and Indian film-makers pursue their governments' separate interests, and as a result we get widely differing depictions of the subcontinent. *Indian Background* is reflective of the British government's withdrawal from India; it displays uncertainty about what sort of allies Indians would now be. *Bassien: An Indian Fishing Village* takes a longer view. It is quietly eloquent about both the transience and the lasting effects of colonial rule. Ultimately, however, films sponsored by democratic governments remain a contradictory form. During World War II, one of the responses of the Allied countries to the complex political situation was an increasingly sophisticated use of film propaganda. Henceforth, the Allied countries have held varying ideals of 'freedom', and governmental film-makers have been closely monitored regarding the ways in which these freedoms have been portrayed.

NOTES

1. Keith Jeffery, 'The Second World War', in Judith M. Brown and Wm. Roger Louis (eds), *The Oxford History of the British Empire: Volume IV: The Twentieth Century* (Oxford and New York: Oxford University Press, 2001), pp. 306–28 (p. 306).
2. Jeffery, 'The Second World War', p. 313.
3. A. J. Stockwell, 'Imperialism and Nationalism in South-East Asia', in Brown and Louis, *The Oxford History of the British Empire: Volume IV*, pp. 465–89 (p. 476).

4. Jeffery, 'The Second World War', p. 322.
5. Ibid., p. 311.
6. B. D. Garga, *From Raj to Swaraj: The Non-fiction Film in India* (New Delhi: Penguin, 2007), p. 62.
7. Judith M. Brown, *Modern India: The Origins of an Asian Democracy*, 2nd edn (Oxford: Oxford University Press, 1994), p. 324.
8. Ashley Jackson, *The British Empire and the Second World War* (London: Hambledon Continuum, 2006), p. 358.
9. Ibid.
10. The Ministry of Information was constituted on 4 September 1939, the day after Britain entered the war. The department had previously been in existence during World War I.
11. James Chapman, *The British at War: Cinema, State and Propaganda, 1939–1945* (London: I. B. Tauris, 1998), p. 138; Gerald Sanger, 'We Lived in the Presence of History: The Story of British Movietone News in the War Years', in Luke McKernan (ed.), *Yesterday's News: The British Cinema Newsreel Reader* (London: BUFVC, 2002), pp. 164–70.
12. Philip Woods, 'From Shaw to Shantaram', *Historical Journal of Film, Radio and Television*, August 2001, pp. 293–308 (p. 297).
13. Woods, 'From Shaw to Shantaram', p. 297.
14. Ibid.
15. H. V. Hodson (Director of the Empire Division of the MOI), letter to Jack Beddington (Head of the MOI Films Division), 11 May 1940 [document in India Office materials held at the British Library. File: L/I/1/684 'Films for Publicity Purposes General File 1939 and 1940'].
16. Ibid.
17. Woods, 'From Shaw to Shantaram', p. 297.
18. Ibid.
19. Garga, *From Raj to Swaraj*, p. 63.
20. Desmond Young, 'Publicity through Films', letter, 29 October 1940 [document in India Office materials held at the British Library. File: L/I/1/684 'Films for Publicity Purposes General File 1939 and 1940'].
21. F. Burton Leach (India Section, Empire Division, MOI) to A. H. Joyce (India Office, Whitehall), 20 February 1941 [document in India Office materials held at the British Library. File: L/I/1/691 'Films from India'].
22. Young, 'Publicity through Films'.
23. Ibid.
24. Garga, *From Raj to Swaraj*, p. 65.
25. Srirupa Roy, 'Moving Pictures: The Postcolonial State and Visual Representations of India', *Contributions to Indian Sociology* vol. 36 nos 1–2, pp. 233–63 (p. 239).
26. Young, 'Publicity through Films'.
27. Garga, *From Raj to Swaraj*, p. 66.
28. Woods, 'From Shaw to Shantaram', p. 31.
29. Garga, *From Raj to Swaraj*, pp. 71–2.
30. Woods, 'From Shaw to Shantaram', p. 298.
31. H. V. Hodson (Director of the Empire Division of the MOI), letter to Jack Beddington (Head of the MOI Films Division), 11 May 1940 [document in India Office materials held at the British Library. File: L/I/1/691 'Films from India'].
32. R. R. Ford (Film Officer, British Library of Information, NY), letter to J. Hennessey (Principal Information Officer, Bureau of Public Information, Home Department,

Government of India), 15 October 1941 [document in India Office materials held at the British Library. File: L/I/1/691 'Films from India'].

33. Garga, *From Raj to Swaraj*, p. 78.
34. Woods, 'From Shaw to Shantaram', p. 300; Ford, 15 October 1941.
35. Garga, *From Raj to Swaraj*, p. 68.
36. Government of India, Dept of Information & Broadcasting, telegram to Secretary of State for India, 2 December 1941 [document in India Office materials held at the British Library. File: L/I/691 'Films from India'].
37. Government of India, 2 December 1941.
38. F. Burton Leach (India Section, Empire Division, MOI), letter to J. F. Gennings (India Office, Whitehall), 22 March 1943 [document in India Office materials held at the British Library. File: L/I/1/692 'Films – India'].
39. Garga, *From Raj to Swaraj*, pp. 92–3.
40. Woods, 'From Shaw to Shantaram', p. 293.
41. Letter from P. N. Thapar, Secretary to the Government of India, 5 January 1943, cited in Garga, *From Raj to Swaraj*, p. 94.
42. 'Note for Cut Motion on 15th March 1944: Defence of India Rule 44A' [document in India Office materials held at the British Library: File: L/I/1/686 'Films for Publicity'].
43. Garga, *From Raj to Swaraj*, p. 101.
44. 'Defence of India Rule: 44A. Control of Cinematograph Exhibitions' [document in India Office materials held at the British Library: File: L/I/1/686 'Films for Publicity'].
45. Garga, *From Raj to Swaraj*, pp. 108–9.
46. Hodson, 11 May 1940. File: L/I/1/684 'Films for Publicity Purposes General File 1939 and 1940'.
47. Thapar, cited in Garga, *From Raj to Swaraj*, p. 81.
48. Winifred Holmes, 'Postscript to India. An account of the Work of Information Films of India', *Sight and Sound*, 1 July 1946, pp. 43–5 (p. 43).
49. *Indian Information*, 1 April 1944 [document in India Office materials held at the British Library. File: L/I/1/692 'Films – India'].
50. Garga, *From Raj to Swaraj*, p. 110.
51. Ibid.
52. R. W. Brock (India Section, Far East Division), letter to A. H. Joyce (India Office, Whitehall) 26 February 1945 [document in India Office materials held at the British Library. File: L/I/1/692 'Films – India'].
53. Chapman, *The British at War*, p. 139; Paul Swann, *The British Documentary Film Movement, 1926–1946* (Cambridge: Cambridge University Press, 1989), p. 154.
54. Jeffery, 'The Second World War', p. 313.
55. Woods, 'From Shaw to Shantaram', p. 297.
56. Sangar, 'We Lived in the Presence of History', pp. 164–70.
57. Thomas W. Bohn and Lawrence W. Lichty, '"The March of Time": News as Drama', *Journal of Popular Film*, Fall 1973, pp. 373–87 (377–8).
58. F. Burton Leach, letter to A.H. Joyce (India Office, Whitehall), 29 May 1940 [document in India Office materials held at the British Library. File: L/I/1/684 'Films for Publicity Purposes General File 1939 and 1940'].
59. Garga, *From Raj to Swaraj*, p. 88.
60. Ibid., p. 89.

61. Ibid., p. 90.
62. Ibid., p. 112.
63. Ibid., p. 113.
64. 'March of Time. No. 1. 10th Year: British Imperialism', *Documentary News Letter* no. 53, 1944; 'British Imperialism', *Monthly Film Bulletin* no. 125, 1944; 'Cinema: The New Pictures', *Time*, 28 August 1944, <www.time.com/time/magazine/article/0,9171,885646,00.html>.
65. Garga, *From Raj to Swaraj*, p. 112.
66. 'March of Time. No. 1', p. 53.
67. Garga, *From Raj to Swaraj*, p. 113.
68. 'March of Time. No. 1', p. 53.
69. *Monthly Film Bulletin* no. 142, 1946; *The Cinema: News and Property Gazette*, 18 September 1946, p. 35.
70. Judith M. Brown, 'India', in Brown and Louis, *The Oxford History of the British Empire: Volume IV*, pp. 421–6 (p. 439).
71. Brown, 'India', p. 444.
72. Brown, *Modern India*, p. 332.
73. Wm. Roger Louis, 'The Dissolution of the British Empire', in Brown and Louis, *The Oxford History of the British Empire: Volume IV*, pp. 329–56 (p. 332).
74. S. Narwekar, *Films Division and the Indian Documentary* (New Delhi: Publications Division, Government of India, 1992), p. 23.

5

Official and Amateur: Exploring Information Film in India, 1920s–40s[1]

Ravi Vasudevan

This paper will draw upon the archival film material of the colonial period in India to explore different currents in the use of film as a vehicle of information. While my larger project will look at documentaries, newsreels, short films (including topicals and actualities) from the work produced by government, film industry, educationists, individual entrepreneurs and amateur or home film-makers, for this essay the focus will primarily be on official and amateur movies between the 1920s and 1940s.[2] The important phenomenon of non-fiction film-making by the Indian film industry impinges on the themes of this essay in two ways. First, the industry provided the rhetorical ground to argue for the usefulness of film in its topical and instructional versions and, relatedly, the need to have compulsory screenings of such films at cinema halls.[3] This came to be incorporated into government policy, if not exactly in the way desired. Second, the local industry was also compelled to develop ties with government initiatives as a result of the various conditions under which limited film stock would be allocated in wartime conditions. Thus, the story of these initiatives necessarily incorporates part of the narrative of local industrial activity as well.

While government initiatives go back to the 1910s, and I will refer to some dimensions of these earlier exercises, my main focus will be on the 1940s, when key long-term formations came into being. These related to the development of policies for production, circulation and exhibition, which were to remain influential after Independence, and also mobilised intelligentsia to assume leading positions in this venture. This was accomplished despite tensions and anxieties resulting from the face-off between the British rulers and the nationalists, which ultimately resulted in the Indian National Congress going into a critical phase of resistance, the Quit India movement in 1942. The second body of material, the colonial home/amateur movie, presents a different set of issues, even while we observe certain overlapping elements between official and amateur films. As I will suggest, the overlap arises from the fact that the film-makers were often part of colonial officialdom, capturing not only home life but official events. There also appear to be instances of an overlap of home and professional worlds, for example, in the use of film to document resources and work practices for business needs.[4] Further research will enable us to garner more precise details about the depositors of this material, the positions they occupied under the colonial regime and in the world of business and enterprise, and the spectrum of functions served by amateur forms. A major consideration will also be the nature of the equipment available for this substantial personalised distribution of film technology, as well as the circuits of amateur film print culture and associational life which provided instruction, advice and community feedback for this hobby. For the present exercise, my purpose has been to take examples that appear to suggest important questions about the nature of film form and technique in such amateur activities.

To fully engage this archive of film material, related research in the print archive will be crucial. An exploration of the British Library's India Office collection and national and state archives in India will constitute a crucial dimension of the broader project from which this essay arises. Particularly important here are the political, public and information departments. The latter department generated official initiatives in commissioning, producing, circulating and exhibiting films. However, there are two frames to consider. The first is the wider orbit within which such official initiatives were taking place. Here, the relatively well-known but under-explored influence of transnational circuits on models of documentary, instructional and training films will need to be considered. These include the influence of important institutions and enterprises such as the Empire Marketing Board Film Unit, the GPO Film Unit and subsequent Crown Film Unit, the Shell Film Unit, the National Film Board of Canada and colonial film units in Africa, Malaya and the Caribbean. This influence was exercised through the presence of figures who were delegated to run new units or function as consultants, such as Alexander Shaw from Britain in the early 1940s, James Beveridge from Canada in the 1950s; it also developed through the circulation of journals such as *Colonial Cinema* and in the information relayed by British trade papers. A transnational company like Shell's Film Unit acquired substantial institutional and film-making presence in various territories.[5] One of the most important agendas for all this would be the analysis of war-related training and propaganda films, such as those that emerged from the Army Film Centre in India. This appeared to have set up a wide menu of audiovisual forms that proved influential in developing new units of instruction in the period after Independence. Another transnational frame of reference emerges in technologies and political apparatuses for circulating and exhibiting film, as in the case of mobile vans, tents and outdoor exhibition in rural areas. In the absence of detail of how such practices worked in the Indian context, I will turn to comparable situations, in this case postcolonial Egypt, to speculate on the social and political circumstances that surrounded the cinematic event.

This agenda relates to institutional histories from the 1920s through to the 1950s, and indicates a line of continuity rather than discontinuity at the time of decolonisation. While some key institutions, state-run film-making and newsreel units were disbanded, key people and policies continued when the new institutions, such as the Films Division, came into being. There were probably a number of different currents which fed into state models and documentary imaginaries, including the Soviet example while, at the level of training, the US was also a reference point for new entrants.[6] Also, if certain national developmental and cultural agendas emerged in the war period, they did not emerge from colonial developmental agendas in an uncomplicated way. Thus, the cultural investments of a generation of film and information intelligentsia were involved in this transaction, and we can see the imprint of this investment in international bodies such as UNESCO.[7]

These issues may appear to be fairly standard: as states are reconstructed, lines of continuity tend to be somewhat inevitable. However, the historical implications of such continuities need to be considered, and here, agendas of development that emerged in the colonial period seemed to retain a potency for a long time after. The functions of film and other media forms in this long historical trajectory need to be better theorised, both within the logic of communication theory around issues such as the rhetorics of textual form and the incidence of infrastructural elaboration; and in film and media theory, in mapping the relation between the profilmic and the types, levels and densities of information or data ratios circulated to putative spectators.

To my mind, the latter set of questions poses significant challenges to historical method. For these derive not from issues of continuity and discontinuity on an institutional plane, but focus on film form and the materiality of film as a vehicle of information, of circulation and recombination. This line of enquiry emerges specifically from observations I make about the amateur film and its characteristic forms. Discontinuities in form, the arbitrary way amateur films combine episodes ranging from domestic subjects to public engagements of various types, suggest the possibility, perhaps even the imperative, of thinking of the form through disaggregation. This opens various lines of comparison and connection between characteristic units in the amateur film and the objects of professional practices. And it also opens the way to reflection on what would constitute an appropriate historical and ethnographic method of engaging with the indexical character of such material, the conditions – in terms of social authority and relations, technological parameters, climatic conditions, built and natural forms – under which spaces, people, bodies, things are imprinted on film. The question of disaggregation, rendering film into separable, unnarrativised or, shall we say, yet-to-be-narrativised units, is further addressed through the phenomenon of the stock shot, its circulation and recombination.

STATE FILM AND MEDIA INITIATIVES IN THE COLONIAL ERA

Central to official deliberations about the use of film were questions of address and reach, how the medium could be deployed to communicate with deeper swathes of the population. The question of address, the way textual form was shaped to appeal to specific audiences, is something I will explore in relation to some of the post-1940s official films. Considerations about infrastructures of circulation related to how new communication technologies could be used to gain access to the broader small-town and especially rural populations. Here we have as yet intermittent information on how substantial this was before more sustained developments took place in the period of World War II. Government information administrators, to coin a term, reviewed the potential of existing entertainment networks. These included the impresario Maurice Bandmann, who was key to the movement of live performers in theatre, circus, acrobatics and dance, as well as film products through a network of theatres that straddled the Eastern world, from Bombay to Hong Kong.[8] However, while war propaganda films were exhibited in Bandmann's theatres and through his network, officials were sceptical about their ability to connect with the populations the government was really concerned to engage.[9] It was argued at this point that if it was decided to show films extensively to 'native' populations, then this would be best done 'by creating a special organization which would ... maintain "projecting outfits" and motor lorries, for which certain initial expenditure would need to be sanctioned'. A small price could be charged for exhibition.[10] A census of the equipment and technical personnel available for such activity was planned, and guidelines were presented of the conditions under which government-approved films should be exhibited. The strictures outlined included, interestingly, the idea that deteriorated film material should not be exhibited as this would reflect poorly on the government. Officials were making an implicit distinction between government films and the more variable quality and conditions of commercial film circulation in touring cinemas, to which, surely, such government exercises would be compared. There was an emphasis too that films should communicate a fixed meaning. Thus silent films and magic-lantern slides would be accompanied by scripts from which lecturers were not to deviate.

We have some insight into official strategies for information dissemination and the way its focus was distributed among technologies of communication and exhibition in the Punjab province. F. L. Brayne, a Deputy Commissioner, developed schemes for village reconstruction, based on identifying and training village guides. These would be key figures in a host of activities relating to health services, marketing, improvement of agricultural techniques, encouraging education, and so on. Such activities would be channelled through village fairs and competitions, and also through folk performances, magic-lantern and film shows. Film occupied a minor position in the overall strategy. There were few films available for such purposes, and these were supplied by the railways, another institution which needs to be investigated when mapping the history of information films.[11] The colonial government also commissioned individual film entrepreneurs such as R. L. Shorey, also from the Punjab, to make instructional films. Shorey had returned from the US after training in film-making and set up a film studio. Later, his son Roop was to be a major producer in the Lahore film industry. The Shoreys also made films for the government in the 1940s, such as *Save for the Future* (1941) and *ABC of ARP: Bombs* (1943), on safety measures during air raids.[12]

While there is some evidence of government involvement in media communication in this earlier period, an altogether different level of initiative took place in the 1940s, both in terms of state investment in film as a medium of governmental communication, and in terms of measures to ensure the medium could reach rural populations. A multiplicity of institutional arrangements existed for the production of films, some based on developing ties with the industry, as with the Film Advisory Board (FAB, 1941–3), others being more directly controlled and managed by the state, as with Information Films of India (IFI, 1943–6). There was also an Army Film Centre, and finally an investment through collaboration with a private entrepreneur to set up an extensive network of mobile vans and projection facilities to carry rural education films into the countryside. Companies such as Twentieth Century-Fox were involved in producing newsreels for Indian audiences through British Movietone, a position subsequently taken by Indian News Parade, a government-controlled newsreel run by William Moylan.[13]

We will revisit some of these ventures to consider their content; here I want to explore how the network of distribution and exhibition was set up in the 1940s. Key dimensions of this propaganda policy were reliant on the industry. Individual film-makers and film companies became involved, either by participating in institutions such as the Film Advisory Board,[14] or by making war-propaganda films, for example studios such as Bombay Talkies (*A Day with the Indian Army*, 1942), Wadia Movietone (*Voice of Satan*, 1940), Prabhat (*The Awakening*, 1941) and National Studios (*Whispering Legend*, 1941; *Road to Victory*, 1943). A further two key elements came into play at this point. The first derived from the pressure the government could exercise on film studios around limited wartime film stock. The film periodical, *Film India*, claimed that the government leveraged war-propaganda films by only ensuring supply to those outfits which would comply with its terms. This was related to a licensing system which continued till the end of the war.[15] The second and very well-known strategy occurred at the point of exhibition, where, under Defence of India rules, the cinema exhibitors were obliged to compulsorily screen government-approved documentaries.[16] Another restriction applied both to production and exhibition, with the feature-film length being restricted to 11,000 feet, and this was the corresponding duration allowed to the main feature in the film programme. The extra showtime was meant to be dedicated to the compulsory shorts produced through IFI. It was said that, in practice, cinema halls advertised main show timings so that people could avoid the government-sponsored films.[17]

B. D. Garga has argued that the Film Advisory Board, and presumably its successor, IFI, continued to demonstrate a concern about which films would work best with which audiences. Two considerations operated. The first was whether a film could be circulated outside the country, i.e., would it communicate with clarity the views and interests of government in the war effort and in how it was managing colonial populations. This was particularly important in terms of the image Britain presented to America as potential war allies. The second related to how far the film was likely to reach in terms of the local population, and decided whether it would be dubbed or not.[18]

Here, separate tracks for the deployment of film and other audiovisual techniques emerged. From the 1940s, provincial governments undertook rural education programmes using mobile vans and projection equipment. Information about efforts in the Bombay presidency indicate that this programme was undertaken in collaboration with a private entrepreneur in photographic equipment, Ambalal J. Patel.[19] One hundred 16mm Kodak projectors were purchased by the government from Patel's Central Camera Company, and films were screened in several districts.[20] It was reported that the films came from Patel's newly started firm, Education Films of India, and that other sources of supply included the Film Advisory Board, though any producer could in principle submit a film for consideration. How this scheme worked, what films were shown, in what settings they were screened and through what local networks of authority audiences were congregated, have yet to be explored.[21]

I want to move sideways and forward in order to speculate on the framework within which this communication strategy emerged. James Beveridge, the Canadian expert who was film advisor to Burmah Shell in India for the development of instructional and documentary film, talked in 1955 of the Films Division's

coordinated scheme whereby all specialized films for the various Ministries of the Centre, are produced by or through Films Division for non-theatrical release to information vans, community projects, and other 16mm channels. This development is of greatest importance as it will mark the evolution in India of specialized, carefully made films to be used functionally in a precise teaching context – a very different thing from release in commercial cinema to audiences gathered solely for entertainment.'[22]

But let us move sideways now, to an entirely different locale, but one perhaps overlapping in its film-pedagogical motivations, its bid to capture and educate 'illiterate' subjects, perhaps even in its understanding of audience identification. Here is the widely travelled Winifred Holmes, propagator of short films for development and cultural understanding, writing from Egypt:

The village to which we had come to see a film-show sponsored by the Egyptian Ministry of Public Health … [was] … a typical agricultural village … [at] the Social Centre – to which the village comes for medical and social services and which cooperates with the Government in running by means of its village committee – a large crowd had gathered. Boys were running from all directions, shoving each other for best places; men, trying to appear as if the film-show were nothing to them, walked there as fast as dignity permitted. Groups of pre-adolescent girls scurried to get good places on the ground as close as possible to the centre of the screen and last of all, women, materializing, as if by magic, silently appeared, draped gracefully and discreetly in their long, black shawls, 'milaya', and sat together apart from the men. There must have been at least a thousand people waiting there.

The Ministry's mobile cinema van flood-lit the scene. The screen and projector were in place and the warm air of an Egyptian Arabic song floated out towards the distant Pyramids, helping the people to forget the day's work and putting them in a happy, expectant frame of mind.

The village headman, 'omdah', had some upright chairs placed for us and with the generous hospitality of Egypt, offered us some Coca-Cola which we drank with pleasure without the fuss of glasses. The village watchmen, 'ghaffirs', their rifles slung round their shoulders, kept order by tapping the more unruly boys none too gently on the back and shoulders with their staves of office. At last everyone was settled, the music ended, the floodlights went out and the Ministry's spokesman talked to us about the films we were going to see. There was a hush and the show began.

Holmes captures here a picture of the institutional setting, authority structures (ministry official, village headman, village watchmen), within an ambience at once rustic and exotic (with an Arabic song floating towards the Pyramids). She further delineates an understanding of how documentary instruction provides the possibilities of audience identification:

The treatment of the subject was apparently just right for the audience, who gave the film their complete attention and made acute remarks while it was going on. The human story of village characters like themselves, acted by professionals with a touch of humour now and then was familiar to their own lives.[23]

Overall, we could speculate that similar understandings and perhaps similar conditions of audience mobilisation operated in India.

For Beveridge, what was imperative was to develop greater precision in targeting audiences and estimating effects:

> It might be said … that the production of specialized films in India, for functional and specific uses, has just begun. Ahead, there lies a whole range of trial-and-error experiences, of testing, audience sampling, evaluating, and comparing various production techniques to assess their effectiveness in reaching audiences of different kinds … .[24]

Positioned as part of a nation-state, rather than a colonial project to deploy film 'functionally', I will nevertheless suggest that there was a line of continuity here, with Indian film-makers, film 'intelligentsia' such as critics, film entrepreneurs such as Patel, and the key institution of the army, all participating in a project of harnessing film to pedagogic and instructional functions. Such instructional drives did not devolve on film alone. During the 1940s and 1950s we can witness a proliferation of associations and institutions promoting audiovisual education more broadly. Bombay State had been an initiator, as it had been with the use of film in rural propaganda. Its Inspector of Audio-Visual Education attributed the powerful emergence of AV techniques of teaching to the army's wartime investment in training technical personnel. The result was UNESCO making AV one of the principal planks, resulting in a large number of training programmes highlighting 'teaching aids like charts, maps, posters, diagrams, models and 35mm filmstrips'.[25] In practice, forms would be combined, and films often used diagram sequences. In her description of health documentaries, Winifred Holmes believed that such techniques had an immediate effect: '"So this is bilharzias!" commented a fellah standing beside us as the diagram representation of the life-history of the disease, from snail host to sufferer, came on the screen.'[26]

Having suggested certain features of government strategy in circulating and exhibiting film and other audiovisual materials for instructional and propaganda needs, let me turn to a select discussion of film content and form. I will cite for my examples the particular 'progressive' axis' FAB and IFI were seeking to put together in some of their film products. *Women of India* (1943) is a case in point, and its investment in the image of modern professional women particularly notable.[27] This was produced by Alexander Shaw and directed by a key figure of the early information film, A. Bhaskara Rao, who went on to be an important Films Division director after Independence. The film opens with an image of Indian women destined to live out a life of constrained options. A marriage procession wends its way around a tree, and cuts to a woman borne along on a palanquin as a voiceover (VO) notes fatalistically that her only destiny is to await marriage and bear children. Having set up this traditional frame, the film leaves it behind. The image track shows us a fashionably dressed young woman getting into a car driven by a young man sporting a solar topi. The image might in another setting be the basis for a censorious viewpoint, but this possibility is rapidly skirted by the VO proclaiming a new generation unbound by traditional conventions. Suggestions of a romantic liaison in this image give way to an investment in the female group, presented in the next shot through a group of young women socialising over tea and cigarettes. 'They know there is more to life than their grandmothers ever dreamt of.' Here and later, the voiceover links this new

Women of India (1943): Women professionals and the war effort; teacher and journalist; double exposure shows two contrasting images of modern Indian women in the same frame

potential to the expansion of cities and new professions. I outline below the succession of images that follow this initial situation and define the film's imagination for modern womanhood. (These divisions do not refer to shot breakdown.)

- group shot of typists and client
- individual typist with war-mobilisation poster, hawai fauji ka taiyari/preparation for air combat, followed by closer view on typist and poster [VO: 'Thousands of girls all over India have jobs in the world of commerce']
- telephone operator
- cloth shop/shop assistant [VO: 'as in the West, emancipation gives the privilege of long hours in offices for small pay']
- doctor, followed by closer view
- image of drawing, with angle, scissor, hand in the frame; cut to female architect discussing the drawing with another [VO: 'As towns grow there is a need for more hands']
- women barristers (two shots) [VO: 'India has had one for the last sixteen years']
- well-known woman journalist interviews film star Surendra, in make-up room in front of dressing table
- teacher [VO: 'None of this is possible without education']^{28}
- group of women students in science class with male teacher
- doctor with blood-pressure machine
- student with microscope
- women painting
- women sculpting with male model on display
- music of the country
- singer and male violinist [VO: 'In the world of entertainment a woman's part is all important; all over India listeners tune in to their favourite tune']
- boy switches on radio

Women of India: Actress Devika Rani

- woman sings in front of microphone with tabla, harmonium and violin in accompaniment
- movies (shots of three film posters/publicity songbooks)
- Actress Devika Rani
- Actress Sadhona Bose
- Women in public debate with men
- All India Women's Conference
- Volunteers work in remote villages: images of women teaching village/small-town kids with close-up on girls
- Message will reach far and wide (women in manual labour, sorting work)
- Girl smoking
- Women playing badminton
- Air travel: woman alighting from plane
- Dancer [VO: 'Not held back by customs but appreciates all that is unique; women will be allowed to play a part in the destiny of this great land, like the women of England, Russia, France.')

There is a particular charm to this work, in its unabashed investment, indeed, celebration of the image of modern young woman, starting with the brash iconography of the debutante, at ease in the public world, in a variety of professions and in sporting activity. The pedagogical function that comes towards the conclusion appears as an add-on, with the organisation of shots and the distribution of narrative attention suggesting that female presence in the modern world, facilitated by education and urban expansion, is key to any broader transformation. Thus institutional and political mobilisation through women's organisation, popular pedagogy and so on appear to emerge from this primary focus.

Key points of departure include the underwriting of the acting profession and of the film industry, which, alongside the images of the female singer relayed to audiences through the radio, signal a startling openness of engagement. There is also a frisson of sexual adventure, both in the opening image of romance in the automobile, in the woman journalist's encounter with the male star in his dressing-room and in the image of the male model displayed for women sculptors. The concluding focus on a considered cultivation of custom through the image of the female dancer appears to return the viewer to the imperatives that such emancipatory drives have to be reconciled with identity needs, specifically of a national sort. But the overwhelming impression left by the film does not gel with this concluding note.

For our purposes, there are two sets of connections which I would like to draw attention to. The first is the remarkable exceptionality of this film in terms of its expansive account of female modernisation. What made this possible? The presence of two elite women collaborators, figures who worked in arts, literary and social reform circles, Tara Ali Baig as commentator, and Premila Rama Rau as screenplay writer, point to the outlines of the circle within which the FAB and IFI were functioning. Raj Thapar in her autobiography wrote of the dense and often incestuous network of leftist playwrights, actors, journalists, radio professionals and commentary writers who had a presence in the media professions of these times.[29] Alexander Shaw, then head of the Film Advisory Board, noted the importance of such intellectuals at a time when the FAB's functions were subject to strident criticism.[30] The group could be said to be both advanced and perhaps removed from some of the more conventional social protocols and patterns of change. It was perhaps indicative of a certain type of power elite that was to prove influential in the years after Independence and beyond. This also suggests why deeper transformations, for example, in rural life, should have this top-down, add-on position in the overall design. It nevertheless remains a remarkable visual documentation of an investment in modern female professions of this time.

A related issue is the special position given to the arts, from painting to sculpture to music and dance, to writerly professions, such as journalism. In these years the FAB and IFI also made films on culture, handicrafts, dance, sculpture, as well as on new industries along with war-propaganda films. Much of this anticipated Films Division work after Independence, and continued to feature in Films Division and Central Film Library catalogues as part of the storehouse of material available in the area of instruction and education up to the 1960s.[31] The film also, of course, highlights the profession of the film actor, symptomatic perhaps of the state film institution's bid to cultivate the film industry. While there were industry representatives on the Film Advisory Board, on the declaration of the Quit India movement, key figures such as the leading industrial film-maker, V. Shantaram, dropped out. Nevertheless, government policies would continue to shape industry involvement, especially around disbursement of film stock against licences, with a baseline 25 per cent amount dedicated to war-related films in the overall pattern of use. And, in turn, there were signs of industrial compliance in war-propaganda films, and in ways which do not always suggest duress.

Even after the Quit India call, the left in particular retained an ambiguous relationship to the war effort, committed as they were to the anti-fascist rationale for war involvement, and despite the failure of the British government to provide an adequate plan for the transfer of power. Thus, K. A. Abbas, the left-wing nationalist film critic, short-story writer, playwright, scripwriter and later director was involved in *Voice of the People* (1943), an IFI film on the democratic awakening made possible by the press, produced and directed by Ezra Mir.[32] Abbas appears in the figure of a newspaper editor, identified as lynchpin to the process of news collection, communication, writing and processing. Abbas was an important figure in the left-wing cultural organisations, the Progressive Writers' Association and the Indian People's Theatre Association. So too was David, the Jewish-Indian actor, who started his career with the fiction film Abbas scripted on journalism, *Naya Sansaar/New World* (N. R. Acharya, Bombay Talkies, 1941). David features in a very skilled war-economy film called *School for Wives* (B. Mitra, Films of India/FAB 1943).[33] The film outlined strategies for housewives to economise on energy consumption in cooking, and to maximise use of all consumable material. It was deftly structured to address the husband through the conceit of a film within a film. The film within a film makes the husband rather than the wife the primary addressee of the home-economics class, deftly combining war-economy messages with advocacy for some change in gender roles.

Another in the 'School' series, *School for Farmers* (date not given, probably 1942, produced by Ezra Mir and directed by A. Bhaskara Rao) has more straightforward pedagogic functions.[34] It is notable however for Soviet-style angles in its opening shots of ploughing, a dynamic carried into the image of children marching with implements to work in the fields. In its portrayal of the schooling process, it also draws upon the armature of audiovisual methods which, as we have seen, were circulating at the same time, with the children presented with toys of factory implements and maps of the land as part of the learning process. There is a startling literalism in its depiction of how knowledge can be brought bodily to relate to agriculture, with children armed with books walking through crops to identify them. Such classification is allied, the commentary informs us, to the teaching of other skills, including arithmetic, the market calculation of the value of crops and packing processes.

While research into this phase of officially sanctioned or 'approved' documentary and short-film-making is perhaps as yet too preliminary to make generalisations, I would note that the vast majority of films related in some fashion to the war, and those specifically devoted to culture and economic development were relatively few. However, even in the war films, issues of economy, gender relations and so on, could appear, perhaps as a sign of the progressive alliance forged through this initiative. The phase remains institutionally critical. It developed the controversial model of compulsory screening that was to be followed by the independent Indian government;

School for Farmers (1942): Marching to work; models of agricultural implements

cultivated personnel for this activity, some drawn from the industry itself, others to come through the route of foreign education and training; and it consolidated the genre of a developmental documentary form.

HOME AND AMATEUR MOVIES

The archive of official movies is considerably complicated by the huge proliferation of home and amateur movies, whose ostensible audience tended to be other family members or friends, perhaps members of an amateur film society or social club. I say ostensible because there might have been professional dimensions to the amateur form as well. Such a distinction is based on observation of the film material, rather than on evidence available through other sources, and thus is entirely speculative and provisional. A proper exploration of the status of some of this work needs to consider the standard repertoire of research questions posed for the non-fiction film: Who commissioned the film? What was the occasion for which it was made? To whom was it addressed?[35] This proliferation appears to have been facilitated by the availability of cheaper and more portable 16mm. cameras from about 1923.[36] For the colonial period, this is a new and startling archive for film history, but also for novel considerations about everyday life, providing as it does a form which moves between the personal and the public. While some amateur films may be devoted to a singular subject, whether related to home or public spaces, including townscapes, infrastructural vistas and workplaces, it was very common for these films to combine such elements. In this format, the films tend to move between the spaces of private habitation and those of social settings, public life and even official engagement. Mostly made by civil servants, army men, planters, businessmen and travellers, these films pose significant challenges to film history. This lies not only in their position on the border between the personal and the official, but also in their bid to show and thereby document the everyday and the event.

Patricia Zimmerman has argued that home movies should be differentiated from amateur films, primarily in terms of a distinction between domestic and public subjects, with the subject of travel in particular distinguishing the amateur film.[37] The latter also brought with it a whole panoply of associations, and journals of the 'how-to' sort. We will see in practice how this difference is difficult to uphold, in terms of the colonial home or amateur movie. She suggests another distinction, which again appears problematic:

> Consonant with explanatory models of a history from below, the history of amateur film discourses and visual practices is always situated in context with more elite, more visible forms of cultural practices such as Hollywood, national cinemas and avant-garde movements, as well as other, larger historical, political and social metanarratives.[38]

Clearly, while the amateur film I am dealing with here may be less visible than public and commercial film formats, it could hardly be called non-elite or part of a history from below. Further, the amateur film has a complicated relationship with discourses of professionalism, displaying as it does complex practices of framing and editing, and the insertion of intertitles. In some cases, one is startled by the achievement of compositional and cutting patterns. By the end of the 1930s, advanced discussions about amateur film techniques were taking place in India.[39]

In the selection of colonial amateur movies I have looked at, there are instances of the classic home-movie format, where the focus is entirely centred on the home, and the addressees appear to be friends and family. A second type is the descriptive diary relating to some aspect of social life, including scenes from the everyday, but sometimes involving more detailed and carefully composed descriptions of agricultural, manufacturing and building processes. Most common is perhaps the third category, where the home segues into wider public events, settings and views. In these instances, the films assume the form of visual diaries, in which shifts in locale and subject matter emerge from the often highly contingent itinerary and interests of the film-maker. We could speculate that on these occasions, the functions of the material range from private consumption, through exhibition for family and friends probably accompanied by oral exposition, but also perhaps to professional requirements that need to be fleshed out through further research.

An example of the first, more clearly defined home-movie genre is available from the Hunter collection,[40] relating to a family based in Meerut, United Provinces, between 1928 and 1932. Three short films are centred around the Hunter family activities, and each starts with a title card 'A GLIMPSE OF INDIA', the words framed by drawings of palm trees and camels (a generic image of the East which could as well have stood for Egypt). The three films are notable for the use of intertitles, and an attempt to build a narrative around the premise that the Hunter family invites the audience for a visit. The first film starts with Mr Hunter making this request via direct address, and spelt out by intertitles and the insertion of a written invitation. After this, the film evokes images of a journey through shots of landscape captured through a train window, and of the train's arrival at a station. The 'visitor' appears completely imaginary, his/her off-screen dimension highlighted when the mother holds the door of the family car open, but a cut precludes our seeing the guest. There follows a journey

Hunter Collection, Film I:
A Glimpse of India

by family car from station to home, and the depiction of the house, the garden and the family at leisure and in play. The next film dwells on the servants, the servants' quarters, the 'bearer', maali or gardener. It then shifts to an extended scene showing washermen in action, beating clothes and wringing them, and ends with the arrival of the fully laundered material at home. The final film recounts the family visit to the hill station of Mussoorie during the summer. The film is notable for numerous intertitles, some printed, some handwritten on a blackboard or a placard; views from train and car to capture movement; static frames, but also shifts to closer views along the same axis. There is an attempt to build a sense of movement, not only by seeing through mobile vehicles, but by moving the camera towards objects and by panning. There is also cutting, but, it would seem, editing in the camera when the film is stopped before the next view is captured.

The Hunter series also displays a substantially different format, what I will refer to as something which inhabits the spectrum between an ethnographic and an industrial diary. This, too, is organised to generate narrative integrity by grounding what we see and read on a singular subject and its exposition. Thus, there are films devoted to irrigation, cotton cultivation, sugar production and road engineering. The irrigation film employs both ethnographic-diary and industrial-diary formats. I use the distinction heuristically, to distinguish a form devoted to a study of a people and their cultural forms, often with a sense of Orientalist curiosity, from another which involves a description of material practices and technologies. The latter appears motivated by an impulse not to capture the cultural particularity of labour or natural-resource usage, but to indicate a transformative logic grounded in new technologies and techniques, or a combination of the old and new. Thus, the irrigation film ranges between showcasing the way new dam and canal construction facilitates irrigation, to featuring traditional forms and the use of animals, with intertitles highlighting these as resources of a traditional and low-tech society. The road-engineering film on the other hand, is quite distinct, organised as it is to show the materiality of a new practice. It was almost certainly an extension of Hunter's professional existence as an employee of the Public Works Department.[41] In fact, at one point during the film, it seems that it is Hunter himself, a figure we have become familiar with from his home movies, who appears to order the unloading of stones from a mule. The film works on the basis of fairly tight descriptive shots, introduced by typed rather than written intertitles. Each segment of the short film is devoted to showing specific elements of the work process, from describing the use of available materials to remetalling, surface painting and maintenance. This is followed by a series devoted to the replacement of an old construction bridge by a modern concrete structure. Here the film provides details about the mixing of sand, cement and concrete, shows how concrete is sprinkled with water for its consolidation, how metal 'reinforcements' are bent, and how concrete is laid in the foundations of the bridge. In contrast to the home movie and the ethnographic diary, the titles are not defined by personalised or cultural references or direct address. There are two instances of personalisation, and of the performance of a skill, which might elicit interest in an audience habituated to higher technological resources. The first is when the wizened guard of the old bridge, about to be dismantled, is placed before the camera, salutes and departs; the second is when the workman carrying bricks is presented from the front, loading one brick on top of another on his head until a veritable little mountain rises above him.

Finally, let us turn to the combinatory form, in which family scenes that take place in the garden give way to the outer world, a feature that is perhaps the characteristic structural pattern of the colonial home movie. This outer world may be variously constituted. It may derive from the official or semi-official frame, including scenes from official visits and inspections, visits to military and regimental displays, and the presentation of what we could call infrastructural or developmental vistas arising from tours, whether formal or informal, conducted by colonial officials. These would include dam, road and canal construction. Such films could even inhabit the genre of the promotional film, as appeared to be the case for a film by Stokes (Ootacamund, Mysore, Madras, 1930–3). Thus films 11 and 12 in this twenty-film collection herald 'a great irrigation project', relating perhaps to the Metur Dam, with title cards providing information about costs and logistics and the material used for the construction. The film features scenes of stone quarrying, and three elaborate, long, panning shots starting from the construction site and overseeing the train carrying the stone. There are also shots of the stone-crushers at work, the machinery they use, the laying of concrete, a view of the towers and a view of the dam (1931).

But often the shots of the 'outside' world are more loosely, observationally organised, so that such vistas (street scenes, scenes of labour practices) may appear to float free of their origins as colonial amateur movie. Sometimes labour practices are enclosed in a colonial ethnographic frame, where groups are defined by iconography of dress, implements and setting, when the Morgans (Lahore) for example, capture tea-garden labourers with their implements, or washermen demonstrate a characteristic flourishing movement in their beating of clothes. The latter image is indeed quite common, perhaps because it is integral to the household, but also one senses because it allows the film-maker to capture graphic movement. But on other occasions, there are quite startlingly organised and sustained scenes of documentation that do not cohere with a colonial ethnography.

An emblematic film of this more loosely, indeed, arbitrarily ordered form is available in the collection of films deposited by the Banks family in Lahore. The films move through the characteristic itinerary of the colonial amateur movie. The first

Banks Collection, Film 1:
Child in the garden

episode is devoted to a child crawling along in a garden. The second and most complex episode is a remarkably sustained segment on the glass-blowers of Lahore. The framing and cutting develop a sense of the interior space of the factory, of the way labour is deployed and specialised, a sense of intense heat from the glow of the furnaces, and a variable response by the workers to the presence of the film-maker, one of whom stares back disconcertingly at the camera. The film then shifts to the Lahore train station, where scenes of everyday activity are captured, an apparently objective frame intruded into by the self-conscious positioning of a white officer on the platform, perhaps the film-maker or a friend making an appearance. The final episode, featuring an exhibition of horse riding for a military regiment, is common-place in subject matter, but displays once again an alertness to camera position and editing, including a sense of how best to frame to elicit maximum effect. Thus there is a recurrence of a particular stunt, in which two soldiers are seated precariously, the horse's hooves going dangerously close to them in the leap. When the manoeuvre takes places a second time, the camera captures the action again, as if to emphasise the risk involved. There is an awareness here of how the physical parameters imposed on the seated men confronting the leaping horse are reiterated in the filmic parameters imposed by the frame on the spectator, the sense of shock relayed through a peculiar doubling effect, where the body tensed and flinching is dispersed from on- to off-screen sites. This clearly may be over-interpretation, but the fact that such films solicit this type of curiosity and engagement indicates the complexity of the material they encompass and, on occasion, the way they give that material form.

The particular format I have described here suggests how a single film can combine forms, starting with home movie, moving into public space in a way that includes the home-movie subject in the frame, through an industrial film component in the glass-blower's factory, and onto the horse exhibition, that official-public setting which the colonial home movie can so easily navigate as an extension of its subject's world. The industrial format echoes, if with greater film-making acumen, the type of detail I referred to in Hunter's film on road engineering. And, in fact, we find that Banks was a representative of Imperial Chemicals, and has other films in his collection which provide

Banks Collection, Film 1: In the glass-blowing factory

detailed accounts of artisanal practices and small-scale industry, for example, saltpeter-mining.[42] There may even have been professional training involved in the dexterity the film displays, as Imperial Chemicals had started a film-making unit in 1925.[43]

There is one conclusion we can arrive at from this juxtaposition of different types of film, official and amateur. This is that there is an overlap between the forms, in that both deal, willy-nilly, with official material, and they even deal with this in an official way. By this I mean that the recurrent movement outwards of colonial amateur movies from home to the official colonial setting – functions, inspections, displays, develop-mental vistas and so on – derives from a similar locus of public authority and may even share the objectives of displaying colonial developmental achievements. On the other hand, this overlap hardly tells the whole story of the amateur form. At one level, the shifting focus of these amateur films can only be unified by the subject who films the changing settings: the colonial officer, traveller, soldier, businessman and so on. However, it would be remiss to view these films only in terms of the colonial, racial or social position, which produced them. Of course, it may be true that certain views, for official functions, visits and inspections, and perhaps even certain perspectives on spaces and structures otherwise available for public view, are privileged by arising from their proximity to or presence as authority. However, there is a more openly and indiscriminately available visibility which these films traverse in their capture of street and bazaar scenes, labour practices and so on. The discontinuities of the amateur form, episodes following each other without any causal logic, lend an autonomous status to the different segments. In turn, they also invite us to consider the unnarrativised segment through a logic of indexicality, of the camera capturing the physicality of people and objects and material life in the world. Following Chistopher Pinney's recent work on colonial photography, the question of indexicality is also one of the relationship between film-maker, camera and the subject and space viewed, and how that relationship is constructed through social and political authority, labour, travel, timing, and the material features of technology and film stock, including the susceptibility of film to the vagaries of climate.[44]

Clearly, the image we see is a surface constructed through a set of relations. It then invites historical and ethnographic research into these relations, of a material, social and technological sort. I want to suggest also a second register. In underlining the autonomy and separability of components in a colonial home movie, we have two options. The first is to combine them with other similar views on these subjects, within a database indicating their source, location, perhaps with a view to creating a thick description, in a Geertzian sense, of how a particular practice, material form, locale is captured through different views, technologies and so on. The second, however, is to emphasise not their indexicality, but their separability, including the possibility of their redeployment. In this sense, the material not only offers us a relationship to things in the world, a physiognomic specificity and irreducibility, but the possibility of entering a second register, that of their generic functions and perhaps an iconic rather than indexical dimension.

This particular form of documentary as matter is best represented by the stock shot, the non-integrated, generic, repeatable, redeployable form of film information. Here I will take an example of an iconic documentary film-maker of those times, P. V. Pathy. A publicity note in the film periodical, *Film India*, remarked that

> Pathy, best newsreel man ... has worked with British Paramount and shot events like the Mysore Wedding, the Bikaner Jubilee, the Baroda Coronation, the Wedding of the Viceroy's Daughter, Haripura Congress Topical and the Quetta Earthquake ... . Pathy has a library of stock film shots during his five-year stay in India: 'Shots of earthquakes, floods, gypsy dances, sunrise, sunset, camel caravans, temples, fairs, mountain parks, landscapes, architectural grandeur, village life, rivers with their sacred associations etc. ... [he] has filed and kept this at his house in Siki Nagar at Vithalbhai Patel Road. Sells at Rs 2.8 per foot for the films. Producers who keep their cameraman waiting alongside a sea shore may as well pay Dr Pathy Rs 15 for the shot and save time and money.'[45]

It is also instructive to note the way that Shell, another key player in the world of information film, also realised the value of retaining an archive of stock shots. It is suggestive to position this value against the backdrop of something Shell official history was proud to highlight, how its own product, oil, would only feature if it was an integral part of the story world:

> Arthur Elton established another basic factor almost from the start. Shell films were in no way to be classed as advertising films. There was to be no heavy-handed waving of the product of the Company name at the audience. In fact, quite the reverse. If oil or petroleum featured in production it was there on the screen as an integral part of the story, not as something 'Made and distributed by Shell' ... .[46]

In counterpoint to this emphasis on how products would be integrated, if at all, to the narrative of public knowledge about nature, resources, peoples and cultures, there was also an understanding of the value of film footage as separable and reusable material.

> With the mass of film footage that the Unit was acquiring, now from many corners of the globe, Elton decided that a properly organized stock-shot library should be formed. He

realised that there were many outtakes or extra shots taken during a film production that should not be junked, but catalogued and used for future productions or as a basis for complete films … .[47]

From questions of discontinuity, segmentation and indexical autonomy, we have shifted registers, to where filmic material is defined as footage, as extra material, as stock, repeatable and reusable. This is where the boundaries between mainstream commercial formats and documentary and newsreel may also be breached, as material of this type finds its way across divisions. Such effects were of course most noticeable in the way newsreel and topical footage was inserted into popular commercial films. In the Indian case, this was especially so with Nehru, actuality footage of whom was used in a number of entertainment films from the 1950s onwards.

These reflections on amateur film forms and on film as excess footage which can be reused give pause for historiographical thought. Disaggregative logics, identifying key scenes, even fragments, rather than whole films, literary texts and other unities, are commonplace to historical method. Sometimes this is deployed for illustration, to explore a dimension or convention of the cultural artefact under review, and its relation to social and political reality. In the instances I cite here, such fragmentation is a structural characteristic of the amateur film object itself. I have suggested that the amateur film thereby provides a more complicated possibility, to explore the bundle of relations that composes the different scenes organised for the camera, demanding a historical ethnography of film practices. The result may require us to assume a distance toward larger ways of positioning filmic material and the way it implicates the subjects in front of or behind the camera. Perhaps this is new ground which, through an exploration of the material, social and imaginative dimensions of media forms will map lateral pathways and connections in the historical landscape.

NOTES

1. Acknowledgments: earlier versions of this paper were presented at the Centre for Historical Studies, Jawaharlal Nehru University, Delhi; the Film and End of Empire Conference, University of Pittsburgh, PA; and at the University of Washington at Seattle. I thank those who made these presentations possible, including Neepa Majumdar, Colin MacCabe and Sudhir Mahadevan. Thanks also to Lee Grieveson for a careful reading of an earlier draft.
2. There was a substantial strand of film-making in the area of non-fiction film by local film companies and individuals that preceded World War II, which will be part of the larger project. Such activities acquired a significant presence in terms of cinema programming, with certain items such as topical films relating to nationalist activities proving popular with audiences. According to *The Indian Cinematograph Year Book* of 1938 (Bombay: Motion Picture Society of India, 1938, pp. 183–204), some 830 short films were produced between 1920 and 1936.
3. Resolution no. 10, *Indian Motion Picture Congress Proceedings*, 1939, urging that

    Provincial Governments should be approached with a scheme for the production of news-reels of Indian events and for such purpose should work in collaboration with the film industry ... . Provincial Governments should assist the Industry ... by making suitable arrangements to see that in every theatre a prescribed length of Indian newsreel is exhibited in every daily programme.

See *Proceedings*, p. 189.

4. I have taken notes from films viewed at the British Film Institute and others at the Centre for South Asian Studies, Cambridge, including material recently put online.

5. See for example, Norman Vigars, *A Short History of the Shell Film Unit (1934–1984)*, Shell Film Unit London, March 1984.

6. When the government announced its decision to 'revive the organization for the production and distribution of documentary films and newsreels', it required most posts, from controllers to directors and scriptwriters to require five to ten years' experience in the line of documentary, newsreel and general film production. This would mean getting people from the disbanded IFI, the film industry or from abroad. Some of the more basic office staff positions were in fact specified for IFI staffers, for example stenographers and so on. See classified advertisements 6 and 18, *Times of India*, 28 January 1948. A number of new hires at this time came from a group of Indians trained at the University of Southern California. Jagat Murari, 'Reminiscences of Films Division', in Jag Mohan (ed.), *Documentary Films and National Awakening* (New Delhi: Publications Division, Ministry of Information and Broadcasting, 1990), p. 49.

7. See, for example, the comments made by Jehangir Bhownagary on how the documentary would help circulate cultural information in the development of the nation. Mohan, *Documentary Films and National Awakening*, p. 51.

8. B. D. Garga, *From Raj to Swaraj: The Non-Fiction Film in India* (New Delhi: Penguin), pp. 25–6.

9. See Foreign and Political, Internal B, May 1919, nos 230–352, National Archive of India (NAI), 'Institution of Propaganda Relating to the War by Means of Cinematograph in India' and 'Creation of the Central Publicity Board'; four films issued by the Cinema Trade committee were exhibited through Bandmann's theatres but 'left the mass untouched'. Notes, Political, A February 1918. I owe this reference to Radhika Singha.

10. Ibid. See also Foreign and Political, Internal B, June 1918, nos 143–5, NAI. This file indicates that Vernon and Co. were making films in India on local topics and offered their services to the government. Letter from Vernon and Co., Bombay 7 November 1917.

11. F. L. Brayne, *The Remaking of Village India* (London: Humphrey Milford and New York: Oxford University Press, 1929).

12. *Information Films of India Annual for 1944*, New Delhi, Government of India, 1944; Ashish Rajadhyaksha and Paul Willemen (eds), *Encyclopedia of Indian Cinema* (Delhi: Oxford University Press, 1994), p. 216.

13. Sanjit Narwekar, *Films Division and the Indian Documentary* (New Delhi: Publication Division, Ministry of Information and Broadcasting, 1992) provides a very helpful account of this period.

14. Desmond Young, Chief Information Officer of the government, noted that, at the inauguration of the FAB, 'efficient production and distribution of films could only be secured with the help of the brains and experience of those who were actively engaged in the industry itself'. Among the industry representatives at this inaugural meeting were Chandulal J. Shah of Ranjit Movietone, Rai Bahadur Chunilal of Bombay Talkies, Chimanlal Desai of National Studios, Baburao K. Pai of Prabhat, M. B. Billimoria of M. B. Billimoria

and Co., M. A. Fazalbhoy of Fazalbhoy Ltd., A. Rowland Jones of MGM (India) and J. B. H. Wadia of Wadia Movietone. See 'War Publicity through Films: Advisory Board Formed', *Times of India*, 5 July 1940.

15. *Film India*, editorial, July 1943.
16. *Film India*, editorial, June 1943.
17. *Film India*, 'Bombay Calling', December 1943.
18. Garga, *From Raj to Swaraj*, pp. 65–6.
19. Ambalal J. Patel, Central Camera Co., advertisement, 'Educating India's Millions', *Times of India*, 22 January 1940, about availability of 16mm films priced at 100–175 rupees per copy. The districts targeted were Ahmednagar, Ahmedabad, East Khandesh and Belgaum. Twenty films were purchased from Patel's Education Films of India for this project. Reported in *Film India*, January 1940.
20. See 'Documentary Films for India', *Times of India*, 23 January 1941.

> Government have purchased a hundred projectors to be distributed amongst the various districts on a population basis. Each projector will be passed on from village to village in each area so that it will be in constant use. Each fortnight a completely new 45 minutes of programmes of films, comprising a newsreel and two other features is to be compiled and distributed by the Director of Information ... . The features will have a definite educational value, many of them dealing with subjects such as health, sanitation, agriculture and social welfare.

The films were silent, partially to do with electricity constraints, but also because of the diversity of languages involved, so that each film would be accompanied by a commentary 'delivered by a competent person'.

21. It was reported that the scheme was an immediate success, with hundreds of people flocking to see the films. See 'Visual Education Scheme: Wide Popularity', *Times of India*, 25 February 1941.
22. 'The Film in India: First Impressions', *Indian Documentary* vol. 2 no. 1, July–September 1955, p. 5.
23. Winifred Holmes, 'The Documentary in Egypt', *Indian Documentary* vol. 2 no. 1, July–September 1955, p. 9.
24. Ibid.
25. G. K. Athalye, 'Audio-visual Education in Bombay', *Indian Documentary* vol. 2 no. 1, July–September 1955, p. 19.
26. Holmes, 'The Documentary in Egypt', p. 8.
27. National Film Archives of India.
28. The double exposure was not part of the film's technique. My flagging of a particular image for capture in the film reel at the National Film Archives fortuitously located an overlap between frames. I was puzzled when I received the image, as I couldn't recognise this particular frame. The film has subsequently gone into storage, and so is not retrievable at short notice. However, the resulting mistake has produced a richly suggestive image.
29. Raj Thapar, *All These Days* (New Delhi: Seminar Publications, 1991).
30. Alexander Shaw noted that the bureaucracy was the main hurdle to the Film Advisory Board but he lauded progressive elements, who were involved. Writing in *Four Times Five*, a Films Division publication, he noted,

With their usual intuition, some Indians saw the possibilities for the future that the idea of a Government Film Unit contained. Left-wing politicians, journalists, intellectuals and fighters for women's rights decided to support our efforts to keep the unit going.

They often had to remain covert because of the Independence movement, but

they gave advice, they opened doors, they showed us the path ... we were surrounded with a goodwill ... *it was important that we should realize that what we were doing was for the future, however equivocal the background of the project and its production might be ... . These were small beginnings, but I hoped they helped to pave the way for the now world-famous Films Division, whose activities have made a pattern for the rest of the world to follow.*

See Mohan, *Documentary Films*, pp. 14–15, emphasis added.

31. It is instructive to see how far back post-Independence governments went in terms of material. IFI and FAB films continued to be used, as is indicated by National Council of Educational Research and Training, *Catalogue of Film*, Vol. 1, 1947–61.
32. National Film Archives of India.
33. Ibid.
34. Ibid.
35. Thomas Elsaesser, 'Archives and Archaeologies: The Place of Non-Fiction Film in Contemporary Media', in Vinzenz Hediger and Patrick Vonderau (eds), *Films That Work: Industrial Film and the Productivity of Media* (Amsterdam: University of Amsterdam Press, 2009).
36. Patricia D. Zimmerman, 'Geographies of Desire: Cartographies of Gender, Race, Nation and Empire in Amateur Film', *Film History* vol. 8 no. 1, Spring 1996, pp. 85–98.
37. Ibid.
38. 'The Home Movie Movement: Excavations, Artifacts, Minings', Introduction to Karen L. Ishikuza and Patricia Zimmerman (eds), *Mining the Home Movie* (Berkeley: University of California Press, 2008), p. 4.
39. Stanley Jepson, 'The Amateur Cinemaniac's Progress: A Vision of What He Can Do in India', *Indian Motion Picture Almanac*, 1938, pp. 399–402. Jepson was the editor of the *Illustrated Weekly of India*, a leading English-language periodical.
40. All amateur films have either been viewed at the Centre for South Asian Studies, Cambridge, or online.
41. From the description of the Hunter papers, see <www.s-asian.cam.ac.uk/overview.html>.
42. See the description of the Banks papers available at <www.s-asian.cam.ac.uk/overview. html>.
43. There was also a film called *The Glassblower*, not dated, in the ICI collection, though this was not set in India. The BFI database refers to it as 'The Story of Homer Last, Glassblower at the ICI Plastics Division; His Interests and Activities'. See <ftvdb.bfi.org.uk/sift/ title/220286>, accessed 14 February 2011.
44. Christopher Pinney, *The Coming of Photography in India* (New Delhi: Oxford University Press, 2008).
45. *Film India*, August 1940, p. 13.
46. Vigars, *A Short History of the Shell Film Unit*.
47. Ibid.

6

Who Needs a Witch Doctor? Refiguring British Colonial Cinema in the 1940s

Philip S. Zachernuk

In the late 1930s, British colonial policy in West Africa complacently asserted a racialist confidence that its self-proclaimed trusteeship would be a long-term affair. Only ten years later, colonial policy had shifted gears, racing through new development schemes down the road toward decolonisation. Before the war, mainstream British culture framed Africans as stable even inert wards in need of protection and gentle tutelage. After the war, Africans would need to be imagined with quite different qualities: as potential partners capable of rapid development and effective self-government. How was this transition accomplished? This story offers a rare insight into this question. It traces how two film characters key to the image of Africa – the witch doctor and the Good African – were refigured, and became new problems. Their development, in the British Colonial Office propaganda feature film, *Men of Two Worlds*, is traced here from their conception in 1942 to their screen debut in 1946. The witch-doctor character began as a perennial convention representing old Africa; his educated African opponent began as a faint, deferential dependant of the stock European hero. By 1946, the witch doctor had been challenged, refigured and then restored in an attenuated form. The educated African blossomed into something of a Renaissance man, but one who risked mental collapse. Through these changes we can glimpse how the Colonial Office muddled forward, initially not fully aware of the problem until invited and uninvited critics obliged them to confront it, and then not completely sure of where to seek a solution, and how to defend it. *Men of Two Worlds* was a major undertaking of the war effort, despite its eventual failure in commercial and critical terms. Shot on location in colonial Tanzania, with equipment that had to be replaced after it was lost in a German naval attack, and then largely reshot in a British studio because much of the expensive Technicolor film stock was ruined, it took three years of director Thorold Dickinson's time. The eventual budget rivalled the £500,000 earmarked for the British Colonial Development and Welfare Act of 1945.[1] The story of this film's production provides valuable insight into how official British thinking about the image of Africa, even when pursued with such commitment and resources, was not really under official control. As the British empire in Africa moved toward its end, official attempts to recast the image of Africa were shaped in a rather *ad hoc* series of stages by a diverse collection of groups. The emergent image remained problematic.

Much of the considerable literature on the invention of Africa stresses, correctly, underlying continuities. Africa remains in American and British minds, for example, exotic, dangerous, primitive.[2] Despite such continuities, the image of Africa is not constant. Means of defining African difference have changed; broad shifts of tone and content have accompanied major changes in West Africa's relation to the Atlantic world, notably with the end of the Atlantic slave trade, colonial partition and decolonisation. But our understanding remains limited in several respects. The process has been seen as rather amorphously linked to changing contexts, saying little about who did the work of rejecting old ideas or creating new ones. Film critics typically deal with the screened image, seldom with the dialogues through which those images were invented or developed. Studies have often been framed within national or continental boundaries, overlooking the influences crossing these arbitrary borders. Significantly, Africans have seldom been seen as active agents in these transformations. The production story of *Men of Two Worlds*, available in rarely accessible detail, can start to transcend these limitations.

BOSAMBO VS JOHN ZINGA

In 1942, when the British Colonial Office conceived its feature-film propaganda project, African witch doctors were familiar – but not uncontested – figures in British American, and African American images of Africa.[3] Witch doctors were 'old bogey men' in the popular images of Africa in the early twentieth century. Novelists H. Rider Haggard and Edgar Wallace used them, and they often reappeared in the empire cinema based on their work, such as *King Solomon's Mines* (1937). These witch doctors deploy magic to excite fear and violence among African commoners, both revealing Africans' ostensible innate primitive nature and challenging Western adventurers. Medical missionaries and colonial health-education films commonly pitted enlightened doctors against witch-doctor opponents.[4] They conveniently encapsulate the essence of imagined African difference and the qualities of African culture assumed to obstruct progress. The African witch doctor in children's literature, similarly, incarnated 'the force of "darkness" which enslaved the continent, a religious imposter beyond redemption, and a perfidious source of intrigue and reprisal against the British presence'.[5]

Good African figures were rare. Empire cinema, like its literary analogues, celebrated the white heroes who braved the dangerous landscape and its hostile inhabitants to impose order and save the natives from their own vices. When Africans fighting these same battles did appear they were almost always dependent inferiors – often servants – incidental to the main drama of old Africa confronting the modern. Literate Africans were more likely to be dangerous misfits unable to cope with the burdens of literacy and worldly knowledge.[6]

There was resistance to this, well illustrated by the career of the African American singer, activist and actor, Paul Robeson. Sensitive to the negative image of Africa in British and American culture, Robeson had been attracted to the 1935 Zoltan Korda film, *Sanders of the River*. Korda screened some footage shot in Africa for Robeson, and assured him the film he and his brothers were producing would reveal the noble qualities of African life, notably songs, and reverse established trends. In the end, by some accounts in the editing process, the final film itself reverted to the familiar.

Robeson's character – 'Bosambo' – came off as a childlike worshipper of the white hero; Africans in general fell into their passive place as victims and beneficiaries of outside manipulation.[7] The film generated considerable profit, but also protest from diasporan Africans in both New York and London. The pan-African activist Marcus Garvey used the occasion to organise a protest in London against the portrayal of Africa in film.[8] Feeling frustrated and betrayed, Robeson helped create the film *Song of Freedom* in 1936 to give his ideas of Africa screen time.[9] Robeson plays the lead as a black British dockworker, John Zinga, descended from exiled rulers of the West African kingdom of Casenga. Zinga first develops an international singing career, then through a song recalled from deep memory learns of his heritage and returns to Casenga to rescue it from the evil hold of the witch doctor who had usurped the Zinga line. He sets it on the road to progress under his guidance, funded by his singing career. Robeson's concern, it seems, was not with using a witch doctor to represent the obstacle to African progress, but rather with the nature of the hero. This film, of which he remained proud, is of a piece with longstanding African American, pan-African traditions which argued the uplift of Africa could be achieved by the return of its civilised sons. It also, in keeping with the spirit of the Harlem renaissance, saw pride and potential in African song as an emblem of how Africa's cultural riches could be harnessed for progress.[10]

West Africans sojourning in Britain, who had taken on the role of explaining African affairs to Britain, also resented and resisted popular misconceptions of Africa. Several books, and the journals *The Keys* from the League of Coloured Peoples (LCP) and *Wasu* from the West African Students Union (WASU),[11] revisited these problems frequently. Efforts to perform and record African music for British audiences also figured in this campaign.[12] The witch doctors and Bosambos on film certainly bothered them, as did the propaganda messages of imperial cinema, notwithstanding the opportunities some enjoyed to play extras in these films.[13] The rare episode of a British government documentary about sojourners such as themselves – a short called 'An African in London', produced in 1941– became a cause of protest rather than celebration because the title role was played by a West Indian.[14] By the early 1940s, then, the power of imperial cinema and Colonial Office documentary film had been felt and criticised by Africans and African Americans.

'LET US BY ALL MEANS HAVE LIONS, TIGERS, WITCH DOCTORS AND CROCODILES'

When *Men of Two Worlds* was first conceived in 1942 by Noel Sabine, a public-relations officer in the Colonial Office, colonial policy and thinking about Africa were in a state of flux. The complacency of the interwar period had been shaken in the face of failed development, headlong social change and African challenge.[15] The Colonial Office initiated a rethinking of policy. The outbreak of war added urgency to the task. The need to appease educated Africans squeezed by wartime demands, defend the idea of empire under the shadow of the Atlantic Charter and reduce American anti-imperial sentiments with a show of progressive reform, pushed new ideas forward. Educated Africans in Britain and in the colonies were being cultivated as allies in both the war effort and the prospect of more active development. The ability of chiefs to combine with modern forms of government came under scrutiny. The Colonial Office guiding idea was moving, falteringly, from the pre-war trusteeship of its 'chiefly' allies to a post-war partnership with educated Africans.[16]

African students in London were aware of these winds of change. But few African or British observers seemed to appreciate yet that this policy shift required a profound reimagining of Africa. In official British eyes, the Africans of Indirect Rule were passive, trapped in their primitive stagnation without the ability or desire to move forward, and distinctly not modern. The African intelligentsia's vision was different: Africans were distinct, and their special qualities needed to be recognised and preserved as the foundation on which they would enter modernity on their own terms. Differences among them arose over what mixture of resources to use, but even the more thoroughly Anglophile among them asserted the continuing relevance of African culture.[17] For both British and West African traditions, the inchoate new policy would require an Africa that was dynamic, capable of fairly quick progress toward modern status. The witch doctor and the Good African became sites of this revision.

Sabine's initial thoughts reveal the state of flux. In terms of form, he wanted a major feature film produced in Technicolor, without public connection to the government, to raise awareness of the emergent colonial policy. But in terms of content, he simply wanted to repackage and present 'incidentally' the propaganda message of a disappointingly dull 1939 Colonial Marketing Board documentary short, *Men of Africa*. This film had packed the purpose but not the punch of Alexander Korda's and Michael Balcon's classic empire cinema features of the 1930s, praising imperial administration as heroic exploit.[18] The synopsis is clear: 'This simple life under the hot African sky was once a life of fear and uncertainty … British rule has brought peace … . But there is still a long battle to be fought with ignorance, poverty, and disease.'[19] Sabine's rough ideas, derived from his experiences in African administration and spun by E. Arnot Robertson, a writer on staff, into a film treatment titled 'White Ants', readily deployed a witch doctor for dramatic effect alongside other familiar elements of colonial fiction.

The central character is District Officer Shearforth, who, disconsolate over a growing estrangement from his selfish wife, struggles valiantly to administer his corner of the empire (understood to be in West Africa). He has the support of the village schoolteacher Hale, a local African who had spent ten years at Achimota College in colonial Ghana, and who represents Africa's potential for change under British guidance. Shearforth is pitted against Africa's hostile environment and unchanging culture, as represented by the destructive swarms of white ants and the witch doctor's resistance to Shearforth's initiatives. The witch doctor, never named, evokes the familiar: an 'old man, with an air of authority, and one who might have been any age, with a cavernous face like a skull. He wore a kaross of wild cat skins, and charms about his arms and legs.'[20] He is revealed to have buried an infant alive as a sacrifice to control locusts, and to have poisoned a child in an attempt to kill the District Officer. He is shown identifying witches, in one case driving a woman to suicide. He combines, then, the ideas of a witch who harms people, and of a witch doctor who finds witches. He does not practise useful medicine. Tired of the witch doctor's obstruction, and seeking distraction from his marital woes, Shearforth decides to fight for 'the soul' of his district. He challenges the witch doctor to kill him by magic or be discredited. When the officer fails to die at the waning of the moon as predicted, the witch doctor withdraws his curse, claiming white men are beyond his power. Hale knows he must now challenge the witch doctor, because 'in the end, it is the Africans who must lift the fear that lies over Africa'. But he is not made of quite the same stuff as Europeans. As he laments to Shearforth,

> For not quite ten years, I have been of your faith. For more than ten thousand, my people have been in Africa, where the ground is soaked in blood, and alive with the terror and the magic made out of spilt blood … . You ask me what I believe about witchcraft. Do you mean with my head or my heart? They aren't the same. You can't wipe out ten thousand years with ten.[21]

Driven by duty, Hale takes on the curse, but from the start is 'wholly African in his distress', wrestling with 'age-old terrors'.[22] As the moon wanes towards the curse's conclusion, the schoolmaster almost succumbs. But, as Hale had predicted, he survives through the steadfast support of Shearforth and his wife.

> What you can do – and you must do – is to stand by us and make it possible for us to come forward; the African doctors and the African teachers; the new Africa that will fight the old evils with the science and the knowledge which you brought.[23]

In the end, Shearforth's estranged wife decides to pitch in with her husband; the recovery of the schoolmaster heralds the rise of Africa.

For the Colonial Office this was 'a grand story of Colonial Administration'. The District Officer's personal strife suitably 'spiced' the story of 'his struggle against the influence of witchcraft', combining 'dramatic influence with excellent Empire propaganda'. And it was excellent propaganda in the established fashion. A colonial hero, supporting a Good African, had defeated 'the sinister influence of the witch doctor' and emerged a better person for his struggle on behalf of the empire.[24]

Perhaps because someone in the Colonial Office sensed this script was not quite in touch with the rapidly changing times, or perhaps officials made their next move simply driven by a search for promising cinematic talent. In any case, at the end of 1942, the Colonial Office secured Thorold Dickinson as director. Their first choice, he was a leading light in British commercial cinema, and not easily released from the army where he had been posted to do film work for the war effort. Dickinson in turn asked Joyce Cary to write the screenplay. Cary and Dickinson, outsiders to the Colonial Office, would challenge conservative positions there with their more liberal imperialist sensibilities.

Dickinson was clearly a man of large talent whose 'politics was in general that of a pragmatic and humane man of the progressive Left'.[25] Although he had no particular connection to African affairs, his *High Command*, a 1937 drama incidentally set in West Africa, took the opportunity to satirise imperial pomposity.[26] Dickinson's position on colonial affairs is clearer in a piece written in 1944, during production of *Men of Two Worlds*. He feared the post-war world would fall back into old and dangerous habits unless pushed consciously forward.[27] New, scientific attitudes needed to replace the 'age-rotten' and 'primitive', in just the way 'sane education' was moving Africa ahead. Dickinson accepted the standard colonial view that Africans' culture was 'two thousand years' behind that of their European 'guardians,' but avoided the common racial explanation for this gap. Rather, African 'tribal society' and Nazi Europe both contained 'the false racial pride, terrorism and opposition to innovation' which needed to be defeated. Dickinson, then, was engaging in a general battle for social progress with a rather ambivalent attitude toward Africans: they were potential allies as long as they left the evils of old thinking behind.

Dickinson keenly recommended Cary as the scriptwriter, after reading Cary's 1941 Liberal Party pamphlet *The Case for African Freedom*. Cary's experiences as a Colonial Officer in Northern Nigeria mostly during World War I, and his four novels based on them, established his credentials for the Colonial Office.[28] Cary's writings foreshadowed British post-war attitudes. Empire was necessary, but had to be done better. Cary aligned himself firmly in 'sympathy with the African masses, suffering under bad conditions of health and pay',[29] but also insisted that Africans lived in 'a museum of disease and frustration'.[30] The renewed purpose of empire was to free Africans from the superstition, fear and hunger in which they languished. The highly educated few had to restrain their demands for power, and the growth of a poorly educated literate population would only confuse matters; viable political progress could only come 'at the end, instead of at the beginning, of a people's emancipation'.[31]

Dickinson and Cary shared with West African activists a desire to initiate progressive change in Africa and to repudiate racialist thinking. But they retained the imperial faith that meaningful change could only come from European civilisation. Africans were capable of progress, but African culture could only colour the imported patterns of change. In a 1944 lecture (when he was well aware of African concerns about his script that we will examine below), Cary asserted that colonial education

> should aim at giving the African, the best of Europe, in art and literature and science. Of course, give him the best of Africa too, give him his own history and mythology and arts. But do not try to keep him to any narrow local pattern.[32]

The two writers were clearly equipped to shift the Colonial Office image of Africa forward from pre-war complacencies, and echoed some positions favoured by African activists. But how were they to translate these broad ideas into effective film propaganda? And how would African activists react to this mixture of liberal openness and colonial hubris?

Striking changes appeared to the two protagonists in the film treatment Cary and Dickinson submitted in April 1943, produced during a tour through West and East Africa preparing for the film shoot. This expensive tour was an important part of the project. Their firsthand experience of Africa shooting on location would allow the filmmakers to counter critics with claims that their treatment was authentic. The plot still turns on the African teacher's victory against the witch doctor's challenge. But the whole marriage plotline is now removed, initiating the gradual erosion of the white officer's centrality and the growing focus on the Good African. Now with the clearly African name Kijana, he is a government scholarship student who had studied music in London for four years, and had become a promising composer in the European style.

He foregoes his musical career, however, honouring his promise to return home as a teacher. The District Officer, now called Rendell, welcomes him as a respected subordinate, hoping Kijana can help convince his 'Litu' people to agree to a resettlement scheme away from tsetse-infested bush. The witch doctor, now named Magole, is still a familiar exotic figure 'in full witch-doctor dress with kilt' and 'big silver rings'.[33] He holds both good and bad powers: he can poison and cure people, and find witches. To save the village from sleeping sickness, he presides over a ritual in which the 'stone-age people' of the village stuff a live ram's stomach with tsetse flies.[34] But Magole has been slightly transformed. He is not just an ancient institution, but also a stranger to Litu, and a former railway clerk. The obstacle he presents thus combines ancient African culture and the *bête noire* of Cary and the Colonial Office: the dangerous, semi-educated clerk.

As we shall see, the film-makers continued to need their witch doctor. But why the Good African as musician, a transformation Arnot Robertson (and many later critics) thought false?[35] We can see here how Cary and Dickinson's quest to recast their characters was shaped by others. Arnot Robertson's teacher Hale quotes at length the late J. K. Aggrey. A widely respected moderate pan-African and staff member at Achimota College in colonial Ghana, Aggrey's most famous message was that progress in Africa required harmony between black and white.[36] The LCP journal *The Keys* evoked black-and-white piano keys as a tribute to Aggrey's vision. Robertson's intent, presumably, was to appropriate Aggrey's endorsement of her message. Cary and Dickinson's more forward-looking message led them to two more contemporary models. Fela Sowande, the pioneering Nigerian composer who melded African and European traditions, was very probably one. He was known to the Colonial Office Film Unit (CFU), and the film-makers. Present in London musical circles from 1935, he often played with Rudolph Dunbar, the Guyanese musician approached in March 1943 to play Kijana (perhaps because of his link to Sowande). Sabine's office was interested in hiring Sowande in April 1943, as the film treatment was being circulated; he was hired in June.[37] Dickinson claimed to be fully aware of Sowande's accomplishments in June when he agreed to Arnot Robertson's suggestion to contact him.[38] As a successful popular figure also willing to work with the Colonial Office. Sowande provided an attractive model for an updated Good African. As we shall see, as the film-makers sought to appease African critics, Kijana acquired more explicitly Sowande's cultural nationalist musical interests. In a real-life parallel, by July 1943, Sowande was liaising with WASU about how the CFU might better serve them.[39]

The second model was Robeson. Film historian Kenneth Cameron sees the Kijana character as directly derived from a 'new archetype' introduced by Robeson in his films, *Song of Freedom* and *Jericho* (1937): the educated African returning to improve his motherland. 'Consciously or otherwise', the Kijana role was 'clearly intended for Robeson'.[40] Robeson had in fact been named by Arnot Robertson in production plans for 'White Ants' written in August 1942.[41] Cary and Dickinson may well have seen in Robeson's response to *Sanders of the River* a template for revising Hale. Zinga's message harmonised with Cary's *The Case for African Freedom*: Africa needed outside agency to break free. He also appeared in tune with West African opinion, having become a patron of WASU in 1935. That Robeson himself deployed the witch doctor vs civilisation plot structure in *Song of Freedom* only made the adaptation smoother.

Evoking both Robeson's musical career and his film plots in the Kijana character made sense.

John Sutro, the producer, seems to have thought the revisions by Dickinson and Cary improved the film so distinctly that he instructed Dickinson not to provide Dunbar – the prospective Kijana – with a copy of 'White Ants'.[42] Response at the Colonial Office accepted the new treatment as a necessary lapse from fine literature to vulgar popular culture. One official compared the original 'delightful little piece of literary Camembert' to the new 'whacking hunk of feature film chalk', but conceded that the 'propaganda element' was 'clearer and more definite' because it was now 'a rattling good film story ... that shows British administration among primitive peoples through appropriately rosy spectacles'. Despite the changes, the Good African remained a colonial dependant; the witch doctor still effectively conveyed the fears and superstitions of Darkest Africa. Wondering about a minor character inserted in this version, the same official remarked 'Let us by all means have lions, tigers, witch doctors and crocodiles, but, of all creatures on earth, not, I beg, a German professor of logic.'[43]

'THERE IS NO SUCH THING AS A WITCH DOCTOR'

This new approach did not, however, please the members of WASU. It was not the Good African that concerned them immediately, nor the colonial development propaganda, but rather the witch doctor. In the spring of 1943 the need arose to find an African actress to play the new role of Kijana's sister. It seems likely that, at least by early April, WASU was approached by Two Cities for help, and that its objections to the film's form were becoming known months before WASU sent a long formal memorandum in late July, followed by another in September.[44] Recalling the *Sanders* episode, the July memorandum raised three main objections:

> (a) the content and representation is contrary to African law and customs; (b) it casts a slur on the prestige of African peoples as a whole and is in no way suggestive of real co-operation between whites and blacks; and (c) it prejudices future relations between African Peoples and the British Empire.[45]

The attack on Magole was not a minor criticism: 'There is no such thing as a witch doctor in African law and custom. It is an entirely European invention.'[46] Africans believed in witches, all agreed, and Africa had various kinds of doctors and healers. Indeed, various British West African governments had 'accorded ... statutory recognition' to different 'professional native doctors', who, like modern doctors, can hurt as well as heal with their knowledge. This indigenous medical knowledge had an essential role to play in the cultural nationalist agenda. When combined as Aggrey had recommended 'with the best from the West', it would create a specifically African modern society. Lumping diverse forms of African medical knowledge into the white man's witch doctor in effect dismissed its potential value. As Solanke stated succinctly in a later letter, 'recognition should be accorded' African medicine 'while scientific improvement should be imported into it in order to fulfil the object and aim of Indirect Rule ... moulding it and establishing it into lines consonant with modern ideas and higher standards'.[47] The members of WASU did not need a witch doctor.

But WASU was not willing to forego the chance to bring the power of cinema to bear on its problems. The memorandum went on to suggest what could 'be substituted for the part played in this film by the so-called witch-doctor and his witch-craft'.[48] It proposed changing the film's setting to the early colonial period. Rendell would be seeking to extend direct British rule over the Litu; Kijana would represent those educated Africans in favour of close and long-term foreign rule. Magole would represent 'the opposite school of thought among the educated Africans', seeking a limited and short-term British presence as seen in Egypt, which had led quickly to 'complete self-government' there. Thus, instead of the superstition vs science structure of the propaganda film, 'the whole film play will turn on' conflict between two African factions dealing with Rendell's attempts to forge an empire.[49]

This suggested revision not only dispensed with the witch doctor, but also would have WASU usurp the Colonial Office propaganda project, and instead place the concerns of West African intellectuals on the screen. The issue for them was not to defend colonial rule, but rather to explore the political divisions among West African leaders as a departure point for designing its future. Here they marked a difference of vision that separated them from both the film-makers and Robeson. The latter approached Africa from the outside, as a stage for the epic struggle of enlightenment vs superstition. Africa would be conquered in the name of progress, it would not generate progress on its own. This plot suggestion wanted to remove the witch doctor so as to speak directly to African concerns about directing progress from within Africa.

The Colonial Office was not inclined to concede WASU's points. A. R. Thomas set the tone, invoking the outsider's lack of excitement with a story steered away from its familiar grand meanings. The suggested plotline was 'unacceptable, partly because of the anti-Imperialist tinge which it would give the film and also because it would turn the film into a very much duller thing'. He wanted to keep to the 'film which portrays Colonial life round an exciting story and with a real human interest and does not (as the Union's revision would) aim at *direct* propaganda in any direction'. A like-minded higher official dismissed WASU and LCP concerns as a pathetic 'inferiority complex', based on an inability to stomach the 'commonsense' view that films on Africa would naturally reveal 'the primitive beliefs and habits of coloured peoples'.[50]

But Thomas could not just dismiss these concerns, for political reasons and also for fear that, without WASU help, the search for female actors would flounder. He asked Sabine to consult the West Africa Department about the weight to be given to WASU complaints, and to check if Two Cities could still 'consider re-casting its theme fundamentally or adapting it in detail so as to take some account of these representations'.[51] The West Africa Department's political assessment indicated that WASU was not worth much worry.[52] Challenged in their views, officials buttressed their claims to superior knowledge of Africa by calling in opinions from various officers with field experience in West or East Africa, which assured Sabine that the witch doctor as portrayed was accurate.[53] But, perhaps because this new question called for additional sources of authority, Sabine also looked for 'African' authentication to secure his position. He passed the film treatment to Ivor Cummings, a minor official whose father was from Sierra Leone. As Cummings later revealed, he was asked to respond 'as an African'.[54] Cummings, who had not seen the WASU memorandum, saw nothing that should offend if people understood it was a fiction intended to support change. 'We have all been conscious of the fact that Witchcraft has been, in many parts of tropical Africa, responsible for the slow progress which has been made in the fields of medicine and education.' He asserted that 'certain aspects of African tribal life and custom must be swept away'.[55]

Thus reinforced with 'a representative body of opinion' that carried both racial and professional credentials to counter WASU claims, Sabine reported to his superiors that he remained

> convinced of the validity of the film. I would draw particular attention to the comments of Ivor Cummings, himself an African ... .To this I would only add that Mr Rudolph Dunbar, who, I venture to say, is at least as jealous of the rights and dignity of coloured people as anyone in W.A.S.U., is himself convinced that the film is well conceived and should have a beneficial effect ... . Incidentally Mr Dunbar who was aware of W.A.S.U.'s protest, ventured himself to express the opinion that the members of W.A.S.U were not really in close touch with responsible African opinion, if they took this view.[56]

In July, the film production company pointed out that Cary and Dickinson had done fieldwork to authenticate their account, reassured by their liberal, imperial paternalism.

> The film's basis is still ... the fact that the coloured man is a human being with all the attributes of the white man even if his mental development has not yet reached that stage. Special prominence is given in the script to the power of witchcraft – a form of superstition still most powerful in Africa, but our treatment of witchcraft is up-to-date and factual and the subject is not treated with mysterious glamour.[57]

Thus reassured, the Colonial Office decided not to push the WASU concerns on the film company, but the sense of anxiety did not evaporate. Instructions remained to 'treat W.A.S.U.'s intervention sympathetically'.[58] A letter sent to WASU and Sorensen at the end of August defended their 'realistic and helpful' approach based on 'received advice from several quarters, including advice from other Africans', but also indicated that 'the script is again being revised, not specially to meet the comments made by W.A.S.U. but in a way which will in fact meet some of their points'.[59] As Sabine stepped back, Dickinson, Cary and Robert Adams (replacing Dunbar as Kijana) worked to continue the conversation with WASU and other Africans. They arranged meetings with WASU through Cummings in October, which were known about by senior officials, but kept officially unofficial.[60] John Sutro might also have arranged further 'friendly discussions' with WASU members in early November.[61] The film-makers still wanted their witch doctor, but they were beginning to recognise that he could not remain unquestioned and unchanged, and that African advice would help them refigure him.

In the context of the WASU protest and these various conversations and deflections, an actual script was produced in late August, to which continual revisions were made through the fall.[62] It would be difficult to closely correlate script alterations with the discussions. For present purposes, it seems clear that both the Good African and the witch-doctor figures were repeatedly revisited over these months, in an attempt to create a more acceptable representation.

Kijana became a yet more accomplished figure, more independent, with a more cogent cultural nationalist position. His music is performed at the British National Gallery in the opening sequence. (This success was now achieved, however, after seven years in England rather than four.) He is hired as a school inspector with the prospect of being a provincial school inspector within a few years. He is much more a social equal to Rendell: they have drinks together at the Boma and play Kijana's composition together on the piano, evoking Aggrey's black-and-white keys in harmony. This time Kijana sees the need to challenge Magole without Rendell's intervention. His music in April had 'a distinctly European quality';[63] now, like Sowande's own compositions, it is explicitly a mixture of African and European ideas. In the climactic scene, as Rendell realises Kijana's own music might win Kijana back from his delirium, he passes the composition to schoolchildren. As they drum, play and sing, he whispers 'Drums Kijana. Your drums. It's your music – real music, about Africa'.[64] Kijana as always recovers, but his mental stress at the climax is now deepened. Special effects portray hallucinations of drumsticks rising off the music score, which he must control to displace Magole's drumming with his own music.

Magole also changes; he is raised above the unexplained African darkness and given both motives and clearer connections to changing colonial society. He is a troubled character who was fired from his railway clerical post for theft; he lives in a hut made of crushed petrol tins, furnished in a mixture of European and African styles. He is no longer dressed exotically, but like the other villagers. But he is still the son and grandson of *mgangas*, now introduced as the authentic local term for witch doctor. He is presented not as a man of magic, but quite clearly as a confidence man, out for power, even the chieftancy, who sees Kijana as a rival for worldly influence. He works not by mysterious but by psychological methods. Thus he secretly positions 'death ju-jus' to play on the fears of the villagers (and Kijana), and convinces the villagers of a curse by secretly sabotaging the new bridge. He is even allowed the chance to deny, however weakly, witchcraft. Magole is asked (by the German professor of logic inserted in an earlier draft) 'You are an educated man – tell me – do you truly believe in witchcraft?' He replies 'No, the people ask me for help and I cure them.'[65]

Perhaps in response to the WASU suggestion that the witch doctor and educated African represent opposed political factions, Magole and Kijana debate.

MAGOLE: You don't belong here. You belong to the whites.
KIJANA: That's a lie. You know I came here to help my people. I want my people to learn all that the whites can teach.
MAGOLE: How to kill people? How to make war with guns?
KIJANA: They stopped our wars.
MAGOLE: And made us into slaves.
KIJANA: They stopped slavery. They made us free.

MAGOLE: What is freedom? If we must live to suit them, and give up our old ways.

KIJANA: New ways come, even by themselves ... . Even in Africa things change. You can't stop them.[66]

Far short of rewriting the plot as a conflict between collaborators and resisters, it is nonetheless a far more explicit statement of political values than was conceivable from the witch doctor in 'White Ants' or the earlier film treatment. The witch doctor was now a debater with political ideas, not just superstitious fears.

Solanke saw some version of the revised script in early November 1943, and thought it a much more 'realistic representation' of African life than the April treatment.[67] He welcomed the scene in which Magole denies practising witchcraft, but remained unsatisfied because the witch-doctor plotline and its false premises remained. He repeated his original objection: because it folds potentially valuable native medicine into the invented witch-doctor figure 'the film naturally ends with the destruction of the Native Medical Institution as a necessary evil. This should not be so.' In its place, Solanke offers again a more 'constructive principle' for the plot which would, like his earlier suggestions, put Africans' issues forward. Magole and Kijana should be presented as 'two educated Africans – patriots or teachers or leaders of their country'. They would represent not the old Africa that had to be destroyed and the new Africa emergent, but rather two contemporary political camps. Magole should be 'a conservative educated African leader', Kijana 'a liberally progressive educated African leader'. The plot could then turn on the struggle of the District Officer to manage this conflict in 'a manner of a constructive co-operation'. The result, still effective for propaganda, would be 'the development of the Litu people on modern lines ... effected in a most happy way without the loss of anything'. Resisting the grand confrontation of the colonial development agenda, Solanke was holding true to his nationalist sense that African culture and African political debates had much to contribute to the development project. Probably more in despair than hope, Solanke concluded. 'If you agree to the above comment and suggestion we think further conference over this matter is no longer necessary.'[68]

In these same months, Solanke also tried to make his criticisms public, pressing the editor of *West Africa*, Albert Cartwright, to publicise his protest. Cartwright first resisted, but came around to accepting Solanke's position that British attitudes did need to change.[69] An editorial finally appeared in April 1944, asserting that cinematic witch doctors were indeed pure European invention, and heralding a new colonial era in which WASU could be consulted about the accuracy of an African film.[70]

Indeed, these script revisions do suggest that the writers, attending to wider discussions, were trying to render a more acceptable Good African. They had taken their cues on rethinking the character from contemporary figures, and although the WASU memoranda wanted this figure to be more tuned to political questions, Kijana was not the focus of its criticisms. In their struggle to make the witch doctor represent actual African opinion rather than a European fantasy, it seems the writers had added another type of African feared in the official imagination: the clever but discontented former colonial clerk. However, because the epic struggle of colonial progress vs African darkness remained in place, Cary and Dickinson still required the cinematic services of the witch doctor in his primal form.

'IN AFRICA THERE WERE GOOD AND BAD *MGANGAS*'

After the fall of 1943 I have no more direct evidence of contact between the film company and WASU, but conversations may have continued. By Dickinson's account, throughout location filming in Tanganyika in 1944 and studio filming in 1945, 'Always we had to prove to the coloured people that our film was to be no "Sanders of the River", that bugbear of every educated person of colour.'[71] Years later Dickinson credited Orlando Martins, the Lagos-born actor playing Magole, with helping to create a co-operative atmosphere on the set.[72] Presumably, this atmosphere involved listening to Africans' input. The Colonial Office also pressured for various changes over these years.[73] In any case, the witch doctor and Good African who debuted in Dar es Salaam, then in London in July 1946, had changed since late 1943.

The Magole on screen falls back toward earlier versions, but retains traces of having been critically reviewed. He still dresses like other villagers, and works by suggestion and trickery. But he is no longer a disgraced railway clerk; he is simply the illiterate heir of a witch doctor lineage from beyond Litu. He no longer denies his witchcraft. An attempt to recognise the existence of legitimate African medicine is undercut by the need to amalgamate in the same figure the dark essence of Africa's backwardness:

> In Africa there were good and bad 'mgangas', and Magole wielded great power over the Litu. The term 'mganga' meant a practitioner in medicine. But the mganga was a healer in the mind as well as the body, and in a country where superstition amounted to almost a religion, the power over the mind was a dangerous weapon in unscrupulous hands.[74]

Traces remained of the debate between Magole and Kijana, and thus of contemporary African politics, but they were diluted and presented in separate scenes. Magole expresses essential resistance to change rather than ambition for power: he both refuses to be relocated and to accept the challenge to place Randall (the new name for Rendell) under a death spell.

> I seek no power over the white man. I am an *African* ... . We like to live in peace on our own fields and reap our own crops. We are Africans and we ask only to live as Africans.[75]

Kisenga (the new name for Kijana)[76] speaks at a school opening, espousing not a strong cultural nationalist position but rather Cary's argument that real freedom required development first, and Dickinson's belief that Africa required above all modern education.

> I want my people to learn all that my white friends can teach them. Knowledge is the only power against man's enemies – disease, superstition and that worst enemy, fear. Fear stands in the way of all progress, not only in Africa but in all the world.[77]

In other ways, Kisenga continues elements of his earlier trajectory. He rises yet again in stature and cultural nationalist achievement. Discussing Kisenga's emergence as a 'new African', Randall assures his peers that 'we didn't put him up to be the carbon copy of a European'.[78] In the opening scene, Kisenga's orchestral concert, now named 'Baraza' after village meetings common in East Africa, was explicitly presented as an accomplished work on an African theme.[79] (On the insistence of a government official, his sojourn in Britain had been increased from seven to fifteen years to account for this artistic achievement.)[80] Kisenga is revived at the climax by schoolchildren performing 'Baraza', highlighting the triumph of modernised but African culture over the sinister African drums, representing fear and superstition.

But, perhaps because Kisenga's new stature was so novel, threatening to violate the boundary between the two worlds of imperial ruler and colonial subject, the final film went to greater lengths than before to enervate him. Sometime late in 1943, Dickinson and Cary had turned their attention to Kijana's psyche. As Dickinson recalled thirty years later, they 'approached a psychiatrist, an authority on racial behaviour, and with his consent we had made our leading African character, Kisenga, a "patient" of his. He vetted his character development throughout the story to make it psychologically authentic.'[81] Whereas his decline under the curse had earlier still been largely attributed to the 'ten thousand years' of Africa in his blood, the film injects a broader and more complex process of alienation and loss of identity. After fifteen years away, Kisenga is terrified when having to cross the crocodile-infested river on the rope bridge that leads to his childhood village. He is ostracised by his villagers as a 'black white man'; his father hardly recognises him when he returns; his mother disowns him, blaming him for his father's death.[82] His sister's fear of Magole erodes Kisenga's faith in himself. During his trying wait for Magole's death spell to take effect, he gradually sheds his tidy European clothes and habits, at one point running bare-chested through the moonlit jungle. During a respite from his ailments, Kisenga retreats to the Boma and wears Randall's clothes. Kisenga becomes lost between his two worlds: 'But what am I? I thought I had two worlds. Now I have none at all.'[83] Hints of hallucination in the climactic scene from 1943 become a full-blown nightmare sequence, hinting at mental breakdown from a collision of cultural, and even racial, identities. Kisenga dreams he is trapped in a tent, at the peak of which hangs one of Magole's death charms. Outside one wall, Magole and his drummers beat their sinister rhythm, outside the other the National Gallery orchestra plays his 'Baraza'. As he struggles to grasp the charm and escape, his arms turn white. When he fights past his father to join the orchestra, his father attempts to strangle him. Magole wields a knife over the pair, the screen is splattered with blood, the scene ends. Kisenga recovers, but the audience is left deeply unsure that the Good African will be able to lead the march of African progress without counselling from his white friends.

'DARKEST AFRICA SLINKS AWAY ...'

Heavily promoted in Tanganyika and Britain on its release, the film evoked much discussion, and remained an unhappy memory in the Colonial Office years later. Opinions ranged widely: not all Africans resented it; and not all British reviewers approved. But the dividing lines from 1943 remained prominent. To *The Times*, the core of the story was that, when confronted with 'the white magic of stethoscope and education ... darkest Africa slinks away into the bush'.[84] African activists in London and abroad objected to 'the film's failure to capture the realities of Africa', showing instead 'the East African as a savage … who believes in magic and witchcraft'.[85] M. C. Peterside, picking up the WASU banner in Solanke's absence, lamented that 'the producers, in spite of all protests and attempts at correction by the West African Students' Union, have insisted on maintaining the fallacy of their plot', and the purely European invention of the African witch doctor. [86] Even Orlando Martins admitted the film did little to erode popular notions of African witch doctors.[87] Equally, Peterside protested Kisenga's mental instability.

> To suit their plot, they have invented a type of African who only exists in the imagination of some people, a man of two worlds, who cannot fit into the European or African society just because he has lived and studied in Britain.

Another African reviewer elaborated: 'the African who returns home from Europe is not regarded by the simplest villager as a white man, and neither does he regard himself as such … . In short, he is not a Kisenga.'[88] In short, Kisenga was another European invention. Dickinson tried to defend his project, claiming he was seeking to rally concerned people around a new vision for Africa's future, free of racialist essentialisms or romantic ideals.[89] Clearly, for all his efforts, he had not created new characters on which the putative partners in the post-war development programme could agree.

Composing new cinematic figures for Africa suited to the era of 'partnership' involved a wide community – as inventors, models and critics – interacting in complex ways.[90] Arguably, the old witch doctor became a problem only when WASU raised the issue. And because this film project required active African participation, African voices had to be heeded. But once the question was raised, and the linked revisions of the witch doctor and Good African proceeded, the circle of participants widened and aligned in ways that crossed racial boundaries and the divisions between rulers and subjects. Arnot Robertson sought posthumous endorsement from Aggrey. Dickinson and Cary challenged conservative Colonial Office thinking with more liberal beliefs. Searching for a new approach, they also combined in their Good African features of the different cultural nationalist projects represented by Robeson and Sowande, and tried to accommodate Solanke. Sabine at the Colonial Office found support from sympathetic people who could claim authentic 'African' status; Solanke and his peers cited American, European and African experts back at them. Cartwright and Solanke deployed *West Africa* to change British popular culture. If the Colonial Office had intended to create a new image under its control it did not.

Men of Two Worlds came into being during crucial years in colonial history. It had the budget and the talent to make a decisive step toward imagining an Africa more suited to post-war policies and ambitions. Film scholars argue that the film marks various important transitions in the cinema of Africa and the empire. Peter Swaab, for example, sees it caught between two worlds, 'not so very far upstream' of *Sanders*, but also engaging debates about African interests and colonial development in new ways.[91] The discussion evoked by the film played forward into later commentaries on screened images of Africa.[92] In the wake of the WASU protest, the Colonial Office launched a review of non-theatrical films about African witchcraft held in British film libraries. The report in December 1943 confirmed fears that they were misleading and harmful, and plans were made to improve on this.[93] Good African characters received more attention in its wake: the disappointment of *An African in London* in 1941 was followed by better-received treatments of West Africans connected to WASU in *Nurse Ademola* (1943) and *An African in England* (1945). It is probable that these subjects reflected Sowande's consultations with West Africans.[94] More powerfully, a 1948 short feature by the Colonial Film Unit, *Daybreak in Udi*, contained the familiar plot of British officials and educated Africans confronting superstitious resistance to development. But the character chosen to represent the old ways turned out to be merely a conservative elder, avoiding many of the hallmarks of the familiar witch doctor.[95] The film won an Academy Award in 1949.

In so far as *Men of Two Worlds* marks a change, one might credit the invited and uninvited critics who persuaded the Colonial Office to revamp the stale vision articulated in 'White Ants'. But the film's failures, including its lack of success in rallying its West African critics around a new development agenda, derive from the odd mixture comprising the emergent image. Robeson's African American agenda for change, while attractive to the Colonial Office because it shared the sense that Africa needed outside help, ran against the West Africans' faith in themselves as the guides for African progress. The weakness of the new image also stems from the film-makers' inability to relinquish the old tenets of empire. Dickinson and Cary fought against blind racism in Britain, but held on to more subtle elements of imperial prejudice. They could not, it seems, finally free themselves of the sense that development in Africa would be an epic struggle, a challenge to the very sanity of the new African. As Hale became Kijana and then Kisenga – as the Good African became a more impressive and accomplished figure – his achievement required education in Britain rather than in Africa, and then this exposure grew from four, to seven, to fifteen years. Their new African needed to become more dependent, not less. For all their efforts, the makers of *Men of Two Worlds* had not fully remade their key cinematic figures to fit with post-war policy. For all their attention to others' ideas, they could not transcend some core empire-cinema values. In the end, the sturdy District Officer remained, and the witch doctor reverted to his essential role as a fictional representation of the African evils British genius would defeat. 'Darkest Africa' would slink away only slowly.

NOTES

1. *Men of Two Worlds* (Thorold Dickinson, UK, 1946). The most complete account of the film's production is Chaim Litewski, 'The "Acceptable" Face of British Colonialism: "Men of Two Worlds"', unpublished MA thesis, Polytechnic of Central London, 1983. Press reports at its release put the cost of this film at £400,000, *Chronicle* (London), 20 July 1946; Litewski, '"Acceptable" Face', p. 22, puts it at £600,000.
2. There is a substantial historiography on images of Africa. See, for example, Douglas Rimmer and Anthony Kirk-Greene (eds), *The British Intellectual Engagement with Africa in the Twentieth Century* (London: Macmillan, 2000); Andrew Roberts, 'The Imperial Mind', in Andrew Roberts (ed), *The Colonial Moment in Africa* (Cambridge: Cambridge University Press, 1990), pp. 24–76; Stephen Howe, *Anticolonialism in British Politics: The Left and the End of Empire, 1918–1964* (Oxford: Clarendon, 1993); Penelope Hetherington, *British*

Paternalism and Africa, 1920–1940 (London: Cass, 1978); James Meriwether, *Proudly We Can Be Africans: Black Americans and Africa, 1935–1961* (Chapel Hill: University of North Carolina Press, 2002); Curtis Keim, *Mistaking Africa: Curiosities and Inventions of the American Mind* (Boulder, CO: Westview Press, 1999); Dennis Hickey and Kenneth Wylie, *Enchanting Darkness: The American Vision of Africa in the Twentieth Century* (East Lansing: Michigan State University Press, 1993).

3. On Africa in cinema, see, for example, Femi Okiremuete Shaka, *Modernity and the African Cinema* (Trenton, NJ: Africa World Press, 2004); Kenneth M. Cameron, *Africa on Film: Beyond Black and White* (New York: Continuum, 1994); Alfred E. Opubor and Adebayo Ogunbi, 'Ooga Booga: The African Image in American Films', in Robin Winks (ed), *Other Voices, Other Views* (Westport, CT: Greenwood Press, 1978), pp. 343–75. Cameron goes further than most to perceive processes and agents of change.

4. Megan Vaughan, *Curing Their Ills: Colonial Power and African Illness* (Stanford, CA: Stanford University Press, 1991), pp. 162–5, 181; Françoise Pfaff, 'Hollywood's Image of Africa', *Commonwealth Essays and Studies* no. 5 (1981–2), p. 106.

5. Kathryn Castle, *Britannia's Children: Reading Colonialism through Children's Books and Magazines* (Manchester: Manchester University Press, 1996), p. 108.

6. On this figure, see Cameron, *Africa on Film*, pp. 96–126, *passim*.

7. *Sanders of the River* (Zoltan Korda, UK, 1935). For the Sanders controversy, see Stephen Bourne, *Black in the British Frame* (London: Continuum, 2001), pp. 14–18; Jeffrey Richards and Anthony Aldgate, *British Cinema and Society 1930–1970* (Totowa, NJ: Barnes and Noble Books, 1983), pp. 13–27.

8. Marcus Garvey to Lord Lugard, 14 October 1936, Lord Lugard Papers, Rhodes House, Oxford, MSS Lugard 11/1 'G–Miscellaneous, 1928–1945', f 3–12; *West Africa*, 12 September 1936, p. 1283.

9. *Song of Freedom* (J. Elder Wills, UK, 1936). See Cameron, *Africa on Film*, pp. 100–2; Barbara Bush, *Imperialism, Race and Resistance: Africa and Britain, 1919–1945* (London: Routledge, 1999), pp. 214–17; and Charles Musser, 'Paul Robeson and the Cinema of Empire', in Lee Grieveson and Colin MacCabe (eds), *Empire and Film* (London: BFI, 2011).

10. See, for example, David Krasner, *A Beautiful Pageant: African American Theatre, Drama and Performance in the Harlem Renaissance, 1910–1927* (New York: Palgrave Macmillan, 2002), p. 3; Meriwether, *Proudly We Can Be Africans*.

11. For example, J. W. de Graft Johnson, *Towards Nationhood in West Africa* (1928; 2nd edn, London: Cass, 1971); Ladipo Solanke, *United West Africa (or Africa) at the Bar of the Family of Nations* (1927; reprinted, London: African Publication Society, 1969). On WASU, see G. O. Olusanya, *The West African Students' Union and the Politics of Decolonization, 1925–1958* (Ibadan: Daystar Press, 1982); Hakim Adi, *West Africans in Britain 1900–1960* (London: Lawrence and Wishart, 1998). On the LCP, Anne Spry Rush, 'Imperial Identity in Colonial Minds: Harold Moody and the League of Coloured Peoples, 1931–50', *Twentieth Century British History* vol. 13 no. 4, December 2002, pp. 356–83.

12. Chris Stapleton, 'African Connections: London's Hidden Music Scene', in Paul Oliver (ed.), *Black Music in Britain: Essays on the Afro-Asian Contribution to Popular Music* (Milton Keynes: Open University Press, 1990).

13. See, for example, Solanke's protest to Rita Hinden of the Fabian Colonial Bureau about a 'primitive people film show', 25 October 1942, Ladipo Solanke Papers, Gandhi Library, University of Lagos (hereafter LSP) 72/9/80.

14. Ladipo Solanke to Rita Hinden, 20 November 1941, LSP 72/8/56c. The actor was Robert Adams, who would play Kisenga in *Men of Two Worlds*. Bourne, *Black in the British Frame*, p. 73.

15. See Frederick Cooper, *Africa since 1940* (New York: Cambridge University Press, 2002); John D. Hargreaves, *Decolonization in Africa* (New York: Longman, 1996).

16. See John E. Flint, 'Managing Nationalism: The Colonial Office and Nnamdi Azikiwe, 1932–1943', *Journal of Imperial and Commonwealth History* vol. 27 no. 2, May 1999, pp. 143–58.

17. On West African thought of this period, see P. S. Zachernuk, *Colonial Subjects: An African Intelligentsia and Atlantic Ideas* (Charlottesville: University Press of Virginia, 2000).

18. Minute, Sabine to Lloyd, 18 August 1943, CO 875/17/6 f 24. (All Colonial Office (CO) and Ministry of Information (INF) references which follow are from the British National Archives, Kew.) Rosaleen Smyth aligns it with Korda's *Sanders*, 'Movies and Mandarins: The Official Film and British Colonial Africa', in James Curran and Vincent Porter (eds), *British Cinema History* (London: Weidenfeld and Nicolson, 1983), p. 132. Interestingly, Femi Shaka places it in a tradition of documentary film-making which, unlike empire cinema, at least recognises Africans as capable of devising and guiding their own development. *Modernity and the African Cinema*, pp. 175–89. Presumably this combined praise for colonial administrators and Africans' potential seemed an appropriate message for Sabine.

19. 'Men of Africa: Production and Distribution', INF 1/200.

20. E. Arnot Robertson, 'White Ants', p. 3, INF 1/218. Compare such figures in children's literature: 'In the tribal ceremonies they were transformed into "repulsive" and "hideous" figures, "dancing maniacs" who donned horrifying disguises.' Their pitiless life-and-death hold over the tribe was manifested in cruel ceremony and blood sacrifices, over which they presided with 'the air of one born to authority, and vindictive in the upholding of it'. Castle, *Britannia's Children*, p. 108.

21. Arnot Robertson, 'White Ants', p. 12.

22. Ibid., p. 41.

23. Ibid., p. 12.

24. Jack Beddington to Paul Kimberly, 10 November 1942, INF 1/218. On British fiction about Africa, see Michael Echeruo, *Joyce Cary and the Novel of Africa* (New York: Africana, 1973), pp. 1–27.

25. Philip Horne and Peter Swaab, 'Introducing Thorold Dickinson', in Philip Horne and Peter Swaab (eds), *Thorold Dickinson: A World of Film* (Manchester and New York: Manchester University Press, 2008), p. 14. Dickinson's position might be usefully located with reference to some critics of trusteeship described in Susan Pedersen, 'Modernity and Trusteeship: The Tensions of Empire in Britain between the Wars', in Martin Daunton and Bernhard Rieger (eds), *Meanings of Modernity: Britain from the Late-Victorian Era to World War II* (New York: Berg, 2001), pp. 203–20.

26. Partially set (and filmed) in Lagos, but not about Lagos, one scene depicts the self-important colonial officer holding his dinner guests stiffly to attention during the playing of 'God Save the King', while the harmattan winds force themselves through the windows and wreak havoc on the dining tables. Jeffrey Richards, *Thorold Dickinson and the British Cinema* (London: Scarecrow Press, 1997), pp. 42–5.

27. '"Where Do We All Fit In?", written for *British Picture News* 10.10.44', typescript, Thorold Dickinson Papers, British Film Institute, London (hereafter TDP), 8/4 (reprinted in Horne and Swaab, *Thorold Dickinson*, pp. 70–2).

28. Cary seems to have been approved on the Colonial Office and Ministry of Information sides because of his proven literary achievements and especially his firsthand experience in African administration. Robertson to Beddington, 30 December 1942, INF 1/218. Certainly his African experience would be played up in the promotional material during production and afterwards. Norman Leys, certainly one of the more radical critics of empire, found in Cary's writings cause to invite him to assume Leys's role on the Labour Party Advisory Committee on Imperial Affairs, resisting the harmful expertise of Colonial Office insiders like Margery Perham and Reginald Coupland. Leys to Cary, 23 August 1941, in Joyce Cary Papers, Oxford University Library, MS Cary, adds.5/f 139. On his distance from mainstream colonial thinking, see Siga Asanga, 'Joyce Cary's Representation of African Reality: a Study of Cary's Novels on Africa', in Wolfgang Zach and Heinz Kosok (eds), *Literary Interrelations: Ireland, England and the World. Vol 3. National Images and Stereotypes* (Tübingen: G. Narr Verlag, 1987), pp. 169–79. Also M. M. Mahood, *Joyce Cary's Africa* (London: Methuen, 1964); Alan Bishop, *Gentleman Rider: A Life of Joyce Cary* (London: M. Joseph, 1988).

29. Joyce Cary, *The Case for African Freedom and Other Writings on Africa*, with an introduction by Christopher Fyfe (Austin: University of Texas Press, 1962), p. 13.

30. Cary, *The Case for African Freedom*, p. 75.

31. Ibid., p. 27.

32. Joyce Cary, 'Primitive Freedom', MS Cary 271/ N. 85 (e), pp. 10–11.

33. [Cary *et al.*], 'Men of Two Worlds, Third Treatment, Revised', pp. 22, 33, CO 875/17/5 ff 2–70.

34. [Cary *et al.*], 'Third Treatment', p. 17.

35. Minute, Arnot Robertson, 28 May 1943, INF 1/218; Raymond Durgnat, *A Mirror for England: British Moves from Austerity to Affluence* (London: Faber and Faber, 1970), p. 79.

36. In 'White Ants', the schoolmaster reads a long, inspiring, even pan-African, passage from Edwin Smith's biography, to the District Officer's approval. See Edwin Smith, *Aggrey of Africa* (London: Student Christian Movement, 1929).

37. Sabine to Fletcher, MOI (draft), 7 April 1943, CO 875/10/9: 'Cinema Propaganda: Colonial Film Unit'. As both Sowande and Dunbar were colleagues and were both approached within weeks of each other, it seems reasonable to assume the producer John Sutro's links to one led to the other. Sutro approached Dunbar at the end of March to play Kijana. Sutro to Dickinson, 29 March 1943, INF 1/218.

38. Dickinson to Arnot Robertson, 30 June 1943, INF 1/218. Sowande was sought again regarding a study of music in CFU films for Africans in 1948. Alan Izod, 'Some Special Features of Colonial Film Production', *The Film in Colonial Development. A Report of a Conference* (London: British Film Institute, 1948), p. 31. He worked until 1950 as musical director in the Colonial Film Unit. Daily Times Magazine, *Who's Who in Nigeria: A Biographical Dictionary*, 2nd edn (Lagos: Times Press, 1971), p. 216.

39. Fela Sowande, Colonial Film Unit, to Solanke, 13 July 1943, LSP 6/8/53.

40. Cameron, *Africa on Film*, pp. 66, 105. There are further similarities of detail between *Song* and the April 1943 treatment of *Men of Two Worlds* that Cameron does not mention. Not only do both returnees use music to defeat the witch doctor, but both are ridiculed by the witch doctor for failing to save villagers with Western medicine. Zinga's kingdom of Casenga evokes the name Kisenga eventually given to the Kijana character. There are also personal links: Robert Adams played both Zinga's friend Monty and the Kijana character; Orlando Martins, the witch doctor in *Men of Two Worlds*, was in both *Jericho* and *Song*. Dickinson and the director of *Song*, J. Elder Willis, had been editor and designer respectively

in Basil Dean's *Sing as We Go* (1934). Rachael Low, *The History of British Film 1929–1939: Film Making in 1930s Britain* (London: George Allen & Unwin, 1985), p. 386; Peter Noble, 'The Cinema and the Negro, 1905–1948', *Sight and Sound* vol. 14, 1948, p. 20.

41. Litewski, '"Acceptable" Face', p. 3.
42. Cable, Sutro to Dickinson, 14 April 1943, INF 1/218.
43. Memorandum, 'Men of Two Worlds', 31 May 1943, INF 1/218. Richards identifies this person as R. Nunn May, assistant director of the Film Division. Richards, *Thorold Dickinson and the British Cinema*, p. 103.
44. WASU, Memorandum on 'A (Proposed) Film Play Entitled "The Men of Two Worlds"', 27 July 1943, LSP 58/2/2; Solanke to Under Secretary of State for the Colonies, 11 September 1943, LSP 58/5/7; also in CO 875/17/6 f 50. The evidence for this timing is scattered. WASU would have been a natural place to turn in answer to Dickinson's request from Tanganyika that Sabine 'contact all available attractive young African women' for the sister role. Dickinson to Sutro, 9 April 1943, INF 1/218. Perhaps as part of this exchange, Ivor Cummings, a black Colonial Office official, was proactively seeking WASU advice about other film issues in April. See Solanke to Ivor Cummings, 13 April 1943, LSP 72/10/23; Fela Sowande to Solanke, 13 July 1943, LSP 6/8/53. Most conclusively, the Labour MP Reginald Sorenson, an active supporter of African interests, wrote to the Colonial Office in May, indicating that WASU was 'very disturbed' by the film idea and intended to write about it. He pleaded: 'If it is at all possible to let the script be altered to avoid any legitimate complaints it would be a substantial service'. Sorensen to Secretary of State for the Colonies, 30 May 1943, CO 875/17/6 f 61. Litewski notes that WASU may have been consulted about the script's authenticity, which was a major concern of Cary and Dickinson throughout. '"Acceptable" Face', p. 13.
45. Solanke to Under Secretary of State for the Colonies, 27 July 1943, CO 875/17/6 ff 62–3.
46. WASU, memorandum.
47. Solanke to Sutro, 18 November 1943, LSP 58/5.
48. WASU, memorandum. The choice of authorities cited to make this case warrants further attention. The July memorandum cites only a white American medical missionary, in the September letter, three African authorities on African medicine.
49. WASU, memorandum.
50. Minute, T. K. Lloyd, 20 August 1943, CO 875/17/6 f 26.
51. A. R. Thomas to Sabine, 2 August 1943, CO 875/17/6 f 20.
52. Minute by K. E. Robinson, 14 August 1943, CO 875/17/6 f 22.
53. Minute by Sabine, 4 August 1943, CO 875/17/6 f 21–2.
54. Cummings to A. R. Thomas, 9 October 1943, CO 875/17/6 f 34.
55. Ivor Cummings to N. Sabine, 2 August 1943, CO 875/17/6 f 19.
56. Minute, Sabine to Lloyd, 18 August 1943, CO 875/17/6 f 24. Robert Dunbar was recommended in part because it was established that he was 'friendly, sincere, and reliable' – a real-life Good African – but Sabine was nevertheless anxious about sending Dunbar to shoot on location in Tanzania. He might get the wrong impression of the colonial system and 'raise rather awkward questions' through the Associated Negro Associated Press, for whom he had worked. See minute by Sabine, 1 May 1943, CO 875/17/6 f12. In the end, for reasons I do not yet know, Robert Adams played this role. Martins recalled later that Dunbar's accent did not fit the character. Taku Falomi, *Orlando Martins: The Legend* (Lagos: Executive Publishers, 1983), p. 33. But Dunbar had raised awareness of the British colour bar in the African American press, and operated a black music club in London in the

mid-1930s with pan-African activist, Amy Ashwood Garvey. Jeffrey Green, 'Afro-American Symphony: Popular Black Concert Hall Performers 1900–40', in Oliver, *Black Music in Britain*, p. 40; John Cowley, 'London Is the Place: Caribbean Music in the Context of Empire 1900–1960', in Oliver, *Black Music in Britain*, p. 63.

57. Two Cities, 'Progress Report No 2', 20 July 1943, INF 1/218.
58. Minute, Sabine to Lloyd, 18 August 1943, CO 875/17/6 f 24.
59. Draft of Secretary of State to Sorensen, August 1943, CO 875/17/6 f 58. Sabine indicated that he intended to act only in response to further WASU action. Sabine to Beddington, 9 September 1943, CO 875/17/6 f 55.
60. Cummings to A. R. Thomas, 9 October 1943, CO 875/17/6 f 34; Minute, A. R. Thomas, 13 October 1943, CO 875/17/6 f 34.
61. Sutro to Beoku Betts, WASU president, 17 October 1943, LSP 58/5; Solanke to Albert Cartwright, 5 November 1943, LSP 72/11/12b.
62. Joyce Cary, Thorold Dickinson, Herbert W. Victor, 'Men of Two Worlds Screenplay', CO 875/17/5, ff 72–261 [dated 2 July 1943]; Joyce Cary, Thorold Dickinson, Herbert Victor, 'Threshold (formerly Men of Two Worlds)', MS Cary 221 [dated 7 October 1943]. The October script also contains handwritten amendments.
63. [Cary *et al.*], 'Third Treatment', p. 1.
64. Cary *et al.*, 'Screenplay', p. 182.
65. Ibid., pp. 140–1.
66. Ibid., pp. 83–4.
67. Solanke to Sutro, 18 November 1943, LSP 58/5.
68. Ibid.
69. Solanke to Cartwright, 19 August 1943, LSP 72/10/64b; Cartwright to Solanke, 9 August 1943, LSP 9/10/7a; Cartwright to Solanke, 23 August 1943, LSP 9/10/7b. Cartwright and Solanke would continue to collaborate in the presentation of West Africa issues. See for example Cartwright to Solanke, 26 August 1944, LSP 7/8/11b.
70. 'W.A.S.U. and Witchcraft', *West Africa*, 8 April 1944, p. 313.
71. Litewski, '"Acceptable" Face', pp. 20–1.
72. Falomi, *Orlando Martins*, p. 87. Over his long film career, Martins pushed for appropriate representation of Africa.
73. See, for example, Beddington to Sutro, 7 November 1944, INF 1/218.
74. E. Fisher, *Men of Two Worlds: The Book of the Film* (London: World Film Publications, 1946), pp. 13–14. The book follows the film dialogue closely.
75. Ibid., p. 36.
76. The name was changed because of 'strong local opinion' gathered in Tanzania, as Dickinson was considering changing the film's title to 'Kijana'. Dickinson to Sutro, 21 January 1944, INF 1/218. The reason was not given, but in current usage in Tanzania 'Kijana' has the connotation of an immature young man. Personal correspondence with Steven Fabian, Dar es Salaam, 15 February 2005.
77. Fisher, *Men of Two Worlds*, p. 44.
78. Ibid., p. 45.
79. Sowande's example was probably close to mind. His *Africana* composition was broadcast on the BBC in 1944; his orchestra played at the *Men of Two Worlds* London premiere in 1946. Green, 'Afro-American Symphony', p. 40.
80. Memorandum by Winnifred Wirrell[?], 31 October 1944, INF 1/218.

81. Thorold Dickinson, 'Men of Two Worlds', March 1976 (notes for a screening of the film in London), 'Men of Two Worlds' file, British Film Institute Library. Dickinson's and Cary's private papers revealed no further clues as to the timing or content of this discussion.

82. A minor plot is established in the third treatment, in which Kijana/Kisenga and Magole vie to save Kijana's father from illness, or from the curse Magole claims white medicine placed on him. Kijana's distress over his father's death becomes more pronounced in each subsequent version.

83. Fisher, *Men of Two Worlds*, p. 70.

84. 'Men of Two Worlds', *The Times*, 18 July 1946.

85. W. W. Awori, *Africa World*, August 1946, quoted in Litewski, '"Acceptable" Face', p. 22. The British Film Institute Library *Men of Two Worlds* file holds many press reviews, many of which are reprinted in Litewski, '"Acceptable" Face'.

86. M. C. Peterside, letter to the editor, *The Times*, 11 September 1946; also M. C. Peterside, letter to the editor, *The Times*, 27 September 1946.

87. '"Men of Two Worlds": Africans and "Witch-doctors"', *West Africa*, 31 August 1946, p. 797.

88. James Ene Ewa, 'Hollywood and Africa', *Leader*, 7 June 1947.

89. Thorold Dickinson, letter to the editor, *The Times*, 19 September 1946; Thorold Dickinson, letter to the editor, *The Times*, 25 September, 1946. Peterside seems to have remained open to further conversation. In a private letter to Dickinson, he insisted that his criticisms were well intentioned.

> I only feel that those who control such an important instrument of public education as the film industry, should use it to improve human relations nationally as well as internationally, for that way alone lies hope for the human race in this atomic age.
>
> Peterside to Dickinson, 14 September 1946, TDP 9/4.

90. On the community involved in discussing Africa in Britain at this time, see P. S. Zachernuk, 'Critical Agents: Colonial Nigerian Intellectuals and Their British Counterparts', in Chris Youé and Tim Stapleton (eds), *Agency and Action in Colonial Africa* (London: Palgrave, 2001).

91. Peter Swaab, 'Dickinson's Africa: *The High Command* and *Men of Two Worlds*', in Horne and Swaab, *Thorold Dickinson*, p. 188. On the place of *Men of Two Worlds* in the history of the cinematic image of Africa, see, for example, Durgnat, *Mirror for England*; Michael Paris, 'Africa in Post-1945 Cinema', *South African Historical Journal* no. 48, May 2003, pp. 61–70; Wendy Webster, 'Domesticating the Frontier: Gender, Empire and Adventure Landscapes in British Cinema, 1945–59', *Gender and History* vol. 15 no. 1, April 2003, pp. 86–107; Marcia Landy, *British Genres: Cinema and Society, 1930–1960* (Princeton, NJ: Princeton University Press, 1991), pp. 96–120; Wendy Webster, 'Mumbo-jumbo, Magic and Modernity: Africa in British Cinema, 1946–65', this volume.

92. Kenneth Little, *Negroes in Britain* (London: Kegan Paul, Trench, Trubner, 1948), pp. 282–4 ('Appendix II: A Note on the Cinema as a Factor in Racial Attitudes'); Oladipo Onipede, 'Hollywood's Holy War against Africa', *Africa Today* no. 3, August–July 1956; J. Koyinde Vaughan, 'Africa and the Cinema', in Langston Hughes (ed.), *An African Treasury* (New York: Crown, 1961).

93. A. R. Thomas to Girkins, 29 October 1943, CO 875/17/7 f 2; Girkins to Thomas, 13 December 1943, CO 875/17/7 f 4-5; C. A. W., 'Daybreak in Udi', *To-day's Cinema: News and Property Gazette* no. 78, 9 August 1949.

94. Bradshow to Watson, 23 March 1943, INF 1/225: Films: An African in England; Smyth, 'Movies and Mandarins', pp. 129–43. The Ministry of Information entertained suggestions from WASU regarding West African material suitable for newsreel coverage. W. Sellers to Solanke, 2 September 1943, LSP 7/1/23.

95. See 'Daybreak in Udi', INF 6/403; Shaka, *Modernity and the African Cinema*, pp. 189–211. This film can be viewed on the Colonial Film project website, <www.colonialfilm.org.uk>.

7

'Johnny Gurkha loves a party': The Colonial Film Archive and the Racial Imaginary of the Worker-Warrior

Vron Ware

The steady development of amateur film technology in the mid-twentieth century has left a priceless legacy of documentary footage shot by British military personnel in the period after 1945. The colonial film archive contains many examples recording military operations in Malaya between 1948 and 1960, before and after the Briggs Plan was introduced as a radically experimental form of counter-insurgency. Among these is a collection entitled 'Operations by 1st Battalion 6th Gurkha Rifles during the Malayan Emergency', shot by Major William Rhodes James, himself a Gurkha officer. The film covers two exercises carried out between 1948–50, the first recording the clearance of Chinese villagers from their homes near the jungle to detention camps under British custody. The catalogue of the Imperial War Museum (IWM) offers a description that helps to paint a picture:

> ... elderly Chinese men as well as women and young children leave the village on foot, laden with their belongings. View from top of mountain range, with displaced Chinese passing in foreground. Gurkhas cross shallow river. British military vehicles. Chinese family stands waiting, looking anxious. Pan over cleared village, where British officer and Gurkha soldiers emerge from hut (presumably having checked for any remaining villagers); children stare at the camera.

Numerous scenes of troops navigating the difficult terrain, whether by river or through the notorious Malayan jungle and chest-high grasslands, reveal a wealth of detail about British attempts to destroy the rising Communist insurgency as well as showing the environment in which the soldiers were required to operate. To an untrained eye, this type of footage can exemplify the difficulties involved in viewing unedited material shot by insiders – especially those military personnel who held a professional stake in the activities being recorded – as distinct from the official footage shot by agencies such as the Malayan Film Unit and used for propaganda purposes. While the individual attempts at documentation have provided useful material for historians of that particular conflict, their handiwork is often experienced as little more than a series of disjointed, fragmented and unexplained glimpses of military life and counter-insurgency warfare. Efforts to interpret this material in the context of compiling a vivid account of Britain's process of decolonisation present substantial challenges. For this reason an audio commentary provided in 2000 by Rhodes James himself transforms his contribution into a very different kind of resource.

Commenting on a brief section in which soldiers enjoy a swim in a river, for example, Rhodes James points out that a large proportion of the Gurkhas were extremely young and only recently recruited from Nepal. He explains that when the Gurkha regiments were divided between Britain and India in 1947, many of the soldiers destined for the British Army opted instead to transfer to the Indian regiments, draining the section of trained men allocated to Britain. This piece of information serves as a useful starting point for discussing the significance of Gurkha troops within the colonial film archive as a whole.[1]

First, it raises the question of why soldiers from Nepal remained under British command after the Indian subcontinent was granted independence. What were the conditions – as well as the circumstances – that enabled Britain to deploy Gurkhas as part of a colonial force in the Malayan Peninsula? Apart from the underlying reasons – both ideological and adventitious – that Gurkha troops under British command were integral to this particular operation, we might also ask: what does their presence within the archive have to teach us today about those lethal links between military policy and racial hierarchy that appeared to set the foundations of the British imperial order in stone? By addressing these enquiries, it might then be possible to compile a more comprehensive understanding of how the medium of film might illuminate the protracted decline of empire.

FROM MERCENARIES TO REGULARS

The strategic importance of Gurkha soldiers in British military history is a topic well documented by specialist historians but routinely passed over in more mainstream accounts of colonial warfare, at least outside the realms of imperialist mythology. Before making any claims for their inclusion in this new colonial film archive there are two issues to be considered if they are to be accorded their due significance. First, the visibility of Gurkha troops actively engaged in British military campaigns across different continents throughout the twentieth century suggests the need for a more critical evaluation of their role in the filmic imaginary of a particular conception of racialised military force. But the status of these soldiers presents a conundrum since Nepal, their country of origin, was never subjected to colonial rule. The Gurkhas' relationship to the British empire was different from the other segments of the global imperial army assembled in Africa, Asia and the Middle East.[2] A second factor is the powerful tradition of Gurkha exceptionalism apparent in the earliest literary and pictorial representations and sustained right through into contemporary media commentary.[3] This discursive tradition demands a critical approach to the available historical resources in order to assess how different representations of their heritage – including the filmic imaginary – serve particular purposes today. In an essay on 'Nepalese Gurkhas and Their Battle for Equal Rights', for example, Ché Singh Kochar-George has argued that 'colonial stereotyping along racial lines' not only occupies a powerful place in the public imagination but also means that 'colonial constructs of difference' continue to influence decisions made by the courts and government.[4]

In the interests of explaining the role of Gurkhas in Britain's wars of decolonisation from 1947–65, the most salient facts are their terms of employment as members of the larger British Army, a connection forged 130 years earlier. In brief, the word 'Gorkha' is derived from the name of the state in west central Nepal that dominated the region throughout the eighteenth century, often referred to as the 'Gorkha Raj'.[5] The unification of Nepal, carried out by a Gorkhali army of legendary force, brought the kingdom into conflict with the East India Company leading to the Anglo–Gorkha war in 1814–16. The pact drawn up at the end of hostilities granted independence to Nepal, and in return, Nepal's rulers agreed to allow Gorkhali soldiers to enlist as mercenary volunteers in the service of the East India Company.[6] Initially, the British colonialists were anxious to protect the northwest borders of its Indian territories from hill tribes and identified their former enemies as more valuable allies than foes.

Over the course of the next four decades, the arrangement proved to be of strategic importance as the British expanded their hold over the Punjab, employing an array of forces including Hindus and Muslims organised within the Bengal Army. In 1857, the two Gurkha regiments played a key role in suppressing the 'Sepoy Revolt' which came to be known as the First War of Independence. Their loyalty to the colonial administration in the face of the nationwide insurgency guaranteed them a role in the British Indian Army which was reorganised after the British Crown took over. By this time, however, there were other factors that determined how this new army was to be managed as a multiethnic force.

The concept of martial races is a crucial factor in understanding why Gurkhas were so valued within British military calculations. As Toby Haggith and Richard Smith explain in *Empire and Film*, early recruitment practices may have been dictated by pragmatism and opportunism on both sides, but colonial military policy would be transformed by new doctrines of racial hierarchy that emerged throughout the course of the nineteenth century.[7] In his book, *The Sepoy and the Raj: The Indian Army 1860–1940*, David Omissi describes how, by the early nineteenth century, the application of racial theory to the governance of the new Indian territories led to the belief that 'some communities possessed inherited traits which made them better soldiers' and this became the 'rationale for recruiting'.[8] As favoured (and tested) components of the British Indian Army, formed as a result of the 1857 war, Gurkhas were recruited alongside many other ethnic and religious groups as part of a 'highly effective, well-trained, all-volunteer force of professional regulars' that supported the wider colonial military order.[9]

The theory of martial races did not refer solely to the selection of effective sources of manpower, however. It was also about the manipulation of ethnic differences in the army, as Tarak Barkawi explains, 'keeping it divided by grouping men in companies of their "own kind" and catering to their religious, dietary, and other customs'.[10] After 1857, the reasoning was that maintaining strict adherence to religious and cultural differences among ethnic groups, such as Sikhs, Punjabi Muslims, Pathans and Hindu Dogras, would keep them from combining against the British. At the same time, it was thought, no situation would arise that would render all the different groups of troops simultaneously unreliable, 'so should there be problems with one class of troops, the others would be available to check them'.

One historic example of the application of this 'divide-and-rule' policy, in which Gurkhas played a significant role, was the Amritsar Massacre in 1919. During a particularly tense period of nationalist protest in the Punjab, Brigadier General Reginald Dyer ordered his troops – consisting of sixty-five Gurkhas and twenty-five Baluchis – to open fire without warning on the crowd assembled in Jallianwala Bagh.[11] Hundreds of unarmed Sikhs and Muslims were killed, many in the crush to leave the park, which was surrounded by buildings on all sides and hemmed in by soldiers. The massacre became 'both a symbol and a cause of the upheaval in nationalist, revolutionary, and other political activity that rocked India for the next twenty years', but it also provided evidence of the relative success of British military organisation.[12]

As we shall see below, prior to this display of loyalty to the British Crown, Gurkha soldiers were deployed in 1914 to 1916 within Europe, and took part in British military operations in Turkey (Gallipoli), Iraq and Palestine, suffering 20,000 casualties. Their record as reliable and fearless warriors in different terrains meant that their numbers were increased in 1939, and throughout World War II over 250,000 were engaged in extensive campaigns in Italy, North Africa, Singapore and Burma.[13] It is estimated that 23,000 Gurkhas lost their lives and over 2,000 awards were earned for bravery. When India became independent in 1947, the ten Gurkha regiments in the British Indian Army were divided between the two countries in a tripartite agreement with Nepal, and after much discussion, wrangling and hand-wringing, four regiments were selected for inclusion within the Brigade of Gurkhas which was part of the reorganised British Army. Those regiments that survived were then immediately put to the test by being sent to protect British colonies on the eastern edge of their crumbling empire.

MYTH-MAKING

There is a limit to how far a list of chronological events can explain the complex body of ideas and representations that developed over the course of the now 200-year-old relationship between the British state and Gurkha forces and it would require a much more comprehensive, multidisciplinary investigation to track the genealogy of myth-making that survives to this day. The colonial film archive has a potentially valuable role in this project, partly because it provides visual, though often silent, proof of the extent of Gurkha deployment within Britain's imperial armies. Perhaps more importantly, by analysing the representation of Gurkhas through the medium of film it is also possible – necessary even – to interrogate ways in which domestic audiences were gradually habituated to the concept of a loyal, obedient and multi-ethnic military force that underpinned the empire as a whole. In order to demonstrate how vital the Gurkhas were in establishing this particular construct of imperial cohesion, I will examine a series of films chronologically, beginning with an example from the early twentieth century.

The first British official film record of any of the war zones in World War I released for public viewing was a film called *With the Indian Troops at the Front Part 1* (1916). Following the outbreak of the war in Europe in 1914, Britain had scrambled to raise extra troops from all over northern India as well as Nepal, designating particular tribal groups as ideal for fighting purposes.[14] By the end of 1915, almost 30,000 of the Indian Corps had fought on the Western Front, and at least 3,000 were killed and over

14,000 injured. In an analysis of this film for the archive, Tom Rice notes that it illustrates 'this distinct Indian force – and more broadly the disparate imperial troops – united within the British army and in their support for the Empire'.[15] Viewed in a different light, as Barkawi points out in his analysis of war as a global process, the contribution of Indian troops in European war zones is an example of the way in which 'India itself has shaped the wider world in far-reaching and significant ways'.[16] 'Were it not for the fact that Britain had raised an army in India,' he suggests, 'the world might have witnessed a German victory in France in the opening months of World War 1.'[17]

In the context of British Army doctrine in India, however, the Gurkhas constituted only one of a series of ethnic groups able to supply military manpower when the empire was threatened from outside as well as internally. As Cynthia Enloe has pointed out in her study of 'ethnic soldiers', Sikh regiments were thought to share many of the same attributes as other 'martial races': strong cultural identity, pride in their own military tradition and reliance on British power to obtain their own political ends.[18] In this extraordinary film, contingents of Sikhs are portrayed carrying out various activities, including wrestling, dancing and digging trenches. One scene is captioned: 'Types of Indian Soldiers in the 57th Wilde's Rifles' and consists of the camera panning over a group of men with beards and turbans.

The film is also notable within this discussion because it features a scene in which Gurkhas are seen polishing their knives or *kukri*, providing the first-known filmic image of this iconic object. The famous curved knife had long functioned as a visual trope in the representation of Gurkhas as fighters, often silhouetted against the sky in prints and paintings from a pre-photographic era. This was true of written histories as well, continuing right up to the present. No description of Gurkha ferocity in battle is complete without the appearance of the *kukri* as a marker of their ethnic origins and martial character. For example, Tony Gould begins his book *Imperial Armies* with an acknowledgment of the knife's representational power: 'About Gurkhas', he writes,

> as about Cossacks, myths and legends abound. The *kukri* is a rich source of mythology: sometimes it is represented as a kind of boomerang; at other times it is said that it cannot be drawn from its scabbard without blood being shed.[19]

The reality, he explains, is that the *kukri* is merely a practical tool, as useful for cutting firewood as it is for self-defence. It provides a starting point because, 'Myths perform a vital function in military lore, establishing the fearsome reputation of – in this case – the Gurkhas for hand-to-hand fighting.'[20] A brief search in the colonial film archive reveals a variety of footage featuring the *kukri* as an emblematic weapon: *Gurkhas at Rest/Head Shaving and Sharpening Kukri/Crossing River* indicates that these customs were judged to be of ethnographic value in recording the special characteristics of Gurkha soldiers as an elite, if expendable, force.

AN EXCITING CRICKET MATCH

The global war of 1939–45 provides a rich setting for demonstrating the value of the film archive in this investigation of colonial militarism. It is in this context that the

Gurkhas' unique historical connection to the British empire begins to influence the way they are represented in comparison with other colonial troops, especially those whose military service was conditional on demands for national independence. We can see this by contrasting the ethnographic documentary *Johnny Gurkha*, produced in 1945, with films that focus on India's contribution to the war.[21] Before that, however, it is important to note that there is significant footage by agencies such as the Army Film and Photographic Unit (AFPU), recording the presence of Gurkha troops in various battlefields across Europe, North Africa, the Middle East and South Asia, which indicates the extent to which they were deployed as a priceless and flexible military asset.

A selection of these films includes *Gurkhas Relieve NZ troops* (no date); *Indian Troops* (no date); *Gurkhas Patrol in Snow* (no date); *Gurkha Troops Enter Tavaleto – 4th Indian Division* (no date). These items provide an enormous amount of historical data on military campaigns, though it is not always clear what is going on or even if scenes are being staged for the cameras. While the 'dope sheets' kept by cameramen deliver valuable insights into circumstances of films, the actual footage can furnish glimpses of military training and of war itself, although both of these entail long periods of inaction as much as scenes of risk and danger.

A fourth film, *Gurkha Battle in the Imphal Area and Japanese Dead at Bishenpur* (1944)[22] contains extraordinary footage from Burma in what has been called 'the forgotten war'.[23] Produced by the Public Relations Directorate, India, the film shows how

> Gurkha infantry, probably of the 17th Indian Division, attack a Japanese position on a ridge near the Tiddim Road during the Battle of Imphal (in Manipur, India) while patrols enter Bishenpur and find abandoned enemy equipment and Japanese dead.

The accompanying synopsis points out that this film is inherently valuable due to the scarcity of footage of this particular battle, although it should be used with care because of the lack of precise information about which Gurkha battalion it shows and the rather 'dubious quality of direction in the stage sequence'.[24]

The staged sequence to which it refers is described in the synopsis, and a brief excerpt will indicate its content:

> A kneeling Gurkha, seen in profile, waves his men forward. Men, after receiving their cue, run down the hillside and one swipes at a small bush with his *kukri* for good measure. Men carry on running down the hillside; one appears to drop something and stops to pick it up, then his hat falls off and he stops again.[25]

Earlier the film had shown more sobering footage, including dead Japanese soldiers, 'one quite contorted'. The secret dope sheet mentions that, as the Gurkha infantry prepared to attack an enemy position on the next hill, it 'took the whole exercise like an exciting cricket match'.[26]

These documentary fragments afford tantalising visual evidence for reinterpreting the historical detail of this global war. It is clear from these films that Gurkhas operated in separate contingents within battle groups in the British Indian Army, which was deployed within a wider multinational force throughout Europe, North Africa, Mesopotamia and Burma. The film, *Commander in Chief's Tour to the 10th Army* (1942), for example, purports to show General Auchinleck inspecting British and Indian troops in Iraq.[27] The film was made by the War Office Film Unit, and shows the general's journey from Cairo to Baghdad, and then to Basra in 1942. Although it mostly consists of military personnel climbing in and out of a plane and inspecting troops, it is the Gurkhas who are notably present in Quayara, northern Iraq, and again in Basra, even though they have been labelled 'Indian troops'.

One aspect of these films by the AFPU is that there is minimal commentary on the training or capabilities of Gurkha soldiers, from which it may be implied that their participation was of a different order than those regiments raised within colonial territories. Although the doctrine of martial races was still a factor in the recruitment of particular groups within the empire, the discourse had evolved, in terms of overt propaganda at least, to one that prized the spontaneous coming together of many different peoples in support of the larger aims of the war against Nazism. So in *Empire's New Armies*, an 'inspirational' piece made by the Ministry of Information in 1941, it is mainly the turbanned Sikh soldiers who represent India as they are filmed carrying out weapons training, PT and unarmed combat.[28] But another promotional film, produced the same year, entitled *India Marches*, provides a fascinating glimpse of British-Indian military culture that also helps to explain why Indian soldiers might have been the subject of promotional films while their fellow Gurkha regiments were not singled out for such treatment.[29]

Re-edited from a longer documentary called *A Day in the Life of the Indian Army*, this item is labelled as 'A brief look at an Indian Army regiment (15th Punjab)'. Wendy Webster has written about *India Marches* in her study of Englishness and empire in the period between 1939 and 1965.[30] The film, she argues, is as much 'a metaphor of Indian self-sufficiency as of imperial unity, and so emphasizes Indian membership of the British Commonwealth and not the Empire'.[31] Unlike their arrangement with Gurkha regiments, which had established their own traditions of recruitment from Nepal, the British were faced with raising manpower in India at a time when the independence movement had reached a critical mass. 'When war was declared,' Webster writes, 'the need to recruit Indians into the military made the impact of productions on Indian audiences a more urgent consideration.'[32] This point underlines the widely differing political context that determined the representation of the Gurkhas to a Nepalese audience.

While the selection from the AFPU is by no means an exhaustive list of the films available, it is enough to illustrate the point that, although the Gurkhas were visible in military documentaries, they often remained below the radar in terms of a heroic metanarrative of colonial subjects 'springing to Britain's side'. In 1943, for example, the film, *The King and His People*, was released by the Ministry of Information in an effort to present a view of empire as both forward-looking and rooted in history. It was produced by British Movietone News, described by John MacKenzie as 'strongly conservative', and narrated by the famous commentator, Leslie Mitchell, whose assuring tones would have been familiar to cinemagoers subjected to patriotic films of this type.[33] One of the more desperate attempts to rally imperialist fervour among a global Anglophone audience, the film centred on the figure of King George VI as a symbol of unity, an embodiment of 'a true conception of monarchy, for the King serves as he rules his people'. Mitchell's voice can be heard proclaiming, 'the British Empire, based on ideas of strength in unity, not force or even self-interest, has one goal: freedom for every living individual'. Needless to say, in the roll-call of colonies and Commonwealth countries taking part in military operations, there was no place for the Nepalese since their pact with the British Crown had a different lineage.

BORN FIGHTERS

Despite the fact that Britain's relationship to its Gurkha soldiers fell outside the terms of colonial governance, the opening scenes in *Johnny Gurkha* show King George VI paying tribute to them, as well as the Viceroy of India who is seen thanking them for their 'gallantry' on eastern fronts. *Johnny Gurkha* was originally produced in two versions, one British and one Nepali, a fact that highlights the 'special arrangement' binding these two countries.[34] The catalogue records that this is 'a film showing the importance and prestige of belonging to the famous Gurkha Regiment', and the format has been edited for the English-language version by the Crown Film Unit for the Ministry of Information. It was made in India in 1945, sponsored by the Interservice Public Relations Directorate in India and produced by the Public Relations Film Unit, India. Narrated in a distinctly American accent, the English version appears to be a promotional documentary aimed at educating Anglophone audiences about the historic traditions of Gurkha soldiers – referred to in the singular as Johnny Gurkha throughout – and their continuing, and very modern, contribution to the war. The final scene shows them scrambling into an aircraft and parachuting out into unknown territory, ready for battle.

This film is an important part of the colonial archive because it ably exemplifies many of the issues that I have raised so far. First, the film clarifies the relationship between Nepal and Britain that permits the Gurkhas to fight as the result of an alliance between the two countries rather than a consequence of colonial rule. Second, the ethnographic terms used to introduce the process that generates the new recruits evoke the underlying concept of a people inherently suited to military work. They are shown to be absolutely rooted in a rural economy, which not only provides them with extraordinary physical strength and abilities (the words 'tough', 'wiry' and 'athletic' recur throughout) but is also the basis of strong community ties to the land. In other words, their 'way of life' ensures that they are able to reproduce perfect soldiers as part of the indigenous culture. They are 'born fighters', 'skilled in peace but deadly in war', and the Gurkha woman is every bit as tough as her man. The community is filmed within its topographical setting, carrying out farming and subsistence activities as well as religious and cultural rituals, such as dancing. 'Right from his early childhood, Johnny Gurkha loves a party', claims the narrator, and 'a good soldier is one who has a happy secure home behind him.'

This last point underlines the third reason why this film is especially valuable in contextualising Gurkha campaigns for reparations and equality today. As well as showing the recruitment, selection and training of young Nepalese men focusing on the mental and physical characteristics required from these willing candidates, there is also a section on how each regiment (often organised along family or tribal lines) maintains its links with home and helps to support Gurkha ex-servicemen after retirement. The system of pensions is underlined as an explanatory factor in keeping the flow of new soldiers going, since one man's pay and pension guarantees a certain standard of living for his extended family throughout his lifetime.

The film therefore draws attention to the reciprocal nature of the agreement between these military labourers and their British employers, a pact in which innately superior martial skills and an enduring sense of loyalty are granted in exchange for economic benefits commensurate with their 'ethnic' and timeless way of life. This was a very different script than one that evoked expectations of autonomy and separation; rather than a metaphor of 'self-sufficiency', which Webster notes as a subtext in corresponding films about Indian troops, *Johnny Gurkha* might have been calculated to produce unease as well as homage, precisely because the future of this relationship was thrown into doubt by the political maelstrom that lay ahead. The British public would have been aware of the high numbers of Gurkha casualties before 1945 as well as the many citations for bravery earned by individual Gurkha soldiers. It is likely then that *Johnny Gurkha* might have played a role in galvanising support for maintaining this mutually convenient arrangement with Nepal in the event of India becoming independent.

In spite of the fact that Nepal lay outside the bounds of empire, *Johnny Gurkha* is a valuable item within the colonial film archive because it shows how the medium contributed to the racial imaginary of this exceptional group of worker-warriors bound to Britain through enduring historical and economic ties. At the same time, it can be approached as a text that marks – though does not explicitly acknowledge – the uncertainty of the closing years of the war.

SENSE OF BETRAYAL

In this final section, we will return to the battlefields of Malaya to assess the value of the film which introduced this essay. It is hard to compress the profound sense of betrayal and shame experienced as a result of the agreement made immediately after Partition in 1947, when four Gurkha regiments were retained for service in Britain's Southeast Asian colonies. Rhodes James's explanation for the tender age of many of his men in 1948–50 requires some elaboration in order to make full sense of what actually happened. The Tripartite Agreement between India, Nepal and Britain was greeted with fury and dismay by many of the Gurkha soldiers, including their British officers, but the decision was final. After much consideration, the individual soldier was allowed to choose 'whether he wishes to remain under the War Office, under the new government of India, or neither'.[35] This was partly a result of the Maharajah of Nepal's desire that the Gurkhas should be consulted about their willingness to serve under the new dispensation.[36] Within each of the four designated British regiments, rumours of new terms and conditions led to resentment, confusion and near mutiny in some cases. Many soldiers were reluctant to go to Malaya and felt they were being tricked, and for various reasons, the majority opted to stay in India where they were already located. One estimate was that about 40 per cent, or less than half of those who might have moved to the British regiments, chose to do so.[37]

This historical background is important to the start of operations in Malaya for several reasons. First, as Rhodes James explains in his commentary, the British were obliged to carry out intensive recruiting in Nepal in order to fill their depleted ranks. Parker describes how Gurkhas were 'still in poor shape' by the time they were massed in Malaya.

> It was, after all, only six months since the great shake-up, and battalion commanders had not had time to train up new recruits or assess their new officers. Few remained who were trained for the rigours of jungle warfare, learned during the latter days of the war.[38]

But the reality was more complicated than a logistical shortage of trained manpower. A second factor that contextualises the use of Gurkhas in Malaya was the changing political climate, which had emerged during the war as a result of independence struggles. Although Nepal was not a British colony, it was certainly affected by revolutionary movements against imperialism. In their exhaustive account, *Forgotten Armies: The End of Britain's Asian Empire*, Christopher Bayly and Tim Harper describe the threat by Communists in Nepal to stem the flow of new Gurkha recruits, citing the fact that opposition parties in India were putting pressure on Nehru to end the use of the 'sacred soil' to recruit for the war in Malaya.[39] British military commanders, already rattled by losing so many to the ranks of the new Indian Army, were indeed anxious not to upset Nehru by appearing to use the British contingent of Gurkhas for nakedly imperialist purposes. In 1948, for example, Britain's ambassador to Nepal 'suggested to the Foreign Office that it would be "unwise" for the BBC and press agencies to draw too much attention to the use of Gurkha troops in anti-communist operations in Malaya'.[40]

This glimpse of some of the political tensions surrounding the deployment of Gurkhas in Malaya disrupts the simple explanation that an endless supply of plucky warriors from the foothills of the Himalayas were ready to pitch in and fight on behalf of the British empire. As the Emergency progressed the British were forced to bring troops from elsewhere, and by mid-November 1951, there were

> seven British infantry battalions, eight Gurkha battalions, three 'colonial' battalions and the Malayan Scouts, two Royal Armoured Corps regiments, one Royal Marine Commando Brigade, four battalions of the Malay Regiment, ten RAF squadrons, two Royal Australian Air Force squadrons and a small naval contingent.[41]

Even this was not enough. Units from the King's African Rifles were imported on a rotational basis – although the development of the insurgency in Kenya prohibited many *askaris* from being sent. A small contingent of Fijian volunteers was also raised, a fact which was to have added significance in the early 1960s when 212 Fijians were recruited into the British Army.[42]

This discussion of the wider politics of augmenting the British military force in Malaya is informed by a number of different sources, of which film is just one medium. The value of Rhodes James's footage during this critical period is not that it supplies details that are unavailable elsewhere, although of course its visual testimony, as with other examples of this type, is remarkable. With the commentary taken into account, it can be made to unlock a pivotal moment in the historic relationship between the Gurkha soldiers recruited in Nepal and the British defence sector which employs them to this day. Rather than speak for itself, however, the film illustrates the potential of the archive to frame critical questions about Britain's colonial past. I have argued that the representation of the Gurkhas as a military force belongs within this project for several compelling reasons. Acknowledging their presence in the archive offers a chance to re-examine the precepts and conditions of military service under the different stages of imperial rule, seen from both British and South Asian perspectives. The British military system in India had a profound impact not just on the administration of the Raj but also on Britain's capability as a European power throughout the twentieth century. The representation of Gurkhas as an exceptional group of soldiers, who continue to be strategically deployed in a global counter-insurgency on Britain's behalf, reveals the durability of colonial constructs of ethnic difference derived from the history of military Orientalism.[43] Their place within the colonial film archive affords another opportunity to dissect and disassemble the racial imaginary as part of a wider project to address the aftermath of European colonial rule.

NOTES

1. This essay examines the history of Gurkhas organised under British military command. However, it is also important to acknowledge that Gurkhas are represented in other military and security institutions throughout South Asia and elsewhere. Apart from significant numbers of ex-Gurkha servicemen working within the private-security sector worldwide, there are Gurkha regiments in the Indian Army, and the Singapore Police Force employs a Gurkha contingent, founded in 1949, whose members are recruited from the British Gurkha headquarters in Nepal.

2. The word 'Gurkha' is an Anglicisation of 'Gorkha' which refers to an ethnoracial group whose origins are imprecise. One account suggests that they were descendants of Rajputs, forced by the Muslim invasion of the thirteenth century to seek refuge in the Himalayan foothills. Tony Gould, *Imperial Warriors: Britain and the Gurkhas* (London: Granta, 1999), p. 32.

3. Ché Singh Kochar-George, 'Nepalese Gurkhas and Their Battle for Equal Rights,' *Race and Class* no. 52, 2010, pp. 43–61.

4. Ibid., p. 44.

5. See 'Ayo Gorkhali' for further information about the history and legacy of the relationship between Britain and its Gurkha soldiers. This website was set up to provide background on the various campaigns for equal terms and conditions, and is endorsed by the Gurkha Museum. It describes itself as a

   non-profit, educational project developed by a small, dedicated team from the Believe Collective, a London-based new media production company. The project's Producer, Roshan Rai, is the son and grandson of British Gurkhas – Major (retired) Maniprasad Rai and the late Captain (Hon.) Dalbahadur Rai, who both served in the 7th Gurkha Rifles.

6. According to the website 'Ayo Gorkhali', a number of Gorkhali warriors also fought with the British against the Nepalese Army. Gorkhali mercenaries had also been recruited by the Sikh leader, Ranjit Singh, in Lahore, and served under him until 1823 when their entire unit was wiped out by Afghan artillery in the Sikh–Afghan War. In other words, the simple history of British imperialists co-opting a group of soldiers for their own ends can be made to reveal a much more complex account of regional affiliations and military work as a form of livelihood rather than loyalty. See <www.ayo-gorkhali.org/index.php/en/timeline/soldiers-of-empire/company-soldiers-become-lahoreys>.

7. Toby Haggith and Richard Smith, '"Sons of Our Empire": Shifting Ideas of "Race" and the Cinematic Representations of Imperial Troops in World War I', in Lee Grieveson and Colin MacCabe (eds), *Empire and Film* (London: BFI, 2011).

8. David Omissi, *The Sepoy and the Raj: The Indian Army 1860–1940* (London: Macmillan, 1994), pp. 23–4.

9. Tarak Barkawi, *Globalisation and War* (London: Rowman and Littlefield, 2006), p. 74. See also Jahan Mahmood, 'Remembrance Sunday – From Allies to Terrorists', 10 November 2010 at <www.thesamosa.co.uk/index.php/comment-and-analysis/society/447-remembrance-sunday-from-allies-to-terrorists.html>.

10. Barkawi, *Globalisation and War*, p. 72.

11. 1920 [Cmd. 681] East India (disturbances in the Punjab, etc.). 'Report of the Committee Appointed by the Government of India to Investigate the Disturbances in the Punjab, etc.', pp. 111–12.

12. Barkawi, *Globalisation and War*, p. 67.

13. Gurkhas were deployed in South East Asia in 1942, where they were forced to surrender to Japanese troops in Singapore. Christopher Bayly and Tim Harper's chronicle, *Forgotten Armies*, describes how they were targeted for recruitment by the second Indian National Army which reformed in internment camps in Malaya in 1943. Christopher Bayly and Tim Harper, *Forgotten Armies: The End of Britain's Asian Empire* (London: Allen Lane, 2007). In Burma, there were Gurkha soldiers in the infamous Chindits, a special force organised by Orde Wingate.

14. For example, the use of the Brighton Pavilion as a military hospital from 1914–16 has resulted in extraordinary photographic archives of Gurkhas, Pathans, Dogras, Sikhs, Jats and Punjabi Muslims who were all part of the Indian Corps. In an article 'From Allies to Terrorists', Jahan Mahmood, who created an exhibition on the British Indian Army for the Ministry of Defence in 2010, writes that, 'In total, Punjabi Muslims (136,126) represented approximately a third of the overall Muslim contribution and were singularly greater than both the Sikh (88,925) and Gurkha (55,589).' See <www.thesamosa.co.uk/index.php/comment-and-analysis/society/447-remembrance-sunday-from-allies-to-terrorists.html>.

15. Tom Rice, 'Analysis', *With the Indian Troops at the Front Part 1*. 1916. (IWM 202). See <www.colonialfilm.org.uk/node/6141>.

16. Barkawi, *Globalisation and War*, p. 64.

17. Ibid., p. 65.

18. Cynthia Enloe, *Ethnic Soldiers: State Security in a Divided Society* (Harmondsworth: Penguin, 1980).

19. Gould, *Imperial Warriors*, p. 1

20. Ibid.

21. See <www.colonialfilm.org.uk/node/5754>.
22. *Gurkha Battle in the Imphal Area and Japanese Dead at Bishenpur* (allocated) MYW/24, <www.colonialfilm.org.uk/node/6482>.
23. Bayly and Harper, *Forgotten Armies*.
24. See <www.colonialfilm.org.uk/node/6482>.
25. Ibid.
26. Ibid.
27. See <www.colonialfilm.org.uk/node/5524>.
28. See <www.colonialfilm.org.uk/node/5723>.
29. See <www.colonialfilm.org.uk/node/5749>.
30. Wendy Webster, *Englishness and Empire: 1939–1965* (Oxford: Oxford University Press, 2005).
31. Ibid., p. 32.
32. Ibid.
33. John MacKenzie, *Propaganda and Empire: The Manipulation of British Public Opinion 1880–1960* (Manchester: Manchester University Press, 1984), p. 88.
34. There is a shortened ten-minute version edited by the Ministry of Information at <http://www.colonialfilm.org.uk/node/5754>. See CIN 231A for the full original version (two reels, 1,771 ft) and CIN 231B which is a Nepalese version (reel 2 only).
35. John Parker, *The Gurkhas: The Inside Story of the World's Most Feared Soldiers* (London: Headline, 1995), p. 226.
36. Gould, *Globalisation and War*, p. 301.
37. Ibid., p. 316.
38. Parker, *The Gurkhas*, p. 232.
39. Bayly and Harper, *Forgotten Armies*, p. 522.
40. Barkawi, *Globalisation and War*, p. 320.
41. Bayly and Harper, *Forgotten Armies*, p. 522.
42. From our military correspondent, 'Fijian Recruits for Army', *The Times*, 7 November 1961; Issue 55232; col. G.
43. Patrick Porter, *Military Orientalism: Eastern Wars through Western Eyes* (London: Hurst, 2009).

FILM/
GOVERNMENT/
DEVELOPMENT

8

From the Inside: The Colonial Film Unit and the Beginning of the End

Tom Rice

In January 1948 the British Film Institute organised a conference entitled 'The Film in Colonial Development'. While speakers at the conference trotted out, as the journal *West Africa* termed it, 'the old rusty arguments about primitive, illiterate peoples ... ad nauseam', they also acknowledged a shift in colonial film policy that was clearly closely aligned to broader political developments.[1] 'Throughout our Colonial Office policy we are working at one main thing', explained K. W. Blackburne, the Director of Information Services at the Colonial Office, 'trying to teach the people of the Colonies to run the show themselves and doing precisely that thing in the film world as in every other field.'[2] Speaking at the conference, John Grierson further outlined the need to create 'a genuine African Unit that can work with native units in other colonies', what he described as a 'Colonial Film Unit with true regard for decentralisation and the part which natives will play in it'.[3]

The conference marks a public shift in colonial film policy, revealed at a moment when the British government was outlining concurrent changes in its political strategies toward Africa. It represents a moment of transition, one marked by uncertainty surrounding decentralisation and the alacrity and extent to which power would be transferred. The discussions address the position, function and structure of the Colonial Film Unit (CFU) and, as throughout the history of the CFU, these film policies were intricately connected to greater political changes.

When the CFU began in 1939, under the aegis of the Ministry of Information (MOI), it sought to produce 'propaganda' films encouraging African support for the war effort. These films often showed scenes of British life to African audiences, exemplified by its first production, *Mr English at Home* (1940). After the war, the role of the CFU began to change in ways that often mirrored the broader processes of decolonisation. At the start of 1946, the CFU sent units to East and West Africa. Now funded by the Colonial Development and Welfare Act and under the direction of the Films Division of the Central Office of Information (COI), the CFU made instructional films for African audiences, as practical instruction replaced more general imperial propaganda. By 1948, the CFU was increasingly looking to take production (and with it expenditure) away from London and into the colonies. The Home Unit now accounted for no more than 20 per cent of the CFU's output and was financed separately as an allied service from the vote of the COI. The increasing marginalisation of the Home Unit is indicative then of this shift in film policy, which closely mirrored changes in political policy.[4]

The Home Unit serves to connect the traditional functions and structure of the CFU with its ultimate ambitions. Its role in filming Africans brought over to London may appear anachronistic within the context of an administrative and film policy that was increasingly looking away from London and towards the colonies. Yet, in filming a series of conferences, tours and public exhibitions, these Home Unit productions reveal some of the ways in which the Colonial Office visualised Britain's changing relationship with Africa and, more significantly, sought to articulate these impending changes to an African audience. The films depict African sportsmen (*Nigerian Footballers in England*, 1949), musicians (*Colonial Cinemagazine 9*, 1947) and leaders (*An African Conference in London*, 1948). They celebrate British interest in the empire (*Colonial Month*, 1949) and show social and political events that sought to challenge popular perceptions of Africa within Britain. The events depicted may promote an increasing autonomy in African political life. Yet, in their largely traditional formal structure, which defined London through its landmarks, institutions and repeated references to the royal family, as the ideological centre from which the empire could be controlled and contained, the films reveal the still tentative and reactionary nature of the British government's moves towards decolonisation.

The films of the Home Unit thus provide a starting point when examining these shifts within colonial film and political policy. In showing official events and tours, they reveal some of the ways in which the Colonial Office and the COI sought to promote and represent a reconfigured empire to the British public and subsequently to African audiences. The demise of the Home Unit and the emergence of local film schools, the first of which opened in Accra on the Gold Coast in September 1948, are a practical realisation of these changes.[5]

Finally, the workings, and in particular failings, of the emerging local units reveal this continuing uncertainty and tension between local administration and centralised colonial policy. Colonial governments utilised film as a means of shaping, defining and controlling imperial subjects, disseminating government information to local audiences. Yet, film was also now more closely aligned to central government policy as by 1950, the Colonial Film Unit was incorporated into the Colonial Office. While the Colonial Office publicly sought to foster decentralisation, the CFU continued to co-ordinate and oversee an exchange of personnel, ideas, films and equipment throughout the empire. These dynamics are most neatly encapsulated in the physical films themselves, which continued to be processed in London. The notion of 'local' African films travelling through London in order to reach their African audiences highlights this ongoing negotiation between the centre and periphery, between broader colonial film policy and local practices, between transnational exchanges and emerging regional cinema cultures. In this period of rapid social and political change, film offers a microcosm of the political processes of decolonisation, often mirroring the stuttering, complex and tentative moves towards independence.

AFRICANS IN ENGLAND: EXHIBITING BRITAIN

In 1940, Winston Churchill said, 'If the British Empire and its Commonwealth lasts for a thousand years, men will still say this was their finest hour.'[6] Never mind a millennium, the empire barely survived the decade as under the post-war Labour government, the imperial map was redrawn. While often unable to keep pace with the changing political situation, the Colonial Office staged a number of events designed to promote and consolidate Britain's relationship with its African colonies. How then did it present this new imperial model to British audiences, and in what ways did the CFU films reimagine these events for African audiences?

At the opening address of the African conference, also held in 1948, the Deputy Prime Minister Herbert Morrison sought to break away from traditional notions of imperialism. 'We must wipe out the word *exploitation*', he began, 'put it amongst the antiques with *piracy* and *slavery*.' In a speech that successfully riled Churchill, Morrison further acknowledged the need for rapid change. 'Let us keep our eyes on the clock and calendar', he stated, adding that

> We in Britain are finding it difficult to adapt our ideas and ways and arrangements quickly enough to the greatly changed needs of the post-war world … a glance at Asia is enough to show the type of trouble which could break loose in your own continent if the right answers cannot be found and adapted much quicker than has ever before been thought possible.[7]

Despite these calls for action, the structure of the conference, which co-ordinated an African leadership within the British establishment, revealed a still conservative and traditional model of colonial authority.

The conference brought over delegates from Africa, many of whom, as *West Africa* noted on more than one occasion, 'were not at all sure why they had been invited or what exactly they were going to discuss'.[8] This was, to an extent, a publicity exercise after the loss of Britain's Asian colonies. The conference sought to illustrate the prominent position now afforded to the African colonies within the empire and, given the intensification of nationalist movements within Africa, encourage loyalty among a British-approved leadership. Furthermore, while the conference discussed moves to decentralise colonial operations, particularly in the development of local governments, the resultant film of the conference largely overlooks the specific details. Instead, the film positions the African leadership within an image of Britain, which is defined by traditional signifiers of British authority, such as landmarks, institutions and, in particular, the royal family. Further films produced during the delegates' tour, including *African Visitors to the Tower of London* (1949), reinforced the notion that Britain was the ideological, economic and geographical reference point against which life in the colonies was measured.[9]

Interwar film had regularly depicted London as the 'heart of the empire' and this image featured in some of the earliest organised film screenings for African audiences. Glenn Reynolds has noted how the outdoor film shows provided as part of the Bantu Educational Kinema Experiment in Tanganyika, Nyasaland, Northern Rhodesia, Kenya and Uganda between 1935 and 1937 often ended with an 'interest' film showing images of London. The film would conclude with a picture of the King and then a performance of the national anthem.[10] In their formal structure and ideological aims, these films of London may appear to mirror the conventions of early colonial travelogues, imagining a world that is deemed 'exotic' and remote to its viewers. While those earlier films of foreign spaces represented the 'primitive' to British viewers, these British travelogues inverted this, providing a visual interpretation of a British notion of 'civilisation' to their African audience.

Certainly, these CFU Home Unit productions reiterate the historical primacy and authority of Britain through this image of London, but important distinctions were also emerging. First, the central role of Africans in the Home Unit productions contrasts with their almost complete absence in interwar pictures of colonials in London. Africa is now positioned at the forefront of the empire.[11] Second, this notion of the imperial centre is supplemented by images of workers and performers travelling outside the metropole. While the initial scenes in *An African Conference* highlight the formal nature of this imperial relationship, later sequences move away from the London landmarks, showing the leaders working with, and learning from, their British counterparts on farms and in factories.

The contrasts between these two sequences reveal the uneasy balance between a traditional imperial relationship, controlled from the centre, and this new model of imperial partnership. When introducing the African delegates in London, the film repeatedly foregrounds and displays those Africans wearing traditional costume as they enter the formal proceedings at Lancaster House. Suited Africans can be glimpsed in the background, while British men and women are shown watching, in the words of the commentator, this 'colourful scene'. Later, when visiting the farm, the Africans appear predominantly dressed in suits, now chatting informally and mingling with the British dignitaries and workers. While the formal sequences in London emphasise the division and the incongruity of the scene, the sequences outside London reveal an apparent transgression across class and gender boundaries, as the Africans talk 'first hand' with British dignitaries, local farmhands and women workers.

Further Home Unit productions reveal this dichotomy between modern co-operation and traditional centralised leadership. For example, *Colonial Cinemagazine 14* (1947) shows colonial students meeting young farmers at Lampeter in Wales, but also a formal Colonial Office tea party in London at which David Rees-Williams, the Under Secretary of State for the Colonies, meets students from Malaya and Hong Kong.[12] This uncertainty over the proper balance between centralisation and decentralisation is similarly apparent in *Colonial Month*. *Colonial Month* is bookended by staged shots of African and British men smoking and chatting informally in London. While supposedly highlighting this modern ideal of partnership and equality, the framing reveals a continued division. This is most acutely revealed in the final staged sequence, which shows the African and British men talking on either side of the frame, before walking off in opposite directions.

These are then often conflicted texts, rendered ambiguous by the uncertainty of the political shifts. *Colonial Month* celebrates the colonies' continued dependence and loyalty to the imperial centre, yet it also acknowledges shifts within this imperial relationship, as it promotes the government's developmental agenda. In one scene, the commentator describes how 'Eda, a little Malayan girl whose father is now studying at Oxford University presented the Queen with a bouquet'. The Queen, as a universally recognisable imperial figurehead, receives gifts from her colonies, yet the commentator also points out here Britain's continued responsibilities and role in educating and training an African (and in this case Malayan) elite.

The example of *Colonial Month*, both as an event and a subsequent CFU film, illustrates some of the complexities and contradictions within the Colonial Office's

Filming Africans in England: colonial 'visitors' attend a tea party at the Colonial Office in 1946; footage of this event features in the CFU Home Unit production, *Victory Parade* (1946) (courtesy of the Imperial War Museum)

representation of Africa. The Colonial Office began organising Colonial Month shortly after the completion of the African conference, as a further celebration and promotion of Britain's modern empire. In publicising the event, the Colonial Office explained why such an initiative was necessary:

> An enquiry carried out by the Social Survey in 1948 revealed that there is astonishing ignorance in this country about the Colonies. This ignorance is particularly unfortunate at the present time when so much depends upon a wise development of Colonial resources in the interests of the Colonial peoples (to enable them to raise their standard of living), of the people of this country (in view of the need for developing imports from sterling sources), and of the people of the world as a whole (in view of the world shortage of food supplies and raw materials).[13]

The Colonial Office stressed that the event would not only stimulate interest in the colonies within Britain, but would also demonstrate this popular support back to the colonies. 'Plans for colonial development can only succeed', it wrote, 'if they receive the whole-hearted support of the Colonial peoples; and one bar to obtaining their support is their feeling that the people of this country are not interested in them and their problems.' Stimulating interest in colonial affairs was, the Colonial Office added, 'of vital importance in the long term if we are to maintain that unity of thought and feeling between Britain and the Colonies which is essential to a survival of the Empire'. A letter from the Colonial Office in February 1949 reiterated the month's dual function:

> There can be few better ways of strengthening these links [between Britain and the Colonies] than by awakening the interest of the British public, and thereby showing the colonial peoples that we in this country are really concerned in their problems and in their development.[14]

In strengthening these links, the staging of Colonial Month hoped to convince the British public of the financial benefits of supporting colonial development. The film of Colonial Month then illustrated this support to African audiences. The Colonial Office reasoned that this, in turn, would ensure that Africans reciprocated this support for colonial development programmes. This again highlights the paradoxical nature of these films. While *Colonial Month* appears to reveal a traditional and regressive imperial identity in much of its structure and content, this was intended in a circuitous way to promote modern 'Africanisation' programmes and to support the work of the CFU's African productions.

Colonial Month was centred around an exhibition in Oxford Street in London, which was intended to organise, connect and display the colonies together within the city. While allowing visitors to 'make their way along a realistic jungle pathway' and to see life-sized models of Africans, the exhibition's prime purpose was to highlight the economic value of the colonies at a moment when public opinion was increasingly opposed to large-scale colonial expenditure. *Colonial Month* reveals how raw materials from the colonies are used in Britain. The commentator notes here 'that this section of the exhibition is most important. It shows very clearly that Britain and the colonies need each other today more than they have ever done before.' The colonies were largely defined within the exhibition by their economic value to Britain, usually in the form of an easily recognisable product. Delineating colonies in economic terms by products was a standard feature of colonial rhetoric (the empire exhibition of 1924–5 was largely organised in this way) and was particularly prevalent in interwar colonial documentary cinema. This emphasis on trade and economic partnership responded to American economic dominance as the Colonial Office sought to enact a form of union by promoting the sterling area, an economic bloc (tied to the pound) of which most colonies and Dominions were a part.

The Colonial Office directly emphasised the economic benefits of hosting colonial workers in Britain, and of continued colonial investment. This is evident in *Spotlight on the Colonies* (1950), which uses much of the CFU Home Unit's material, but which was overseen by the government's Economic Information Unit for British cinemagoers. 'To us in the factories at home, this plan for mutual exchange may seem remote', the commentator notes, 'but we are – every one of us – a part of it; for if the colonies are to send us the food and raw materials we're short of, we must send them the tools to do the job.' The press release for the film followed a similar rhetoric. 'If the Colonies are given our continued help,' the release concluded, 'we shall in the coming years have staunch partners on our common road to progress.'[15]

Dr Rita Hinden, a socialist campaigner on colonial issues who initially advised on *Spotlight on the Colonies*, argued that the government was instigating a shift here. 'The trouble in the past was that only the economic interests of Britain were considered, and colonial economies were geared to suit British needs,' she explained in 1948.

> It is now a matter of *mutual* advantage, each country concentrating on producing what it is best suited for – even though we may not have yet succeeded in convincing all the colonial peoples that it is as above board as that.[16]

The CFU served in part then to convince the colonial audiences of the benefits of this 'development'. This is achieved not by foregrounding the economic value of this

Fulham footballer John Finch coaching the Nigerian footballers on their tour of England in 1949 (courtesy of BFI National Archive)

alliance (as in Britain), but rather by referencing imperial trade as a further means of partnership. For example, in *An African Conference*, the delegates visit the Bourneville factory and watch the export of 'good African cocoa', seeing the 'process through from beginning to end'.

This imperial partnership was also imagined through a series of tours that the Colonial Office arranged, which sought to challenge British perceptions of the colonies. In May 1947, the Gold Coast Police Band embarked on a four-month tour of the UK, which was featured in *Colonial Cinemagazine 9*, while in August 1949, the Nigerian football team, the first to leave West Africa, embarked on a five-week tour. Historian Phil Vasili argued that the selectors

> wanted the players to present a collective face to the British public that went some way to dispelling racial myths about Africans and which would also stand testament to the positive contribution made by the expatriates, confirming the legitimacy of their presence in the colony.

Fourteen of the eighteen Nigerian footballers were civil servants, and another two were teachers. The team's player/secretary Kanno had been educated in England and had thus, it was deemed, 'acquired the refinements necessary for the public engagements'.[17]

The films of the tours reveal an overarching, central colonial presence, both formally in deploying a British voiceover and also in their staging as they depict a collective African group gathered around, looking up at, and learning from, a single British figure. This reiterates one of the primary functions of the tours: to emphasise the successful role undertaken by British leadership in the social development of colonial subjects. In writing about the Nigerian footballers, the CFU quarterly, *Colonial Cinema*, argued that 'the team did not take long to establish a fine reputation not only for fast, clever football but also for excellent manners and sporting behaviour on the field'. An editorial in the magazine added that 'of even greater importance than their technical ability was the fine atmosphere of sportsmanship they left along their trail'.[18]

The tours of Africans to England reveal the difficulties that the Colonial Office faced in promoting 'Africanisation' to British audiences. In order to highlight African 'readiness' and 'social development', the Colonial Office defined the Africans in relation to supposedly British ideals and customs, in this case 'sportsmanship' and 'fairness'. This process threatened the African identity of these figures, yet conversely, public responses to the tour reasserted perceived African 'characteristics', albeit in a regressive manner that played on established notions of primitivism and dominant racial assumptions. For example, newspaper reports of the Nigerian footballers' tour of England were preoccupied with the cultural differences between the Nigerians and English players, noting in particular that the Nigerians played barefoot. 'If during the next month, you see a full back put a football on the spot for a goal kick and hoof it beyond midfield with his bare foot,' a *Daily Mirror* report began, 'there's no need to cringe. He likes doing it. In fact, he prefers it that way'.[19] Reports of the Gold Coast band suggested that British audiences were particularly curious as to whether the musicians were playing the music from a score. One report even claimed that during a performance, the lighting crew switched off the lights 'out of curiosity and doubtfulness'. 'To the surprise of the audience', the report added, 'the band stopped playing abruptly.'[20] Such assumptions and stereotypes were similarly evident in the press coverage of the tour. *African Affairs* commented on the 'foolish British press descriptions of the Gold Coast Police Band as "Jungle Musicians"'.[21]

These events and tours showed Africans in Britain at a moment when immigration and questions of citizenship were once again prominent in public discourse. The British Nationality Act of 1948, which instituted a new status of 'Citizen of the United Kingdom and Colonies', elicited broad discussion on the position of colonials within a British identity. At the same time, increased immigration and reports of race riots in Liverpool positioned black men and women more visibly in Britain (and potentially altered the ways in which African viewers would now perceive Britain). For African audiences, the films sought to dispel any notions of racial animosity, most notably in *Nigerian Footballers*, which shows crowd scenes of 7,000 Britons and Africans cheering together in Liverpool. They emphasise African recognition and validation within Britain, as both *Nigerian Footballers* and *Colonial Cinemagazine 9* conclude with shots of British crowds applauding the African performers. Furthermore, they aim to reassure African audiences of the care and welfare provided for those Africans now living in Britain. This is most notable in the uncomfortable analogy in *Colonial Cinemagazine 8* (1947), which shows African animals well looked after in their new homes in London Zoo. It is significant that, given both fears within Britain over immigration and the moves towards self-government, these films largely define the Africans as 'visitors'. The films frequently show Africans waving goodbye and note that the colonial men will take their accrued knowledge back to their own countries and form the political leadership there. The films suggest then a move back to the colonies, yet they crucially outline the importance of British instruction, values and economic co-operation in these moves.

The films of the Home Unit may appear increasingly anachronistic by 1949, as film production and colonial administration began to move away from London and into the colonies. Yet these films reveal the still tentative and complex nature of this move, both in their formal structure and in the events that they depict. They also anticipate impending shifts in film policy. Presaging the work of the film training schools, the films show British leaders training skilled African workers and performers, and high-light the economic motivations behind colonial policy. In representing events and tours organised by the Colonial Office, they also envisage an increasingly prominent role for film within colonial administration. This would be more fully realised in 1950 when, as part of the major restructure of the CFU, full control of the unit shifted from the Films Division of the COI to the Colonial Office.[22] This long-proposed move to the Colonial Office ensured that film policy was now more closely administered as part of the remit of a single, central organisation in Britain. Paradoxically, at the same time, the Colonial Office advanced its plans to decentralise. This negotiation between a central policy overseen from London and the work of local colonial governments was a defining feature of these last years of colonial rule.

TRAINING AFRICANS

When the Home Unit shut down in 1949, it had a staff of three. Two of these were cameramen, Sydney Samuelson and George Noble, who were immediately reassigned to the colonies, joining the recently formed Nigerian and Gold Coast Film Units. They were charged with working alongside the local film workers, who had trained at the CFU's first 'school of instruction' set up in Accra in September 1948. Further training schools followed, in Jamaica in 1950 and Cyprus in 1951, while the CFU also contin-ued to train colonial students in London.[23] In describing the work of the first school of instruction in Accra, *Colonial Cinema* stated that 'One of the long-term objectives of the Colonial Film Unit and perhaps its most important one is the creation of an organisation in each colony to produce its own films.'[24] The formation of these schools illustrates these moves to develop local film production – a move away from the work of the Home Unit – but their ongoing organisation through the CFU suggests that this was still part of a central film policy.

Martin Rennals, one of six students to attend the West Indian school, recognised this as a problem when he criticised the school for its failure to cater specifically for the 'cultural characteristics of the local audiences', and to 'relate the methods of production to the customs and ways of life' of the West Indians.[25] The school was announced by William Sellers, the head of the CFU, at the end of a month-long tour of the West Indies in December 1949 and was then run by R. W. Harris and Gareth Evans, who had also run the first colonial training school in Accra.[26] Certainly the training programmes highlight the transfer of personnel and ideas across British territories, but there are also regional deviations based on institutional racial assumptions and imperial hierarchies.

In Africa, the film school had catered for what its convener referred to as 'the ignorance of cinema convention', following the approach of William Sellers in arguing that African audiences would have different cognitive responses and required 'extreme simplicity' in their films. Yet in Jamaica, the convener noted the influence of American and British 'sophisticated pleasures' in the 'cosmopolitan' West Indies and suggested that no dispensation was required for the local audiences.[27] Furthermore, the CFU scrapped plans to set up a film school at Makerere College in Uganda in 1949, after East African officials argued that no suitable students could be found and that the 'proposed training course may be overloaded beyond the capacity of African trainees'.[28]

The example of East Africa reveals the continued importance of racial prejudices in colonial film policy and it also highlights the tensions between the central and local authorities. The CFU had sent out ten technicians under the control of H. L. Bradshaw to Kenya, Uganda, Tanganyika and later Zanzibar, at the start of 1949. Briefed with the task of founding a government film service in the East African territories and of training Africans to 'make educational films themselves for their own people', the unit operated for less than a year.[29] Throughout this year, the film personnel in East Africa were in almost constant disagreement with their bosses in London. At a conference of Information Officers in Nairobi in June 1949, 'the territorial delegates unanimously expressed a lack of confidence in the London Administration of the Colonial Film Unit'. The feeling was evidently mutual. H. M. K. Howson, the Films Officer of the COI, complained about the poor standard of the unit's work and their 'low reputation' at home and overseas. The breakdown in communication was such that the COI wrote to John Grierson, who was planning on visiting East Africa in December 1949, asking him to 'do a job for this side of the house' by chasing up the CFU store accounts in East Africa. The COI representative explained that he had asked for the accounts on six occasions, but had had no response. He concluded by asking Grierson 'Would you please apply a rocket?'[30]

When the unit was shut down, the delegates threatened legal action against Howson and signed a lengthy petition in which they complained that they had suffered 'innumerable setbacks by not having a well-organized and intelligent backing from England'. However, the acrimonious closure of the unit was largely a result of the restructuring of the CFU within the Colonial Office, a change ironically championed by the East African delegates.[31] Funding now moved from London to the colonies, and while the Gold Coast and Nigerian governments met the costs of their nascent units, the East African government was not willing to do the same. This reorganisation had a number of repercussions as I have suggested. First, the colonial governments were now financially responsible for film production and so film became more closely integrated into local government policy. Second, the Colonial Office was now in charge of the CFU, positioning film more prominently within a single, centralised British colonial administration. This paradox is at the heart of colonial film-making in the latter years of empire, as the CFU is caught between idealising centralisation and trying to foster decentralisation.

Speaking in 1952 at a conference entitled 'New Direction in Documentary', the Director of the Colonial Office Information Department, C. Y. Carstairs, outlined the altered role of the CFU. 'It makes no films and it gives no orders', he began,

> but it performs a whole series of services without which the Colonial Cinema as a whole would certainly suffer. It edits films, attends to titling, sound dubbing, and recruitment of staff, the ordering of equipment and stock, the running of the 'raw stock scheme', and training; it collects and disseminates information by means of its quarterlies and sponsors research.[32]

This decentralised model was still promoting transnational modes of distribution and exhibition, of personnel, ideas, stock and material throughout the empire. This approach largely followed the suggestions of 'The Film in Colonial Development' conference which, with no 'colonials' among its seven invited speakers, had proposed a similarly ambiguous and tentative model of decentralisation. John Grierson had argued for local film production 'created from the inside by and for the Colonial peoples themselves' which he suggested should be integrated more fully into local government administration. However, he had also proposed a central 'School of the Colonies' to administer and oversee a cultural exchange of films, personnel and ideas throughout the empire.[33]

In discussing the changes made to the CFU, Carstairs acknowledged that these 'Africanisation' policies were certainly not entirely idealistic, but were once again driven by financial considerations. 'The European staff of Colonial Film Units do not live soft, but they are still a relatively costly item', he claimed, 'it is important on cost grounds alone, even if there were no others, to train likely local lads for the work.'[34] The Colonial Office's organisation of Colonial Month had acknowledged and re-sponded to a growing backlash in Britain to colonial expenditure. Furthermore, for all the rhetoric of 'Africanisation' in film and administrative policy, Carstairs and his colleagues at the Colonial Office continued to validate traditional theories of colonial spectatorship and institutional racial assumptions. When discussing the limitations of the film-training programmes, Carstairs argued that such limitations satisfied the requirements of the intended audience. 'Trainees are turning out a type of straight-forward film', he argued, 'eschewing frills, but strong in content and local touch, which very closely fits the stage of film education which their audiences have reached.'[35] Even as late as 1954, when Harold Evans, a colleague of Carstairs at the Colonial Office, discussed the closure of CFU training programmes, he still emphasised the value of this centralised body. 'It does seem to us', he stated, 'that a fatherly eye will have to be kept on the output of some of the smaller units for some time to come.'[36]

The CFU's training programmes may have been presented as evidence of the government's Africanisation drive, yet they again reveal the complexities and contin-uing caution in this process. The Colonial Office continued to co-ordinate and oversee these schemes, which often perpetuated established colonial rhetoric. Rather than revealing a new model of African film-makers and production, the programmes selected trainees from various government departments to produce short instructional films, which closely followed CFU conventions and which were then processed in London. Upon completing their training, the workers became part of the newly formed local units, yet the roles that they assumed again demonstrated the limitations in this Africanisation process even as moves towards decolonisation gathered pace.

THE FILM UNITS IN OPERATION

In 1953, the Gold Coast Film Unit produced a two-reel comedy, which was used as part of a 'vigorous and prolonged campaign' to promote the work of the local council and to outline recent changes to local government.[37] *Progress in Kojokrom* represents the latest stage in this decentralisation process, showing democratically elected African

The Gold Coast Film Unit disseminated government policy to local audiences; here a Mass Education team outlines scenes from the 1950 GCFU production, *Amenu's Child* (courtesy of the Public Relations Office, Gold Coast)

leaders and councillors, and depicting an idealised, Western model of government to its African audience. Yet while the completed film sought to highlight the successful completion of this Africanisation process, its production reveals once more the continuing challenges and failings in this move to develop an African leadership.

Progress in Kojokrom is typical of the ways in which colonial governments used film in this last decade of colonial rule. It was shown by a fleet of mobile cinema vans and, according to government reports, reached an audience of 1.5 million. The film was supplemented by government pamphlets ('Your Council and Your Progress') and was often followed by a discussion with a local council member.[38] Sean Graham, the head of the Gold Coast Film Unit, noted the importance of these films to the government. 'In an illiterate society they [films] are the only means government has of speaking to the people with authority and understanding', he explained in 1952, 'far from being a luxury, [films] are at the forefront of the drive to help Africans to help themselves.' Graham recalled regular meetings at which different government departments would propose suitable subjects, as the units were now more closely aligned to local government, working with and propagating specific policies.[39]

Despite these moves to decentralise and to develop local production, emerging 'local' units often worked to similar ends in disseminating government policy, indicating an ongoing exchange of ideas, personnel and exhibition practices throughout the empire. The Colonial Office and the shadow of the CFU continued to influence and direct these units, yet there were also significant regional variations in their operations. While the Nigerian Film Unit (NFU) 'remained very much in the pragmatic mould of the CFU in terms of the kind of films produced', the Gold Coast Film Unit deviated from colonial-film orthodoxy in the formal techniques that it used to address its African audiences, rejecting the 'special technique' espoused by William Sellers and the CFU. [40]

Writing in 1952, George Noble explained that '[m]ostly, the films made by other units in the Colonies were small, single-reelers. Sean Graham decided to make longer films, story films, films about the Africans themselves, played by themselves, in their own land, about their own people'.[41] Noble's comments suggest that this model of Africanisation, what Grierson referred to as a 'genuine African unit', was now realised in the Gold Coast. Images from the making of *Progress in Kojokrom* also show a predominantly African crew working alongside the all-African cast. Speaking recently, Graham rejected the suggestion that this was a colonial unit. 'No, "colonial" was a dirty word in my vocabulary', he stated, 'we were a local unit.'[42]

Graham's comments highlight once more this tension between the 'local' and 'colonial' or, as the East African example suggested, between regional practices and central policy. Yet it is important to recognise that the 'local' does not necessarily equate to what we might understand as 'African', but rather to an administration run by Europeans working and living in the colonies. Indeed, the Gold Coast Film Unit was certainly not a fully realised model of large-scale 'Africanisation'. The example of *Progress in Kojokrom* demonstrates a continuing British presence, both on screen through the voice-of-God narration and off screen where, despite employing 'about 20 African junior technical staff', the directors and writers were predominantly still European.[43] Indeed, the opening credits feature exclusively European personnel, while the soundtrack for the film and, in particular the ways in which the characters repeatedly switch between English and local dialects, reveal again the gradual and uncertain nature of this process of Africanisation.

In outlining the desire for a modern African unit, neither Grierson nor Graham suggested that this should comprise an entirely African leadership although Grierson did call for men who would make this their 'lifework'. 'It is no longer a question of people dropping into Africa to make a picture', he had challenged, 'We have got to create a body of men who live and work with the African problem, who are the African problem in its creative aspect, knowing it and living with it.'[44] Sean Graham also emphasised that an understanding of the local culture should be a prerequisite for this work, but this was certainly not always the case, as the units continued to import European personnel on short-term contracts. Graham frequently complained that the European writers and film-makers brought out to assist the unit, such as Ray Elton, Louis MacNeice and Montgomery Tully, did not understand the local culture. Writing in 1952 to Basil Wright, who worked from London as an associate producer on *The Boy Kumasenu* (1952), Graham complained about Tully's failure 'to make any friends among the Africans'. 'The man is so sensitive that I cannot push him out into the village and tell him to make friends with the locals', Graham wrote, 'Yet I cannot see what good it will do our scripts for Tully to swap confidences with the Europeans in the club.'[45]

The Gold Coast Film Unit
in action, *Ghana Today* vol. 1
no. 22, 25 December 1957

The example of the West African units reveals the regional variations in this
colonial framework and these may again reflect the varying levels of political
advancement within the regions. Sydney Samuelson, who worked briefly for the NFU,
stated that the Gold Coast Film Unit was 'way ahead of us' in terms of its production
and organisation and argued that this reflected the more progressive nature of the
Gold Coast as a country and as a government.[46] The operations of the film units
evidence again the close links between local administrative and film policy. Indeed the
NFU was reorganised into smaller regional units throughout the decade in accordance
with broader constitutional changes, although once more these smaller units continued to produce, exhibit and utilise film in very similar ways.

To an extent then, the developments in these units mirrored the social and
political changes in the respective countries. The often tentative moves towards
decolonisation are played out on screen, yet the organisation of the units is indicative
of the failings in this process. While *Progress in Kojokrom* espouses moves towards self-
government and this much-vaunted 'Africanisation', the units themselves largely fail
in their oft-quoted aim to develop local film-makers and ultimately, Europeans
continue to occupy prominent positions as independence approaches.

CONCLUSION

This essay has focused predominantly on government policy and on how local and
central administrations tried to prepare and then respond to rapid, largely unforeseen
shifts within the empire. The events staged in London and the work of the Home Unit

sought to articulate the Labour government's new policies on Africa to British and African audiences, outlining moves to decentralise colonial operations, promote colonial development and encourage gradual progress towards self-government. The training programmes and resultant local units then revealed the contradictions, challenges and failures in instigating these moves.

Yet the rise of nationalist and resistance movements throughout Africa in the post-war era highlights the fact that colonial governments could not always control the pace of the progress towards decolonisation. Similarly in cinema, there is evidence of an increasing African presence escaping the control of the colonial governments. While governments maintained Europeans in what they believed to be senior positions of responsibility, they failed to recognise fully that, in the context of African cinema, the responsibility lay elsewhere. Europeans headed the units and held what were widely perceived as the most significant roles in film production (as directors and writers), yet it was African people that invariably relayed these messages directly to the audiences. In recent conversation with Sydney Samuelson and Sean Graham, both spoke independently of the problems that they faced in delivering official information to culturally diverse audiences, and acknowledged the importance of the often untrained travelling commentator, who would translate the English script into different local dialects. Sean Graham noted how local commentators often developed their own narratives, moving away from the script and from the official line. 'I was appalled at the divergence, what was on screen and what they said', he stated. 'In most cases the showings of the film were useless', Samuelson added, suggesting that the commentators were often 'showmen', adding their own interpretation to the film or generating comedy by responding to the action on screen.[47] The mobile exhibition of these films often occurred without a European presence, and it is perhaps here that we should look to understand better the development both of African cinema culture but also inadvertently of this more fully realised African voice within cinema. The local commentator may then provide an example of an African presence in this cinema, the revealing emergence of a new voice, at times resistant to government pedagogy, as independence approaches.

NOTES

Most of the films mentioned in this essay are now available to view online at 'Colonial Film: Moving Images of the British Empire', <www.colonialfilm.org.uk>. I would like to thank Lee Grieveson for his help on earlier drafts of this essay, and Colin MacCabe and Emma Sandon.

1. 'Film Talk … African Outlets … Non-White Britons', West Africa, 24 January 1948, p. 59.
2. K. W. Blackburne, 'Financial Problems and Future Policy in British Colonies', The Film in Colonial Development: A Report of a Conference (London: BFI, 1948), p. 35.
3. John Grierson, 'The Film and Primitive Peoples', The Film in Colonial Development, p. 13.
4. Tom Rice, 'Colonial Film Unit', 'Colonial Film: Moving Images of the British Empire', <www.colonialfilm.org.uk/production-company/colonial-film-unit>. For a closer consideration of this development in cinema, see Rosaleen Smyth, 'Images of Empires on Shifting Sands: The Colonial Film Unit in West Africa in the Post-war Period', this volume.

5. In the same month that the CFU launched its training school in Accra, the Colonial Office directly contacted William Sellers, the head of the CFU, requesting that his unit film the forthcoming African conference in London. The CFU was asked to film the visiting delegates 'both at the formal proceedings at Lancaster House and during their visits and tours in London and the Provinces'. The Colonial Office explained that this was with a view 'to providing suitable publicity for this important Conference in the Colonial territories, particularly in Africa'. Letter from H. C. Cocks of the Colonial Office to William Sellers, director of CFU, dated 27 September 1948, 'African Conference in London', INF 6/55, accessed at the National Archives, London.

6. Hansard, House of Commons, 18 June 1940, Volume 361, Cols 787–98.

7. *West Africa*, 2 October 1948, p. 996.

8. 'Colourful Scene as the Delegates Arrive', *West Africa*, 2 October 1948, p. 996.

9. Additional films include *Colonial Cinemagazine No. 20*, which showed the delegates visiting the zoo and *Colonial Cinemagazine No. 21*, in which Nigerians studying in England greeted the Oni of Ife.

10. Glenn Reynolds, 'The Bantu Educational Kinema Experiment and the Struggle for Hegemony in British East and Central Africa, 1935–1937', *Historical Journal of Film, Radio and Television* vol. 29 no. 1, March 2009, p. 64. See also Tom Rice, 'Bekefilm', <www.colonialfilm.org.uk>.

11. In films such as the Empire Marketing Board's *One Family* (1930) or *Heart of an Empire* (1935), the Dominions and India feature, while Africa is barely a footnote.

12. This is again apparent in *Colonial Cinemagazine 15* (1947) where colonial students learn about co-operative methods at Loughborough College.

13. Letter from A. A. W. Johnson of the Empire Advisory Unit to Sir E. Graham Savage, Chief Education Officer, LCC, dated 14 January 1949, INF 12/350, accessed at the National Archives. Johnson explained that the survey had revealed that 'only a quarter knew the difference between a Dominion and Colony: a half could not name a single Colony correctly: only a third knew that the Colonies do not pay taxes to us'.

14. 'Colonial Month – 1949', INF 12/350; 'Letter from Colonial Office, February 1949', INF 12/350, both accessed at the National Archives.

15. 'Spotlight on the Colonies', INF 6/1337, accessed at the National Archives.

16. Rita Hinden, 'The Empire', in Donald Munro (ed.), *Socialism: The British Way* (London: Essential Books, 1948), p. 283.

17. Phil Vasili, 'Colonialism and Football: The First Nigerian Tour to Britain', *Race and Class* vol. 36 no. 4, 1995, pp. 60–1.

18. 'Nigerian Footballers in England', *Colonial Cinema*, December 1949, p. 68; *Colonial Cinema*, December 1949, p. 55.

19. 'Bare Feet Give Them a Kick', *Daily Mirror*, 30 August 1949, p. 6. Cameraman Sydney Samuelson, who filmed the tourists' first game against Marine Crosby in Liverpool, recently recalled specifically filming the feet of the Nigerians as they came on to the pitch, although the commentator makes no mention of this. 'Personal Interview with Sir Sydney Samuelson', conducted by Tom Rice and Emma Sandon, 15 June 2010.

20. 'Police Band', Ghana Police Website, <http://64.226.23.153/others/band.htm>.

21. Henry Swanzy, 'Quarterly Notes', *African Affairs*, October 1947, p. 188.

22. The shift to the Colonial Office saw the closure of the Home Unit. The Colonial Office explained that 'With the transfer to the Colonial Office, the Unit will no longer be

responsible for producing any films to project Britain to the Colonies.' There were still requests for these Home Unit productions though. The Governor's office in the Gold Coast wrote in September 1950 that

> It is hoped that the Colonial Film Unit will continue to cover news items in the United Kingdom which are of interest to Africans: for example the recent film "Nigerian Footballers" enjoyed a great success in the Gold Coast.

'Colonial Film Unit: Long Term Policy', CO 875/52/1, accessed at the National Archives; 'Colonial Film Unit Estimates for 1950/51', CO 875/52/2, accessed at the National Archives.

23. The Accra and Jamaican training schools each comprised six students selected from government departments, while the school in Cyprus had nine students from Cyprus, Mauritius, Hong Kong and the Sudan. The short training courses in London had catered for fifty-one visitors by the end of 1951. See Tom Rice, 'Colonial Film Unit', <www.colonialfilm.org.uk/production-company/colonial-film-unit>.

24. 'The School of Instruction, Accra, Gold Coast', *Colonial Cinema*, December 1948, p. 78.

25. Helen-Ann E. Wilkinson, 'Limited Core Technology Transfer: The Case of the Moving Image Industry in Jamaica' (unpublished thesis, York University, Ontario, 1994). See also Tom Rice, 'Jamaica Film Unit', <www.colonialfilm.org.uk/production-company/jamaica-film-unit>.

26. The CFU produced a detailed geographically non-specific 'Syllabus for Film Training Schools' and in some respects the school endorsed established colonial film-making conventions, for example, in focusing on instructional 16mm films and promoting parables that followed the 'Mr Wise and Mr Foolish' format.

27. G. Evans, 'The Colonial Film Unit's West Indian Training Course in Jamaica', in *Visual Aids in Fundamental Education: Some Personal Experiences* (Paris: UNESCO, 1952), pp. 130–9. Evans further argued that the purpose of the Jamaican school 'was to train West Indians in the art of film production so that they can make films *of* and *for* their own people in an environment that they alone thoroughly understand'.

28. Quoted in Rosaleen Smyth, 'The Post-war Career of the Colonial Film Unit in Africa: 1946–1955', *Historical Journal of Film, Radio and Television* vol. 12 no. 2, 1992, p. 170.

29. 'Colonial Film Unit. Expansion of Activities', CO 875/26/2, accessed at the National Archives.

30. Letter from COI to Grierson, dated 2 December 1949, G5:6:4, accessed at the John Grierson Archive, University of Stirling.

31. 'Colonial Film Unit: East African Project; Possible Abandonment of Educational Film Production', CO 875/52/4, accessed at the National Archives. *Colonial Cinema* stated that

> in certain respects this organisation was cumbrous, unsuitable, and not as efficient as it might be. It was proposed as a first essential (sic) that the Colonial Film Unit should be removed from the control of the COI and placed under that of the Colonial Office.
> *Colonial Cinema*, June 1950, p. 27.

32. 'New Directions in Documentary: Report of the International Conference Held at Edinburgh August 25–26, 1952', G6:42:1, accessed at the John Grierson Archive, University of Stirling.

By the end of 1950, the CFU had ceased all production, and over half of its twenty-nine staff had been made redundant. The CFU continued to use its quarterly *Colonial Cinema* as a means to direct, determine and disseminate the theoretical and practical approaches to film production and exhibition in the colonies. Its ongoing raw-stock scheme provided film in areas that were too small to have their own units, such as Somaliland, Sierra Leone, the Gambia and Malta.

33. Grierson, *The Film in Colonial Development*, pp. 12–13. 'We want, for this school, not only the experience of the Colonial Office', Grierson stated,

> we also have to know what is being done elsewhere and bring world-wide experience to bear on our problem. We will need a first-class library, a growing and developing information service, an exchange of teachers and lecturers and other people interested in colonial problems.

34. 'New Directions in Documentary', p. 15.
35. Ibid.
36. Letter from Evans to Sir Robert Fraser, 19 June 1954, INF 12/505, accessed at the National Archives.
37. Colonial Office, 'Report on the Gold Coast for the Year 1954' (London: HMSO, 1954), p. 120.
38. Tom Rice, 'Progress in Kojokrom', <www.colonialfilm.org.uk/node/2566>; 'The Impact of Information Services on the People of Ghana', *Ghana Today*, 25 December 1957, pp. 4–5.
39. Sean Graham, 'The Work of the Gold Coast Film Unit', in *Visual Aids in Fundamental Education*, pp. 77–87; 'Personal Interview with Sean Graham', conducted by Tom Rice, Emma Sandon and Peter Bloom, 5 February 2010.
40. Ikechukwu Obiaya, 'A Break with the Past: The Nigerian Video-Film Industry in the Context of Colonial Filmmaking', forthcoming in *Film History*. The NFU was run by Lionel Snazelle, a disciple of Sellers, who had filmed many of the recent CFU films in Nigeria. Its first production, *Smallpox*, a health parable that adopted the 'Mr Wise and Mr Foolish' format is indicative of the NFU's acceptance and continuing enactment of established colonial-film conventions.
41. George Noble, 'Cameraman on the Gold Coast', *Colonial Cinema*, June 1952, p. 36. Graham saw himself as a 'storyteller', in contrast to Sellers and Snazelle, who he suggested were 'educators really'.
42. 'Personal Interview with Sean Graham', 5 February 2010. There is little evidence of the West African units working together. Sean Graham did visit the Nigerian Film Unit and shared equipment with them on occasion, but he personally clashed with its head, Lionel Snazelle, and saw himself in 'ferocious competition' with them. See letter dated 8 August 1952, accessed at BFI Special Collections, BCW 1/16/1.
43. 'Gold Coast Film Catalogue, 1949–1954' (1954).
44. Grierson, *The Film in Colonial Development*, p. 13.
45. 'Letter from Sean Graham to Basil Wright, dated 28 July 1952', accessed at BFI Special Collections, BCW 1/16/1.
46. 'Personal Interview with Sir Sydney Samuelson'.
47. Ibid.; 'Personal Interview with Sean Graham', 5 February 2010. Graham suggested that he subsequently sought to manage the commentators more closely, yet he did not attend the

screenings himself. Writing in 1951, William Sellers also acknowledged a need for closer supervision of the commentators. 'Experience has shown the need for checking all translations before they are used in public,' he wrote, although there is little evidence to suggest that this was done. William Sellers, 'Mobile Cinema Shows in Africa', *Colonial Cinema*, December 1951, pp. 77–82.

9

Images of Empires on Shifting Sands:
The Colonial Film Unit in West Africa in the Post-war Period

Rosaleen Smyth

The British colonial government first adopted film as an integral part of the administration of its African colonies during World War II with the setting up of the Colonial
Film Unit (CFU) in 1939 to make propaganda films to ensure the support and loyalty
of the largely illiterate African population. But almost immediately plans were hatched
to enlist the CFU and the mobile cinema vans it used in this war propaganda blitzkrieg
in post-war mass-education campaigns to implement development education. This
was not only to include areas such as health and agriculture and the promotion of
more productive economic structures, abandoning 'the economic conservatism of
indirect rule',[1] but also education for citizenship and for eventual self-government.
Films now became a vital part of a new post-war policy of developmentalism, initially
designed to legitimise the perpetuation of colonial rule and rescue the bruised international image of Britain's colonial trusteeship, which had been damaged by numerous
national and international critiques on the eve of the war. When political decolonisation became inevitable, film had a psychological role to play in ensuring that sufficient
goodwill was retained to persuade the former colonies not to sever their ties with the
home country and remain, as the Secretary of State for the Colonies noted in 1948,
'part of the Western world'.[2]

World War II had produced an epic moment in the changing relationship between
state and society with the Beveridge Report and the introduction of the welfare state
in Britain, which had its counterpart in Britain's African colonies with the Colonial
Development and Welfare Act (1940 and 1945). Governments were now expected
to act as 'agencies of social betterment'.[3] The Act brought into British colonial
administration in Africa a new era of state-sponsored social-welfare initiatives.
The new post-war developmentalism had to be – and importantly be seen to be –
conducted for the welfare of the colonial people themselves and not just for the
economic benefit of the imperial power. This more altruistic post-war interpretation
and representation of 'development' required colonies to produce ten-year development plans and included mass-education campaigns that were developed in the
seminal report of the Colonial Office Advisory Committee on Education in the
Colonies, *Mass Education in African Society* (1944).[4] The CFU, under the leadership of
William Sellers, projected the moving visual imagery for the mass-education onslaught.
Sellers himself had played a pioneering role in the development of public-health films
in Nigeria between the wars, along with Dr Patterson in Kenya. Their initiatives and
the Bantu Educational Kinema Experiment (BEKE, 1935–7) in East and Central Africa

The Colonial Film Unit shooting on location in West Africa, 1946 (cameraman, Peter Sargent) (courtesy of Overseas Film and Television Centre, London)

represented the first significant attempts to use cinema in adult education in Britain's African colonies. Now after the war the CFU was set to take these initiatives to the next level.

When William Sellers led the CFU team to the Gold Coast in January 1946, *Colonial Cinema* commented: 'At last, the long term work had begun of instruction, of mass education, helping to develop self reliance and to break traditional ground so that the seeds of progress in health, industry and agriculture could be planted.'[5] But how long term was it to be? The sands were shifting rapidly under the increasingly fragile edifice of the British empire. The informal economic empire, American-style, was now in the ascendant; the spectre of metropolitan liberal democracy presiding like a benevolent autocrat over a cluster of African colonies was about to be gone with the wind. A 'New World Order' based on the principles of the Atlantic Charter was being constructed under the canopy of the United Nations. Its agencies would soon assume oversight of the many development and welfare issues being identified in the less-developed areas of the world, including Britain's African bailiwick. How did the CFU adjust to this tumultuous era in West African history when its mission evolved to include not only the promotion of its developmentalist objectives but, with the end of empire on the horizon, the maintenance of the ties that bind?

COLONIAL OFFICE POLICY AND THE MOVING OF THE GOALPOSTS

Between 1946 and 1950 CFU crews were producing development films in West Africa. In 1947 their development mission was injected with a new urgency when the Secretary of State for the Colonies, Arthur Creech Jones dramatically revised Britain's colonial policy. Suddenly the life expectancy of the empire was reduced from a leisurely eighty years to twenty. Under Andrew Cohen, the dynamic new head of the Colonial Office's Africa Division, the major objective given to the new director of the Colonial Office's information department, Kenneth Blackburne, was 'to assist in the maintenance of a powerful British Commonwealth of Nations' and ensure that the ties of friendship survived into the postcolonial era.[6] In 1948 the British Film Institute sponsored a conference on 'The Film in Colonial Development'; here the consensus was that the success of development film depended on the production process being Africanised.[7]

The Africanisation process was set in motion by the Film School held in Accra in 1948–9 and after that by the emergence of the Gold Coast and Nigerian Film Units, in which Africans were mainly employed as technicians. While the CFU pulled its crews out of Africa in 1950, some agency services continued to be provided till 1955, when the colonies were asked to finance their own film production. The CFU changed its name to the Overseas Film and Television Centre and transformed itself into a service station for the autonomous production units in the colonies and a training centre for film and television crews. The British connection remained.

The CFU in West Africa might have been intent on the uplift of the 'backward masses' but the educated elites were marching to a different drum. Fired by ideas of nationalism, anti-imperialism and pan-Africanism and influenced by experiences in the US and the UK, African elites were intent on seizing the moment. The Atlantic Charter had given them a potent political vocabulary with which to challenge the legitimacy of British rule. They were also quick to challenge the continuance of visual imperialism, the projecting of Britain's role in Africa in terms of a civilising mission that had been characteristic of feature films from *Sanders of the River* (1935) to *Men of Two Worlds* (1946) and the British government-sponsored documentaries *Men of Africa* (1940) and *Here Is the Gold Coast* (1947). The West African Students' Union in London complained to the Colonial Office about *Men of Two Worlds* for its message that, in the pursuit of a modernisation project in East Africa, a highly educated African could never quite break free of traditions that would prevent him from being the equal of the white man in the modern world. In West Africa itself the radical anti-imperialist press fanned the fires of confrontation. The volatility was not confined to the educated elites. Ordinary Africans, bombarded by war propaganda, had supported the war effort, dug for victory and put up with wartime deprivations. More than 1 million Africans had fought in World War II. Now returning soldiers were expecting to be rewarded for their efforts. In West Africa there was a revolution of rising expectations.

In the Gold Coast the swollen-shoot virus was attacking the lifeblood of the economy, the cocoa plant. When the Agriculture Department instituted a drastic campaign against the virus, it sought the aid of the cinema officer of the Gold Coast information branch, which resulted in the film *Swollen Shoot* (1946). The CFU assisted with the scripting and editing. The film showed the diseased leaves and pods that result when the trees are planted too close together and sunlight cannot penetrate. An agricultural officer, a village chief and several cocoa farmers are all involved in the story; the farmer who does not 'cut to control' is reduced to poverty, the wise farmer prospers. The Agriculture Department's campaign generated mass rural discontent in the cocoa districts of southern Ghana, which was exploited by Kwame Nkrumah, who had returned to Ghana at the end of 1947 at the request of the newly formed United Gold Coast Convention (UGCC). This party, composed of lawyers, merchants, British trained scholars and powerful chiefs, had been formed in 1947 with the goal of bringing about self-government in the shortest possible time for the Gold Coast.[8] Dissatisfied with the elitism and gradualism of the UGCC, Nkrumah broke away and formed the Convention People's Party (CPP) in 1949, with the motto 'self-government now'. Nkrumah introduced a new-style mass political party drawing support from the disaffected masses, including the cocoa farmers, who flocked to the CPP banner, along with youth organisations, trade unions and veterans.[9]

Other films that have an obvious link with the political and economic unrest in the Gold Coast are *Pig Farming* (1950) and *Modern Homes for Africans* (c.1948). In Accra in February 1948 a peaceful protest by disgruntled ex-servicemen related to the non-payment of promised pensions and the lack of employment opportunities turned into a riot when they were fired upon by police. The incident is seen as marking the beginning of the process of independence for the Gold Coast as Ghana and provided martyrs for a nascent political movement.[10] It is not a stretch to see a connection between the riot of 1948 and *Pig Farming*, for the film shows how a resettlement officer in Accra helps an ex-serviceman to use his gratuity wisely by investing in pig farming. He first takes a course at Pokoase farm arranged for him by a resettlement officer in Accra; then, upon graduation, starts his own profitable piggery, which encourages his friend to also embark on pig farming. *Modern Homes for Africans* addresses the urban housing crisis in Accra, and a 1947 Cinemagazine item shows homes being constructed from laterite bricks in Kumasi.[11]

DEVELOPING SELF-RELIANCE, BREAKING TRADITIONAL GROUND AND PLANTING THE SEEDS OF PROGRESS

The Mass Education Report had recommended the production of films to promote organisations like co-operative societies, explaining their principles and functions and the benefits that might accrue to the community; and to popularise small-scale industrial undertakings and cottage industries showing the social and economic advantages they might bring.[12] It also recommended that those who had had a more advanced education should be seen devoting themselves to mass-education work.[13] *Weaving in Togoland* (1948), *Better Pottery* (1948) and *Good Business* (1947) can all be seen to follow these guidelines.

Weaving in Togoland (1948): 1) Demonstration of weaving on broader loom; 2) Chief admires cloth (courtesy of British Pathé)

Two Gold Coast films made about rural industries were designed to modernise traditional practices, one weaving, and the other pottery. In both we see the exercise of individual initiative to break 'traditional ground'. In *Weaving in Togoland*, students from Achimota College, in co-operation with the chief, demonstrate more advanced methods to increase productivity and quality using a wider, more modern loom. The villagers accept the innovation and spinning and weaving become a full-time industry. More cotton is grown, producing more work for dyers. Material prosperity ensues. Before the new looms, there were fewer than 100 children at the village school, but now there are 200 – there are more teachers, bigger buildings and a new infant school. Diet is improved as more varieties of food become available at the local market and better-quality stone houses are built. *Weaving in Togoland* was adapted for showing to non-African audiences under the title *Weaving in a Gold Coast Village* and in 1949 *Weaving in Togoland* featured in a British Pathé newsreel.[14] *Better Pottery* opens with a woman making pots by hand, 'a method as old as the craft itself', but an enterprising man, Awasu, grows rich and prosperous by introducing the factory method; he has a moulding shed and a kiln and hires the villagers, men and women, to work for him. The narrator stresses that the workers are 'well rewarded for their labour'.

The Nigerian film *Good Business* is designed both to promote the co-operative business model and the historic new Cocoa Marketing Board. During the colonial period, the British promoted co-operatives as a strategic tool to group rural producers into clusters, so that essential export commodities such as cocoa could be collected more cost effectively. Marketing boards originated in wartime arrangements for the orderly marketing of West African produce and the protection of UK supplies of raw materials. In 1947 the Nigerian Legislative Council established under the Richards Constitution approved the establishment of the Cocoa Marketing Board, the first of a number of such boards introduced into Nigeria with the aim of establishing producer prices and farmers' incomes through fixing prices at remunerative levels. Marketing boards were to constitute the main instrument of agricultural price policy in Nigeria till 1986.[15]

The thin storyline of *Good Business* dramatises the stages through which Lawani's cocoa harvest passes, from picking to marketing and export. On business matters Lawani consults his son, Belo, who has been to school. The commentary talks of farmers sticking together to get good prices. 'Lawani is a wise man because he realises that alone he is weak but several farmers together are strong and important.' The cocoa beans are fermented and put out to dry in a compound. Belo then takes the beans to sell at the co-operative society, where they are weighed and graded by 'the trustworthy society', which pays the correct rate, and invests ten shillings with the society. Belo helps his father with the bookwork and Lawani attends a co-op meeting in the evening. Lawani and the secretary are then sent to resell the beans to the marketing union. Here he sees the completion of the whole marketing process as he learns that his union has been allocated 400 tons of shipping space in a boat scheduled to depart in forty-eight hours. The climax of the operation comes when we see the cocoa being taken by lorries and trains and then loaded onto the ship.[16] 'The whole business, from farm to ship's hold, is entirely in the hands of Nigerians.'

Good Business, described by one Colonial Office official as 'a most valuable account of an achievement of the kind that home and foreign critics of British colonial rule usually claim to be non-existent',[17] was adapted for showing to non-African audiences under the title *Nigerian Cocoa Farmer* (1948).[18] Like *Weaving in Togoland*, it was used as national and international propaganda for the Colonial Office's post-war policy of developmentalism and the rehabilitation of the image of Britain as a benevolent trustee.

Village Development (1948) is a classic of the post-war community-development model as promoted in *Mass Education in African Society*. The Mass Education Report stresses repeatedly that the emphasis should be on the education of the community as a whole, and that the villagers themselves should be encouraged to take the initiative. 'Some colonial communities, for example, already take a great pride in the sanitary conditions of their villages ...' and showing the accomplishments of one village might encourage other villages to follow suit.[19] (The term 'mass education' was replaced after the war by 'community development' with the United Nations Educational, Scientific and Cultural Organisation (UNESCO) preferring 'fundamental education'. Mass education was thought to have an unfortunate political resonance hinting at 'an inferior kind of education specially designed for primitive peoples').[20]

When the CFU team consulted with government departments in Lagos, one suggestion was that films could be enlisted to promote specific development projects: wells, roads, dispensaries. The locale chosen was the Udi Division of Eastern Nigeria where the District Officer, E. R. Chadwick, was a keen pioneer in the field of functional education.[21] Since his arrival in Udi in 1942, Chadwick had been responsible for a number of social initiatives: a leper colony, roads and bridges, successful mass-literacy campaigns, co-operative shops, dispensaries, maternity homes and, finally, water supplies, all projects planned and carried out by various villages. When the first small film on road-building proved useful in motivating intervillage competition, the CFU team of director Lionel Snazelle and cameraman Freddie Lagden returned to Udi Division. There they scripted and shot more footage on development in Udi. The exposed film, together with a full script, was sent to CFU headquarters in London for processing, editing and the addition of an English commentary.[22] In the completed film, *Village Development*, Chadwick is shown consulting with village elders and chiefs to find out what development projects the local people wanted.

The success of *Village Development* led to the Crown Film Unit's dramatised documentary, *Daybreak in Udi* (1950), directed by Terry Bishop and set in the same district, using the same cast. The film opens with a mass-literacy class in a village compound in the Unama District of Udi Division, then cuts to Chadwick (himself) shown adjudicating a family legal matter in his office. Two young African teachers arrive to seek his help to build a maternity home. He agrees to meet with the villagers but encounters opposition from an elder, Eze (Joseph Amalu), who feels it is a trick to take their land, setting up the dramatic conflict between old versus new, mistrust versus trust, traditional versus modern. But the people agree to clear land, make blocks and proceed with the scheme. Eze and his followers threaten the workers, but fail to stop the project. A midwife from town is hired and the new hospital gets its first patient. When night falls, Eze and other dissidents, dressed in masks, try to frighten the midwife away. But when Iruka (Fanny Elumuze), one of the young teachers, throws boiling water at the intruders, it is they who take flight and the baby is born safely. At the opening of the maternity home Eze is seen sitting near Mr Chadwick, symbolising a rapprochement between the traditional and the modern. As the film ends, Chadwick tells the viewer that progress brings 'power, spirit, unlimited and unknown possibilities and destinations' and suggests that progress should be the ultimate goal of their society. *Daybreak in Udi* is featured in UNESCO's 1953 *Reference Library Catalogue*,[23] and won an Academy Award in 1949 for the Best Documentary Feature Film, gaining priceless international publicity for the repackaging of Brand Britain as a benevolent trustee.

When the Crown Film Unit arrived to start filming, the venture was attacked in the nationalist press as 'yet another film unit come out to our country to depict us as naked savages and unfit to rule ourselves'.[24] Nigerian journalist and film critic, J. Koyinde Vaughan expressed his frustration about the continued centrality of the 'civilising mission' in colonial films, which 'extolled the virtues of her colonizers, police officers, District Commissioners, Civil Servants and Settlers'. These heroes are portrayed as the embodiment of civilisation. The black man's role is to be 'patronized, uplifted and governed'.[25]

The Colonial Office policy on *Mass Education in African Society* is mouthed by Mr Chadwick when discussing the maternity-home project with its two young proponents.

> I know your village well, the people really want progress but they are not quite sure yet how to go about it … . Your people are farming people; farmers all over the world are naturally suspicious of new ideas … . This community development is a new thing; it requires the leadership of men and women like yourselves who have seen a higher standard of living but haven't lost touch with the people they come from … .

Chadwick went on to caution them against doing anything that would 'interfere with the traditional ways of doing things in the village' and suggested to Irika that she should try to persuade the village women to form a co-operative society to pay the midwife's salary.[26]

What commentators on *Daybreak in Udi* have so far overlooked is the significance of the mass-literacy class that opens the film. This reflects the importance placed on adult literacy in *Mass Education in African Society*, which reported that

> The evidence from the Dutch Colonies, and from the Chinese and Russian mass education movements, is overwhelmingly strong on the importance of adult literacy as an essential means of achieving all-round progress. We endorse that view and therefore, place adult literacy in the forefront of the mass education programme.[27]

COLONIAL FILM UNIT: PUBLIC-HEALTH FILMS AND THE EVOLVING INTERNATIONAL SUPERSTRUCTURE

Public-health films are a special subgenre of the instructional film that has had a long and continuing history. Before the war both international organisations and the Colonial Office were involved in fostering instructional health films. According to the CFU's George Pearson, Sellers's chief assistant in London, 'health education is definitely the First Directive of the Film Unit' and 'the noblest purpose in our film programme'.[28] But health-education films can also be seen against a wider background of the growing awareness of international health issues that sparked initiatives in the early twentieth century by the Rockefeller Foundation, which accelerated in the wake of World War II. This is exemplified in the work of United Nations International Children's Emergency Fund (UNICEF)[29] and the World Health Organisation (WHO)[30] and in the broader case of films in fundamental education, UNESCO. Indeed, the link with colonial instructional films is very strong, given that UNESCO's first Director-General (1946–8), Julian Huxley, had been a prime mover in the promotion of development films in the interwar years, and a member of the Adult and Mass Education Sub-Committee responsible for the report, *Mass Education in African Society*.[31]

The objective of *Yaws* (1945), a ten-minute black-and-white silent, is to show how the Gold Coast medical service solved the problem of the treatment of yaws among a widely scattered population. The film opens with some searing close-ups of yaws victims. A van brings a vaccination team to a village; the equipment is unpacked; and a 'living scene' of the vaccination process projected: a woman is vaccinated in the backside; a young boy leads a blind woman with a stick. The co-operation in the campaign between the chief, the African medical assistants and European officials is emphasised. The general structure of health services in the colonies at the end of the war comprised, on the one hand, fixed urban centres, a hospital, dispensary and treatment centre, as we will see in the first post-war CFU film in Nigeria, *Fight Tuberculosis in the Home* (1946), and, on the other, mobile units serving rural areas and performing large-scale mass vaccinations as seen in *Yaws*.

The mass-treatment approach, as exemplified in *Yaws*, has received a critical press from Megan Vaughan in her book *Curing Their Ills*. She lamented that people were being herded into vaccination tents, treated as 'subjects', with cultural and social sensitivities ignored. But, as she also notes, 'In this sense, the colonial medical campaign was very little different to medical campaigns in Britain and elsewhere, and conformed to the stereotype of biomedical practice as objectifying and alienating.'[32]

In the historical context, medical anthropology was not as sophisticated as it is today; and, given the extent of the epidemics, the shortage of doctors and dearth of rural facilities, the mobile-vaccination approach bore an irrefutable logic. In the global context, UNICEF's first interventions in Nigeria were related to endemic disease control through mass campaigns, beginning with leprosy and yaws. In August 1956 WHO's first meeting to co-ordinate yaws campaigns took place in Accra, where a regional approach was adopted.[33]

The first CFU health film made in Nigeria was the Sellers's production, *Fight Tuberculosis in the Home*, a thirty-minute black-and-white and, in the original version, silent film. TB was becoming a menace in crowded urban areas in many colonies, spreading rapidly due to crowded living conditions, inadequate ventilation and insufficient attention to hygiene. In some places the mortality rate was as high as 50 per cent of deaths from all causes. The subject had been given priority by the medical department in Lagos and the film was sponsored by Britain's National Association for the Prevention of Tuberculosis.

The film is set in an urban compound, where a builder, his wife and three children and six labourers share a two-roomed house. The louvres are stuffed with rags to keep out draughts; a sick man with a racking cough spits in the courtyard; the sputum gets mixed with the sand that the builder's wife is using to scour the dirty dishes. One of the labourers and the son of the house go to the hospital, where they are diagnosed as having TB by a European doctor. An African technician examines the sputum through a microscope, but the European doctor comes to the lab to double-check his diagnosis. The doctor then phones a European official, who dispatches an African sanitary inspector to the family's home. The remainder of the film is concerned with showing how the living quarters are cleaned up, alternative accommodation found for the labourers and the boy nursed back to health. His bed is put on the veranda where he can get plenty of fresh air. A set of crockery is set aside for his sole use and a bowl of disinfectant provided for spitting. Significantly, after the African sanitary inspector has directed all the operations, a European official turns up just to recap on all the instructions that have been given. The boy, even while sitting listlessly on the veranda, is always seen with a book in his hand and sometimes reading it. The strong link between the Colonial Film Unit and UNESCO is underlined by the fact that *Fight Tuberculosis in the Home* was added to the UNESCO film library and appears in its 1953 catalogue with added sound.[34]

FILM AS AN INSTRUMENT OF SOCIAL AND POLITICAL PROPAGANDA: EDUCATION FOR CITIZENSHIP

The Grierson tradition of using film as an instrument of propaganda to provide public information and education 'to bridge the gap between the citizen and the wider world' was a driving force in the work of the CFU. Grierson had argued that cinema should be a 'deliberate social instrument ... outside on the barricades of social action'.[35] It was an indispensable part of the administration of the modern state and, as developed in *Mass Education in African Society*, of Britain's colonial empire, especially so since the majority of its African colonial subjects were illiterate.

The Mass Education Report noted that the acceleration of social and economic change happening in Africa (and elsewhere) demanded an education in citizenship, which would enable people to see themselves as part of larger communities that went beyond 'narrow sectionalism'. The report went on to recommend films about local government and the production of news films of world, regional and local interest, promoting an awareness of what was going on in their regions, provinces and districts. This all aimed to broaden horizons in general and develop a '"national" outlook' among people of a territory.[36]

The Mass Education Report did not anticipate how swiftly local government would proceed toward self-government. In Nigeria, where the political landscape was dominated by the sharp ethnic divisions of the east, west and north and the numerical dominance of the Islamic north, the road to Independence would be particularly tortuous. The first constitutional steps are paraded in *Towards True Democracy* (1947), a record of the first session of the Nigerian Legislative Council under the Richards Constitution, a film made in conjunction with *Western House of Assembly* (1947), showing the first session of the Western House of Assembly of the Nigerian Western Province. *Towards True Democracy* showed 'the way in which Nigerians are being initiated into the tasks of self-government' and emphasised the role of the British not only in modernising Nigeria with technological infrastructure but also teaching the people to be 'good citizens'. The Richards Constitution was highly unpopular because Africans were not involved in the consultations and most of the chosen Africans were either chiefs or nominees supported by the Governor, with the members for Lagos boycotting the assembly. In 1948 the new Governor, Sir John Macpherson, announced plans to revise the document.

The cinemagazines produced by the CFU between 1946 and 1949 were government propaganda to promote the development and welfare projects as well as the mission to enlarge the horizons of the target audience. *Cinemagazine No. 14* (1947) features 'Agriculture in a Nigerian African School'; *No. 17* (1947) combines 'Nigeria – A New Industry, Fruit Drinks' and 'Malaya – New Homes for the People'; *No. 23* (1947) has 'Nigeria – a Modern Method of Palm Oil Extraction' followed by 'Gold Coast – Houses That Last'; while in *No. 27* (1947), the topic is 'Gold Coast Government starts canning factory'. Cinemagazine items focusing on regional connections included *No. 10*, 'Inter-colonial Sports Nigeria v Gold Coast, Lagos 1947', and *No. 7* (1947), which combines coverage of an East African spinning and weaving centre in Nairobi with the 1st Boy Scouts' jamboree in West Africa held in Lagos in 1947, opened by the Chief Scout, Lord Rowallan.

Some cinemagazine segments continue the policy started by the CFU during the war, aiming to reinforce the ties between the colonies and the metropole, stressing the idea of inclusiveness that was so important in soliciting African support for the war effort and, in the changing post-war landscape, inculcating a sense of a Commonwealth identity. This strategy is seen in *Nurse Ademola* (1943), which featured the daughter of the Alake of Abeokuta training at Guy's Hospital, London. *West African Editors* (1944) showed a party of West African journalists on a visit to Britain in 1943, which included the anti-imperialist Nnamdi Azikwe, editor of the radical *West African Pilot*, who in 1944 founded the first political party in Nigeria with nationwide pretensions, the National Council of Nigeria and the Cameroons (NCNC);

Durbar at Accra (1949):
British Governor, Sir Gerald
Creasy, speaking at the
installation of a new chief
(Ga Manche) (courtesy of
British Pathé)

it ultimately became identified with the southern region and Azikwe himself was to become first President of Nigeria. Post-war examples include *No. 27*, 'African Students Visit Fire Brigade HQ', *No. 4* (1947), where African students are guests of the Federation of Young Farmers' Club in Lampeter in Wales, and *No. 16* (1947), which sees African students engaged in a classic English ritual, a tea party at the offices of the Royal Empire Society, where they meet the newly appointed Governor of Nigeria Sir John Macpherson and his wife prior to their departure for Nigeria. The vintage example of this strategy is the celebrated *London Bus* (1950) in which two African students travel around London on the iconic red double-decker.

'Durbar Ga State Council', *Cinemagazine No. 25* (1949) presents rich visual imagery of the 'ornamentalism' of empire, with the colonial peoples being included in a larger entity than just the village or nascent state, but the British empire in its uneasy transit to the Commonwealth.[37] When the new Ga Manche, chief of the ethnic group traditionally associated with the Accra region, is presented to the Governor, the viewer is treated to bands playing, crowds milling, groups singing and dancing, lots of national robes and umbrellas, drumming and an elephant float. The Governor arrives with a mounted escort of lancers. The chiefs then file past and shake hands with Governor and Lady Creasy. The Governor formally welcomes the new Ga Manche, and wishes him every success as the 'voice-of-God' commentator intones, 'this is a symbol of a growing partnership in West Africa'. The Governor drives off happy 'that the Ga state has a new paramount chief who will lead his people with understanding and wisdom'. This imperial pageantry was reproduced by British Pathé as 'Durbar at Accra' (1949), but the *realpolitik* was in the noises off.[38] In January 1948, a Ga chief had organised a general boycott of all European imports and this had been followed by the game-changing Accra riots in February. In 1949, the year of the durbar, Nkrumah founded the CPP, Africa's first mass political party. In 1950 Nkrumah was to be imprisoned after he called for countrywide boycotts and a strike, in the name of 'positive action'. When general elections were held in 1951, the CPP won decisively despite the imprisonment of Nkrumah, whose release to form the colony's first African government was filmed by British Pathé. When the Gold Coast became Ghana at Independence in 1957, it was not the end of the durbar. In 1961 the British Pathé newsreel carried the item 'Durbar for Queen', which shows the Queen and Prince Philip attending two durbars in Ghana, one in Kumasi and the other at Cape Coast, during an official visit.[39] The ornamentalism continued after the midnight hour.

TOWARDS THE END OF EMPIRE: THE TIES THAT BIND

In the reinventing of Britain's relationship with its soon to be liberated colonies, great importance was placed on the mystique of royalty and pomp and ceremony, as illustrated in the above story of the durbar, but also on higher-education connections, the visual nurturing of wartime memories and sports diplomacy.

West Africans had long been lobbying the Colonial Office for universities to be established in West Africa but, while indirect rule through traditional chiefs remained the political pattern, it was considered counterproductive to encourage the growth of an independent African intelligentsia who would have no place in that system. An intelligentsia developed anyway as determined Africans found their way to British and American universities. The introduction of the Colonial Development and Welfare Act in 1940 signalled a radical change in policy. As it had become clear that self-government would happen sooner rather than later, it was also both practical and politic to establish universities in West Africa to train the new elite. That members of this elite have affiliations with the British education system was also highly desirable. The Colonial Office was distrustful of the radicalising effect that American universities had had on West African students. Both Azikiwe and Nkrumah were American-educated. With Independence around the corner, the goal was now to ensure that the independent West African countries would remain within the Commonwealth, and a crucial plank in that policy was to introduce university colleges in West Africa with strong links to the British university system.[40]

Opening of University College – Gold Coast (1948) captures the ceremonial flourishes of this event, which took place on 11 October. The visual archive includes the speech of the Governor Sir Gerald Creasy, paraphrased in the commentary, the obligatory garden party, and bands and drumming as well as a significant combination of traditional chiefs from Ashanti and the north, representing that distinctive feature of British colonial Africa – indirect rule-plus representatives of the backbone of the economy, cocoa farmers. The commentary talks of close co-operation between African and European elements in the inauguration of this university;[41] and this in the year that the Gold Coast led the charge of Britain's African colonies towards 'self-government now'. On 17 November 1948, the Secretary of State for the Colonies Arthur Creech Jones turned the first sod at the founding of Nigeria's first university college, a milestone recorded in the CFU's *Foundation Day Ceremony at Ibadan University College (Ibadan, Nigeria)* (1949). African and European staff in academic robes file past the seated chiefs; and an exhibition of drawings and models of the new university and hospital is on display. In *West Africa's New University* (c. 1949), students are shown attending lectures in a temporary building; featuring both an African and a European lecturer are featured. The physical university may not yet have been built but on celluloid university education on the British model had commenced in Nigeria.[42]

The Colonial Film Unit helped to ensure that the victory of the Allies in World War II, to which so many Africans had contributed, was enshrined in the collective, affective memory; films that make such direct contact with the emotions are a potent force in the process. The mythologising began with *Victory Parade* (1946) and continued in the Gold Coast in *Remembrance Day* (1940s?) and *Grand Military Tattoo – Accra* (1950s?).[43] At the Remembrance Day service in Accra at the Cenotaph, the Governor, European officers and police and African chiefs all lay wreaths. The highlights of the *Grand Military Tattoo* included marching bands, jeeps pulling gun carriages, drill displays and two men on motorbikes firing at bottles as they passed. The intertitle 'Modern Battle' was followed by a 'Mock battle with gun carriage, model tanks, and Japanese officer killing wounded soldiers'.[44]

Sport has proved to be one of the most enduring links between Britain and the former colonies in the postcolonial era, a masterstroke of public diplomacy. *Cine-magazine No. 4* (1946) focuses on a 'University football match in which A. Osokway from Nigeria leads Oxfords against Cambridge'; and in *No. 5* (1946), a Nigerian prince takes part in the long jump and high jump in a Britain vs France athletics meet in London. But the greatest efforts were made in the realm of football; and today, with many of the former colonies probably more interested in England's Premier League than their own football competitions, that strategy has certainly worked. We can see the seeds being sown in the CFU films *Nigerians v Leytonstone* (1949), in which a Nigerian team plays Leytonstone, which had twice won the then amateur FA Cup, and the riveting *Nigerian Footballers in England* (1949). According to Phil Vasili, between 1949 and 1959, Britain made a determined effort to expand sporting ties, with teams from the Gold Coast and Uganda following in Nigeria's path.[45] The football tour not only served as good propaganda for Britain's colonial development and welfare mission but showing the film in Nigeria also helped to promote a sense of national identity (as recommended in *Mass Education in African Society*). The *Annual Report on the Colonies in 1950* noted that the football tour of England 'aroused nationwide interest and enthusiasm in Nigeria';[46] and, as Tom Rice reports in his comprehensive entry on *Nigerian Footballers in England* on the 'Colonial Film: Moving Images of the British Empire' website, an editorial in *West Africa* suggested that the tour 'had also made a small contribution to Nigerian nationhood by focussing the attention of Nigerians on "our" team'.[47]

AFTER THE CFU

The 1944 report *Mass Education in African Society* recommended that:

> An initial step towards the creation of colonial film producing units is the training of selected colonial personnel who have a genuine appreciation of the heritage of their peoples as represented in their music, customs, folklore, arts and history, and an insight into their present social problems. A high standard of general education would obviously be a necessary qualification for selection and training.[48]

In 1948–9, a six-month film training school was conducted in Accra, with trainees from the Gold Coast and Nigeria. The Nigerians included Adamu Halilu Fajemisin, A. J. Atigba and Malam Yakubu Aina. The aim was to train pupils to a standard that would enable them to film local events in newsreel fashion and also to produce simple instructional films of more lasting importance. Instruction was in 16mm film with some assistance from a CFU 35mm unit. Three student productions have been recorded, *Basket Making* (1946), attributed to the Gold Coast students and *Copra* (1949), attributed to the West African students. In *The Good Samaritan* (1949), produced by the Nigerian students 'entirely without guidance', the chief passes by the beggar on the roadside but an ordinary citizen comes to his assistance! *A Film School in West Africa* (1949) showed the school in progress.[49] The training scheme was successful to the extent that the Gold Coast Film Unit was organised on a professional basis in 1949 immediately following the course and a Nigerian Film Unit followed a year later. Europeans continued to lead both units.

The Gold Coast Film Unit led by Sean Graham, a Grierson admirer, set out to make more sophisticated social-message films, with more complex characters and more interesting narratives that were rooted in the local customs and culture rather than the rudimentary Mr Wise and Mr Foolish formats of the CFU films in the Sellers style. The first attempt *Amenu's Child* (1950), written and produced by Graham, was made for the medical department's campaign to reduce infant mortality and formed the centrepiece of a mass-education campaign organised by the public relations officer and the Department of Social Welfare 'to train village leaders in Child Welfare'.[50] The film uses the traditional idiom of storytelling that was a popular art form in the Gold Coast. Before the titles a drummer beats two talking drums as the narrator says, 'Listen and gather round ...'. Set in Togoland, the film describes how Amenu's child, Essi, dies because her mother consults a traditional doctor instead of taking her to the clinic. 'It is the story of how new ways of feeding children came to an African village ... it may be true, it may not be true ...'. In *Colonial Cinema*, the Oxford-educated G. B. Odunton, an African member of the Gold Coast Unit, praised *Amenu's Child* for trying to avoid the patronising commentaries and simplistic plots favoured by the CFU.[51]

Amenu's Child was used in conjunction with both interpersonal communication, instructors who had prepared notes, and other forms of media like posters and pamphlets. This multi-pronged approach, with the addition of broadcasting, had been recommended in the Mass Education Report. While the Gold Coast's chief social development officer reported that the campaign featuring *Amenu's Child* was highly successful,[52] its attempt at authenticity did not win over Koyinde Vaughan: 'This naive film, with its stereotyped characters and all-too-simple presentation of the conflict of ideas, gives as is usual with Colonial Office films a rosier picture of life under British rule than the facts will allow.'[53] *Amenu's Child*, like Seller's *Fight Tuberculosis in the Home*, achieved the distinction of being added to UNESCO's film library.[54]

Graham's biggest international success was *The Boy Kumasenu* (1952), the first full-length feature film to be made by a government film unit in West Africa. The film, its Eurocentric feel highlighted by the use of a narrator and a score by British composer Elizabeth Lutyens, is the parable of a boy fisherman who abandons his village for the excitement of Accra and in economic desperation embarks on a life of petty crime. (Juvenile delinquency was a theme flagged for possible film treatment in the Mass Education Report.) Kumasenu is rescued from delinquency by an African medical doctor who arranges for him to be apprenticed to a driver of motorboats. He is reunited with his family and, as a fisherman using a motorboat – in a heavy piece of symbolism – combines the old world and the new. The film was praised by Jean Rouch for not presenting the intrusive Western culture as 'synonymous with progress' to the detriment of African traditions.[55]

The Gold Coast Film Unit made other social-message films aimed directly at local audiences rather than courting the international community employing what is now described as the edutainment format. This can be seen in *Progress in Kojokrom* (1953), showing 'taxation and the dependence on it of developmental work', another theme straight out of the Mass Education Report, and the entertaining *Mr. Mensah Builds a House* (1955), a propaganda film to promote the government's rural housing-assistance scheme.[56] However, there proved to be almost too much social realism in the nursing-recruitment film *Theresa, the Story of a Nurse in Training* (1955), described by Rouch as 'a shattering document about the difficult life of nurses'. After some deliberation, the government reluctantly agreed to the film's release, 'fearing that there would not be a young woman in Ghana with enough courage to embark on such a testing career'.[57] In contrast, *I Will Speak English* (1955) is a straightforward English-language lesson, an exemplary demonstration of the communicative theory of foreign-language teaching and a pedagogical advance on the opening sequence in *Daybreak in Udi*. The Gold Coast Film Unit took the social-message film to a new level, pushing the genre beyond the simplistic binary opposition of the Mr Wise and Mr Foolish format, which in a colonial setting appears racist and degrading, and looked forward to the flowering of the social-message film in the development communication films of the late twentieth and early twenty-first centuries.

The Federal Film Unit, which succeeded the CFU in Nigeria, was more typical of government information and public-relations film units found in other parts of the empire and Commonwealth, promoting and explaining government programmes and projects, emphasising modernisation initiatives and memorialising events of ceremonial and political significance as well as continuing with mass education/community development projects. The Federal Film Unit was headed from 1950 to 1960 by Lionel Snazelle, a former CFU employee, and in its organisation reflected the colony's federal structure, with ten mobile film units: three in Kaduna, two in Ibadan, three in Enugu and two in Lagos. Towards the end of the decade, the information services of western and northern Nigeria produced public-relations films promoting a strong visual identity of their own regions, contributing to the ethnopolitical consciousness that continues to be a characteristic of Nigeria in the twenty-first century.

In keeping with the primacy of health-education films in the CFU's original remit, the first major production of the Nigerian Film Unit was *Smallpox* (1950), which Snazelle scripted and directed in association with the Nigerian medical department. *Smallpox* addresses two widespread problems in this era of the mass-vaccination campaigns: people hiding when vaccination teams arrive and the failure to report smallpox outbreaks in some villages. Snazelle's script followed the hackneyed and by now controversial Mr Foolish format. When a sanitary inspector arrives in a Nigerian village to vaccinate people against the disease, 'Foolish Alabi' refuses and takes off to visit his friend Tijani in a neighbouring village, where there just happens to be a smallpox outbreak. Although Tijani is very ill, Alabi fails to report the outbreak and soon after he returns home, falls ill. After being diagnosed with smallpox, he finally tells the doctor about the outbreak in Tijani's village. When a vaccination team is sent in, Tijani and several others hide. 'This ignorant concealment', says the narrator 'is one of the main reasons why this disease is given a big chance to spread.' Alabi recovers in hospital but Tijani goes blind. Two graduates of the CFU film school, J. A. Otigbah and Mallam Yakuba Auna, were production assistants on the film, which, despite its ideological shortcomings, is reported to have enjoyed great success in Nigeria, helping many people to overcome their fear of vaccination. It was subsequently shown widely in other colonies, with particular success in Tanganyika.[58]

The Nigerian Film Unit continued to make films of the village-development genre epitomised by the CFU's *Village Development* (1948) and then reinvented for international propaganda purposes in *Daybreak in Udi*. What is remarkable about the Nigerian Film Unit's approach to the genre is the contrast between *Community Development in Awgu Division, Nigeria* (1949) and *Nigeria Community Development in Ahoada Division* (1950). In the Awgu Division the white District Officer continues in the tradition of Mr Chadwick and is shown orchestrating housing, health, irrigation and transport projects organised by individual villages in conference with the elders and councillors.[59] But just one year later in the Ahoada Division version there is no white district officer in sight. It is Nigerian officials who are seen consulting with the elders on various projects, and in one sequence with a group of women who appear to be senior village figures. Projects include the building of roads and of cement steps down to the river where previously women collecting water had to negotiate a treacherously slippery slope; the construction of two community schools and of new houses in the village; the widening of village streets and the cleaning up of the village market, including an inspection of the butcher's stall. The intertitle tells us 'The Chief Is Pleased at the Progress in Building and Street Widening'. In the 'Elele Domestic Science Class' sequence we see girls washing, using steam irons, sewing (with one operating a Singer sewing machine), embroidering, cooking and seated at a table eating the fruits of their labour, with broad smiles on their faces. In a baby-feeding lesson, three girls seated in a row are shown spooning some liquid into the babies' mouths with Ovaltine and Nestle's tins in evidence on the bench in front of them. The last scene, a cameo of the 'Englishness of Empire', echoes the CFU's very first film, *Mr. English at Home* (1940). The camera zooms in on a newly completed modern brick house. In front of the house a man seated in an armchair is reading a newspaper; his wife pours him a glass of water from a jug on a table before sitting in a corresponding chair to embroider while their two children sit on the ground playing cards.[60] *Mass Education in African Society* noted that

> the Colonial Film Unit's 'Mr. English' gave a picture of English life which, to many Gold Coast Africans who saw it, was a vivid revelation of some of the basic facts in European civilisation of which they had hitherto only a vague conception ... .[61]

Here we have some more 'vivid revelations' being mimicked in an African setting.

Education for citizenship is the goal of *Count Your Blessings* (1952–3), made to overcome resistance to the 1952 census. The unfortunate Kubara, a census enumerator, gets beaten up and his posters repeatedly pulled down when he tries to explain the census to the village of Nsoka; another enumerator, Ebenezer, encounters a more welcoming environment in Waranya village, where he receives co-operation from the chief's daughter, a primary schoolteacher. But, more broadly, 'education for citizenship' in the context of the runup to Nigerian Independence, inevitably spotlights the vexatious 'national question'. Back in 1944, the Mass Education Report suggested that films be utilised in such broad-brush terms as 'education for citizenship' and the creation of a 'national outlook', not realising how quickly the colonies would be taking the leap into nationhood. And in Nigeria, the political and administrative foundation, on which an organic nation could be built, was particularly fragile. There was no sense of an emerging Nigerian identity or concept of Nigerian citizenship. What the tripartite division of the colony into three distinct ethnic and regional divisions inevitably promoted was ethnonationalism. It is ethnonationalism that we see at work in the struggle to find a constitution that would satisfy competing regional interests, with the protagonists being ethno/ regional political parties. *Nigeria's New Constitution* (1952) sets out to explain the new provisions introduced under the Macpherson Constitution of 1951; the elections to set up regional legislatures in northern, eastern and western Nigeria; and the meeting of the new legislatures at Kaduna, Enugu and Ibadan.[62] There would be two more constitutions before Independence in 1960, with the final version providing a federal structure that it was hoped would balance regional interests, though inevitably the north's numerical dominance would be a potent political factor.

Self Government for Western Nigeria (1958) celebrates this milestone, achieved by the western region in 1957, in an eighty-five-minute colour film produced by the information services of the western region. The new premier of the western region Chief Obafemi Awolowo had written in 1947 in *Path to Nigerian Freedom*, 'Nigeria is not a nation. It is a mere geographical expression',[63] and, in 1950, went on to found the Action Party to advance Yoruba interests in the campaign to oust the British colonisers. That did not stop his pragmatic exploitation of the ornamentalism of empire to heighten the legitimacy of the new government. The visit of the Princess Royal was the highlight of the self-government celebrations, attracting extensive press coverage; and the presentation of a mace to the new legislative council established a symbolic link with the venerable British parliamentary tradition.[64] Obafemi Awolowo had an acute understanding of the importance of the mass media as a government public-relations and information tool, not only to communicate with the citizens of the western region but also as a visual projection of regional identity for local, national and international consumption.

The northern region, too, marked its attainment of regional self-government in 1959 with the release of a public-relations film, *Giant in the Sun*, sponsored by the northern information services, produced by Victor Gove Productions in London and narrated by the distinguished BBC commentator, Wynford Vaughan-Thomas. *Giant in the Sun* is another celebration of ethnonationalism, underscoring the fact that no visible concept of nationhood embraced the whole of Nigeria. The 'giant', which the film introduces to a global plus local audience is not the new nation of Nigeria scheduled to achieve Independence the following year, but the northern region distinguished by its numerical dominance and adherence to Islam. Nigeria was a 'cleft country'[65] before it ever achieved Independence and the cleavages were only being reinforced by the regional film divisions of the Nigerian Film Unit devoting their resources to promoting their own regions on the local and international stage.

Giant in the Sun pays homage to British developmentalism and the beneficence of Britain's colonial stewardship, demonstrating how many new mechanised industries have been introduced, with a series of plants and factories producing items such as textiles, canvas and rubber shoes, cosmetics, confectionery, bottles and tinned foods without losing sight of the older traditions as evidenced in the dye pits of Kano. Traditional methods of pottery and weaving are now being enhanced by the introduction of more modern techniques. Huge new crushing mills have been introduced to beef up the groundnuts export industry, the mainstay of the regional economy. An African doctor ministers to the sick with a nurse in attendance, and local technicians peer through microscopes; Vaughan-Thomas speaks authoritatively of the work of the government in its efforts to control trypanosomiasis affecting humans (as well as Fulani cattle), the fight against leprosy and improvements in health care. The climax of all these developmental efforts is that now Nigeria is on the verge of achieving Independence and becoming part of the British Commonwealth of Nations;[66] for the British government propagandists at the Colonial Office: mission accomplished.

CONCLUSION

The CFU and its offshoots the Gold Coast and Nigerian Film Units managed to adjust their operations with some dexterity as the sands began to shift under the crumbling edifice of the British empire. The West African Film School set in motion the process of Africanisation of film production and gradually the more patronising elements of the development film disappeared in the later work of the Gold Coast and Nigerian Film Units. African film-makers were not to be in at the launch as well as the landing, however, till after Independence. The work in the area of health-education films was of particular interest to UNESCO and films about this and other development issues continue to be produced at both the national and international level by coalitions of state and non-state actors, with a leading role being played today by the British government's Department for International Development. The ideas of Grierson and Stephen Tallents that have had such a formative influence on the role of film in Britain were mirrored in the work of the CFU and its successors. Film had become an essential part of colonial government for many reasons: to manage public opinion; to educate citizens about the workings of modern government, and community development and welfare issues; to promote a sense of national and in Nigeria, regional identity, as well as the encompassing Commonwealth identity; and, following Tallents, as a weapon of public diplomacy to promote a positive image of Britain's colonial administration in the colonies, in the UK and abroad.

NOTES

1. Public Records Office (PRO) National Archives, Colonial Office (hereafter CO) 9847/38/3, R. E. Robinson, [research officer, Colonial Office African studies branch], memorandum, 'Some Recent Trends in Native Administration Policy in the British African Territories', no. 1 [nd; 1947].
2. CAB 21/1690, A. Creech Jones, 'Organisation for Colonial Development', memorandum to Cabinet by the Secretary of State for the Colonies, 2 March 1948.
3. W. M. Hailey, *Native Administration and Political Development in British Tropical Africa*, report by Lord Hailey, with introduction by A. H. M. Kirk-Greene, [London: 1942], rev. edn (Liechtenstein: Nendeln, Kraus Reprint, 1979), p. 305.
4. Colonial Office Advisory Committee on Education in the Colonies, *Mass Education in African Society*, Colonial No. 186, 1944.
5. W. Sellers, 'Address to the British Kinematograph Society, December 1947', *Colonial Cinema* vol.6 no.1, 1948, p. 9.
6. 'The Information Department – Colonial Office Policy and Re-organisation', Blackburne to Jeffries, 11 June 1947, CO 875/42/6143302.
7. British Film Institute, *The Film in Colonial Development; A Report of a Conference* (London: BFI, 1948); Rosaleen Smyth, 'The Post-war Career of the Colonial Film Unit in Africa: 1946–1955', *Historical Journal of Film, Radio and Television* vol. 12 no.2, 1992, pp. 164–5.
8. Kwame Botwe-Asamoah, *Kwame Nkrumah's Politico-cultural Thought and Politics: An African-centered Paradigm for the Second Phase of the African Revolution* (London: Routledge, 2005), p. 101.
9. Francis K. Danquah, 'Sustaining a West African Cocoa Economy: Agricultural Science and the Swollen Shoot Contagion in Ghana, 1936–1965', *African Economic History* no. 31, 2003, p. 43.
10. D. Killingray, 'African Voices from Two World Wars', *Historical Research* vol.74 no. 6, November 2001, p. 442.
11. See <www.film-images.com/searchDB.jsp?page=2&>.
12. Colonial Office, *Mass Education in African Society*, pp. 41–2.
13. Ibid., p.13.
14. See <www.britishPathé.com/record.php?id=59543> accessed 2 August 2010.
15. F. S. Idachaba and G. B. Ayoola, 'Market Intervention Policy in Nigerian Agriculture: An Ex-post Evaluation of the Technical Committee on Produce Prices', *Development Policy Review* vol. 9 no. 3, 1991, p. 285.
16. See <www.colonialfilm.org.uk/node/888>.
17. D. M. Williams to Rigby, 5 August 1947, INF 12/293/105239.
18. See <www.colonialfilm.org.uk/node/759>.
19. Colonial Office, *Mass Education in African Society*, p. 41.
20. Colonial Office Information Department, Notes on Education in the Colonies, Memo no. 24, October 1961.
21. E. R. Chadwick, 'Fundamental Education in Udi Division', *Fundamental Education* vol. 1 no. 4, 1949, pp. 9–21; and E. R. Chadwick, 'Communal Development in Udi Division', *Oversea Education* vol. 19 no. 2, 1948, pp. 627–44.
22. Peggy Medina Giltrow and David R. Giltrow, 'Films of the Colonial Film Unit', paper given at 'Film and Empire' conference , Imperial War Museum, London, 10 April 1981; David

Giltrow, 'Films: Daybreak in Udi. 1948. Central Office of Information Crown Film Unit. Terry Bishop', *American Anthropologist* vol. 81 no. 3, September 1979, pp. 736–7.

23. United Nations Educational Scientific and Cultural Organisation, *Film Reference Library Catalogue*, September 1953, UNESCO, Mass Communication Department, p. 26, <unesdoc.unesco.org/images/0017/001795/179538eb.pdf>.

24. T. Bishop, 'Film-making in Udi', *Spectator*, 1 April 1949, p. 431.

25. J. Koyinde Vaughan, 'The African and the Cinema', in L. Hughes (ed.), *An African Treasury* (New York: Crown, 1960), p. 87.

26. See <www.colonialfilm.org.uk/node/252>.

27. Colonial Office, *Mass Education in African Society*, p. 14.

28. George Pearson, 'Health Education by Film in Africa', *Health Education Journal* vol. 7 no. 1, March 1949, p. 39.

29. United Nations International Children's Emergency Fund (UNICEF) *1946–2006 Sixty Years for Children*, November 2006, E document, <www.unicef.org/publications/files/1946-2006_Sixty_Years_ for_Children.pdf> accessed 14 August 2010.

30. World Health Organisation, *Public Health Work in Africa, Ten Years of Progress*, 1958, Brazzaville, WHO Regional Office for Africa. Supplement 1959, <whqlibdoc.who.int/publications/1948-60/14565.pdf>.

31. Julian S. Huxley, 'Report on the Use of Films for Educational Purposes in East Africa', 1930, CO 323/1252/3025/1; Rosaleen Smyth, 'The Cinema and Britain's African Colonies in the Inter-war Years: The Stirrings of Globalisation', conference on 'Colonial Film: Moving Images of the British Empire', Birkbeck College, University of London, 7–9 July, 2010.

32. Megan Vaughan, *Curing Their Ills* (Cambridge: Polity Press, 1991), p. 52.

33. WHO, *Public Health Work in Africa*.

34. See <unesdoc.unesco.org/images/0017/001795/179538eb.pdf, 26>.

35. Jacquie L'Etang, 'John Grierson and the Public Relations Industry in Britain', *Screening the Past: An International Electronic Journal of Visual Media and History*, 1999, <www.latrobe.edu.au/screeningthepast/firstrelease/fr0799/jlfr7d.htm>.

36. Colonial Office, *Mass Education in African Society*, p. 41.

37. David Cannadine, *Ornamentalism: How the British Saw Their Empire* (London: Penguin Books, 2001).

38. Film Images London Ltd, <www.film-images.com/searchDB.jsp>; <www.britishPathé.com/record.php?id=59548>.

39. See <www.britishPathé.com/record.php?id=74844>.

40. Nwauwa Appollos, 'The British Establishment of Universities in Tropical Africa, 1920–1948: A Reaction against the Spread of American "Radical" Influence', *Cahiers d'études africaines* vol. 33 no. 130, 1993, pp. 247–74.

41. See <www.film-images.com/searchDB.jsp>.

42. Ibid.

43. See <www.colonialfilm.org.uk/node/1579>; and see also <hansard.millbanksystems.com/written_answers/1946/jul/24/service-contingents-film-record>.

44. See <www.film-images.com/searchDB.jsp>. I have not seen either of these films but they are both described as CFU films and more precise dating than that given on the website is needed.

45. Phil Vasili, 'Colonialism and Football: The First Nigerian Tour to Britain', *Race and Class* vol. 36 no. 4, 1995, pp. 55–70, quoted by Tom Rice, 'Nigerian Footballers in England', <www.colonialfilm.org.uk/node/1444>.

46. C. E. Newman, 'Nigerian Sport in 1950', *Annual Report on the Colonies: Nigeria, 1950* (London: HMSO, 1951), pp. 131–2, quoted by Rice, 'Nigerian Footballers in England'.
47. Vasili, 'Colonialism and Football', p. 62.
48. Colonial Office, *Mass Education in African Society*, p. 43.
49. See <www.film-images.com/searchDB.jsp?>, pp 1–7.
50. A. R. G. Prosser, 'An Experiment in Community Development', *Community Development Bulletin*, June 1951, p. 52.
51. G. B. Odunton, 'One Step Ahead', *Colonial Cinema* vol. 8 no. 2, 1950, pp. 29–32.
52. Prosser, 'An Experiment in Community Development', p. 54.
53. Koyinde Vaughan, 'The African and the Cinema', p. 92.
54. See <unesdoc.unesco.org/images/0017/001795/179538eb.pdf>, p. 5.
55. Jean Rouch, 'The Awakening African Cinema', *UNESCO Courier* vol. 15, 1962, p. 14.
56. Colonial Office, *Mass Education in African Society*, p. 31; <africa.berkeley.edu/MRG/2009July.RevMod.FilmFlyer.pdf>.
57. Jean Rouch and Steven Feld, *Ciné-ethnography* (Minneapolis: University of Minnesota Press, 2003), p. 66.
58. C. Y. Carstairs, 'Information Services as an Aid to Administration', *Journal of African Administration* vol. 5 no. 1, January 1953, p. 4.
59. Tom Rice, 'Community Development in Awgu Division, Nigeria', <www.colonialfilm.org.uk/node/1054>.
60. National Film and Sound Archive, Australia.
61. Colonial Office, *Mass Education in African Society*, p. 1.
62. Seee <www.film-images.com/searchDB.jsp>.
63. Obafemi Awolowo, *Path to Nigerian Freedom*, with a foreword by Marjorie Perham (London: Faber and Faber, I947).
64. Tom Rice, 'Self Government for Western Nigeria', <www.colonialfilm.org.uk/node/1819>.
65. Samuel. P. Huntington, *The Clash of Civilizations* (London: Simon & Schuster, 1997), p. 137.
66. See <www.colonialfilm.org.uk/node/1820>.

10

The End of Empire: The Films of the
Malayan Film Unit in 1950s British Malaya[1]

Hassan Abdul Muthalib

INTRODUCTION

The history of British Malaya in the decade leading up to Independence in 1957 must be looked at from a political and economic perspective. The British had much to lose economically if they were to grant Independence to Malaya. They therefore made sure that political power would be in the hands of the conservative Malay ruling class while the non-Malay capitalist class was allowed its hold on business. The arrival of Sir Gerald Templer in 1952, with his strategy to 'win the hearts and minds of the people', fitted in perfectly with the overall scheme of things. Templer employed psy-war strategies against the Malayan Communists, and as part of this also made effective use of the films produced by the Malayan Film Unit (MFU). The documentary films projected an image of the people as heroic and progressive, working side by side with the British in defending the nation and supporting the leaders in the Independence talks.

This essay will look at some of the films made by the MFU between the years 1947 when the first film was made, and 1957, the year Independence was granted to Malaya. The films will be analysed to identify the methods and strategies employed by the MFU to create the image of an (imagined) community working together for the benefit of the nation, blissfully unaware of the propagandistic intent. This analysis will reveal the crucial role played by the Malayan Film Unit and how its films contributed, in no small measure, to winning the fight against the Communists as well as setting the stage for the smooth transition of power to Malayans.

THE MALAYAN FILM UNIT

After World War II, and the Japanese occupation of Malaya, the returning British set up the British Military Administration (BMA). The Malayan population was grappling with grim, post-war realities: price inflation, food shortages and scarcity of medicine. The BMA, though, quickly became known as the 'Black Market Administration'. Corruption, cronyism, murders, kidnapping and extortion became rampant. The people's frustration with the BMA's methods of handling the economy resulted in a strike in January 1946. The suppression of the strike by the BMA did not go down well even with British soldiers. A demonstration to commemorate the fall of Singapore to

The entrance to the MFU in Bangsar, Kuala Lumpur, c. 1963 (courtesy of Filem Negara Malaysia)

the Japanese was violently broken up by police, prompting a rebuke on the police action from Lord Louis Mountbatten himself.[2]

By April 1946, the BMA gave way to a civilian government. As agitations for Independence surfaced, the British found that it would be far easier to side with the conservatives among royalty and aristocracy. To achieve the ends of empire, the British 'repressed and eradicated a whole spectrum of left-wing parties that were socialist in orientation but not necessarily communist'.[3] It was in the earliest stage of this government, and in the very same month, that a fortuitous event led to the establishment of the Malayan Film Unit whose documentary films were to play an important role in the attempted winning back of the Malayan people's faith and confidence in the colonial masters. A benign but fully orchestrated portrayal of the country subsequently made it to the screen, and, for better or worse, became an important visual record of Malaya and its people in the most turbulent period of its modern history.

The MFU was set up in Kuala Lumpur, Malaya, in June of 1946. It had first germinated as an idea in 1943 in the mind of Mervyn Sheppard when he was interned as a prisoner of war during the Japanese occupation in Changi, Singapore.[4] With the end of the war and civilian rule, he became the director of the Department of Public Relations. Some time in May, 1946, Ralph Elton, a film director with the Crown Film Unit (CFU), arrived. Elton, together with a camera crew, had been dispatched by the CFU in London towards the end of the war to accompany Allied forces in Operation Zipper to cover the retreat of the Japanese but Japan's surrender put paid to those plans. Elton then stayed on to make a documentary, *Voices of Malaya* (1948), and also covered the official surrender of the Japanese in Singapore and Kuala Lumpur together with the British Army Film and Photographic Unit (AFPU). The AFPU had been disbanded in Singapore and all its equipment was waiting to be sold off. Elton told Sheppard about the equipment that would soon be bought by a film production company.

Sheppard's dream of establishing a film unit was rekindled and he immediately made an appointment with Sir Edward Gent, the Governor, to discuss the matter. In less than a week, the film equipment was acquired and transported to Kuala Lumpur.

Film and the End of Empire

Gillie Potter and H. W. Govan discussing a production outside the MFU Studios in 1947 (courtesy of Filem Negara Malaysia)

The nucleus staff of the unit was made up of a few locals who had accompanied Elton around the Peninsula for the making of his documentary. Sheppard persuaded Elton to be the first director of the Malayan Film Unit. Elton returned to England to wind up his affairs but became ill and died before he could return.[5] Harry William Govan, who had been enlisted to be a writer and a trainer with the MFU, subsequently took over as its first director.[6] Together with R. E. D. (Gillie) Potter,[7] a combat cameraman who had also been with the AFPU, he trained the locals in all aspects of film production as well as writing the film scripts and narration himself.

THE MALAYAN FILM UNIT'S EARLY STEPS (1947–50)

Thanks to Govan and his staff, the unit took only about a year to get to its feet, and by June 1947 the first documentary to come out was, appropriately, *The Face of Malaya, No. 1*, a review of the current housing problem that portrayed the government as looking out for the people's welfare. It was the earliest example of the kind of propaganda that was to emerge from the MFU. The same year also saw a record number of films in the form of 'eight cinemagazines, two topical reviews, one commercial newsfilm and three trailers'.[8] The fledgeling unit's success resulted in a report by the Film Unit Advisory Committee being tabled at a meeting of the Legislative Council. As related in the *Malay Mail* at the time, Article 21 of the report commenced favourably with the words: '[T]he members of the Committee wish to record their appreciation of the high technical standard reached by the Unit and of the impressive progress made in training local Asian technicians ...'.[9]

By the end of 1949, the MFU was a permanent feature of government. The outstanding film of the year was *The Kinta Story*, written and directed by Govan about

An MFU crew with a British contract director on location in one of the islands in Malaya, c. 1948; the cameraman is Lee Meow Seong, one of the pioneers of the MFU (courtesy of Filem Negara Malaysia)

tin mining in the Kinta Valley and the Communist threat. The film made its international debut at the Edinburgh Film Festival in 1950 and was a harbinger of the international accolades that were to follow over the next decade. *The Kinta Spirit*, a ten-minute film on the Home Guards in the Kinta Valley was on 'the new spirit' of the Home Guard forces (made up of ordinary citizens), who were now well trained and armed, and were full of confidence in facing the threat from the enemy. The film was an example of how the image of what Benedict Anderson has called an 'imagined community' was projected on Malayans as a group perceiving themselves as coming together to rebuild the nation.[10] The British presence was kept carefully in the background and this would be the *modus operandi* in the films to come. Post-war colonialism was benign but 'refracted the production of knowledge and structured the conditions for its dissemination and reception'.[11]

Commissioner-General Malcolm MacDonald's advice to the Colonial Office was that he believed the Chinese were 'highly susceptible to visual propaganda'.[12] In March 1950, the producer-in-chief of the Australian National Film Board, Stanley Hawes, arrived on an invitation from the Malayan government to look into the purpose and role of the MFU and provide recommendations. Among his suggestions were:

Studio shoot for *The Knife* (1952) (courtesy of Filem Negara Malaysia)

Film and the End of Empire

Sir Henry Gurney looks at the proposed model of the new studios (made by Gillie Potter on extreme left); next to Gurney is B. H. Hipkins, the second head of MFU (1951) (courtesy of Filem Negara Malaysia)

Films chosen or produced for this purpose will lose their effect if they are too obviously propagandist. They should aim without being blatant at familiarising as many people as they can possibly reach with the positive advantages of democratic government, and with the strength and positive achievements of the British Commonwealth of Nations. They must be screened regularly and constantly, one after another at definite intervals, so that their effect is cumulative.[13]

Hawes understood the power of film as propaganda, and having noted the early success of the MFU's films, he was extremely positive in his report of the capabilities of the staff. Funds were subsequently made available to increase the MFU's local and European staff. Public screenings of the MFU's films were still limited as, by the end of 1950, there were only twenty-three mobile units available. At the urging of Hugh Carleton Greene, Staff Officer of Emergency Operations, the number was increased to fifty-three.[14] A former BBC man, he, too, knew the importance of visual propaganda in the fight against the Communists. The MFU's role became crucial during the Emergency and, in fact, became 'a blessing in disguise for the youthful Unit, now entrusted with a frontline role in the battle for the hearts and minds of the people'.[15]

THE MALAYAN FILM UNIT GETS INTO STRIDE (1951–3)

Over the next few years, the MFU, true to the symbol of the leaping tiger in its present title, began to brandish its claws. Production doubled in 1951 and 1952. The films were also shown in cinemas before the main feature, with mobile units of the Information Department travelling into remote villages to screen them. Soon, the films became a fixture of Malayan life and were eagerly awaited to such an extent that when the present title with the tiger came on accompanied by its stirring theme song, the audience would spontaneously break into applause.[16] Mobile-unit field officers reported that the screenings of Malay newsreels in villages were 'exceedingly popular with the rural audiences'.[17] The people were, however, not to know that the

Crew on location in a
rubber plantation (1952)

documentary films were as much a construct as the feature films that they were used
to watching in the cinemas.

The MFU's leadership realised that the films could become a potent force in
contributing to the social, political, cultural and economic 'transformation' of Malaya.
To commemorate the seventh year of its founding, *Seventh Anniversary of Malayan Film
Unit* (1953), was made. A gala performance of the MFU's films was held, leading to an
increased awareness among the Malayans of the works of the MFU. A local magazine,
Young Malayans, heaped praise on the MFU, declaring enthusiastically that

> It came as a revelation to most people that not only was the technical standard so high, but
> that films could be so obviously valuable as a means of instruction, of breaking down racial
> barriers, of interpreting the customs and culture of one community to another, and generally
> being a uniting factor in the growth of Malaya towards nationhood.[18]

The year's Annual Report complimented the MFU and its achievements: 'The
confidence placed in the ability of local men to take charge of all the technical phase
[sic] of film-making was fully justified.'[19]

But what was conveniently omitted from the films or the reviews was the reality
that, even with the impending end of empire, the British presence would continue
through its business interests in Malaya in tin, rubber and later, palm oil. Independence was definitely going to come with a price.[20] The population at large – aside
from the business community – was not really aware that the economy of Malaya was
actually contributing more revenue to Britain than all the other colonies combined
through its export of rubber and tin. Malaya's net contribution to the gold/dollar pool
in 1946 alone was US$118 million compared to the total net contribution of US$37
million of all the other colonies.[21] Britain was not going to let this goldmine slip away
from its grasp but funds were short in the early years of the return of the British. Help

Film and the End of Empire

came unexpectedly in the form of another conflict. The Korean War in 1950 created a demand for raw materials and this elevated the prices for rubber and tin to record heights.

At this time, the Communists in Malaya were beginning to gain the upper hand. Morale was low among the people and the economy was under threat. Lieutenant-General Sir Harold Briggs formulated what came to be known as the Briggs Plan. One of its strategies was to starve out the Communists by cutting off their food supply, which was being coerced from (mostly) Chinese squatters living at the fringes of jungles and remote areas. Sir Henry Gurney (High Commissioner from 1948–51), in a massive exercise, brought a sense of direction and urgency and moved half a million squatters into what were called New Villages. These villages were, in actual fact, more like prisons. Movements were restricted with food being rationed to avoid it falling into the hands of the Communists. This created hardships for the villagers but, whether they liked it or not, they were forced to accept the resettlement. To give a positive portrayal of the efforts, the MFU brought out a number of documentaries, among them *A New Life* (1951), which focused on the resettlement and purported that life was actually better in the New Villages than it had been previously.[22] The MFU went further by showing the voluntary resettling of a farmer with *Our New Home* (1952). This was British propaganda to counter that of the Communists, which claimed that the New Villages were actually concentration camps. The gunning down of Gurney in the same year actually helped to fuel anger against the Communists. The MFU quickly produced a solemn documentary called *Tribute to Sir Henry Gurney* (1951) that included a scene of the Malay sultans of the various states of Malaya accompanying the cortège, thus lending legitimacy to Gurney and the colonial presence in Malaya.

THE 'PICTURISING' AND MOBILISING OF MALAYANS THROUGH THE FILMS OF THE MFU

In a policy document of 1940, the image of a 'British Commonwealth of Nations' was promoted:

> It is not the Nazis and the Gestapo who have the goods to deliver, so to speak, for the post-war world, but the British Commonwealth. This is true because the Empire has been gradually transformed from being a political organisation owing obedience to central authority in London to an association of free and equal partners.[23]

The mobilisation of the Malayans during the Emergency in the civil service, military, police and other agencies, was to show that the fight was not just between the British and the Communists but was through an 'association of free and equal partners'. This was the consistent image endemic in the films of the MFU right from its inception and up to the Independence talks in London. A heroic image of the Malayan leaders and the common people was consciously constructed. The British were shown working alongside them as colleagues and not as their masters. Sir Gerald Templer, noted for his harsh and dictatorial manner, was inevitably portrayed as a mild-mannered man, who was always smiling and mingling with the ordinary people and shaking their hands wherever he went. This was in line with the order given to the MFU to make Templer 'the hero' in every film that he appeared in.[24] The MFU films gave the impression that everything was alright with the country. The people appeared cheerful and happy and the country seemed to be on its way to prosperity.

The colonial masters did not seem to have regarded their largely illiterate subjects as highly intelligent or able to interpret the information given to them. In August 1949, Commissioner-General Malcolm MacDonald had advised the Colonial Office that he believed the Chinese were 'highly susceptible to visual propaganda'. Stanley Hawes's report on the MFU in 1950 was in a similar vein: 'The advantage of films over other media of information when dealing with illiterate population makes it the best for the purpose.'[25] A note from H. M. K. Hawson of the Colonial Office indicated that 'it seems to be generally recognised that films have an important role to play in an area where illiteracy is the norm'.[26] In the *Empire News* of 3 August 1950, the article 'BBC to Blast Truth to Russia' proposed Singapore as the headquarters for revealing the 'truth' about the Korean War:

> On the orders of the Government, the BBC is to blast the truth on the Korean war to the peoples of Russia … . Linked up with the BBC all-out drive will be the distribution in the Far East of films countering Communism. The films will be so produced as to be easily understood by primitive uneducated people.[27]

This writer's many interviews with Gillie Potter, one of the trainers and film-makers of the MFU, and also with some of the pioneers, however, reveal that, while the British personnel at the MFU never underestimated or looked down upon the locals, it was the government that dictated the way that the MFU was to approach its productions. This is borne out by the fate of the first head of the MFU, Harry Govan, who, in the initial stages had tried to make social-realist films, showing two points of view. This had not been acceptable to the powers-that-be and as a result, his contract was not renewed upon its expiry.[28] Govan's wife, Valerie, confirmed to the writer Govan's strong, independent streak.[29] Even the contract directors who came from London were put under the same constraints.

Almost every single MFU film produced from 1947 onwards used a narrator to describe the events as they transpired on screen. As a consequence, there was only a one-way communication with the point of view always being that of the MFU. What was projected in the films was an obedient and agreeable populace receptive to whatever was being planned or implemented by the government. A frequent technique was the use of binary opposites. The films would begin with a visual representation of the wrong way to do something. The negative results would be revealed and then the whole situation would be re-enacted, showing the correct procedures. *Acting on Information* (1952) was a training film featuring four Communists planning a strike. The Police Field Force men are portrayed as lacking in discipline. They are fired upon by the Communists and many of them die. A re-enactment shows a more disciplined Force. The earlier scenes are repeated and the correct procedures followed. The result is success over the Communists.

Hugh Carleton Greene had already urged the MFU in 1949 to make full use of the entertainment medium to 'coat the pill' of propaganda to render the films and their messages more palatable to the local audience.[30] And so began a new style of presentation in the MFU films that would go on to become its trademark – the story approach. The straightforward journalistic style had been the norm since 1947 but now the story approach was adopted in order to engage more effectively with the people. This would later be followed by docudramas, employing professional actors. The story approach used locals as actors where they would be directed to do whatever was relevant to the story. This method was effective and provided the verisimilitude needed to deliver the message.

The story and docudrama conventions employed the classic narrative three-act structure. Malayans of all races were already accustomed to the form from their traditional performing arts such as the *wayang kulit* (shadow play), *bangsawan* (Malay opera), Chinese opera and Indian theatre. A glaring difference was that the voices of the subjects were never used in the MFU films. A voiceover conveyed to the audience the import of what was on screen. Generally, the plot would begin with the protagonist faced with a problem; in the middle, he would face tribulations; a solution would then be offered to him by a third party (representing the authorities), and it would all end happily when the subject accepts the solution. This structure can be seen in *Before the Wind* (1953) and *Hassan's Homecoming* (1954). In *Before the Wind*, a debt-ridden traditional fisherman is introduced; he then discovers that he can take a loan at low interest from a co-operative to buy a motorboat; at the end he returns with a big catch and is able to repay his debts. *Hassan's Homecoming*'s subject is also debt-ridden. He then learns about the village co-operative; a good harvest ensues and he has a feast with his family. Such endings went down well with the populace as paying off debts and putting food on the table were the priorities for everyone at the time.

A conspicuous example of the classic three-act structure is found in *Abu Nawas* (Cyril Randall, 1954). Its style was modelled on the feature films of the time, made in Singapore. These films would invariably have the hero and heroine breaking into song with little motivation very early in the film. This became the reference for the British film-makers and so, in *Abu Nawas*, in the very first minute, the heroine is introduced singing a song. She waxes lyrical about how life is so good in Malaya that even the birds are singing. And exactly on cue, the sound of chirping birds is heard loud and clear on the soundtrack. What was depicted in *Abu Nawas* was actually an artificial representation of the Malays, modelled on the films made by Indian directors in Singapore that were themselves copies of those made in India. And as usual, the Malays were associated with village life while the Chinese were seen as businessmen in the towns. The same construct appears in *Hassan's Homecoming*. Hassan is seen working hard in the rice fields and when he sells the rice, it is to a Chinese middleman. Interestingly, this image of the Malays being rural and identified with agriculture continued to be perpetuated in MFU films even after Independence.

British colonial policy at the turn of the nineteenth century had been greatly influenced by the colonial administrator, Sir Frank Swettenham. He did not think that the Malays had the traits to succeed in a modern economy and considered the Chinese as probably more suited to it. It was deemed better to keep the Malays 'on the farm'.[31] Education, said Swettenham, was 'to make the Malay children better farmers rather than offer them any wider views of life. The longer the Malay is kept away from the influence of civilisation, the better it will be for him.'[32] Sir Hugh Clifford, British

Resident, also argued that 'the goal of preserving the culture of the Malays was not at odds with improving their economic position ... the answer was to make Malays better and more efficient farmers'.[33] As a consequence, the school curriculum was restricted to

> simple reading, a little mathematics, and religious teaching. Malay education was not geared towards the changing needs of Malaya and had the effect of tying the Malays to their traditional agricultural pursuits. It did not train them for a more active role in the development of their country.[34]

Political awareness among the Malays had begun to rise in the 1920s and 30s due to the economic depression but it had been confined principally to writers. But in three and a half years of occupation, the Japanese had 'planted the seed of nationalism into younger Malays in the country'.[35] The Japanese occupiers harped on the image of the British running away from Malaya by screening propaganda films that 'celebrated the Asiatic spirit'.[36] After the war, Malay anti-colonial sentiments and agitation, were, however, mainly centred in Singapore, a Crown colony, and only surfaced in newspapers and novels. None of this appeared in the Malay feature films of the period. This is not surprising as the censors would have followed the directives of the British Board of Film Censors that would 'allow only those films that endorsed British rule ...'.[37] While some of the feature films from Singapore were social-realist films and critical of the Malays, in Kuala Lumpur, the MFU films tended to almost glamorise their image, focusing on 'the creation of heroes, who would lead their communities and the nation-state by their example'.[38] But in both instances, the Malay community was portrayed as 'one more comfortable with, and suitable to, a rural ideal'.[39] This, of course, fell in line with the British practice of identifying the three main ethnicities by their economic functions. Neither was a common language promoted as a means to unite the races. As a general rule, the MFU films were made in Malay, English, the Chinese dialects and Tamil. The 'unity' that was depicted on screen between the races was one that was imagined and constructed by the colonial masters. In reality, the three major races were separated by language and profession.

WINNING HEARTS AND MINDS: THE FILMS OF THE MFU DURING SIR GERALD TEMPLER'S TENURE (1952–4)

General Sir Gerald Templer arrived on 7 February 1952 to spearhead the fight against the Communists. He had come armed with directives from the British cabinet:

> ... Malaya should in due course become a fully self-governing nation ... there must be a common form of citizenship for all who regard the Federation ... as their real home and the object of their loyalty. It will be your duty to guide the peoples of Malaya towards the attainment of this objective and to promote such political progress in the country as will ... further our democratic aims for Malaya ... the Malays must be encouraged and helped to play a full part in the economic life of the country, so that the present uneven economic balance may be redressed ... . The Government will not lay aside their responsibilities ... until they are

Sir Gerald Templer on a visit to the Malayan Film Unit upon his arrival in Malaya in 1952; here he is in the editing room with Abd. Shukor Hassan, a dubbing editor; in the background is Ow Kheng Law, an associate producer and one of the pioneers of the MFU who would later become the first Director-General of the MFU and the first Director-General of Radio-Televisyen Malaysia in 1963, the government broadcasting station (courtesy of Filem Negara Malaysia)

satisfied that Communist terrorism has been defeated and that partnership of all communities, which alone can lead to true and stable self-government has been firmly established.[40]

Of course, there was a condition attached to all the 'benefits' for Malaya. The British in Malaya would have 'a worthy and continuing part to play' after the attaining of self-government.[41]

Even a cursory look at MFU's films during Templer's time in Malaya would reveal that as High Commissioner and Director of Operations, Templer was to follow the British cabinet's directive to the letter. One of his first actions was to visit the MFU and impress upon the senior staff what he wanted to achieve. He brought in Tom Hodge, a member of the Foreign Office, as the head of the MFU. Templer took the fight against the Communists in a new direction with two kinds of operations: 'physical and psychological warfare conducted by the police and the army, and psychological operations by using films aimed at the general public'.[42] All of Templer's strategies to fight the Communists were made manifest in the films of the MFU. Many left-wing Malays had also joined the Communists and so some films were directed specifically at the Malay population. In *Imam Sermon* (1952), a Muslim religious leader speaks to the Malay Regiment about the Communist ideology and explains how it goes against the teachings of Islam. But he omitted mentioning that those Malays had not actually given up their religion.[43] *Self Help* (1952) was about a group of Malays under threat by the Communists. They voluntarily decide to resettle themselves in a new area where they will be within easy reach of government services. They form a Home Guard and successfully repulse an attack on their new homes by Communists.

The Big Kitchen (1952) depicted a central kitchen where rice was cooked and distributed based on the number of persons in a family in order to avoid provisions falling into the hands of the Communists. The film showed the scheme in operation

MFU crew shooting
The Big Kitchen (1952)

and how it actually benefited the people in the New Village. To downplay the seriousness of the situation, some children were directed to bring in utensils to take home the cooked rice, and when weddings took place, it was shown that adequate food was available for the celebration. Throughout the film, the people in the village were seen as being cheerful and content with the situation. *Proudly Presenting Yong Peng* (1953) depicted the new-found security in the New Village of Yong Peng, situated in the southern state of Johor, where the people were seen to be happy and living together in permanent communities. Yong Peng was promoted as a stirring example of progress where the villagers and the government appeared to be working in close partnership. 'Success' was seen to be achieved if the people were obedient and supported the (colonial) state.

The gathering of intelligence by the Special Branch was a key factor in the success of the campaign against the Communists. Citizens were offered generous rewards for providing any information that could lead to the capture of the terrorists. *The Magic Word* (1952) demonstrated how information could lead to the successful capture or killing of Communists. The police are shown reacting quickly to information given by a citizen, resulting in a confrontation with several Communists, who are killed in the battle. *Operation Starvation* (1951) and *Starve Them Out* (1954) exhorted the people not to support the Communists and showed the government's strategies for denying food to them. The success of the strategy is demonstrated with Communists giving themselves up due to hunger. *Surrendered Enemy Personnel* (1952) and *More Communists Give Up* (1953) became invaluable psychological tools. As a result, many Communists gave themselves up voluntarily. They in turn persuaded their comrades in the jungle to surrender and were handsomely rewarded for it.

In *Jungle Fort* (1953), the fight is taken deep into the jungles where aborigines had been coerced into helping the Communists. To provide protection for them, security forces and police build fortified posts in the jungle. Jungle fort centres in Kuala

Lumpur send provisions and medicine by planes, dropping them by parachute. The aborigines, who had been practising shifting cultivation, agree to stay put and build a permanent camp. Their plantations are guarded by the soldiers and their children are taught to read and write by them. *Operation Termite* (1954) depicted the security forces launching a combined air–ground operation against the Communists in the jungle. Planes drop carpet bombs on hideouts. Soldiers then parachute down to the bombed areas and kill many Communists in a skirmish. *Malaya – We Serve to Defend* (1954) showed how the Federation was advancing towards military preparedness. The local defence forces included the Royal Malayan Navy, Malay and Federal regiments, the Malayan Auxiliary Air Force and the Civil Defence Corps. Future officers are seen being trained at the newly established Military College in Port Dickson. The image of the nation's security being in safe hands runs throughout the film.

The MFU had obviously taken to heart Hawes's recommendations that a consistent effort should be made to create an image of the British contributing to the well-being and security of the Malayan peoples. *Chik's Great Adventure* (1953) was about youthful enthusiasm and being of service to the community. A young Malay boy, Chik, joins the Boy Scout movement. The aims and objectives of the Scout movement are revealed through his activities. *Youth in Action* (1953) showed young people of all races being prepared for their place in society. *Fight for Your School* (1954) aimed to make parents aware of Communist infiltration into schools. *Rohani Steps Out* (1953) was about the Women's Institute of the Federation of Malaya. Rohani, a shy woman, joins the local branch where she learns many things from member instructors of all races. At the end of the film, Lady Templer herself shows up (as the white cultural benefactress). She describes the successes of the Women's Institute all over the country. The image of women as home-makers was reinforced rather than showing them as participating in more public and political activities. The idea of the Women's Institute was actually mooted by Dato' Onn Jaafar, the Chief Minister of Johor (who had rallied the Malays to protest the Malayan Union).[44] It was also he who had arranged for Lady Templer to be the president but the closing graphics pay tribute only to Lady Templer and her efforts in setting up 250 institutes nationwide. As usual, the benevolent British image was promoted.

The Letter (1953) portrayed an Indian couple in the rubber estates (where the largely illiterate Indians were predominant), receiving an important letter and taking it to be read by a half-educated person, which leads to a serious misunderstanding. They visit a schoolmaster who straightens things out, resulting in the couple deciding to send their children to school while exhibiting no desire to read and write themselves. In *Eggs Galore* (1954), a rural family gets better results after a visit to a model chicken farm at one of the government's experimental stations. *Food for Strength* (1954) focused on the importance of children being given proper food before they set out for school. Workers were assured of their future through *Worry Free* (1954) which depicted the establishment of the Employees' Provident Fund and portrayed how it was managed and run by the federal government for the benefit of the ordinary worker. However, these films did not address the more pressing issues of the day – low wages, poverty and unemployment.

The plight of Malay fishermen and the solution to their economic woes were foregrounded in *Before the Wind*. Storms frequently force traditional fishermen to abandon their fishing trips as they are not able to venture far out to sea. The officer of the local Rural and Industrial Development Authority (RIDA) convinces a fisherman that he can overcome the problem by using a motorboat. The fisherman's application to buy a motorboat is speedily approved. The fisherman returns with a big catch and his previous debts to a middleman are paid. The film appeared to be more of an advertisement for RIDA, an agency that had been set up by the government, which projected an image that the Malays were being helped economically.

Hassan's Homecoming exhorts Malay rice planters to improve their lot by joining the village co-operative. Hassan's family had called a medicine man to tend to his sick father. He quickly brings a doctor but it is too late. Hassan borrows rice seeds from a rich man but the repayment is crippling. He then becomes a member of the village co-operative and is given a loan at very low interest. Hassan reaps a bountiful harvest and has a good dinner at home with his family.[45] Through this film, the rural Malays were subtly called upon to change their lot and break from the vicious cycle of debt. Hassan was projected as the new progressive-minded Malay (symbolically shown arriving by train from the city). He initiates a break from the outdated traditions his family is mired in, such as the belief in traditional healing rather than modern medicine. The doctor and the co-operative (symbols of modernity) offer the Malays a way out and, in effect, the Malays were exhorted to do away or 'forget' elements that would thwart the realisation of 'a new nation' and continue their lives as farmers.

Abu Nawas was Malaya's first feature film and was part of the anti-Communist campaign. It starred not only Singaporean actors but also surrendered Communists.[46] The Communists are shown harassing a Malay villager and his girl. The villager teams up with a Chinese friend and together they gather information about the Communists. The police and army then come into the picture and in a climactic fight, the Communists are killed. At the end of the film, the hero and his girl march with the soldiers while singing a patriotic song.[47] As with *Hassan's Homecoming*, the British policy of divide and rule is blatantly obvious in *Abu Nawas*. Ethnic groups were identified with particular occupations: the Malays with agriculture in the villages while the Chinese were associated with business in the towns. A social and economic reconstruction was desired but what consistently appeared on screen was a call for the transformation of culture with the agenda for capitalist gain kept hidden in the background.

The year also saw the end of Templer's service in Malaya. The MFU's *Malaya Says Goodbye* (1954) depicted his departure with his wife, Lady Peggy Templer, from Kuala Lumpur in May 1954 after a job obviously well done. The MFU, together with the police and army, had played a significant role in accomplishing many of Templer's objectives. In turn, Templer's psychological warfare strategies through the MFU films had also helped to enhance the skills, experience and creativity of the staff of MFU. This was to stand them in good stead for the next phase in the country's development – setting the stage for the attainment of Independence.

TOWARDS A SELF-GOVERNING INDEPENDENT NATION

As early as 1953, the people of Malaya were already encouraged to be actively involved in village politics but this revolved around the (British-approved) Alliance Party, made up of the three ethnic races. The leftist parties had been conveniently banned, with many of their members having been thrown into prison. This was a prelude to the people's involvement in national politics. The MFU reacted to these developments with *The People's Choice* (1953), which was about the election of local councils. In *Letter from Home* (1954), a young Malay policeman in the city receives a letter from his mother. She is excited at the prospect of local council elections in their village and she tells him how it all transpired. It showed creatively how village women were able to accept the changes taking place in the country. The MFU's role in awakening the people as to their rights and kindling their sense of nationalism cannot be under-estimated. Creative ways were invented to deliver these messages. The *Election Song* (1954) was a lively rendition on screen (and radio) in all the major languages by one man, the versatile Zainal Alam, a radio personality. The tune and lyrics, coupled with his inimitable style, made the song popular with young and old and was reused in other elections for many years. Many other radio personalities were roped in later.

Malaya Votes (1955) showed the voting process and how the people were eager to participate in the general election. The fact that elections were held took the wind out of the sails for the Communists as it appeared to demonstrate the people's overwhelming support for the Malayan leaders. As a consequence, the Alliance Party, made up of the major races, ended up with a landslide victory. *Chief Minister Speaking on the Amnesty* (1955) and *Labour Minister's Speech on Amnesty* (1955) suggested that the Communists give themselves up. Tunku Abd. Rahman, the Chief Minister, reiterated that there was now no more reason for them to bear arms as the nation would soon be independent. Tunku (as he was popularly known) then had peace talks with Chin Peng, the leader of the Malayan Communists. The talks were part of a segment in a newsreel, *1955: The Year in Malaya* (1956) and demonstrated the cordiality of the meeting which was conducted in a gentlemanly manner. This further enhanced the benevolent image of the government led by Tunku. Tunku came across as a leader who had united the races and was leading Malaya towards Independence.[48] Like all of the MFU's films, it was, in reality, an image constructed on the editing table by the British film-makers – and it worked.

In *Merdeka Mission* (1956), Tunku is depicted being given a rousing send-off to London by the leaders and the people. He and his delegation are given a warm and friendly welcome when they arrive. The negotiations are shown to be cordial and visually constructed as a meeting of equals. Tunku meets Malayan students and teachers, who are studying in the UK. They are portrayed breaking into spontaneous cheers when he announces the impending independence. This 'heroic' image of Tunku is repeated in other films 'indirectly signifying British acceptance of Tunku as their choice for leading the nation'.[49]

Milestones to Merdeka (1957) chronicled the events from the early days of the Emergency to the first general elections. The members of the cabinet are represented as dynamic, proactively travelling the country personally to investigate its development. The Independence talks are depicted positively, setting the stage for the declaration of Independence. *Merdeka for Malaya* (1957) covered the official Declaration of Independence on 31 August 1957 and the symbolic departure of the British High Commissioner. The people's joy is shown in the celebrations that were held all over the country. The realities of self-government are seen in a solemn ceremony where the

King and the Prime Minister are sworn in. The King then opens Parliament and outlines the policies of the new government. The people and leaders were depicted as being of one community, finally in full charge of the nation.

On the political front, the British presence was depicted as being benevolent and still necessary even after Independence. In *Merdeka Mission*, Malaya's continued dependence on the British is shown to be necessary throughout the film. The narrator notes Tunku's expression of thanks at the London talks for the previous loans from the British government and his hopes for further loans. Students and teachers still needed to be trained in the United Kingdom. Military cadets are seen in training at Sandhurst availing themselves of British military expertise. Addressing the Malayan people on camera in the film, Tunku lays the blame for colonial rule on his ancestor who signed a treaty and gave away Penang to the British, and on other sultans, who later signed away Malaya. Back home, Tunku is shown as being greeted everywhere in the manner of a hero. The overall image that emerged was that of the Malayan delegation returning with a well-deserved 'victory' after the colonial masters had 'acceded' to all their 'demands'. The film was constructed with iconic images and stirring commentary and the audience was never in doubt as to the 'victory' that had been achieved under the leadership of Tunku Abd. Rahman. And in confirmation of this fact, Tunku was then conferred with the title of Father of Independence.

CONCLUSION

The Malayan Film Unit had, undoubtedly, contributed immensely to the nation and, at the same time, carved a niche for itself in the making of acclaimed documentaries during the post-war and pre-Independence period. This success must be attributed to the staff who worked tirelessly and uncomplainingly and, at times, ventured beyond the call of duty. In those early days, there was no such thing as division of labour. Everybody did everything 'including repairing the attap sheds, painting the walls with black creosote, mixing cement and laying out the brickpaths in between the assigned tasks of film-making'.[50] By 1953, there were 135 men and women employed at the unit made up of all races: seventy Malays, thirty Chinese, twenty-two Indians, nine Eurasians and four Europeans. Working under conditions that were hardly conducive to a film studio, they, nevertheless persevered in a spirit of camaraderie.

In this respect, the MFU appears to have paralleled the early tottering steps of the fledgeling Malayan nation with its diverse ethnicities and problems on its way to self-government. Just as Malaya was being prepared for self-rule, the MFU itself was made ready for local management. By the time the MFU celebrated its seventh anniversary in 1953, four locals had proved their worth as film directors as well as many other staff in various other capacities. General Templer himself paid tribute to the staff in a special write-up about the anniversary in the *Malay Mail*: 'The work that they are doing in showing Malaya to Malayans is of the greatest importance in the task of nation-building which lies ahead of us …'.[51] In the article, Tom Hodge, the head of the MFU then, noted that the MFU's films 'must grow out of a local culture and the only way our men will learn to direct films is to be given a chance to direct'.[52]

The Malayan Film Unit successfully articulated the late colonial mission: promoting a Malayan 'nationalism and national culture ... through new techniques of collaboration. This stood at the apex of the colonial mission. Nowhere was political contest more evident than in the propaganda and sponsorship of cultural renewal.'[53] The MFU produced and disseminated propaganda in a manner intended by the colonialists to foster elements of patriotism and a sense of nationalism. Indeed, the early films of the MFU did project a modern nation that 'heroically' emerged from the ashes of war through the 'hard work' of the Malayans themselves. The MFU then went on to chronicle the history of a plural society at work and leisure and one that was content under colonial rule. The screening of these films through mobile units became an event in rural areas and entrenched the image of a colonial government that appeared to be sincere in improving the lot of the people. With the run-up to the granting of Independence, MFU's films focused on Malaya's leaders and their sincere desire to build a truly independent nation. However, what was kept discreetly in the background was Britain's hand in the choice of the political leaders of the new nation – those who were amenable to the colonial masters and would safeguard their economic interests. Nevertheless, MFU's films stand as a record of the nation's and its people's post-war history. Certainly the MFU's films were on the whole propaganda with the aim of furthering the ends of empire, but they are also now a record for posterity and a testimony to the spirit and dedication of the men and women who made them – both locals and British. They showed Malaya to Malayans during a crucial part of the history of the country – and then became themselves, a part of that history.

NOTES

1. I would like to acknowledge the invaluable assistance of Dr Khoo Gaik Cheng, Dr Hatta Azad Khan, Dr Timothy Barnard, Norman Yusoff, Kay Gladstone, Valerie Govan and Rachel Govan in various capacities in my research and writings on the MFU.
2. T. N. Harper, *The End of Empire and the Making of Malaya* (Cambridge: Cambridge University Press, 2001), p. 81. Lord Mountbatten was Supreme Allied Commander of Southeast Asia at the time.
3. Khoo Gaik Cheng, 'Filling in the Gaps of History', *Studies on Southeast Asia* no. 51, 2010, p. 250.
4. Noted by Mervyn Cecil ffranck Sheppard in his Foreword, 'The Fulfilment of a Dream', in the souvenir programme of the official opening of the new studios of the MFU (renamed Filem Negara Malaysia – FNM), on 24 August 1965. Sheppard had arrived in Malaya as a colonial officer in 1928. He later converted to Islam and became Abdul Mubin Sheppard.
5. Elton's date of death is uncertain. A member of the staff of MFU, Goh Meng Huat, who had joined up in 1947, told the writer that Elton had died of tuberculosis. Tuberculosis and malaria were rampant at the time in Malaya. Elton may have contracted the disease during his travels up and down the Malay Peninsula. However, an entry on the internet mentions the year of his death as 1968, <www.screenonline.org.uk/people/id/513790/index.html>.
6. Harry William Govan was with the AFPU as combat cameraman and served in the Burma Campaign. He was originally going to be second director with the MFU. He subsequently took over as the head.

7. Ronald Edward David 'Gillie' Potter was seconded to the MFU by the British Army as an art director. He married a local Eurasian girl and went back to England in 1957 where he became famous for his visual-effects work in commercials and feature films.

8. Anonymous, 'Short History of Filem Negara Malaysia', in the souvenir programme of the official opening of Filem Negara Malaysia, 1965, p. 44.

9. *Malay Mail*, 12 September 1948, p. 5. The following year, MFU was declared a permanent feature of government and a grant was given to build new studios.

10. Benedict Anderson, *Imagined Communities, Reflections on the Origin and Spread of Nationalism* (Pasig City, Philippines: Anvil Publishing, Inc., 2003), p. 6.

11. Anis Loomba, *Colonialism/Postcolonialism* (London: Routledge, 1998), p. 62.

12. Kumar Ramakrishna, 'Telling the Simple People the Truth: The Role of Strategic Propaganda in the Malayan Emergency', *Journal of the Malaysian Branch of the Royal Asiatic Society* vol. LXXV Part 1 (2002), p. 53, quoting Susan L. Carruthers, *Winning Hearts and Minds: British Government, the Media and Colonial Counter-insurgency, 1944–1960* (London: Leicester University Press, 1995), p. 94.

13. 'Malayan Film Unit: Proposed Investigation and Reorganisation (1949–50)'. Hawes Report, British Archives, CO 537/6571, p. 41.

14. Before coming to Malaya in September 1950, Carleton Greene was with the BBC in London as head of the German service and was involved in anti-Nazi propaganda during the war years.

15. Anonymous, 'Short History of Filem Negara Malaysia', p. 44.

16. This writer can attest to the fact, having seen numerous films of the MFU at his primary school as well as in outdoor screenings in his hometown in Penang.

17. Ramakrishna, 'Telling the Simple People the Truth', p. 53.

18. Anonymous, 'Short History of Filem Negara Malaysia', p. 46

19. Ibid.

20. In his book, *British Business in Post-colonial Malaysia, 1957–70: Neo-colonialism or Disengagement?* (New York, Routledge, 2004), p. 37, Nicholas J. White argues, however, that British businessmen did not have it that easy with the Malaysian government. They were frequently frustrated by policies and decision-making. And that British businesses in Malaysia and Singapore had more to fear from international capitalism than from international Communism.

21. Richard Stubbs, *Hearts and Minds in Guerrilla Warfare: The Malayan Emergency, 1948–1960* (Singapore: Eastern Universities Press, 1989), p. 18.

22. Dato' J. J. Raj, Jr, *The War Years and After* (Selangor Darul Ehsan, Malaysia: Pelanduk Publications, 1995), p. 108. Dato' Raj noted that Hamzah Sendut of the University of Malaya observed in 1955 that, in of one of the New Villages (Rasah), a 'social revolution' had actually been started, resulting in better hygiene, medical and educational facilities, a forum for discussion and youth clubs.

23. Cited in James Chapman and Nicholas J. Cull, *Projecting Empire: Imperialism and Popular Cinema* (London: I. B. Tauris, 2009), p. 51.

24. 'Personal Interview with John Nettleton', 5 January 2000. Nettleton, who was in charge of the editing department, told the writer that Templer did not like the films made under B. H. Hipkins (the head of MFU then) and brought in Tom Hodge from the Foreign Office. Hodge gave the order to foreground Templer in every film made by the MFU. He would sit next to Nettleton and personally approve the rough edit.

25. 'Colonial Development and Welfare: Malayan Film Unit (1950)', British Archives, CO717/195/5, p. 48.
26. 'Malayan Film Unit: Proposed Investigation and Reorganisation (1949–50),' British Archives, CO 537/6571, p. 21.
27. *Empire News*, 3 August 1950.
28. 'Personal Interview with John Nettleton', 2003.
29. 'Personal Interview with Mrs Valerie Govan' in Clevedon, England, 2007.
30. Ramakrishna, 'Telling the Simple People the Truth', p. 56.
31. Jim Baker, *Crossroads: A Popular History of Malaysia and Singapore* (Singapore: Marshall Cavendish International (Asia) Pte. Ltd., 2005), p. 196.
32. Ibid.
33. Ibid., p. 197.
34. Ibid.
35. Harry Miller, *Prince and Premier: A Biography of Tunku Abd. Rahman* (Singapore: Eastern Universities Press), p.69. Miller argues that the Indonesian nationalistic currents at the time were also an influence.
36. Harper, *The End of Empire and the Making of Malaya*, p. 45.
37. Chapman and Cull, *Projecting Empire*, p. 16.
38. Hassan Abdul Muthalib, ' "Winning Hearts and Minds": Representations of Malays and Their Milieu in the Films of British Malaya', *Southeast Asia Research*, March 2009, p. 61.
39. Ibid.
40. Miller, *Prince and Premier*, pp. 123–4.
41. Stubbs, *Hearts and Minds*, p. 144. This was one of the reasons why the Malayan Communists rejected the granting of Independence, saying that the British would continue to have a say in Malayan matters. Citizenship for the Chinese and Indians had actually been proposed earlier in the People's Constitution by the joint PMCJA-PUTERA alliance in 1947–8.
42. Hassan Abdul Muthalib and Wong Tuck Cheong, 'Gentle Winds of Change', in Aruna Vasudev, Latika Padgaonkar and Rashmi Doraisamy (eds), *Being and Becoming: The Cinemas of Asia* (New Delhi: Macmillan India, 2002), p. 310.
43. In an interview with Wan Khazim Wan Din (2007), a former member of the leftist group, Angkatan Pemuda Insaf (API), the writer was told that the members of the United Malayan Nationalist Organisation (UMNO) went around telling the simple village folk that the Malay leftists who were with the Communists were no longer Muslims. Relatives and friends stopped visiting them, resulting in Wan Din leaving his village for Singapore.
44. Mohd Abid, *Reflections of Pre-Independence* (Selangor Darul Ehsan, Malaysia: Pelanduk Publications, 2003), p. 96.
45. For a detailed analysis of this film, see the writer's article 'Winning Hearts and Minds'.
46. 'Personal Interview with Long Hin Boon', 2003, a member of the MFU staff, who was the Chinese-language interpreter for the film. Though completed in 1954, the film was only shown in 1957, and only then, briefly, as it was considered sensitive to the Chinese population. This was because all the Communists in the film were Chinese with Malays only shown as their victims.
47. For a detailed analysis of this film, see Abdul Muthalib, 'Winning Hearts and Minds'.
48. However, when the film was shown in the cinemas, the audience applauded Chin Peng when he appeared on screen. Reported in the *Straits Times*, 6 January 1956, p. 4, and quoted in Tom Rice, *1955: The Year in Malaya*, <www.colonialfilm.org.uk/node/2545>.

49. Abdul Muthalib, 'Winning Hearts and Minds', p. 60.

50. *Malay Mail*, 31 August 1953, p. 5.

51. Ibid.

52. Ibid.

53. Harper, *The End of Empire and the Making of Malaya*, p. 11.

INTERVIEWS

Abdullah Zainol, Elias Mydin, Goh Meng Huat, Goh Meng Kwee, Hamzah Hussin, Hasan Rashid, Ismail Kulop, John Nettleton, Long Hin Boon, Mohd. Ali Hanafiah, R. E. D. (Gillie) Potter, Salmah Sodhy, S. Suppiah, Valerie Govan, Wan Choon Guan, Wan Khazim Wan Din, Wong Khye Weng, Woon Kee Fee, Yeoh Gaik It.

PROJECTING
AFRICA

●

ⅠⅠ
Projecting the Modern Colonial State:
The Mobile Cinema in Kenya

Charles Ambler

During the 1940s and 1950s a small number of official cinema vans made regular circuits through the Kenya countryside, just as they did in British colonial dependencies across Africa and elsewhere in the British empire. Often interrupted by bad weather, impossible road conditions and mechanical breakdowns, these van tours took movie programmes to Kenyan towns, market centres and remote communities, each year attracting audiences in the hundreds of thousands. The van team typically parked near a government office or school to set up the apparatus and early arrivals listened to radio broadcasts, looked at posters or were given newspapers and magazines to read. After sunset, the show began and the hundreds and often thousands in the audience experienced the spectacle of movies lighting up the night – on a screen nineteen feet in the air and measuring eight feet by six. No matter that the films were short documentaries and dated comedies, the mobile cinema became enormously popular, with commentators bringing the movies alive over loudspeakers that could be heard several miles away.[1] These cinema shows were part of a larger and highly uneven effort to use film to advance the objectives of British imperial rule during this period of both reinvigorated colonial occupation and increasingly aggressive anti-colonialism.

Officials were often enthusiastic about the potential of film as a tool of education and propaganda in British Africa; and a substantial scholarship has documented the development of official film policy and explored the content of films produced and shown.[2] It is easy enough to ridicule the heavy-handed and dull didactic movies that were stock elements of the mobile cinema. Writing as early as 1954 on 'Kenya's Answer to the Mau Mau Challenge', C. J. M. Alport noted that, when it came time for historians to assess British colonialism, 'one of the conclusions reached might quite easily be that we bored the African peoples'.[3] But the record of colonial film shows in Kenya tells quite a different story. Large and generally enthusiastic audiences regularly turned out to see these shows; and local officials, both African and European, were passionate supporters of mobile cinema. Although imperial policy focused on the films themselves as tools of education and propaganda, accounts of the actual practice of mobile cinema in Kenya reveal that it was the spectacle of cinema shows, rather than the movie content, that drew in audiences and made colonial officials strong advocates for government film shows.[4] District officials, working in small towns and rural areas, saw these film shows as important elements in a broader effort to project a new, explicitly modern, image of the colonial state.

During the 1920s the Colonial Office became increasingly convinced of the potential power of officially sanctioned film as an instrument of propaganda that could be engaged to support the broader interests of the British empire, to promote the development or 'welfare' of colonial people, particularly in Africa, and to provide an alternative to commercial cinema, regarded at the very least as banal and at worst dangerous.[5] The Advisory Committee on Education in the Colonies sent Julian Huxley to East Africa in 1929 to assess African reaction to didactic films and he concluded that they were 'the most powerful weapon of propaganda which we have at our command'.[6] Three years later the Colonial Office and the Commission on Educational and Cultural Films produced a widely read report on *The Film in National Life* restating Huxley's view at the same time that the Carnegie Corporation-funded study of the Copperbelt concluded that film should be used to help migrant workers from rural areas adjust to modern urban life. This suggestion in turn inspired the Bantu Educational Kinema Experiment (BEKE), also backed by Carnegie, which produced thirty-five films in East and Central Africa between 1935 and 1937, mostly on agriculture and health, that were shown by the film-makers themselves in mobile-cinema tours across these regions, exciting a new generation of colonial officials committed to 'native welfare' and development.[7] A 1939 quasi-official memorandum on the 'Education of East African Natives by Means of Mobile Cinema Projection Units' proposed the creation of a network of exhibition halls in the more prosperous and densely populated districts of Kenya that would be served by mobile projection units circulating on a regular schedule.[8] Although the memorandum declared the jury out on the effectiveness of film as an educational approach in rural East Africa, there seemed little question that the author, Ambrose Coghill, was convinced of the modernising potential of film. 'There can be no doubt', he wrote, 'that the method suggested would considerably expedite the Government's object of ultimately turning the African into a self-governing and responsible citizen.'[9] The East African governments, however, remained unconvinced of the effectiveness of film propaganda, doubtful that Africans would pay to see didactic films, and especially worried about the costs involved.[10]

WORLD WAR II AND THE EXPANSION OF MOBILE CINEMA

The outbreak of World War II rapidly shifted official attitudes toward film propaganda. The Ministry of Information established a Colonial Film Unit that produced propaganda movies to support the war effort and provided some cinema vans to take those films into rural areas in Africa.[11] The films produced documented the progress of the war and the development of the war machine, thus urging Africans living in the British colonies to contribute to the war effort. Pressed by the Colonial Office, the film unit gradually broadened its approach somewhat to embrace a more general educational mission that encompassed the development of a 'national' outlook.[12] Within months the new policy was reflected on the ground in Kenya. A retired colonial official, Arthur Champion, returned to the administration to develop the mobile-cinema effort. Almost immediately, Champion grasped the key role of local commentators in the programmes, encouraging them to tailor their comments to the local situation and inject humour. Champion was adamant that attendance should be entirely voluntary and that officials, African or European, should not be required to attend.[13]

From the very beginning, however, the mobile-cinema exhibitions involved the performance of local state power. The chiefs, sub-chiefs and headmen (local men appointed by the British as administrators) who attended were given special chairs at the front and opportunities to speak using the microphone.[14] Predictably the maintenance of order at the shows was a major concern. Children were seated in the front and the sexes were segregated. Those who brought stools or chairs were required to sit toward the back. Imposing order meant mediating competing local understandings of hierarchy, with one report noting that

> considerable difficulty was experienced, especially at first, in inducing those who considered themselves privileged persons of some importance or who occupied official positions in the Native Administration to realise that by standing up or sitting on chairs they obscured the view of the less fortunate ones behind them.[15]

At around sundown a short talk would be given to local students, teachers and other educated people regarding the progress of the war; printed materials would be distributed; and there would be a programme of recorded or live music in the local language. 'Just before it was dark enough to start the pictures', Champion reported,

> I made it a habit to deliver an address on the Empire and their Majesties and the Royal family, and at the same time presenting to the leading chiefs pictures of the King, Mr. Winston Churchill, the Union Jack, and suitable posters to put up in their homes and offices.[16]

If there was a programme the following day, there would be a talk on the causes of the war and the ways that African communities could contribute to a British victory. The programme of films usually lasted about an hour and a half and always ended with a patriotic movie and the playing of 'God Save the King'.[17]

There was little difficulty in attracting audiences, and according to Champion, although children were big fans of Charlie Chaplin, the 'bulk of the audience, even the women, were more attracted by welfare, war, and agricultural pictures and especially those depicting the home life and agricultural activities of the artisan, peasant and working people in Europe'.[18] In 1940 and 1941, for example, film tours attracted large numbers of people in central and western Kenya, with nearly 100,000 people attending thirty shows in the western Kenya province of Nyanza alone in 1940.[19] A confidential report from September 1941 described a tour in the area surrounding Kisumu disrupted by breakdowns and rain. A show in Kisumu town was held in the large covered market that was 'very unsuitable for a large and highly excitable audience'. With a crowd of more than 4,000 squeezed in, 'chaos and noise ruled throughout', with the commentary rendered entirely inaudible. The tour's organiser, Arthur Champion, felt that any 'propaganda value' attaching to the films had been lost, but these conditions did little to deter audiences, who attended subsequent shows in Kisumu and neighbouring areas in very large numbers – underscoring the Provincial Commissioner's claim that the shows were 'universally appreciated'.[20] Whether the PC's additional assertion that the films were 'doing a lot of good' was true depended on what it was that constituted 'good'.[21]

Champion's detailed report of a cinema circuit through the Rift Valley and western Kenya in late December and early January 1941–2 illustrates the impressive scope of the new mobile-cinema programme and the diversity of those who attended. After putting on eighteen shows in Nairobi for students and military personnel, Champion headed for the Rift Valley, where the shows attracted hundreds and in some cases thousands of people. The two showings in Eldama Ravine, for example, pulled in 600 and 1,800. In Eldoret there was an audience of 2,300 and in Kitale about 2,000. In less populated areas sometimes only a few hundred showed up and occasionally response was less than enthusiastic. One show was given to about 400 Suk pastoralists of whom, supposedly, only five or six had ever seen a film. According to Champion's account, 'the audience seemed overwhelmingly mystified by the whole performance'. On the other hand, a few days later a 'dull response' was attributed to the fact that an audience was largely made up of wage labourers, a group thought to be more 'sophisticated than their brothers in the reserve' – an argument that was belied by the large crowds attending the same film shows in towns and other commercial agricultural areas. Part of the success of the showings depended on the quality of the local-language commentator whom organisers managed to recruit. Subsequent shows attracted anywhere from 800 to 3,000.[22]

Although there can be little question that the film shows were quite popular, officials may well have inflated attendance numbers. No doubt the very officials whose position and roles were spotlighted at the film-show spectacles also applied pressure on people in their areas to attend, knowing full well that the success of film shows, determined by attendance and order, would be a measure of their effectiveness higher up the bureaucratic chain. In April 1942 a central government circular on the 'Government Mobile Cinema Unit' emphasised the need to ensure local support for the shows by having 'senior tribal Policemen' accompany the van and local tribal police guarding it. Local authorities were congratulated on the 'maintenance of order and the marshalling of the audience' for shows, but the circular stressed the need to continue and enhance those efforts.[23]

The official records of cinema tours during the war years afford only a very limited impression of the mobile-cinema experience. Although colonial officials had earlier argued for the importance of evaluating the effectiveness of films as educational tools, reports offer little information on the particular films shown and even less on audience response to them. Officials certainly showed little interest in determining how or whether films changed attitudes or behaviour. Instead, reports focused almost exclusively on documenting the numbers in attendance and the presence or absence of local dignitaries. In a typical example, at Mambarze, three chiefs and a number of headmen were present and made speeches to a crowd of 1,300.[24] By January 1942 Champion had presented more than 400 shows to many thousands of people, including 'huge audiences' in Kisumu town.[25] A month later, Champion reported on a thirty-three-day tour that he regarded as the most successful thus far: with forty-seven shows attracting 68,000 people. In the tea plantation area of Kericho, more than 4,000 attended a show and in Kisii more than 3,000 came each day on successive days. The shows were often preceded by radio broadcasts and informal 'short addresses on the war'. During downtime on this particular tour Champion and his crew also shot footage of stock inoculation and various 'bad agricultural practices' for later showing with appropriate accompanying commentary.[26] A typical programme included various didactic films such as *The Two Brothers* (1939, a film with African actors illustrating the dangers of venereal disease), wildlife movies, war films such as *Drums in the Desert* and *War Came to Kenya* (1942, a sound film on the impact of the war in Kenya that was still being shown a decade later) and movies illustrating the imperial regime such as *Governor's Visit to AAPC, Nanyuki*, shot in Kenya and *The King's Men* (footage of the king visiting the armed forces). In addition, entertainment films such as *Showdown*, a cowboy 'talkie' were included in programmes.[27]

Champion retired as head of the mobile-cinema unit in April 1944 after a final tour through western Kenya that included forty-six shows in forty-nine days, attracting an audience of approximately 103,000, or an average of 2,200 per show.[28] According to the press account of his retirement, Champion had supposedly become known to Africans all over Kenya as 'Bwana Cinema', having over the course of almost four years put on nearly 800 performances to a total audience exceeding a million people.[29] Without question, Champion was an enthusiastic advocate for the mobile cinema, referring to it as a 'unique agent for propaganda to the Africa'.[30] He stressed its importance in promoting improvements in agriculture and public health and the potential he saw in linking film shows with programmes in local schools. He cited the growing numbers of women at film shows as a measure of the spread of modern ideas, noting that

> it has often been difficult to get women to come to Barazas [meetings held by chiefs and other officials] as it is against their tribal custom, but now they attend the cinema shows in ever-increasing numbers and show the keenest interest.[31]

Champion also made it clear that a central purpose of the mobile cinema was 'telling the people in the Reserve what the British Empire stands for and they themselves are an important part of it'. What he stressed in practice, however, was respect for the imperial state rather than information about the war effort. He took particular pride in the fact that previously oblivious audiences now understood the 'etiquette of standing to attention and removing hats during the playing of the National anthem', and now readily stood for 'God Save the King' at the end of the programme and remained respectfully silent.[32]

The film shows in fact increasingly involved rituals of state power and imperial patriotism. Captain A. G. Dickson, the officer in charge of the mobile propaganda unit of the East African Command claimed that the unit had reached more than a million people during the course of the war. Movie showings were certainly accompanied by talks and distribution of printed propaganda, but even more importantly, also by various displays by African members of the forces in handsome uniforms, climaxing in the firing of weapons.[33] According to a welfare officer's 1942 report on a film tour in western Kenya,

> the greatest welcomes were at Subakuria where the Cinema was received by a guard of honour and at Kendu where a crowd of 6,000 was exceptionally well disciplined and where after a full programme of 2½ hours, the Chief asked specially that his people should also see *The Two Brothers* and they gave it the best reception I have ever experienced.

At Maseno, home to one of Kenya's leading Anglican mission stations and schools, 'the School marched down to the Recruiting Depot', apparently inspired by the film show to support the imperial cause.[34] As the war effort ramped up, the film-show spectacle took on an increasingly martial quality. In conjunction with a mobile film show in Kisumu in March 1943, the East African Command preceded it with a display in front of the District Commissioner's office that included physical training by forces members, combat demonstrations, displays of armoured cars, mortars, bren guns and an inspection of the unit – until the film show began at 9pm.[35] After one of the shows in the Luhya area of western Kenya, an African was supposedly overheard to say after the weapons had been fired, 'it is better to be the friends of King George than his enemies'.[36]

By the end of the war Captain Dickson had managed to reinvent himself as something of an authority on the mobile cinema, publishing articles in metropolitan journals and making the case, as did many others, for applying the supposed great success of wartime film propaganda to the task of colonial development in the post-war age.[37] This was part of a broader call for a modernised and sympathetic approach to imperial rule that would involve mass education to transform colonial societies.[38] One of those involved in the East Africa Command mobile-cinema project, arguing that demobilised African soldiers should be co-opted into helping to educate people in rural areas, even cited Lenin's argument that it was the task of the Red Army veteran to 'make the deaf villages hear'.[39]

MOBILE CINEMA IN THE POST-WAR ERA

This developmentalist impulse led at the end of the war to the establishment of the Colonial Film Unit, with its mission to produce and distribute didactic movies. By the late 1940s, the CFU had twelve production units in eight countries in East and West Africa; but enthusiasm for mass education through film always ran substantially ahead of financial support, with colonial governments still unconvinced of the efficacy of film and suspicious of the dangers they associated with it. In Kenya the effort to develop welfare and information services not only ran up against budgetary constraints, but strong opposition from settler interests and conflict over what shape propaganda should take in a racially stratified society like Kenya.[40] The newly created African Information Services (AIS) received only minimal state support and its limited activities were viewed with suspicion by both the district administration and the white settler community. An ambitious plan to develop information centres that would include film shows fizzled out and the Kenyan government's media presence remained weak and haphazard into the early 1950s. Until late in 1946 only one mobile cinema van was in operation, when a second was added.[41]

Commercial interests also saw possibilities in bringing educational film to African audiences and, amid the general recognition of the potential of cinema, the Kenyan government received a number of requests from individuals and businesses seeking to establish private mobile film shows in rural areas. In 1946 African Sound Studios, based in Nairobi, approached the government with a plan to set up commercial mobile cinemas, similar to those that were operating successfully in outlying areas of Britain.

The Kenya Information Office was sceptical about this enterprise's potential for success, noting issues with crowd control and the collection of admission fees. Although some officials saw this as a good way to involve private enterprise in a broader educational mission and make up for the lack of public funding, the government ultimately concluded that, given 'conditions in Native areas', it was not the right moment to introduce commercial mobile cinema.[42] Official files on the 'Use of Cinematography' from that period make it clear that Nairobi officials feared the problems that might result when poorly capitalised businesses or businessmen attempted to profit from film shows but failed to provide adequate crowd control and offered 'inappropriate' movies.[43] A 1948 circular from the Deputy Chief Secretary underscored this view that 'it is at the present time undesirable to encourage commercial mobile cinemas to operate in this way', in the 'native areas for exhibition to African audiences'.[44] Although Africans still had only limited opportunities to see commercial films, the discussions that took place at this time over film censorship also reflected a broad consensus that African film shows should remain largely a state monopoly.[45]

The reluctance of the administration to permit private enterprise to enter the market for film shows in rural areas was expressed in the typical paternalistic rhetoric of colonial officials, voicing deeply held fears of the disruptive potential of commercial markets. At the same time, the opposition to commercial film shows seems to have reflected an understanding on the part of many officials of the important symbolic role that these film shows could play in buttressing the colonial regime. With private enterprise blocked and state funding limited, the mobile-cinema enterprise continued through the 1940s, with a small number of decrepit cinema vans touring the rural areas of the country. Nevertheless, film shows continued to be major community events, drawing large audiences of people who often travelled very considerable distances to see films. And many district officials became convinced that these shows represented an important opportunity to build support for the colonial regime. In Fort Hall District, in the Kikuyu-speaking region of central Kenya that would five years later be at the heart of the Mau Mau rebellion, the mobile cinema was already a popular fixture of local life in 1946. The District Commissioner clearly had his doubts about the efficacy of the propaganda films being shown and instead, perhaps predictably, suggested organising mobile-cinema tours in which film shows would occur in conjunction with sports and athletic competitions – in effect an extension of the wartime cinema shows that combined films with physical training and weapons displays.[46] Local administrators and mobile-cinema staff stressed the popularity of the cinema van and the role that the film shows and associated activities could play in changing attitudes toward the government in what was regarded as a highly politicised district.[47] A typical stop on a 1946 tour included several educational films, such as *Local Native Councils*, *Better African Homes*, *British Empire at War* and *Africans Visit Social Welfare Centres in England*, as well as athletics competitions, a dance, lectures on agricultural practices, social services and recreation, sports instruction and music from a record player.[48]

Three participants in a social-welfare course, Gibson Mwangi, Paul Gathii and Francis Thuku, accompanied the October 1946 tour through Fort Hall District and shared their reactions to shows that typically attracted 3–4,000 people. In addition to expressing the general frustration with interruptions caused by rain, two of the men concluded that cinema entertained but did not instruct. They noted especially 'actual antagonism to instruction when at the showing of a terracing film askaris [African police] had to check members of the audience who were using strong, antagonistic language in the vernacular', to argue that they already knew how to look after their own soil.[49] Although the third observer, Mwangi, was more optimistic about the educational benefits of films, all three noted that documentary films, for example on education in Britain, were often interpreted politically, as illustrating, in this instance, the disparity in wealth and resources between the metropole and colony. They also reported that in some of the more remote areas the cinema van was met by 'general suspicion' regarding the intentions of the white officer and his staff. This suspicion was by no means misplaced, since the Information Services staff regularly touted the opportunities for intelligence-gathering and surveillance that cinema tours represented – even if the district administration was wary of such activities.[50]

Among the early targets of the post-war mobile-cinema programme were the relatively impoverished Kamba-speaking districts of Kitui and Machakos, east of Nairobi, where prewar protests had attacked state efforts to reduce livestock herds. In the late 1940s, this area became the focus of a concerted effort on the part of the administration to combat soil erosion – notably including the use of media vans.[51] This was a rare case in the history of mobile cinema in Kenya of a close alignment between mobile film shows and specific development policies, yet the emphasis in the reports was still less on the specific impact of films on agricultural practices than on the broader role of the film shows in building support for the government. Mobile-cinema staff had been warned to expect 'unrest and in places, hostility to the Government', in Machakos but, despite some evidence of political activism, they met no antagonism.

Predictably, the accounts of the tours through Kitui and Machakos placed emphasis on the maintenance of order, reporting that, with a couple of exceptions, the large crowds that turned out were easy to control. Notwithstanding their apparent affection for cinema, local people were characterised as 'ultra conservative and distrustful of European ideals and ideas, with the exception of a growing worship of the "almighty dollar" '. And the tours often encountered the argument that previous agricultural recommendations had not worked out and that traditional crops and agricultural practices were more reliable. Once again, the cinema tour reports were as much about gauging political sentiments in this rural area as they were about documenting the efficacy of the films shown.[52] In July 1947 a tour, using a new van with the capacity to show sound movies, included twenty-five shows that each attracted crowds of between 1,000 and 5,500. The two-day stop at Kangundo, regarded as a centre of political activity, drew in almost 10,000 at two shows, although it was thought that, given the equipment, shows ought to be limited to a thousand. The tour report noted that 'it was significant that crowd control during shows was very much easier this year'.[53] Apparently anxious to use the colonial-film apparatus to co-opt African politicians, officials permitted the local Kenya African Union (KAU) leader, Paul Ngei, to make an announcement over the PA system at one of the Kangundo shows. They were surprised and disappointed when he used the mike to urge the crowd to attend an upcoming KAU meeting.[54]

Most problems, however, had no direct political instigation, as in the case of the trouble that occurred in Kangundo two years later when some elders objected to the standard rule of seating women and children in front. A good deal of arguing went on for about fifteen minutes until the operator was able to restore order and continue the show, which included a number of additional disruptions. The District Commissioner's report makes it clear, however, that his primary concern was not with the actions of a few elders, but with the absence of the chief and tribal police from what he clearly regarded as an official event.[55] Such problems arose occasionally at film shows across the colony, typically caused by alcohol and demands on the part of senior men that they be accorded appropriate deference.[56] Disruptions may have been rare, but audience control and behaviour were nevertheless standard elements in the evaluation of cinema tours and colonial authorities acted forcefully when problems arose. In 1949 at Chepterwei in the Nandi District the local headman easily handled a few drunks at the first of three shows, but on the following day he was absent and

> the audience were most unsatisfactory. There were too many drunks and too much noise. Fighting broke out and the Headman's Tribal Policeman was hit over the head when attempting to restore order. The show was completed but it was most unsatisfactory.[57]

When the film-show operator warned those present that if their behaviour didn't improve the show scheduled for the following night would be cancelled, he was shouted down. Since the headman could not be found the next day, the show was cancelled and a report made to the local chief and the District Officer that placed as much weight on the derelict headman as it did on the unruly audience.[58]

For the most part, however, the tours were uneventful. Over the course of several circuits, between April and July of 1947, many tens of thousands of people in Kitui and Machakos saw movies focusing on soil conservation, manuring, thrift, dam building and hygiene.[59] According to Information Services reports, 'an attempt was made after some cinema shows to measure the reaction of the crowd to the films shown, but with indifferent success, though loud acclamation was recorded by the children to the humorous items', a reminder that all of the film programmes included some movies purely designed for entertainment.[60] The officer in charge of the tour noted growing support, including among women, in the area for soil conservation and reported that 'several Chiefs asserted that this was largely due to propaganda by the Government Mobile Cinema – a very gratifying thought if true, and I personally have no doubt that this is the case'.[61]

Such confident assertions of the link between cinema shows and welfare policy were relatively rare, however and, as the audiences for film shows mounted into the hundreds of thousands across the country, district officials seem actually to have become less interested in the direct educational impact of films and more concerned with the value of the film shows themselves.

By 1950, district officials in Machakos and in districts across the colony continually pressed and occasionally begged the Information Services to send the mobile cinema vans into their districts. The Information Services meanwhile had to make do with outdated equipment, limited staff and a library of ageing movies. Mobile-cinema tours in Machakos in the late 1940s and early 1950s typically included from twenty-five to more than sixty shows.[62] One tour in late 1949 had to be cut short after only six shows but still attracted a total audience of more than 9,000 from the area not far from district headquarters.[63] At times the shows were quite minimal. Plans for a van tour with three driver/operators for July of 1950 in Machakos included only one film, *Trees Are Cash*, that had been made in Uganda, and a filmstrip. District officials complained relentlessly about the quality of the films, the lack of variety and the problem of mechanical breakdowns.[64]

Why was it then that district officials pushed so hard and enthusiastically for the mobile-cinema tours – with all the technical problems, challenges of audience management and disappointment over movies that were worn and out of date? As is apparent in official concern with the location of shows – preferably near government buildings, schools and so forth – and with the presence of local officials, these shows had come to be regarded as important spectacles of the local imperial state – a state that these officials very much wished to associate with advanced technology and modernity.[65] Whatever the problems, the shows generated enormous excitement. Thousands of local people crowded together as night fell, waiting with anticipation for the magic of motion-picture technology, brought to them by the agents of British colonialism, to illuminate the screen and carry them off into other worlds. George Nthenge, who was in charge of a van in Machakos during that period, affords us a rare glimpse of the excitement that followed the mobile cinema vans, recalling that 'cinema then was a miracle, almost … it was popular with all the people including seniors'.[66] As the cinema tours were increasingly run by African staff, the presence of these men, with their education and knowledge of English and their progressive values, only served to underscore the modernising agenda of the cinema spectacle.[67] Thus, the often intimate involvement of district officials in planning tours and their preoccupation with the quality of apparatus and image were not at all surprising. In fact, it is quite clear in the requests made by some officials for particular films that their preferences were driven not by the subject matter as much as by the physical quality of the celluloid print.

As the pleading entreaties of rural district officials make clear, by the late 1940s, a new generation of colonial administrators had come to see mobile cinema shows as an important strategy for reinventing the colonial state in a modern form. They lobbied aggressively for visits from the mobile vans and argued for as many film shows as possible in each tour.[68] A 1949 note from a local chief requesting a visit from the mobile cinema suggests that the fascination with the possibilities of cinema as a tool of administration had extended to the grassroots, to local African members of the colonial bureaucracy.[69] Officials in the Rift Valley, like those elsewhere in Kenya, were film-show enthusiasts. In May 1950, the District Commissioner in relatively remote Tambach strongly requested the mobile cinema, complaining that there had not been a show in the district for more than a year.[70] The cinema tour was finally scheduled for July and attracted large audiences. Over the course of twenty days, covering nearly 1,000 miles, the 'mobile information unit' presented twenty-five shows reaching an estimated total audience of more than 19,000. Specific attendance data showed that as many as 3,000 turned out for some shows and as few as 100 for others. The 'main propaganda theme' of the shows was 'soil conservation, co-operation and hard work', but officials seemed little interested in whether the films presented advanced these goals or not. Instead, again, they focused on numbers in attendance and audience behaviour. Each show typically included four or five films and no filmstrips.[71] In contrast, a cinema tour in Elgeyo Marakwet in October 1951 was deemed something of a failure because attendance was 'fair or even less than fair', with shows typically attracting 400 or 500 people, but some only thirty, forty or fifty, possibly because of a conflict with some local ceremonies. Following one show, it was necessary 'to write to the Chief of Sambiri Location to call for a larger audience and he himself or his headmen to attend the next show'.[72]

An African mobile-cinema operator reported that a three-week tour in 1950 in Uasin Gishu and Elgeyo Marakwet Districts in the Rift Valley received a good reaction everywhere. The programme included playing records and broadcasting radio shows. Attendance went as high as 3,000, many of the programmes attracted over 1,000 people and quite a few had between 500 and 1,000 people in attendance. There was no mention of which films were shown or the impact of those particular films.[73] A year later the District Commissioner of Elgeyo Marakwet commented that local audiences preferred war movies, films about the royal family, empire travelogues and how-to movies about agriculture – essentially the only types of films that were available.[74] In contrast to Central Africa and other British territories, Kenyan audiences had little access to commercial entertainment films such as the Westerns that were hugely popular elsewhere. Audiences in Kenya had to content themselves with the old comedies that were stock elements in mobile-cinema and public film shows and look for 'action' in the World War II documentaries that were still being shown in the early 1950s. Wartime audiences had found films showing footage of officials visiting munitions factories boring, but they loved scenes of actual combat.[75] The Crown Film Unit's movie on the blitz, *London Can Take It* (1940) apparently caused a great deal of excitement when it was shown.[76] By 1950, the World War II documentaries like *Why We Fight: Tunisian Victory* (1943), or *White Battle Front* (1941) on war in Russia were still the staples of film libraries.[77] A report of a cinema-van tour through Nandi District in 1950 noted that 'almost everywhere some of the attendants [members of the audience] expressed their wish to see some films on the last World War'.[78] In 1951 the District Commissioner in Marakwet begged to be sent 'any news films which you may have which have definite entertainment value for unsophisticated audiences', for example, war documentaries. His film list included *Victory Parade* (1946), *Masai Cattlemen*, *Laughing Gas*, *Plainsmen of Barotseland*, *Cinemagazine*, *Tapeworm* and the perennial standard, *Mr Wise and Mr Foolish*, an updating of the movie *The Two Brothers* that dramatised the dangers of syphilis.[79]

The report of a 1950 Commission of Inquiry into the African Information Services and its efforts to reach African audiences revealed that there was considerable 'public doubt' as to its efficacy.[80] The commission detailed a long list of problems, in particular noting the 'very low' quality of the African press, general inefficiency and limited activity. The Information Services was conceived at that time as a central unit for the production and distribution of all kinds of media, including 16mm films, filmstrips, booklets, pamphlets, posters, radio programmes, photo displays and recordings.[81] There was not much to show for that ambition, however. Information services were in practice scattered among various departments, sometimes centralised and other times based in the districts and towns. There was little co-ordination among the various enterprises, and few of them were at all well funded. Mobile cinema received considerable attention in the report. At the time of the investigation, the AIS had four mobile-cinema units operating and in the first six months of 1949 gave almost 500 shows to more than 600,000 African viewers. In light of these numbers, the mobile cinema represented a relative success story for the Information Services, at least from the point of view of the members of the official commission.[82] The commission ultimately recommended the appointment of higher-level staff and a more ambitious effort in which the Information Services would clearly align its efforts with the 'task of promoting the accepted policy of raising the standard of living of the majority of the inhabitants of this country as soon as possible, and the maintenance of tranquility and good relations'.[83]

The AIS soon put forward an information plan with the mobile cinemas at the heart of a multimedia effort, with the film shows serving as centrepieces for the distribution of various print material and also opportunities to expose audiences to phonograph recordings and radio. In 1950, Tom Askwith promoted this more comprehensive approach in his newly created role of Commissioner for Community Development. He asked district officials to request specific films and to plan tour itineraries so that vans could remain in one place for more than one day to allow for the distribution and sale of printed materials and for programmes beyond the film show. Each 'multimedia' van would be equipped not only with the film projector but a public-address system, a turntable, a filmstrip projector, pamphlets, posters and publications from the East African Literature Bureau.[84] The vans would also be used to promote radio, which was then very much in its early stages, with few Africans owning receivers and the signal weak except in Nairobi and Mombasa. The mobile-cinema radio broadcasts were seen as a bridge to the creation of a network of permanent community centres where newspapers and magazines would be distributed and people could gather for film shows and radio broadcasts.[85] The director of the AIS even proposed a project in which cameras would be purchased and distributed to community centres, allowing local people to make and then watch their own films.[86] Amid a rhetoric that stressed the education and development potential of a comprehensive media approach, the plan nevertheless emphasised the 'importance of purely entertainment films as a leavening in education programs' and noted the increasing difficulty in obtaining 'humorous films commercially of a kind which appeal to Africans'.[87]

In an atmosphere of growing political unrest and activity in Kikuyuland and elsewhere in Kenya, the central administration, pressured by settler interests, remained ambivalent about information services aimed at the African population. In 1951, steps were taken to further centralise and develop the African Information Services, but the mobile cinema, and other mass-education efforts, remained substantially unchanged.[88] As Kenya moved toward violent rebellion, the idea of thousands of people assembled after dark for outdoor cinema shows suggested not the pageantry of the local state but a potentially dangerous assemblage of rebels and malcontents. And, although the technical apparatus of film presentation might certainly advance the interests of colonialism in Kenya, there was increasing division over what those interests were and also growing fear that, once that apparatus was in place, it could be used for other purposes, just as the political leader Paul Ngei had seized the mobile-cinema microphone at a meeting in Machakos District in 1947 to advertise his cause.

THE MOBILE CINEMA IN THE EMERGENCY ERA

In late 1952 with the outbreak of the Mau Mau rebellion, the Colonial Office and the Kenyan government moved to develop a propaganda campaign that would quiet white settler anxieties; project an image of the conflict in Britain and the rest of the world as an atavistic struggle of reactionary 'tribal' forces against modern Kenyans; and reassure ordinary Kenyans in the areas of conflict and beyond of the advantages of British colonial rule. But, with a weak information service and a colonial state leadership obsessed with the idea of psychological warfare, it would be more than a year before any local propaganda plan began to take shape.[89] A 1964 overview of the history of film in East Africa published in the journal *Transition* claimed that official film production in Kenya in the 1950s was largely a reaction to Mau Mau and that the informational films produced on topics like cotton production, fishing, tuberculosis, the importance of tax payment and government operations were part of a 'large concerted government campaign using posters, radio, exhibits, etc'.[90] It is difficult, however, to find evidence that this was the case. It is certainly true that the mobile-cinema programme expanded during Mau Mau, but only gradually; and the cinema shows of the mid-1950s seem to have differed little from those of the preceding decade.

Despite its supposed commitment to strengthening African 'loyalist' support within the country, the Kenyan administration in fact focused most of its propaganda efforts on an audience outside Kenya, notably in Britain itself. Some scholars have alluded to extensive propaganda campaigns undertaken by the Kenyan government to oppose Mau Mau and in particular to expose instances of violence and terrorism, but the evidence is elusive.[91] Certainly, the colonial regime's highest priority was to produce media materials for external consumption, including the Hollywood films like *Something of Value* (1957) and others that conveyed British imperial perspectives to American and European audiences.[92] Given the expense and complexity of producing films and the security concerns surrounding film shows, it is perhaps not surprising that the anti-Mau Mau campaign did not really surface explicitly in the mobile cinema.

Even before the onset of the rebellion, the Provincial Commissioner in Nakuru in the Rift Valley had held meetings with employers, government officials and others with a view to devising 'means of combating the activities of the Maumau [sic]' in that area that had already experienced considerable political violence. One outcome of those meetings was a decision to step up entertainment and information activities such as the mobile cinema. The film show held at Njoro in January 1950 on commercial premises was 'certainly very well received by the Africans, of whom not less than 1,500 attended the show in the evening'. The films that were shown on that evening 'were not made specially to combat the Maumau [sic] and were looked on largely as entertainment' but, in keeping with the existing approach to mobile cinema, such a strategy was regarded as both desirable and effective. Reflecting the racism that permeated Kenyan society at that time, European officials and especially employers often argued that entertainment such as film shows and 'healthy pursuits' such as athletics would divert Africans from political engagement. But at the same time, the mobile cinema was also seen to be bolstering the state and building its legitimacy as an agent of progress and change for Africans. The proprietor of the company where the Njoro film show took place noted that 'there can be no doubt that the seeds of the propaganda showing what was done for the African must bear fruit in due course'.[93]

But with officials in Nairobi preoccupied with a military and police campaign that would ultimately criminalise a substantial proportion of the male Kikuyu population, there was little interest in and fewer resources for a concerted media effort to reach out to the general population.[94] Film shows were apparently suspended in the areas where the rebellion was centred and state information and media programmes remained fragmented and meagrely funded. In a statement that is remarkably half-hearted and more than a little revealing, the Deputy Governor wrote in September 1953 that

> we do most heartily agree in the need to offset the inevitable effects of the Security Force operations, and to bring some laughter and joy back into the lives of the people. Cycling clubs, more football, an extension of African broadcasting, cheaper radio sets, redefusion and bands, the Scout movement, an African civil servants' club, open-air cinemas ... quite a lot of new stuff is going on.[95]

Notwithstanding a persistent imperial rhetoric that linked media, and film in particular, to lofty goals of civil education and economic development, the Deputy Governor's point could hardly be clearer: mobile cinema and other similar programmes were elements of a disconnected policy to divert Africans from political activity. Moreover, it was quite plain that 'quite a lot of new stuff' was not in fact going on.

By 1955, the Information Department had expanded its mobile-cinema effort to include a total of seven film vans and ten smaller 'information vans'. The cinema vans followed monthly itineraries, arranged by provincial Information Officers.[96] The central administration urged that these be used as part of concerted, well-organised 'campaigns' to advance particular projects or programmes, for example, in public health or agricultural practices, but district records documenting film tours provide little evidence of such systematic efforts. A 1955 report from the Department of Information and Propaganda acknowledged somewhat reluctantly that 'many people agree that film shows for Africans are essential', and that a growing number of government departments were using film and that several had established their own mobile-cinema units. Still the results were clearly very uneven, with some areas described as 'flooded with film shows, and others are starved'. This haphazard situation was cause for official concern, regarding both the lack of co-ordination and financial waste. Each cinema van cost £2,500 and the costs associated with running them were considerable; and a major concern of the central administration was that high costs had led individual government offices to cut corners, hiring unqualified and insufficient staff, in order to get mobile-cinema vans into the field, in the process blunting the potential impact of the film shows.[97] In violation of official policy, the Department of Community Development and Rehabilitation, for example, actually borrowed films from the Information Department library for free and then charged admission. Nairobi officials worried too that they were losing control over the content of film programmes. Some local officials regularly showed films using equipment their offices had purchased – in one case a locally made film that included images of 'the bodies of Mau Mau "terrorists" '.[98] Showing such movies led to debates that once more revealed the absence of consensus around information policy, but it is not difficult to imagine that this kind of footage had the kind of appeal for some audiences that brought them back again and again to watch dated World War II propaganda films.

Not surprisingly, officials welcomed the new multimedia information vans. By 1955 the Information Services was experimenting with sending small spectacles on the road, embracing and elaborating on the notion of the mobile cinema 'performing the state'. The new ABS (African Broadcasting Services) Entertainment Unit travelled in two vehicles with eleven African staff and a European officer-in-charge. Three of the staff provided technical support, but the other eight were professional entertainers who performed as a band and as an acting troupe.[99] Each performance required that a stage be constructed; the shows took place in open air just after sunset and lasted about an hour and a half. The unit carried its own lights and loudspeakers and, in a significant break with the past, a small admission charge was sometimes collected. After the formal show there were African dances.[100] Reports from the district indicate that these performances drew large crowds and were very popular, both with local people and with the district officials, who once again saw opportunities to connect their administrations to these very modern and sophisticated enterprises. More modest information vans travelled on local circuits carrying record players and tape recorders as well as microphones and an amplifier. Often these vans were simply employed at meetings to provide amplification for speeches but they could also supply music. With the tape recorders, staff could record interviews and music on the spot – which could in turn be played back to a local audience or broadcast later on radio. The vans also had radios that could be amplified, as the Kenyan government expanded its broadcast capacity. Vans also carried various printed materials, photographs and posters. A silent-film projector allowed movies to be shown to audiences of up to 500.[101]

The actual experience of the mobile-cinema shows seems, however, to have been largely unchanged. An outraged report from a District Commissioner regarding a cinema tour in the Rift Valley in early 1955 makes it clear that there was certainly no concerted effort to engage the mobile cinema as a propaganda tool to counter Mau Mau – even in this area quite close to the focus of much of the resistance activity. The District Commissioner protested the last-minute arrangements, the small number of films offered and the poor quality of at least one of the films.[102] He described one Saturday-evening cinema show as a disastrous embarrassment: the movies were repeatedly interrupted by the film breaking; the movies shown, *Tribal Dances of Kenya*, *London Zoo* and *Queen Elizabeth*, were old and worn and difficult to see on a poor-quality cloth screen. He also noted that the van driver seemed to be using the van for personal purposes.[103] Within a few months a new information van had been assigned to the area, equipped with a public-address system, a tape recorder, radio, record player and a better projector – but one that was not suitable for the large film shows that were the centrepiece of mobile-cinema operations.[104]

For local officials the purpose of the mobile cinema remained unchanged: that films entertain the audiences, that they be good quality and that the projectors and other equipment function efficiently. The shift toward the multimedia information vans underscored the role of mobile cinema in the technological spectacle of imperial rule, but only powerful projectors permitted shows that attracted the huge audiences that could symbolically demonstrate state power: a disciplined audience in thrall to the moving images playing across the screen, overseen by the agents of the colonial government – District Officers, local chiefs and headmen, and also very importantly those Africans, the van drivers and cinema operators, who managed the technological apparatus. Hence the preoccupation of officials with advance notice, proper organisation, disciplined film showings, appropriate behaviour by van operators, high-quality footage and especially the smooth operation of the equipment itself.[105] These preoccupations also help explain why in late 1955 a District Commissioner again based in the Rift Valley complained bitterly when van tours were cancelled without notice or explanation. With considerable petulance, he went on to note that the mobile cinema teams avoided tours into the districts where population density was lower and roads more difficult – revealing in the process an attitude of almost desperate need for these instruments of modernity in their 'unfashionable districts'.[106]

In any case, the mobile-cinema tours continued to attract many hundreds of thousands of people each year. During 1956, for example, the Machakos District mobile-cinema van was continuously on tour and 89,000 saw films. The film shows were supposedly an element of an anti-witchcraft propaganda campaign that had begun in 1955; but once again the documents make no mention of which films were shown or how it was that these would have combated witchcraft.[107] In 1956 the Information Services did, however, organise a cinema campaign to encourage voter participation in the areas of the country (outside the districts involved in Mau Mau) that were participating in the colony's first multiracial elections. In the Rift Valley two cinema vans offered two showings each day of a twenty-minute film that had been produced in six different African languages and that was shown across Kenya. Based on recent cinema tours, officials anticipated very substantial audiences even in the relatively less populated pastoral areas: 11,000 in Uasin Gishu, 13,000 in Elgeyo, 6,000 in Baringo, 20,000 in Nandi, 7,000 in West Suk and 4,500 in Trans Nzoia – a total of about 60,000.[108] Officials felt it necessary to stress the relative novelty of a film campaign that had an explicit educational message, because they feared that too many children would turn up for film showings that many would presume to be entertainment.[109]

Given the types of films that were included in typical mobile-cinema shows, there was little concern about the appropriateness of movies for African audiences. Like other British colonies, Kenya had a censorship board that reviewed, categorised and sometimes cut or even banned the popular films that were imported for commercial exhibition. With the still small African audience for these films confined to a few urban theatres, censorship attracted little interest until the 1950s. Then, predictably, worries about the impact of popular films intensified with the onset of the Mau Mau rebellion and the number of films banned increased substantially.[110] At the request of the Special Branch, the chairman of the Board of Film Censorship provided a summary of the board's policy on the Westerns that were very popular at that time in Kenya and across the continent. These guidelines were predictable in respect to the kinds of scenes that the board considered unsuitable:

> Violent conflict between White man and Red Indians, attacks by the latter on and the over-running of wagons, forts or homesteads, with the killing of White women. Scenes emphasizing the conquest of Indian country, often by treachery, and the evictions of its inhabitants ... scenes of cold blooded shooting at close quarters.[111]

Yet the board stopped short of condemning Westerns, regarding many as harmless and stressing that the board could not make 'hard and fast rules'. For those disturbed by the sight of African youths dressed in cowboy attire, the board chairman noted that 'small boys in England regularly adopt this costume' and noted that the cowboy was a 'romantic character'. In short, the chairman expressed scepticism that this kind of film had much if any impact on actual behaviour.[112]

This issue became more urgent in 1955 when Nairobi City Council developed a plan to offer film shows for African residents in the Nairobi Stadium that would include commercial movies. This plan raised predictable concerns among central government officials, increasingly concerned about urban unrest and just a year after Operation Anvil had removed large numbers of the Kikuyu residents from the city.[113] While the council intended in effect to take the mobile-cinema concept into urban neighbourhoods, in addition to offering various kinds of public-service films, the plan also involved showing commercial movies, advertisements and charging admission.[114] A leading colonial official feared that 'many films pass the Censorship Board which are not suitable for showing to Africans in large doses, e.g. Cowboy films' and members of his staff likewise worried that 'a surfeit of cowboy and gangster films might have a most undesirable effect on the behavior of audiences'.[115] Once again, however, local administrators, the very people charged with maintaining order, seem to have been much more concerned with providing entertainment, building the credibility of government, and not incidentally generating revenue than they were about any supposed dangers associated with cinema. A year later, as Mau Mau was increasingly contained, movies were being shown routinely on a commercial basis in the Nairobi council welfare halls apparently without incident.[116]

CINEMA AND THE END OF BRITISH RULE

In the late 1950s, the reach of the mobile cinema steadily expanded and audiences grew rapidly; yet even as colonial officials made more insistent efforts to link the colonial state to this symbol of modernity, the age of the colonial mobile cinema was ending. In the final years of colonial rule, Kenya and other African dependencies increasingly opened rural areas to commercial capitalism and at the same time embraced new state-centred electronic media – radio and television. As the massive effort to suppress the Mau Mau rebellion wound down, private interests began to develop ambitious plans for building theatres and taking movies into the countryside – plans that many paternalistic officials once again resisted as they had in the immediate post-war period. But in this instance, they were unsuccessful in warding off business interests.[117] In the late 1950s proposals for commercial film showings in rural areas increased in number and in 1958 East African Film Services (EAFS), based in Nairobi, proposed a mobile-cinema programme that would include didactic films and that would be supported through fifteen minutes of advertising for each ninety-minute show.[118] By 1959 this company was sending out regular mobile film shows, exhibiting mostly entertainment films, in the rural areas that had previously been the hotbed of Mau Mau as well as other regions of the country. The business was apparently only marginally profitable, however, and the company abandoned its ambitious plans for local film production; instead the EAFS mobile film shows offered the usual mix of newsreels, wildlife documentaries and musicals as well as the advertising shorts that paid the bills.[119] At the same time other companies entered the market, including Factual Films Ltd, which was operating a cinema van in the region around Kisumu in 1959.[120] Various versions of mobile cinemas would in fact continue for many years as quaint reminders of its earlier history.

Notwithstanding the expansion of film enterprises in the countryside, in the 1960s the audience for commercial films in Kenya remained very small and movies ceased to be a major concern of officials. In much the same way as the local government officials during the 1940s and 1950s had perceived an opportunity to link the fortunes of the state to the magic of movies, the officials of late colonial Kenya and their successors in independent Kenya attached their fortunes to radio and television.[121] During the late 1950s, the expansion of broadcast services and the increasing availability of relatively cheap radio sets made radio, held firmly in the hands of the state, a much more efficient way to embrace the populace than the relatively expensive mobile cinemas, with their uncertain schedules and their tendency to break down. Television gradually expanded in the 1960s and, although far less pervasive than radio, nevertheless brought motion pictures directly to many hundreds of thousands of people.[122] And even if in Kenya, as in many African countries, the optimistic plans to develop local programming were quickly set aside in favour of dated foreign products, there was solace to be had in the fact that more than once viewers might see on television some of the very same films that had once lit up the night in the Kenyan countryside.

NOTES

For research assistance and comments on the manuscript, I would like to thank Gordon Omenya, Myles Osborne, James Burns, Kenda Mutongi and Cullen Haskins.

1. Kenya National Archives (hereafter KNA): 'Government Mobile Cinema Annual Report for 1944, Nyanza Province, Stage and Cinema General, 1945–7', PC/NZA/2/7/92.
2. James Burns, *Flickering Shadows: Cinema and Identity in Colonial Zimbabwe* (Athens: Ohio University Press, 2002). Note in particular also the pioneering work of Rosaleen Smyth, including 'Movies and Mandarins: The Official Film and British Colonial Africa', in James Curran and Vincent Porter (eds), *British Cinema History* (Totowa, NJ: Barnes & Noble Books, 1983), pp. 129–256; 'The Post-war Career of the Colonial Film Unit in Africa: 1946–1955', *Historical Journal of Film, Radio and Television* vol. 12 no. 2, 1992, pp. 163–77;

and 'Britain's African Colonies and British Propaganda during the Second World War', *Journal of Imperial and Commonwealth History* vol. 14 no. 1, 1985, pp. 65–82.

3. C. J. M. Alport, 'Kenya's Answer to the Mau Mau Challenge', *African Affairs* vol. 53 no. 212, 1954, p. 245. I have myself been guilty of this. See Charles Ambler, 'Popular Films and Colonial Audiences: The Movies in Northern Rhodesia', *American Historical Review* vol. 106, 2001, pp. 81–105.

4. Brian Larkin also stresses the importance of official film shows in his study of media in Nigeria, *Signal and Noise: Media, Infrastructure, and Urban Culture in Nigeria* (Durham, NC: Duke University Press, 2008).

5. Smyth, 'Movies and Mandarins', pp. 129–43; and see also Lee Grieveson and Colin MacCabe (eds), *Empire and Film* (London: BFI, 2011).

6. Quoted in Smyth, 'Movies and Mandarins', p. 130.

7. KNA: Director of Education, Circular, 26 June 1936, Provincial Commissioner, Nyanza, 'Law and Order: Cinema Shows, 1931–43'; Education Department to Provincial Commissioner, Nyanza, 16 August 1938, Provincial Commissioner, Nyanza, 'Law and Order: Cinema Shows, 1931–43', PC/NZA/3/15/157, nos 18 and 35.

8. KNA: Ambrose Coghill, 'A Memorandum on the Education of East African Natives by Means of Mobile Cinema Projection Units', enclosed in Secretariat Circular, 6 July 1939, PC Nyanza, 'Law and Order: Cinema Shows, 1931–43', PC/NZA/3/15/157, no. 49. This report was produced at the instigation of J. Russell Orr, by the Central Information Bureau for Educational Films, Ltd. Orr was the first Director of Education in Kenya.

9. Ibid.

10. In 1939 the African audience for commercial film shows remained very small. See KNA: District Commissioner, Kisumu to Provincial Commissioner, Nyanza, 13 December 1939, PC Nyanza, 'Law and Order', no. 68.

11. Smyth, 'Britain's African Colonies and British Propaganda during the Second World War'; and Joanna Lewis, *Empire State-building* (Oxford: James Currey, 2000), pp. 47, 102.

12. Advisory Committee on Education in the Colonies, *Mass Education in African Society*, 1944, quoted in Smyth, 'Movies and Mandarins', pp. 133–4.

13. KNA: A. M. Champion, 'The Mobile Cinema in Africa', 1944, enc. in Kenya Information Office to Chief Secretary, 26 May 1944, Mobile Cinema Units, 1942/52, Use of Cinematography, CS/2/8/75, no. 21. Champion was a former missionary and early British officer in Kenya. He was posted in a number of different areas, but he was a central figure in the events surrounding Giriama resistance to British rule in 1912. See Cynthia Brantley, *The Giriama and Colonial Resistance in Kenya, 1800–1920* (Berkeley: University of California Press, 1981).

14. Champion, 'The Mobile Cinema in Africa'.

15. Ibid.

16. Ibid.

17. Ibid.

18. Ibid.

19. KNA: Provincial Commissioner, Nyanza to District Commissioners, Nyanza Province, 7 November 1940, PC Nyanza, 'Law and Order', no. 178. During the war, the Kenyan government invested considerable sums in additional equipment for the mobile cinema. See KNA: Welfare Activities: 'Report of Action as from 24th April to 23rd July 1941'; and 'Sixth Progress Report: East Africa Command Welfare Activities – Report of Action as from

1st July to 30th November 1942, Confidential, War Welfare Activities, 1939–1948', PC/CP.13.4/1 (information from Myles Osborne).

20. KNA: A. M. Champion, 'Confidential Report of Government Cinema Unit (not to be distributed below heads of department)', 19 September 1941 and Provincial Commissioner to A. M. Champion, 22 September 1941, PC Nyanza, 'Law and Order', nos 210 and 211. Also, 'Bwana Cinema Retires after Useful Sojourn', *East Africa Standard*, 10 April 1944, enc. in KNA: 'Organisation and Establishment, Information & Propaganda, 1941–44', CS/2/8/35.

21. KNA: Provincial Commissioner to A.M. Champion, 22 September 1941, PC Nyanza, 'Law and Order', no. 211.

22. KNA: Arthur Champion, 'Report of Government Mobile Cinema Unit for the Period Dec. 17 to Jan. 11, 1942 (confidential)', 13 January 1942, PC Nyanza, 'Law and Order: Cinema Shows, 1931–43', PC/NZA/3/15/157, no. 232.

23. KNA: Secretariat, 'Government Mobile Cinema Unit', Circular Letter no. 34, 21 April 1942, PC Nyanza, 'Law and Order', no. 248.

24. KNA: Champion, 'Report of Government Mobile Cinema Unit for the Period Dec. 17 to Jan. 11, 1942 (confidential)'.

25. KNA: PC Nyanza to District Commissioners, 27 January 1942, PC Nyanza, 'Law and Order', no. 211.

26. KNA: A. Champion, 'Report of the Government Mobile Cinema Unit for the Fortnight Ending Feb. 8, 1942, 11 Feb. 1942', PC Nyanza, 'Law and Order', no. 236.

27. KNA: 'Mobile Cinema – Rachwonyo', Welfare Officer to Directorate of Pioneers and Labor, 5 March 1942, PC Nyanza, 'Law and Order', no. 245.

28. 'Bwana Cinema Retires after Useful Sojourn'.

29. Ibid.

30. Ibid.

31. Ibid.

32. Ibid.

33. Lewis, *Empire State-building*, p. 210.

34. KNA: Mobile Cinema – Rachwonyo.

35. KNA: Headquarters, Western Kenya, Kenya Defense Forces, Kisumu to Provincial Commissioner, Nyanza, 8 March 1943, PC Nyanza, 'Law and Order', no. 255. Also, 'East Africa Mobile Propaganda Unit'; 'Dynamic Propaganda', reprinted from *East African Standard*, 21 January 1944; and 'Programme of Mobile Propaganda Unit', East Africa Cinema Unit, DC/KPAT/1/13/6
nos 1, 2, 3.

36. KNA: 'Draft Programme for Mobile Information Units', n.d. [*c.* 1946], Information and Propaganda, Africans, 1941–57, CS/1/10/44.

37. Lewis, *Empire State-building*, p. 212.

38. Ibid.

39. KNA: 'Draft Programme for Mobile Information Units'.

40. Lewis, *Empire State-building*, pp. 257–61.

41. Ibid., p. 259.

42. KNA: Chief Secretary to East Africa Sound Studios [1946], Chief Secretary, Information and Propaganda. Use of Cinematography, CS/2/8/48, no. 78A. See also PC/NZA/2/7/92, Stage and Cinema General Services, for documentation of several proposals during the 1940s.

43. KNA: Chief Secretary, Information and Propaganda. Use of Cinematography, CS/2/8/48, notably minute no. 73.
44. KNA: C. H. Thornley, Deputy Chief Secretary, Circular Letter, 'Cinematograph Exhibitions in the Native Areas', 9 March 1948, East Africa Cinema Unit, DC/KAPT/1/13/6, no. 111.
45. Gareth McFeely, 'Film Censorship in Kenya', unpublished paper, African Studies Association, Annual Meeting, 2009.
46. KNA: DC, Fort Hall, to Information Officer, Nairobi, Government Mobile Cinema Unit, 8 November 1946, CS/2/8/117.
47. KNA: Captain P. R. G. Hutchison, Officer in Charge, Mobile Information Unit, to the Information Officer, Nairobi, 31 October 1946, CS/2/8/117, no. 1.
48. KNA: A note on the experiences of and comments by men in the social-welfare course who went on tour with the Information Office mobile propaganda unit in the Fort Hall Reserve, Appendix 2 in ibid.
49. Ibid.
50. Ibid. Joanna Lewis has documented the tension between the district administration and welfare staff around this issue in *Empire State-building*.
51. KNA: 'Memorandum on a Visit to Machakos to Discuss the Initiation of a Propaganda Drive in the District', enc. in Acting Information Officer to Chief Secretary, Sir Gilbert Rennie, 29 January 1947, Information and Propaganda, Africans, 1941–57, CS/1/10/44.
52. KNA: Major W. S. MacLellan Wilson, 'Notes on Impressions Gained after a 3 Months' Tour of the Machakos Reserves with the Government Mobile Cinema from 23rd April 1946 to 28th July 1946', Information and Propaganda, Africans, 1941–57, CS/1/10/44.
53. KNA: 'Report on the Tour of the Government Mobile Cinema in Ukamba from 1st July to 28th July 1946', Information and Propaganda, Africans, 1941–57, CS/1/10/44.
54. KNA: Report of Machakos Tour of Mobile Cinema Van, July–August 1947, enc. in Acting Information Officer, 'Mobile Cinema Van Tour of Machakos', 30 August 1947, Information and Propaganda, Africans, 1941–57, CS/1/10/44. Ngei would later be detained during the Mau Mau emergency and would eventually be a minister in the independent Kenyan government.
55. KNA: DC, Machakos to African Information Services, 4 August 1949, DC/MKS/8/3, no. 38.
56. A year later, the Machakos District Welfare Office instructed the local chief in Iveti location, close both to Kangundo and to the district headquarters, to arrest two men from the area who had a caused a disturbance at the mobile film show a couple of days earlier – which had left two gramophone records broken. KNA: District Welfare Officer to Chief Kalovoto, Iveti Location 13 June 1950, DC/MKS/8/3 no. 105.
57. KNA: 'Report on Nandi District Safari – Nov. 3rd 1949 to Dec. 3rd', no. 4 Mobile Information Unit, East Africa Cinema Unit, DC/KAPT/1/13/6.
58. Ibid.
59. KNA: Major W. S. MacLellan Wilson, Kenya Information Office, 'Report on Machakos Tour of the Government Mobile Cinema, 23rd April – 18th May 1946', Information and Propaganda, Africans, 1941–57, CS/1/10/44.
60. KNA: 'Report on the Tour of the Government Mobile Cinema in Ukamba from 1st July to 28th July 1946'.
61. KNA: 'Report of Machakos Tour of Mobile Cinema Van, July–August 1947'.

62. KNA: No. 1 Mobile Information Unit, 8 December 1949, 'Report on Shows Given in Machakos District, Nov.–Dec. 1949', DC/MKS/8/3, no. 74; Office of DC, Machakos, 22 May 1950, DC/MKS/8/3, no. 102.

63. Ibid. The poor road network into rural areas made it difficult and even dangerous to get film shows into many areas. Rain frequently cut tours short or forced alterations. One tour in 1950 ended in southeastern Machakos District after a van overturned. See KNA: Telegram, 18 July 1950, DC/MKS/8/3, no. 111.

64. KNA: Press Liaison, African Information Services, to DC, Machakos, 8 May 1950, DC/MKS/8/3, no. 100.

65. I draw my argument here in part from Larkin, *Signal and Noise*, esp. pp. 86–9.

66. Myles Osborne, 'Changing Kamba, Making Kenya, c. 1880–1964', PhD dissertation (Harvard University, 2008), pp. 181–2.

67. These employees were sometimes from the districts where the vans were travelling but often were not. The employment criteria for a Machakos District mobile-cinema van driver/operator were that the individual come from the 'tribe' that dominated that district, that he have the appropriate driving licence and an elementary knowledge of English – qualifications that were not that common in 1950. See KNA: 'Vacancy – Mobile Cinema Driver/Operator', 18 February 1950, DC/MKS/8/3, no. 85; one mobile-van tour team in 1950 in Machakos District included three driver/operators, two of whom (including the commentator) were Kamba and one identified as Kikuyu. See KNA: Press Liaison, African Information Services, to DC, Machakos. On the progressive values of a van operator, see 'Report (from Mobile Cinema Van Manager) on a Visit to Machakos', DC/MKS/8/3, no. 170.

68. KNA: 'Proposed Tour in Kitui District, July 1949, African Information Services, Mobile Information Unit', DC/MKS/8/3, no. 29. Employers also pushed for film shows. For examples from Machakos, see KNA: DC/MKS/8/3, no. 106 among a number of requests.

69. KNA: 'Note from a Chief Requesting a Visit from the Mobile Cinema, 10 January 1949', DC/MKS/8/3, no. 4. In the Kenyan administration 'chiefs' were individuals appointed in the local areas to represent the colonial government. These were increasingly, by the 1940s, men with some education.

70. KNA: DC, Tambach to Information Officer, 18 May 1950, DC, Elgeyo Marakwet District, 'Saucepan Radios, 1949–1957', DC/TAMB/3/18/4, no. 124.

71. Ibid.

72. KNA: Tour Report – Elgeyo Marakwet District, 5–27 October 1951, DC, Elgeyo Marakwet District, 'Saucepan Radios, 1949–1957', no. 58.

73. KNA: W. K. Chelulei, African Field Officer, 'Report on Tour of Uasin Gishu and Elgeyo Marakwet District, 2 Sept. – 21 Sept. and 16 Oct. 1950', Elgeyo Marakwet District, 'Saucepan Radios, 1949–1957', no. 13.

74. KNA: DC, Tambach to Information Officer, 29 March 1951, DC, Elgeyo Marakwet District, 'Saucepan Radios, 1949–1957', no. 4.

75. Smyth, 'Movies and Mandarins', pp. 134–5.

76. Ibid., p. 135.

77. KNA: African Information Services, Kenya, List of Films Available in Library (1950) in Information Services to DC, Tambach, 14 February 1951, DC, Elgeyo Marakwet District, 'Saucepan Radios, 1949–1957', no. 16a.

78. KNA: 'Report on Tour of Nandi District, no. 4 Mobile Information Unit to African Information Services, 13 Oct. 1950, East Africa Cinema Unit', DC/KAPT/1/13/6, no. 190.

79. KNA: DC, Tambach to Officer in Charge, 'Mobile Cinema Unit, AIS, 21 Sept. 1951, DC, Elgeyo Marakwet District, 'Saucepan Radios, 1949–1957', no. 52. See also Megan Vaughan, *Curing Their Ills: Colonial Power and African Illness* (Cambridge: Polity Press, 1991), pp. 180–99.

80. Colony and Protectorate of Kenya, *Report of the Committee of Inquiry into the Information Services*, Nairobi, Government Printer, 1950, p. 1. (My thanks to Myles Osborne for providing the information from this document.)

81. KNA: 'African Information Services', Commissioner for Community Development, Circular Letter, 13 December 1950, DC/MKS/8/3, no. 125.

82. Colony and Protectorate of Kenya, *Report of the Committee of Inquiry into the Information Services*, p. 3.

83. Ibid., pp. 6–7.

84. KNA: T. Askwith, Commissioner for Community Development, Circular Letter, 'Mobile Cinema, 5 Dec. 1950', East Africa Cinema Unit, DC/KAPT/1/13/6, no. 192.

85. KNA: 'African Information Services', Commissioner for Community Development, Circular Letter, 13 December 1950.

86. Ibid.

87. Ibid.

88. KNA: Commissioner for Community Development to Provincial Commissioners, Circular Letter, 9 April 1951, DC/MKS/8/3, no. 129.

89. Susan Carruthers, *Winning Hearts and Minds: British Governments, the Media and Colonial Counter-insurgency, 1944–1960* (London: Leicester University Press, 1995), p. 146.

90. Jane Banfield, 'Film in East Africa: A Report', *Transition* vol. 13 (1964), p. 18.

91. Most recently Daniel Branch, *Defeating Mau Mau, Creating Kenya: Counterinsurgency, Civil War, and Decolonization* (Cambridge: Cambridge University Press, 2009), p. 58. Also Luise White, 'Separating the Men from the Boys: Constructions of Gender, Sexuality, and Terrorism in Central Kenya, 1939–1959', *International Journal of African Historical Studies* vol. 23 no. 1, 1990, p. 18.

92. David Anderson, 'Mau Mau at the Movies: Contemporary Representations of an Anti-colonial War', *South African Historical Journal* vol. 48, 2003, pp. 33–51.

93. KNA: R. G. Knight, Beeston Timber Co., Ltd, Njoro, 24 January 1951 to PC, Nakuru, 'Information and Propaganda, Use of Cinematography, 1943–51', CS/2/8/86.

94. See David Anderson, *Histories of the Hanged: The Dirty War in Kenya and the End of Empire* (New York: W. W. Norton, 2005); and Caroline Elkins, *Imperial Reckoning: The Untold Story of Britain's Gulag in Kenya* (New York: Henry Holt, 2005).

95. Quoted in Carruthers, *Winning Hearts and Minds*, p. 166.

96. KNA: 'Cinema for Africans, Director of Information to Secretariat, 20 May 1955, Ministry of African Affairs, Cinema for Africans, 1955–1961', OP/1/904, no. 1.

97. KNA: 'Production and Distribution of Films' [1955], Chief Secretary, Information and Propaganda, Use of Cinematography, CS/2/8/66, no. 135.

98. KNA: 'Cinema for Africans, Director of Information to Secretariat, 20 May 1955, Ministry of African Affairs, Cinema for Africans, 1955–1961'.

99. KNA: 'The ABS Entertainment Unit', enclosed in Director of Information to Provincial Information Officer, Eldoret, 27 October 1955, DC, Elgeyo Marakwet District, 'Saucepan Radios, 1949–1957', no. 267A.

100. Ibid.

101. KNA: 'Uses of the Information Van', enclosed in Department of Information, Rift Valley to District Commissioners, Information Services, 26 February 1956, DC, Elgeyo Marakwet District, 'Saucepan Radios, 1949–1957, no. 300.

102. KNA: DC, Tambach to Provincial Information Officer, 16 February 1955, DC, Elgeyo Marakwet District, 'Saucepan Radios, 1949–1957', no. 188.

103. Ibid.

104. KNA: Provincial Information Officer to DC, 9 March 1955; and Department of Information, Rift Valley to District Commissioners, 12 May 1955, DC, Elgeyo Marakwet District, 'Saucepan Radios, 1949–1957', nos. 197 and 208.

105. See Larkin, *Signal and Noise*, esp. pp. 86–9.

106. KNA: DC, Tambach to PC, Rift Valley, 18 October 1955, 'Saucepan Radios, 1949–1957'.

107. KNA: 'Machakos District Annual Report', 1956, DC/MKS/1/1/33. (Information provided by Myles Osborne.)

108. KNA: Provincial Information Officers to District Commissioners, 30 April 1956, DC, Elgeyo Marakwet District, 'Saucepan Radios, 1949–1957', no. 315.

109. KNA: Provincial Information Officer, Upper Rift Valley, 'Cinema Campaign – Registration of African Voters, 30 April 1956', 'Saucepan Radios, 1949–1957'.

110. McFeely, 'Film Censorship in Kenya'.

111. KNA: 'Notes on Film Censorship Board's Policy toward "Westerns" supplied at the request of Special Branch', handwritten, C. Brown, Chairman of the Board of Film Censorship, Department of Information, AHC 16/25, no. 11.

112. Ibid. The Northern Rhodesia Censorship Board similarly saw its role as substantially symbolic. The board's action calmed popular fears about the impact of film although board members largely doubted that film viewing inspired criminality. See Ambler, 'Popular Films and Colonial Audiences', p. 93.

113. See Anderson, *Histories of the Hanged*, pp. 200–22.

114. KNA: Chief Secretary to Director of Information, 18 July 1955, no. 5 and Record of a Meeting Held in Central Government Offices, 4 August 1955 re. Coordination of Government Film Policy, Director of Information to Secretariat, 20 May 1955, no. 9, Ministry of African Affairs, 'Cinema for Africans, 1955–1961', OP/1/904.

115. Ibid.

116. KNA: Officer in Charge, Nairobi Extra-Provincial District to Secretariat, 16 May 1956, Ministry of African Affairs, 'Cinema for Africans, 1955–1961', no. 19.

117. KNA: J. E. S. White, 'Cinema Services for Africans', enc. in J. E. S. White to Director of Information, 16 January 1957, Ministry of African Affairs, 'Cinema for Africans, 1955–1961', no. 43/2.

118. KNA: Ministry of African Affairs, Circular, 8 October 1958, Ministry of African Affairs, 'Cinema for Africans, 1955–1961', no. 78.

119. KNA: Director of Information to Provincial Commissioner, Central Province, 10 January 1958; East African Film Services to Ministry of African Affairs, 15 March 1959, Ministry of African Affairs, 'Cinema for Africans, 1955–1961'; J. M. Richmond, East African Film Services to District Commissioner, Nairobi, 17 March 1959; J. M. Richmond, East African Film Services to Permanent Secretary, Ministry of African Affairs, 26 March 1959; J. M. Richmond, East African Film Services to Minister of Finance and Development, 2 May 1959; East African Film Services to Ministry of African Affairs, 15 September 1960; East African Film Services to Ministry of African Affairs, 20 August

1959, Ministry of African Affairs, 'Cinema for Africans, 1955–1961', nos. 77, 91, 99, 103, 112, 113 and 116.

120. KNA: Managing Director, Factual Films Ltd, Nairobi to District Commissioner, Kisumu, 11 December 1959; Simba Cinemas Ltd also operated mobile cinemas in western Kenya. See W. A. Mortimer, Simba Cinemas Ltd, to District Commissioner, Kisumu, 15 January 1960, Publications and Records, Mobile Information and Cinema Units, DC/KSM/1/28/113.

121. Banfield, 'Film in East Africa', pp. 19–20.

122. KNA: Ministry of Information, 'The Kenya Broadcasting Corporation: A History of Progress', n.d. [1963], Ministry of Broadcasting, AHC/18/82.

12

Poverty and Development as Themes in British Films on the Gold Coast, 1927–57

Gareth Austin

Viewing even a sample of the several dozen films made during the last thirty years of colonial rule in what is now Ghana yields much of interest for historians of Africa and empire. This chapter describes and analyses the films' treatment of poverty, physical and economic welfare, and economic development in Ghana from the late 1920s through to the late 1950s.[1] As well as supplementing the important materials on the 'Colonial Film' website <www.colonialfilm.org.uk>, it is hoped that this exercise will encourage further study of the portrayal of problems of, and policies on, poverty and development in the films made in other colonies in Africa and elsewhere.

This essay is based on a double process of selection. The 'Colonial Film' database lists more than seventy-five films under 'Ghana'.[2] At the time of writing, twelve of them could be viewed online. This essay is based on this subset, plus two others with Ghanaian content that I was able to watch at workshops organised by Lee Grieveson and Colin MacCabe as part of the 'Colonial Film' project. Thus the initial selection was made by the project team, and so constitutes what they considered the most interesting of the films. I made a further selection, by deciding to focus on economic welfare and development. This essay will highlight those of the fourteen that are particularly pertinent to this theme. Readers should bear in mind that the points offered below might require some revision if the whole corpus of colonial films on Ghana were examined.

The films provide evidence additional to, and in some ways different in kind, from that available from the written word. First, for historians familiar with the written sources on the matters concerned, the films serve to test what we thought we knew: which is valuable even when the outcome is confirmation rather than revision or refutation. Second, the footage and commentary sometimes reveal things at one or other end of the lens that are not found at all, or not so clearly, in the written sources: providing new information and/or raising new questions. The following enlarges on these two points in turn.

THE FILMS AS A TEST OF, AND AS ANOTHER WAY OF TELLING, THE STANDARD STORIES

Taking the films I have seen in chronological order, they fit rather neatly – almost surprisingly so – into the received periodisation of their era. The interwar films epitomise the era of 'high' colonialism. They convey a sense of colonial rule as set to endure, if not for ever, at least indefinitely and for a long time. Africans – the word used is 'natives' – are depicted as the passive beneficiaries of colonial peace and European technology and economic initiative.

In the silent film *West Africa Calling* (1927), commissioned by the Conservative Party in Britain, a title asserted that 'Years ago West Africa was an unexplored country of forest … swamp … and desert' (ellipses in the original). However, 'British enterprise has changed all this.' The purpose of the film was to persuade voters in Britain that 'workers at home benefit by the policy of developing the Empire'. Though the link is never made explicit in the film itself, the intention was apparently to make British workers more willing to accept the Conservatives' proposal to erect a tariff wall around the British empire. The nine-minute film was to be shown at political meetings around Britain by means of the party's own fleet of cinema vans.[3]

If *Castles and Fisher Folk* (1933), made for the chocolate manufacturer Cadbury, was a sales pitch, this was even more indirect. The film does not mention the company, and seems intended to entertain a British audience with soft-focus shots of 'beautiful' castles and muscular fishermen. It was shown in British cinemas.[4] Like the longer commercial features on empire that were produced in the same decade, *Castles and Fisher Folk* can be seen as offering escapism to British audiences, not least in the context of the Great Depression.[5] An acknowledgment that the castles were built or maintained for the Atlantic slave trade comes only at the very end, and then only in the form of an allusion in the voiceover to the British having ended the trade:

> [T]hese days … the forgotten fortress is a resting house, where the Englishman can shelter for the night as he journeys through on his official round to find out how best to care for and help the native races of West Africa.

Neither film recognised Africans' contributions to their own prosperity. *West Africa Calling* even referred to the growth of export agriculture in the passive voice and with the implication that the innovators were British. A title stating 'New industries have been introduced such as cocoa growing' accompanied brief footage of a European giving instructions to African workers, before adding the words 'and rubber'. Actually, rubber exports from what is now Ghana predated European involvement in its production; indeed in Ashanti it predated colonisation.[6] Cocoa growing was introduced by a combination of missionary, African and colonial government agency. But the extraordinary growth in exports of cocoa beans, from nothing in 1890 to being the largest exporter in the world twenty years later, was overwhelmingly the result of African investment and risk-taking.[7] In short, the growth of export agriculture in the Gold Coast was mainly an achievement of Africans as producers and entrepreneurs. In 1920 Sir Hugh Clifford, former Governor of the Gold Coast, observed to the Legislative Council of Nigeria (of which he was now governor-general), that

> Agricultural interests in tropical countries which are mainly, or exclusively in the hands of the native peasantry … are capable of a rapidity of expansion and a progressive increase of output that beggar every record of the past, and are altogether unparalleled in all the long history of European agricultural enterprise in the Tropics.[8]

Film and the End of Empire

A film which I have not seen, *Cocoa from the Gold Coast* (1936), made for Cadbury, did at least make clear that 'the plantations all belong to the natives'.[9]

The interwar films that I have seen – whether made for the metropolitan government,[10] the Conservative Party or Cadbury – resound with self-satisfaction and confidence, assumed or (quite possibly) real. British complacency about colonial domination is arguably epitomised in the absence of African voices in these films.[11]

The wartime films are very different. Part of the difference is signalled (again, at least in the sample I have seen) by the replacement of the word 'natives' by 'Africans'. These films were made by the government with the evident intention of strengthening support in British West Africa for the participation of African soldiers in the imperial war effort, through enrolment in the Gold Coast Regiment.[12] The films repeatedly and explicitly present the war as a team effort: Africans are no longer seen as passive recipients of European advice. The contribution of Gold Coast civilians to the imperial war effort was noted in silent newsreels produced by British Army film units in 1942, showing Africans engaged in producing cocoa beans and using them to manufacture soap, as a wartime expedient.[13] Naturally, the main emphasis was on Africans' military contributions (and indeed a total of over 70,000 men from the Gold Coast served in the British armed forces during the war).[14] The voiceover in *Africa's Fighting Men* (1943) observed that 'Africans have played their part in this war, from the Abyssinian campaign to the victory in Sicily.' It went on to claim that 'These men are among the finest troops in the Empire, and they are at their best when fighting in the bush.' The Gold Coast Regiment's sappers were shown assembling a ferry in six minutes. It was a task requiring skill and discipline as well as sustained effort in carrying the equipment, though the voiceover emphasised the physical: 'the great strength and endurance of the African is an invaluable asset in work like this'. The footage shows the West African troops training, marching or preparing. According to Tom Rice's analysis accompanying the film on the 'Colonial Film' website, African critics, in particular, criticised the lack of action footage. The same criticism applied to *West Africa Was There* (1945), made for the UK Ministry of Information, which followed and hailed the efforts of the West African divisions in a successful advance in 1944–5 during the Burma campaign. Still, the 1943 film showed a Nigerian pilot taking off and then landing, under the appreciative gaze of half a dozen white air-force men. The same film asserts 'The colonial people ... have shown that they can take their place ... side by side in the battle for freedom.'

The films of the later 1940s and early 1950s express the heightened post-war commitment to 'colonial development'. The complacency about colonial rule, its longevity and responsibilities, that had been apparent in the interwar films was replaced by a clear sense that African self-rule was the future (though still not yet the immediate future), that much needed to be done before then to combat poverty, and that colonial development, too, was a team effort. The government-supported films made for British audiences were now aimed at persuading metropolitan taxpayers, notwithstanding their own post-war shortages and the continuation of rationing, to put their hands deeper into their collective pockets. A secondary aim may have been to reconcile Americans to the British empire, to try to show Britain's major ally that the empire was no embarrassment: that British colonialism was developing poor countries rather than exploiting them. *Here Is the Gold Coast* (1947) presented a rather detailed (thirty-five-minute) and certainly emphatic case for the programme of metropolitan investment mandated by the new Labour government in London. The film was shown in Britain and overseas, including in the US, where it was distributed by British Information Services (BIS).[15] The opening titles of the film proclaimed 'The colonies are the responsibility of the British people'; and that of a total of £120 million to be spent on colonial development and welfare in the next decade, £3.5 million was earmarked for the Gold Coast. The film proceeded to show explicitly the need for such expenditure. Very significantly, it also depicts African elders in the Northern Territories in the act of paying tax. The implicit message is that Africans were doing what they could to help themselves, and were therefore deserving of subsidy from the metropole. In this respect *Here Is the Gold Coast* already presented a theme that would recur after Independence in Western public discussions of development aid.

In *Here Is the Gold Coast* the problem of how to improve living standards was implicitly seen as entirely a matter of overcoming natural obstacles. This was reiterated in *Spotlight on the Colonies* (1950), an eleven-minute film for British audiences sponsored by two UK government agencies, the Central Office of Information and the Economic Information Unit. The British narrator acknowledged that 'The colonies have all had their difficulties', and proceeded to give a list: all of them problems of the physical and pathological environment. Again as in *Here Is the Gold Coast*, but more forcefully, *Spotlight on the Colonies* proclaimed the shared nature of the economic mission on which Britain and her colonies were embarked: 'Our common road to progress', 'this enterprise of mutual prosperity', 'a common partnership'.

The commentary in *Here Is the Gold Coast* was delivered by an African, Augustus Engmann. He addresses the British audience directly, explicitly on behalf of the Africans of the Gold Coast. The British role in ending the slave trade is acknowledged, but their earlier participation in it is also mentioned, though less emphatically. The terms of address are 'you' and 'us', and the tone is respectful but not without pride. The British audience is told very firmly 'our history did not begin when you first took a hand in it'. Again, 'we have to follow your ideas; but we have our own laws too'. In 1950, two years after the riots in the Gold Coast triggered an accelerated transition to Independence, *Spotlight on the Colonies* remarked (with implicit reference to recent legislation) that not only do the British and the people of the colonies 'work together' but also 'We share a common citizenship.' On the face of it the latter assertion denies the prospect of Independence, and, further, of Independence as a nation-state. That prospect, however, was affirmed implicitly both by the language of citizenship in the 1950 film, and in Engmann's (or his scriptwriter's) use of 'us': his identification of the whole population as a single people. It was only a generation since the originally separate colonies of the Gold Coast colony, Ashanti and the Northern Territories had been constitutionally united as the Gold Coast (and British Togoland remained in principle partly distinct, being a United Nations mandate). In the 1953 film *Progress in Kojokrom* and again in the 1955 production *Mr Mensah Builds a House*, an African government minister appeared towards the end, introducing initiatives taken by what were effectively transitional administrations in Accra, with African participation (by 1955 amounting to internal self-rule). The year 1957 brought not only Ghanaian Independence but also – inevitably – a film, *Freedom for Ghana*, to mark the event.

This sequence of films thus appears to confirm the standard narrative of change during the later colonial period, from 'high' colonialism to decolonisation via the war and post-war 'developmental' colonialism. Besides doing that in a very interesting way, this run of films also appears to confirm a major feature of colonial thinking and rhetoric: the emphasis upon the value of technological fixes, usually capital-intensive, stemming from scientific research and perceived best practice elsewhere in the colonial or metropolitan world. This was epitomised in a remark in *Spotlight on the Colonies*, that locusts 'can't stand up to air attack' (i.e. aerial spraying). In *Here Is the Gold Coast*, the commentator made the following remark about the farming methods of the savanna peasants: 'the earth yields unwillingly to their primitive toil, in which all must join'. 'The circle [of low output and low food intake] can only be broken if their ways of agriculture are changed.' This was surely true,[16] but over the decades successive European recipes for transforming the productivity of farmers in this and other parts of tropical Africa had failed, not least because the earth there 'yields unwillingly' to capital-intensive methods too, eroding rapidly when subject to deep ploughing, for example, and this in a context where the use of large animals (for traction, and indeed for dung) was inhibited by sleeping sickness.[17] I have shown elsewhere that the advice given to cocoa farmers by the colonial Department of Agriculture tended to be economically inefficient given the structure of costs under which the farmers operated. It was not until 1940, with the discovery of the viral origin of the cocoa disease known as swollen shoot, that scientific research on Gold Coast farming began to get ahead of African best practice.[18] To judge only from the titles and short summaries of the series of films of instruction for cocoa farmers in the Gold Coast,[19] the films echoed the well-meaning but usually misconceived advice given verbally to farmers by touring agricultural instructors. Let us turn to issues on which the films enable us, not merely to refresh, but to go beyond the evidence of the written sources.

WHERE THE FILMS OFFER EVIDENCE THAT GOES BEYOND THE WRITTEN SOURCES

This section presents impressions of two issues on which the films provide additional evidence for students of poverty and development otherwise reliant on archives and oral history: first, colonial and perhaps also African attitudes regarding 'social capital'; second, aspects of the history of nutrition and physical welfare.

As Independence approached, the government made greater use of film for various purposes, including to promote the accumulation of what has come increasingly to be called 'social capital', in the sense of investment in social contacts, mutual support and cohesiveness. The clearest examples of this are comedies made by the Gold Coast Film Unit, which were shown around the country by touring cinema vans. The above-mentioned *Progress in Kojokrom*, in thirty-six minutes, sought to persuade people of the social value of supporting the introduction of elected local government, including by paying the rates (a form of local tax). It told the humorous tale of a bloody-minded and outspoken male schoolteacher who initially resisted the message before, after salutary experience, becoming an enthusiastic convert to the benefits for all of being a good citizen, as it was now defined.

Mr Mensah Builds a House (also mentioned earlier) was again thirty-six minutes in length, though in colour. It was as didactic as *Progress in Kojokrom*, but promoted a different dimension of social capital. It showed the hard-working and thrifty Mr Mensah retiring from his job in the civil service. After he and his supportive wife had enjoyed the acclaim of his colleagues at a retirement party, they head out of Accra in order to start their new lives in the house that Mr Mensah has been building for three years. Responsibility for overseeing the construction had been entrusted to Mr Mensah's nephew Kofi, and Mr Mensah had furnished him with funds to complete the house. The retired couple arrived to find that the house was no more than a frame; young Kofi had squandered the money entrusted to him on drinking, betting and on his grasping girlfriend.

The makers of *Mr Mensah Builds a House* apparently sought to convey two lessons. One was to recur frequently in the pleas made to their citizens by the leaders of newly independent African states: that government was beneficent and helpful, but that the members of a community also needed to help themselves. Thus the new government Department of Rural Housing could and did help Mr Mensah finish the house, and with modern machinery, while the labour was supplied not by expensive hired labourers but rather by the community. The other lesson was about the risk of betrayal of trust. The specific form in which this theme was developed in the film is not European but rather reflects the matrilineal culture of the Akan-speaking populations of southern Ghana. In this system, the ideal line of inheritance was from a man to his sister's son. The relationship between maternal uncle and heir was (and is) the subject of much attention in Akan culture, as, more generally, is the issue of trust and of betrayal by family members (the latter being fundamental to Akan notions about the source of witchcraft, for example).[20] Thus, at least on the cusp of Independence, a government film used an indigenous frame of reference as a means of coupling advocacy of thrift and community self-help with warnings about the risk of being cheated by those close to you. It may be worth comparing this kind of government story with the Akan tradition of Ananse stories, which rely on the figure of a trickster spider to convey moral tales.

Last but most importantly, we turn to poverty. *Here Is the Gold Coast* contains relatively extended footage from the Mamprussi District in the Northern Territories. It included arresting frames of men working the fields, their arms and legs thin to or beyond the point of emaciation. The accompanying comment was 'This is a village which is losing the struggle: its soils are exhausted and its people's bodies are too', thus implicitly confirming the impression that they were unhealthily thin rather than fit. When the film was shown in Britain, African students condemned this very scene as reaffirming the traditional European perception of Africa as backward.[21] But the film showed Africans as hard-working and intelligent. For instance, an Accra market scene featured young boys sitting at a table playing draughts. Moreover, the visual acknowledgment of the existence of malnutrition in 1947 was in drastic contrast to the stance previously taken by the colonial administration in the Gold Coast.

In the late 1930s the Colonial Office in London had instigated a major investigation of 'Human Nutrition in the Colonial Empire'. A dietetic officer, Dr F. M. Purcell, was appointed for the Gold Coast in 1939 and it was he who wrote the final report on the surveys in the Gold Coast, which were carried out in different ecological and economic zones in 1939–40.[22] Purcell's report was not published. He protested unsuccessfully to his superiors about this, a conflict that led to his resignation. In response, he submitted his material to the *West African Review*, which published large extracts, with photographs, in articles in 1943 and 1946.[23] Purcell explained his decision to go to the press in a letter to the editor of the weekly magazine *West Africa*, towards the end of 1943:

> Apparently because it contained a few facts which might cause official embarrassment (unofficially it was explained to me that 'no one may starve in the British Empire'), the report has been suppressed. It seems to me no less than my duty to make public the state of affairs, especially in view of complacent expressions of faith in the well-being of the Colonies. It is right that those who are sincere in their interest in the welfare of Colonial peoples should be confronted with unequivocal truth.[24]

In 1944 an official in Accra referred to Purcell's allegations as 'scandalous'.[25] Yet just three years later the government was publishing images – moving images, in both senses – of malnutrition. The contrast in official attitude is even more vivid if one takes into account the fact that the still photographs supplied by Purcell, or at least those published in the press, were particularly of the Northern Territories, and were accompanied by comments highlighting the effect of seasonal hunger, in the months before the harvest.[26] The survey on which Purcell based his findings about the north had been conducted in Mamprussi, a few years before the film footage was shot in the very same district.[27]

The contrast in government attitudes may be partly attributable to the fact that the film was produced by the UK Central Office of Information rather than by the Gold Coast government (the Gold Coast Film Unit did not yet exist). Jérôme Destombes has documented a difference in attitude regarding the urgency of research and possible action on nutrition between the Colonial Office in London and the Gold Coast administration – the former being much more alarmed and active about the problem.[28]

Here Is the Gold Coast contained further footage and commentary yielding grounds for official embarrassment: 'These women have [walked] for five or even ten miles to carry home the muddy water that may bring disease to their families', while 'In the water that should gladden us, the mosquitoes multiply.' These statements were preceded by an implicit plea for mitigation of any criticism of the British record on poverty: Engmann made it clear that the Northern Territories are 'the most backward part of our country' and followed this immediately with the comment, placed as if it was explanatory, that it was 'only fifty years' since it came under British rule. Even so, while Gold Coast students in London may have found the film embarrassing, it represented a new official frankness about all that colonial rule had *not* achieved; hence the reason for belated urgency in taking up the task of development after the war.

Research still in progress offers another angle on the evolution of poverty over the colonial era in the Gold Coast, and the depiction of malnutrition as late as 1947, and in Mamprussi in particular. A current project has assembled and is analysing quantitative evidence on changes in the physical welfare of the population of Ghana during the colonial era. Army recruitment records provide the source: data on the heights, birth dates and geographical provenance of the thousands of African recruits to the Gold Coast Regiment. The work is not yet complete, but certain findings are clear. First, the average heights of recruits from all over Ghana increased over the colonial period.[29] Had the colonial government processed in this way the information it collected, it would have been able to point to some improvement under the British flag (whether or not the causes of improvement had much do with colonial rule as such). Second, the popular belief in Ghana that northerners (those from the savannas) tend to be taller than southerners (at least, those from the forest zone) was true, though the gap was reduced during the colonial decades.[30] So Ghana is an unusual case in the anthropometric literature, because the people from the poorer region (the savanna hinterlands) were (and still are) on average taller, and therefore on average had been better nourished in childhood, than the people from the wealthier region (the forest zone, with its lands bearing minerals and export crops). The most plausible explanation so far for this apparently anomalous finding comes from Purcell's own report. Despite his general emphasis on inadequate food consumption in the savanna, especially the problem of seasonal hunger, he also found that 'during the all important growing years, the diet of the N[orthern] T[erritories] child contains qualitatively superior protein and more calcium', mainly thanks to the northern custom of giving children peanuts (a savanna crop) to take with them to the fields, to consume during the day.[31]

What does a viewing of the 1947 footage contribute to the evidence on diet? Primarily, a sense of perspective. Judging from recent quantitative research, the inhabitants of Mamprussi were on average better fed than they had been at the turn of the century. In childhood at least, they were also on average better fed than their more cash-prosperous neighbours in the south, where northern men migrated seasonally in their thousands to earn money, especially as labourers on cocoa farms. Yet many northerners were still very poorly fed; for we can assume that a government propaganda film would hardly have shown such potentially subversive images if they had been highly unrepresentative.

CONCLUSIONS

The films under discussion are significant for historians of Africa and empire, and in this case, for specialists on colonial Ghana in particular. This is partly because they provide a – highly selective – record of aspects of African and imperial history, and partly because they were intended to shape history: as tools for influencing perceptions and behaviour, variously within the colony, the imperial metropolis and even beyond. How much effect these mostly short films had on the public(s) at which they were aimed is hard to determine, and I have not tried to gauge that here. Rather, I have considered what the changing choices of images and accompanying words 'tell us' about the colonial period.

Viewing the available sample of films in chronological order, they reinforce the established view of the basic pattern of change within the period, especially regarding the transformation during the 1940s in the sense of urgency among the British (whether government officials or not) about development as a policy. That reinforcement is interesting in itself, but there are also surprises. The most striking of these, in my view, was the frankness with which one post-war government film observed poverty and malnutrition in northern Ghana. This is significant for what it reveals about the techniques engaged to sell 'developmental colonialism' to the metropolitan taxpayer, and because the images furnish a kind of evidence about the reality of poverty itself. Interpreting that (as with any other) evidence requires relating it to other kinds of sources. As the last section illustrated, such a juxtaposition may yield paradoxes and ironies. Thus for academic specialists, as potentially for students and public – in the former colony, the former metropolis, and beyond – the treatment of poverty and hunger in these films readily inspires critical reflection.

NOTES

1. I thank Colin McCabe for the opportunity to research and write this paper, Lee Grieveson for pursuing the paper, and Tom Rice for facilitating my access to the films that were available online.
2. Unfortunately these do not include what appears to have been the first British film made in Ghana. This was the work of R. S. Rattray, the colonial anthropologist-administrator, during his ethnographic research in Ashanti. Fragments survive in the Pitt-Rivers Museum in Oxford (Andrew Roberts, 'Africa on Film to 1940', *History in Africa* vol. 14, 1987, pp. 196–7, 218).
3. Lee Grieveson, 'The Cinema and the (Common) Wealth of Nations', in Lee Grieveson and Colin MacCabe (eds), *Empire and Film* (London: BFI, 2011).
4. According to Tom Rice's notes accompanying the film on the website <http://www.colonialfilm.org.uk/node/63>.
5. On the feature films, see Teresa Hoefert, 'Imperialism in British Films during the 1930s', in A. G. Hopkins (ed.), *The Imperialism of the Great Powers: Six Studies* (Geneva: Graduate Institute of International Studies, 1991), pp. 129–51, especially p. 148.
6. Raymond E. Dumett, 'The Rubber Trade of the Gold Coast and Asante in the Nineteenth Century', *Journal of African History* vol. 12, 1971, pp. 79–101; Kwame Arhin, 'The Economic and Social Significance of Rubber Production and Exchange on the Gold and Ivory Coasts, 1880–1900', *Cahiers d'études africaines* vol. 20 nos 77–8, 1980, pp. 49–62.
7. Polly Hill, *The Migrant Cocoa-farmers of Southern Ghana*, 2nd edn (Hamburg and Oxford: LIT and James Currey with International African Institute, 1997); Gareth Austin, *Labour, Land and Capital in Ghana: From Slavery to Free Labour in Asante, 1807–1956* (Rochester, NY: University of Rochester Press, 2005).
8. Quoted in Ann Phillips, *The Enigma of Colonialism: British Policy in West Africa* (London: James Currey, 1989), p. 85.
9. According to Rice's notes, <www.colonialfilm.org.uk/node/790>. Actually, the statement in the film was a slight exaggeration: some Europeans established cocoa and rubber plantations early in the colonial period, and European ownership of plantations was not quite extinct by 1936. See Gareth Austin, 'Mode of Production or Mode of Cultivation: Explaining the Failure of European Cocoa Planters in Competition with African Farmers in Colonial Ghana', in William Gervase Clarence-Smith (ed.), *Cocoa Pioneer Fronts: The Role of Smallholders, Planters and Merchants* (Basingstoke: Macmillan, 1996), pp. 154–75.

10. Specifically, *The Official Record of the Tour of H.R.H. the Prince of Wales Part 3* (1925). The tone is conveyed in the titles describing a durbar in Accra: when it 'ended, the parade ground still presented an ever-changing panorama of barbaric splendours'.
11. British complacency was shaken by the cocoa hold-up movement, especially by the hold-up of 1937–8, when collective action by African producers and brokers, refusing to sell cocoa to the European firms, paralysed the commercial economy and provoked anger and recrimination between the local administration and the European companies. The best introduction remains John Miles, 'Rural Protest in the Gold Coast: The Cocoa Hold-ups, 1908–1938', in Clive Dewey and A. G. Hopkins (eds), *The Imperial Impact: Studies in the Economic History of Africa and India* (London: Athlone Press, 1978), pp. 152–70, 353–7.
12. For context see David Killingray, 'Military and Labour Recruitment in the Gold Coast during the Second World War', *Journal of African History* vol. 23 no. 1, 1983, pp. 83–95.
13. *Scenes Showing the Manufacture of Soap from Cocoa Beans on the West Coast of Africa* (1942). I have not seen this film, so rely on Rice's account of the film on the website, <www.colonialfilm.org.uk/node/2023>.
14. Killingray, 'Military and Labour Recruitment in the Gold Coast during the Second World War', p. 94.
15. Rice's notes accompanying the film, <www.colonialfilm.org.uk/node/1280>. BIS was a UK government agency.
16. As Platteau has observed for sub-Saharan Africa generally, cautioning against over-optimism about the potential of indigenous farming methods. See Jean-Philippe Platteau, 'The Food Crisis in Africa: A Comparative Structural Analysis', in Jean Drèze, Amartya Sen and Athar Hussain (eds), *The Political Economy of Hunger* (Oxford: Oxford University Press, 1995), pp. 445–553.
17. For a general survey of the significance of resource constraints, and human responses to them, in African economic history, see Gareth Austin, 'Resources, Techniques and Strategies South of the Sahara: Revising the Factor Endowments Perspective on African Economic Development, 1500–2000', *Economic History Review* vol. no. 3, 2008, pp. 587–624. On the relative success of African informal experimentation, the classic is Paul Richards, *Indigenous Agricultural Revolution: Ecology and Food Production in West Africa* (London: Hutchinson, 1985). For an account of how the biggest colonial project for agricultural transformation in West Africa was obliged to adjust to the demands of African farmers and their environment, see Monica M. van Beusekom, *Negotiating Development: African Farmers and Colonial Experts at the Office du Niger, 1920–1960* (Portsmouth, NH: Heinemann, 2002).
18. Austin, 'Mode of Production or Mode of Cultivation', pp. 154–75.
19. Again to be found on the Ghana section of <www.colonialfilm.org.uk/>.
20. A near-contemporary study was M. J. Field, *Search for Security: An Ethno-psychiatric Study of Rural Ghana* (London: Faber and Faber, 1960).
21. Rice's notes, <www.colonialfilm.org.uk/node/1280>.
22. Public Relations and Archives Administration Department, Ghana (PRAAD), Accra branch, file ADM 11/1/1294, 'Human Nutrition – Standing Committee to Study the Important Question of': F. M. Purcell, 'Final Report on Nutrition Surveys in the Gold Coast 1940'.
23. The controversy is examined in Jérôme Destombes, 'Nutrition and Economic Destitution in Northern Ghana, 1930–1957: A Historical Perspective on Nutritional Economics', *Working Papers in Economic History* no. 49/99, Department of Economic History, London School of Economics, pp. 25–8, 48–51.

24. Quoted in Destombes, 'Nutrition and Economic Destitution in Northern Ghana, 1930–1957', p. 50.
25. PRAAD, Accra, file CSO 8/1/245, Minute by J. K. Lockwood, 9 February 1944.
26. According to Destombes, 'Nutrition and Economic Destitution in Northern Ghana, 1930–1957', p. 50.
27. PRAAD, file ADM 11/1/1294, 'Human Nutrition'.
28. Destombes, 'Nutrition and Economic Destitution in Northern Ghana, 1930–1957', pp. 44–51.
29. The project is being undertaken by Alexander Moradi, Gareth Austin and Jörg Baten. For a very preliminary summary, see Alexander Moradi, 'Confronting Colonial Legacies – Lessons from Human Development in Ghana and Kenya, 1880–2000', *Journal of International Development* vol. 20 no. 8, 2008, pp. 1107–21.
30. Ibid.
31. Purcell, 'Final Report on Nutrition Surveys in the Gold Coast 1940'.

13
Mumbo-jumbo, Magic and Modernity: Africa in British Cinema, 1946–65

Wendy Webster

After World War II the official narrative told about the empire renamed it as the British Commonwealth – what Queen Elizabeth II in the Christmas broadcast of her coronation year called 'an entirely new conception' that bore no resemblance to the empires of the past. The Commonwealth, as the Queen defined it, was 'a world-wide fellowship of nations, of a type never seen before' in which 'the United Kingdom is an equal partner with many other proud and independent nations'. This 'new conception' was intended to modernise the empire, although not everybody remembered to use the new vocabulary. But the Queen also stressed that some territories were 'still backward' – not yet ready to be 'proud and independent' equal partners – although Britain was 'leading them forward to the same goal' of Independence.[1] In the aftermath of war, colonies in South Asia – India, Burma and Ceylon – gained Independence. India, Pakistan and Ceylon joined the Commonwealth. The Queen did not identify which territories were 'still backward', but in her coronation year (1953) Britain intended to keep its colonies in Africa.

British cinemas were important sites for the consumption of images of Africa, especially before the spread of television ownership from the mid-1950s. Africa and Africans featured in cinema programmes – in advertisements, newsreels and feature films. Wildlife photography was a significant part of the imagery produced, but in the immediate aftermath of war and the 1950s there were also narratives that told of schemes for development and welfare in line with the 'new conception' of the Commonwealth. The educated African was a significant newcomer in several feature films, but at the same time, for much of the 1950s, Africa was shown as 'still backward' – a continent of mud huts and mumbo-jumbo. With the onset of colonial war in Kenya in 1952, film and newsreel showed the Mau Mau as atavistic savages.

Kenneth Cameron argues that Africa in British cinema was 'our Africa' and when it ceased to be British, 'the camera looked elsewhere: there was no iconography for an Africa without British power'.[2] Decolonisation was rapid from 1960: British colonies that were 'still backward' in 1953 were fast becoming 'proud and independent' less than a decade later. But during the transitional period when decolonisation was gathering pace, British cameras did not look elsewhere. Independence ceremonies were widely filmed for newsreels and this period also saw the production of an extra-ordinary group of travelogues on Africa. Newsreels and travelogues are relatively neglected in work on British cinema, but their contribution to imagery of Africa was considerable, especially in the early 1960s.[3] Both proclaimed a 'new Africa', characterised as modern.

This chapter explores some of the stock images and sound through which British film homogenised Africa's varied and complex histories, cultures and peoples. In tracing a shift to an image of a new and modern Africa in the first half of the 1960s, it looks at the way this image – of independence within the Commonwealth and of leisure opportunities for whites – obscured loss of imperial power. Within this shift, there were considerable elements of continuity: in the production of Africa as spectacle, the representation of white–black relationships and reworkings of the idea of Africa as a 'white man's' continent. But laments for loss of imperial power surfaced occasionally in feature films.

LATE COLONIAL AFRICA

An African living in Britain wrote to *The Times* about the first post-war feature film with an African setting – *Men of Two Worlds* (1946). 'Is the object of the new film to boost British rule in Africa?' he asked. 'If so', he continued, 'is it a credit to Britain to advertise to the world that after over half a century of British rule, Africa is still one vast mass of jungle and naked people living in round huts?'[4] Other Africans living in Britain had made a similar critique earlier, when *Men of Two Worlds* was still in production during World War II. Lapido Solanke, secretary-general of the West African Students' Union (WASU) protested to the Colonial Office that it perpetuated the 'erroneous idea that modern progress among indigenous Africans is usually rendered abortive owing to the alleged overwhelming influence and complete domination which witch-doctors exercise over the Chiefs and people of every African community'.[5] The Colonial Office dismissed WASU's protests, and privately considered that 'the whole attitude of mind underlying the letter from WASU seems ... to be unreal and to result from an inferiority complex'.[6]

British cinema often cast white actors in blackface in the role of Africans. Between the wars the numbers of black actors increased, particularly in films that starred Paul Robeson. Both *Sanders of the River* (1935) and *Song of Freedom* (1936) provided roles for black women, with Nina Mae McKinney and Elizabeth Welch, both African Americans like Robeson, starring as Robeson's wives. Robert Adams from British Guyana was a black actor who had had parts as Africans in *Song of Freedom* and *Old Bones of the River* (1939), but his first lead role was as Kisenga in *Men of Two Worlds*. The film opens in London where he is performing his own composition as a solo pianist at a wartime concert in the National Gallery, wearing a suit and bowtie, accompanied by an entirely white orchestra and acclaimed by a white audience.[7]

Criticism of representations of Africans in British film came from black actors as well as black audience members. Robeson later repudiated *Sanders of the River*. Adams appeared in a BBC discussion on colour prejudice in 1943 that, through a subsequent decision, was never broadcast, and criticised the depiction of Africans in films that showed 'the white man in the bush surrounded by half-naked savages. People tend to accept such things as being typical of all negroes.'[8] But he exempted *Men of Two Worlds* from this criticism in an interview about the film:

> If all my screen parts were as dignified, moving and human as the one in *Men of Two Worlds*, then one might soon be able to influence cinemagoers in the right direction. And if they see

negroes playing cultured, intelligent people often enough, they will begin to realize that the coloured man is not necessarily a superstitious hymn-singing buffoon.[9]

Old Bones of the River had made an educated African into a comic figure, with an opening title announcing: 'Darkest Africa. Where ... a handful of Englishmen rule over half a million natives, teaching the black man to play the white man.' As Adams's comment suggests, serious treatment of 'cultured, intelligent' Africans played by black actors was new to British cinema after World War II.

Despite Adams's comments on his own role, *Men of Two Worlds* and other films about late-colonial Africa retained stock sounds and images – drums, mumbo-jumbo, mud huts, witch doctors, the bush. Urban African settings were thin on the ground in the 1950s. In *Men of Two Worlds*, at the end of his concert performance in London, Kisenga announces his decision to go back to Africa, and is recruited to help combat an outbreak of sleeping sickness caused by the tsetse fly. The action of the film moves quickly to African villages. There is the same quick movement from urban to bush setting in *Where No Vultures Fly* (1951) and *Simba* (1955). Both begin in Nairobi, but this urban setting is shown only briefly and associated with whites – with the family life of Robert Payton (Anthony Steel) in *Where No Vultures Fly* and in *Simba* with the airport where Mary Crawford (Virginia McKenna) meets Allan Howard (Dirk Bogarde), arriving from England on a visit to his brother. Only *Cry, the Beloved Country* (1951) featured extensive urban as well as rural settings, showing Johannesburg as a place that corrupted African villagers.

Most newsreels were still made in black and white in the 1950s, but Technicolor had been characteristic of a range of feature films on empire in the 1930s, enhancing the spectacle of expansive imperial landscapes. The spectacle of African landscape and its wildlife in Technicolor was an important part of the pleasure that *Where No Vultures Fly* offered its audience. Filmed on location in Kenya and Tanganyika, it modernised the traditional safari narrative, telling the story of Robert Payton's quest to preserve wildlife and his struggles to establish a National Park in Kenya. The *Daily Mail*, commenting on its selection for the 1951 Royal Command Performance, suggested that it would have been an ideal choice if Prince Charles – then three years old – had attended, and called it 'a pleasant picture, especially for children'.[10] Placing a family at the centre of the film – Robert and Mary Payton (Dinah Sheridan) and their son Tim (William Simons) – marked another departure from the traditional safari narrative, strengthening its credentials as family entertainment. At times it resembled George Cansdale's 1950s BBC television programmes, introducing the audience to dangerous, lovable or strange animals and their young. Tim adopts many of these as pets and uses the park as a type of adventure playground. The film's popularity at box offices led to the production of a sequel in 1954 – *West of Zanzibar* – also starring Anthony Steel.

Donna Haraway comments: 'In establishing the game parks of Africa, European law turned indigenous human inhabitants of the "nature reserves" into poachers, invaders in their own terrain, or into part of the wildlife.'[11] These are the three recurrent images of Africans in *Where No Vultures Fly*. Ivory poaching is masterminded by a European, but it is Africans who kill elephants with poison spears. The Masai tribe is portrayed as a major threat to the conservation project should its members enter the National Park with their diseased cattle. Over shots of the tribe and the cattle,

Payton's narrative voice informs us: 'Queer lot the Masai, just as they were a thousand years ago. The only tribe that's managed to resist civilisation completely.' Other Africans dance and sing for European spectators, providing a spectacle-within-a-spectacle as audiences in British cinemas watch British audiences in Africa watching Africans. The *Daily Telegraph* review praised the spectacle of majestic scenery and wildlife, and added as an afterthought: 'As for the natives, I found them all enchanting.'[12]

Africans are assigned subordinate roles in *Where No Vultures Fly* – as *askari*, poachers and villagers they say little. But Kisenga has considerable dialogue to speak in English in *Men of Two Worlds*. A review in the *Liverpool Evening Express* praised the film's director – Thorold Dickinson – for his decision to make all his characters speak English: a language strongly associated with civilisation.[13] Even so, sound contributed to the representation of African primitivism in the film. Chanting and drumming accompany the witch doctor's activities, which take place in darkness. It is Kisenga who identifies the witch doctor's sound with primitivism. As the witch doctor prepares to put a curse on him, he says: 'Hurry up with your mumbo-jumbo.' But despite this dismissive verdict, he is shown as increasingly defeated by the witch doctor's curse, falling ill and driven mad particularly by the sound of drums: 'I wanted only one thing – to stop those drums.' He is made to attribute this to his African identity: 'Fifteen years in England, what's that against ten thousand years of Africa in my blood.'

Modernity in the film belongs to the British in their efforts to combat sleeping sickness – a crusade mounted by District Commissioner Randall (Eric Portman). Catherine Munro (Phyllis Calvert) is a key figure in this crusade. As a doctor she represents rationality, expertise and Western medicine – she is shown taking samples of blood from unwilling Africans to test for infection and scrutinising slides down a microscope. Kisenga also assists Randall, representing the theme of partnership. He has spent many years in Europe and is employed to persuade Africans to move away from infested areas. One message of the film is that, as a Western-educated African, he is a key figure in African modernisation. But this message is undercut in the sequences that show his illness, which Munro identifies as a nervous breakdown. From his early confidence in London, the rapturous reception of his music and his circle of admirers, he is reduced to a pitiful state – crying, sweating, shaking. The project of the British, and of the film, is the defeat of the witch doctor, and the battle between the forces of progress, represented by the British, and the forces of darkness, represented by the witch doctor, becomes a battle over whether Kisenga will die or not. Randall saves the day, organising African children to sing music that Kisenga has composed, so drowning out the sound of the witch doctor's drums. Despite the film's concerns with partnership, it is benevolent British paternalism that ensures Kisenga's recovery.

Witch doctors, superstition, drums and primitivism took on increasingly savage and violent associations in the context of colonial war in Kenya. *Simba* – a feature film about the war – begins with African violence. Before the credits come up, there are shots of an expansive landscape, familiar from *Where No Vultures Fly*, where an African man is riding a bicycle along a path in daylight. Dismounting to investigate cries for help, and propping his bike against a tree stump, he discovers a white man, lying seriously wounded on the ground. Instead of ministering to him, the African proceeds to butcher him. *Safari* (1956) has a similar opening: the murder of a white child.

The white family featured strongly in film on colonial war in Kenya, offering an image of stability and order now threatened by the violence of the colonised. Bill McConville, reporting for Pathé newsreel, showed a family living on the outskirts of Nairobi. Brian is in his pyjamas stroking the family dog and Susan, his sister, is sitting on her mother's knee. A gun on the arm of the chair demonstrates the insecurity of this tranquil scene as their mother reads them a bedtime story.[14] *Simba* sets white home, family and community against African violence and primitivism. After the sequence where an African butchers a helpless white man, the film moves to white modernity in a sequence at Nairobi airport. Allan Howard's arrival there promises reunion with his brother as well as romance with Mary Crawford. But this is a shortlived moment. Immediately they reach his brother's farm he finds it wrecked and his brother murdered by the Mau Mau.

White women like Catherine Munro, Mary Payton and Mary Crawford were increasingly significant figures in post-war film on Africa, suggesting the extent to which domestic, romantic and familial imagery was incorporated into a genre that had previously focused on white masculinity as expansive, active and virile. The figure of the independent and emancipated woman could signify modernity. Catherine Munro in *Men of Two Worlds* is formidable and sometimes domineering. She smokes and on occasion wears trousers and drinks whisky. But white women could also invest films with a personal and liberal register that softened the image of Britons, gesturing towards a discourse of Commonwealth.

This is particularly the case with Mary Crawford in *Simba*. Her work is similar to that of Catherine Munro in *Men of Two Worlds*, bringing the benefits of Western medicine to Africans, but is represented as prompted by her concerns for Africans, emphasising her compassion rather than her expertise or authority. Moreover, Mary acts as an assistant to an African doctor – Peter Karanja (Earl Cameron) – an educated African like Kisenga, and the central black African character in *Simba*. In many ways Mary's image is aligned with Karanja's rather than with a British man, for they not only work together, but are also the chief exponents of liberal views on race. Within a film that is concerned to represent a variety of white attitudes to Africans, it is Mary who speaks for a position broadly in line with the Commonwealth discourse of a multiracial family of nations, identifying this as a feminised discourse through its associations with welfare. Mary's work in the dispensary, however, is also associated with the idea of her independence as an emancipated woman and, like white females in other colonial war films, she carries a gun to protect herself against African violence. She therefore presents an image that resonates both with the liberalism of Commonwealth discourse, and the idea of the emancipated and courageous woman.

African family life was rarely shown after 1945. *Men of Two Worlds* was exceptional in its portrayal of an African family group – Kisenga's return to Africa after fifteen years in England brings reunion with his mother, father and sister. More commonly Africans were associated with family and relationships through their connections with whites. *Simba* shows Africans in domestic interiors as 'houseboys' or as Mau Mau who invade white homes to ransack, steal and kill. African women can be glimpsed occasionally as part of African gatherings, but say nothing. With the exception of the 'houseboys' and Karanja, African men are shown either alone, as sinister figures with criminal or murderous intent, or as a rampaging mob.

After the sequence depicting Allan's brother's ransacked farm, *Simba* moves to Mary's home – another farming family – and a domestic scene as her mother pours coffee, and Mary argues with her father over the nature of Africans. Domesticity and family work to show whites as settlers – people who belong in Kenya through a network of attachments to their families and to the land which they own and farm. This image of white civilisation in opposition to the Mau Mau is strengthened by the juxtaposition of a white meeting with a Mau Mau ceremony. White families are among those assembled at the meeting, which is prompted by the murder of Allan's brother. The Crawford family of Mary and her parents are prominent. The Mau Mau ceremony resembles the witch-doctor sequences in *Men of Two Worlds*. Primitivism is evoked as much through sound as visuals, with chanting and drumming that become ever more frenzied and utterances that, unlike the debates at the white meeting, are incomprehensible to an English-speaking audience.

Simba ends with an image of an African child – Joshua (Huntley Campbell) – focusing on a close-up of his face. Early sequences are careful to establish that he is a victim of Mau Mau violence – abandoned, and wandering aimlessly around the farm. In one of the few references to African family in the film, Allan's servant tells him: 'He belongs to nobody. No family at all Bwana. Mau Mau kill all of them.' Despite the focus on violence against white settlers, Africans were also shown as victims of Mau Mau, endorsing the view that British action in Kenya protected Africans. A newsreel on the Lari massacre in 1953 warned viewers that the story contained 'harrowing scenes', but stated that 'British Pathe News believe that only by showing them can the situation be brought into its true perspective.' It depicted burnt corpses, and shots of African children in hospital, ending with a close-up of a child's burnt face.

Wholly missing from this imagery was the British violence extensively documented by Caroline Elkins and David Anderson.[15] By the end of the war, over 1,000 rebels had been hanged and there was some anxiety in London about the scale of executions. Winston Churchill advised that 'care should be taken to avoid the simultaneous execution of any large numbers of persons', to avoid the impression of brutality and mass executions.[16] Even so, newspapers reported that 'collective punishment', justified in some reports as an appropriate response to the murder of Commander Meiklejohn and the serious wounding of his wife in their Kenyan home, involved women and children rounded up by dogs and men carried off in chains.[17] In 1959, newspapers also revealed that eleven Kikuyu detainees at Hola detention camp had died as a result of beatings, while sixty more had been seriously injured. But it was the Hollywood film, *Something of Value* (1957) that showed torture by the British. While British newsreels showed detainees behind barbed wire, chaining and torture of detainees were never shown on British film.

In both *Safari* and *Simba* the focus on African violence raises questions about who can be trusted, presented from a white perspective. In *Safari* such questions are quickly dispatched: the murder of the white boy at the outset of the film is committed by one of the most trusted 'houseboys'. In *Simba*, there remains a distinction between loyal and disloyal servants. In an attack on the Crawford farm, some servants let the Mau Mau in, while others are themselves murdered. Suspicions extend to Karanja. Whether he can be trusted is a point of dispute between white settlers, particularly between Mary Crawford and Allan Howard. Some believe him to be the local leader of the Mau

Mau. Kenneth Cameron points out that Jomo Kenyatta, a Western-educated African like Karanja, was suspected of being the founder of the Mau Mau.[18] The British acted on these suspicions, imprisoning and then detaining Kenyatta from 1953 to 1961. *Simba* shows suspicions of Karanja to be completely unfounded. The local leader of the Mau Mau is in fact his father.

In the final sequences of the film, Karanja's father repudiates him, telling Africans who have gathered to attack Allan's farm: 'He's not my son, he's a white man.' Karanja has a different view of his relationship with Africans. He rejects Allan's statement that they are 'a bunch of howling savages'. Claiming them as 'my brothers', he goes out to speak to them. His speech is shot from the perspective of Mary and Allan who stand watching behind Karanja, and it is Mary, interpreting for Allan, who speaks his words for a Western audience: 'Will you follow my father and bring more misery and suffering among our people? Or will you follow me and those like me?' His father not only repudiates him, but moves to kill him with a machete. The only African family relationship that the film portrays is filicidal.

Karanja has said earlier, speaking of white settlers to Mary: 'nobody quite trusts me'. His death is not at the hands of his father, who is killed by Allan, but at the hands of Africans, who advance on him like a 'bunch of howling savages' and fatally wound him. In *Men of Two Worlds*, the same accusation of being a white man is levelled against Kisenga and he inhabits a similar narrative of unbelonging. Returning to Africa in early sequences he repeatedly refers to it as 'home' but, as he becomes ill, he tells his sister: 'I thought I had two worlds. Now I have none at all.' Both *Men of Two Worlds* and *Simba* show a white male and female – Randall and Munro, Allan and Mary – coming together over the body of an African man who is on the point of death. As they are united in their care for the African man, these are images that produce a strong contrast between the idea of his unbelonging and white connectedness.

If these films assigned a narrative of unbelonging to Western-educated Africans, *Cry, the Beloved Country* was distinctive among late-colonial films in applying such a narrative to urban Africans. It shows modernity not as a gift bestowed on Africa by the British, but as a corrupting influence on Africans. Their journeys from rural South Africa to Johannesburg separate them from their families and lead them into crime and immorality. Ndotsheni, the African village where the film begins and ends, is the place where Africans can remain uncorrupted – their real home. Made from a liberal and Christian perspective, the film foregrounds the lives and work of South Africans who hold liberal views on race, both black and white. Two African Americans star – Canada Lee as Stephen Kumano and Sidney Poitier in his second major screen role as Theophilus Msimangu. Both play Christian priests.

In *Come Back Africa* (1959) – the first anti-apartheid film made clandestinely in South Africa – Lewis Nkosi, playing himself, says of *Cry, the Beloved Country*: 'The liberal ... wants the African from the country, from his natural environment, unspoilt.' Nkosi is speaking about the novel by Alan Paton on which the film was based, but his comment could apply equally to the film. Mark Beittel, while emphasising Paton's opposition to the National Party and its policies, observes the compatibility between the film's message and 'the basic tenets of apartheid'.[19] Even so, the liberal perspective of *Cry, the Beloved Country* distinguishes it from other late-colonial films whatever their gestures toward liberal ideas. It portrays African family life, however damaged by the corrupting influence of the city, features roles for African women and attributes emotional and psychological complexity to its main African characters. And, unlike most films of the period, it portrays the ethnic heterogeneity of the population of South Africa.

The foyer exhibition at the premiere of *Safari* in a London cinema in 1956 demonstrated the gulf between *Cry, the Beloved Country* and other late-colonial films. On display were 'all the splendours and primitive pageantry of African peoples', including hunting artefacts and a bevy of African female dancers.[20] *Safari* was a particularly clichéd film, complete with dangerous wild animals, white hunter, crocodile-infested river and performances of dancing as well as Mau Mau. But the exhibition, while entirely inappropriate for *Cry, the Beloved Country*, would not have been altogether out of place for many other films of the period. Most films reduced African diversity to a set of stock images and sounds, undercutting their gestures towards a liberal perspective. Ania Loomba's observation about the contradictions of colonialism and WASU's criticism of *Men of Two Worlds* applied to many films of the period: they showed Britain civilising its others while at the same time fixing them into otherness.[21]

MAGIC AND MODERNITY

The villain of *Where No Vultures Fly*, the European who is masterminding ivory poaching in Robert Payton's National Park, tells Payton in their last encounter that Africa is finished: 'there's nothing in it for the white man. One day that black scum is going to take it over.' In response, Payton proclaims there to be a 'new Africa' but this notion remains vague, consisting mainly of his own determination to preserve wildlife, his confidence that Africa is still a white man's country and his belief that Africans are 'black brothers'. In the early 1960s, the idea of a 'new Africa' became a staple part of newsreels and travelogues on Africa and was defined more precisely: Africa was modern. *Modern Uganda* promoted Africa as an alluring holiday destination. Its commentary concluded: 'Africa's changing fast but some parts of it are trying to keep the magic with the modernity.'[22]

Modern Uganda was one of a range of travelogues released in 1961 that included *Kenya Story*, *Zanzibar Story*, *Tanganyika* and *Uganda*.[23] All showed the same tourist attractions and facilities, homogenising Africa. Newsreels of the Queen's tour of Ghana and West Africa, also in 1961, offered another kind of travelogue.[24] Both newsreels and travelogues were made in Technicolor, giving them the edge over British television, which did not broadcast in colour until 1967, and then only on one channel. The urgent and dramatic tones of earlier newsreels on colonial war were gone. Voiceovers in coverage of the Queen's tour continued to be serious, but in most of the travelogues they assumed the tones of an ingratiating salesman.

The nations that the Queen visited in 1961 had either gained Independence or were on the cusp of Independence. Decolonisation prompted further newsreel imagery of Independence ceremonies that bore many resemblances to the Queen's tour: military parades, cheering crowds, displays laid on for royal visitors. The regatta that the Queen watched in Sierra Leone may have seemed particularly familiar to alert members of cinema audiences. Newsreels of Sierra Leone's Independence celebrations in April had shown the Duke and Duchess of Kent watching the same regatta. Newsreels on Ugandan Independence showed crowds cheering the Duke and Duchess of Kent. 'Not in any sense a goodbye', it declared, 'for Uganda has asked to be and has been accepted as a full member of the Commonwealth of which the Queen is head.' Pathé's newsreel of the Queen's tour, entitled *Drums for a Queen* (1961), showed elaborate preparations, the vast distances that Africans travelled on foot to see her and the cheering crowds greeting her everywhere. Such imagery, familiar from royal tours of empire, marked a sense of continuity: the transition to Commonwealth. The British might no longer rule but they retained connections, influence and popularity.

The iconography of Independence-day ceremonies was well established by the early 1960s and not peculiar to Africa: members of the royal family in attendance, the lowering of the Union Jack at midnight, but also the emphasis on former colonies joining the Commonwealth, buttressing Britain's claims to remain at the centre of a global community. There was considerable focus on members of the royal family in a characteristic range of shots: their plane landing, descent down steps, their stay at Government House and the handover of constitutional instruments to the new African leader. Although there was occasional reference to 'strife' or 'trouble' preceding Independence, newsreels never showed decolonisation as a response to nationalism. Rather the presence of members of the royal family and the handover of the constitutional instruments conveyed the impression that independence was a gift graciously bestowed by the British.[25]

Travelogues focused particularly on the spectacle of wildlife – what *Modern Uganda* called 'the Africa of the story books' and *Kenya Story* called 'the natural splendour that *is* Africa'. But this was modern magic. Mervyn Cowie, the figure on whom the character of Robert Payton in *Where No Vultures Fly* was loosely based, makes a brief appearance in *Kenya Story*, but his struggles are over – the National Parks well established and no longer dangerous and difficult territory. There is also a reference to Masai tribesmen, but they no longer pose the threat of disease. Instead they yield evidence about the distinction between reserves and Parks – 'the Masai tribe ... with their herds of cattle and goats' can live on reserves where 'the reasonable need of the human being must take precedence over the animal'. *Rhodesia* (1964), pointed up the modernity of a safari, 1960s-style. A rather aggressive voiceover explains over shots of lions: 'without ever leaving our motor road, here we are face to face with the untamed monarch of the animal world'.

Born Free (1966) supplied a different angle on the conventional spectacle: lions in domestic surroundings. Like *Where No Vultures Fly*, it received a Royal Command Performance. Based on Joy Adamson's autobiographical account of raising a lion cub, and set in Kenya, it made no reference to the recent colonial war. Joy Adamson's husband, played by Bill Travers in the film, had been recruited with his game scouts, to help the police and Home Guard in the campaign against the Mau Mau. In his diary, he described tracking and killing Mau Mau in the language of the safari: a hunt for particularly dangerous game. In *Born Free* he is presented as a caring husband and animal lover, who shares Joy Adamson's (Virginia McKenna) project. All the travelogues repudiate the big game hunt. 'The only shooting visitors do here is with a camera', explain voices over shots of tourists' attempts at amateur wildlife photography. Wild animals may still be dangerous, but as in *Born Free*, in increasingly tamed surroundings, they can be easily caught on camera.

Earlier films had depicted modernity as a gift bestowed by the British on Africa. But in the travelogues it is white tourists, not Africans, who are its beneficiaries. As well as visiting safari parks and beaches, they enjoy the modern facilities on offer – all in bright sunshine. Africans serve them drinks, chauffeur them about in cars and steer them in catamarans. In *Zanzibar Story*, after their arrival on a luxury liner, they are borne away on rickshaws. The voiceover comments: 'The rickshaw boys are the first to enthuse about visitors, and the visitors are the first to enthuse about the rickshaw boys. Zanzibar is a happy island.'

Cities, neglected in 1950s films, are more prominent in travelogues. As places of white leisure and consumption, they advertise Africa's modernity. Africans are happy to service tourists in cities, and their traditional crafts also afford retail opportunities. Various travelogues show tourists purchasing African wood-carving, drums and beadwork.

When Africans, like wildlife, supply their share of magic, this generally takes place outside cities. African performance, particularly of dancing, was a recurrent image in newsreels as well as travelogues, offering one of the many spectacles-within-spectacles – British audiences watching tourists or members of the royal family in Africa watching Africans. The first words of *Uganda* are 'darkest Africa' over shots of women dancing and the sound of drums. The voiceover explains: 'This is an Africa unspoilt by motor cars and modern influence, the hidden face of Africa that Europeans seldom see.' *Kenya Story* declares Kenya 'a modern country with modern ideas' but comments over its final shots of dancing that 'river men dancing is as old as civilisation itself'. No tourists have penetrated the 'darkest Africa' of *Uganda*: a professional has filmed the dance. But in *Kenya Story* and other travelogues, African dancing, like wildlife, is easily caught on tourists' cine-cameras.

In *African Safari* (1962) the magic of Africa extends to a vision of primordial people. This travelogue lays out what it calls a 'magic carpet' on which cinema audiences travel with tourists in South Africa. First they view the wildlife, particularly the land of the white rhino and then they proceed to the land of the 'red blanket peoples'. This is different from routine safaris, the narrative emphasises, one where wildlife cannot be easily photographed from cars, a journey into remote wilderness: 'untamed Africa'. Over shots of a South African village and its peoples, it describes a 'quaint settlement', where a 'happy-go-lucky people' lead 'leisurely lives' and have been 'by-passed by any of the fierce changes of modern life'. In other British media, there was widespread condemnation of South Africa by 1962, especially after the 1961 shootings at Sharpeville, but travelogues did not engage in politics. As *Rhodesia* instructed its audience: 'Forget for a moment any controversy there is about Southern Rhodesia and see it as what it's becoming – an exciting holiday land.' Even so, the message of *African Safari* is clear: black Africans are happy to live under apartheid.[26]

Both the travelogues and the newsreels obscured loss of imperial power. But feature films of the early 1960s did register such loss, although sometimes this was very sketchy. *Death Drums along the River* (1963) updates *Sanders of the River*, but Sanders (Richard Todd) is a policeman, not a District Commissioner and travels on speedboats. Where the 1935 Sanders ruled 'tens of millions' of Africans, the 1963

Sanders deals with criminals who are mainly European – the villain of the film is Austrian. Unlike the original 1935 film, starring Paul Robeson, there are no distinctive African characters. Most do not have speaking parts, and serve as an exotic background to the story about whites, particularly in a tribal funeral ceremony with drums, singing and dancing. The film is set in a fictional colony, and in the present or the recent past: Sanders is asked what he will do when the colony becomes independent. His reply – 'stay on, for as long as they'll have me' – would have been inconceivable in 1935. The 1935 film began with an intertitle announcing that 'tens of millions of natives' are 'guarded and protected by a handful of white men'. The updated Sanders remains a guardian of order and decency, but the world of British rule is over.

Sammy Going South (1963) has not been read as a film that registers loss of imperial power, but its opening during the Suez Crisis and its portrait of the impact of this late-imperial conflict on the ten-year-old boy of the title (Fergus McClelland) mark out an end-of-empire theme. The Suez debacle proved humiliating for Britain. The film shows it as devastating for Sammy. It opens in Port Said, with shots of Sammy, at home, hearing his parents rowing over whether they should send him to his Aunt Jane (Zena Walker) in South Africa for safety. After his home is bombed and his parents killed, he is displaced and orphaned. An Egyptian friend promises to care for him, but proceeds to beat him up, calling him an 'English pig'. Sammy then undertakes the journey to Aunt Jane alone. The journey involves conventional imagery of Africa – wildlife, vast expanses – and a conventional theme about how Sammy is tested, discovering his manhood when he shoots a leopard. Even so, Sammy is a frail imperial hero – a small boy, alone, sometimes forlorn, who has to dodge and run away from people who threaten to deflect him from his goal: South Africa. As a white boy he is powerful only in fantasy: he invents a story in which his family employed many servants and his father whipped one of them. A man he meets identifies his journey as a pilgrimage and it is one that became increasingly common. Decolonisation in Africa prompted a movement of white people to South Africa, which remained a bastion of white rule. Like the travelogues, *Sammy Going South* makes no mention of apartheid, representing South Africa as an entirely appropriate destination for a pilgrim.

Guns at Batasi (1964) is distinguished from other films of the period by its explicit concern with loss of imperial power and its setting in an unspecified ex-colony where the British no longer rule. The early 1960s saw increasing criticism and repudiation of the Commonwealth in Britain.[27] Although the ex-colony is a member of the Commonwealth and the British Army still plays a role there, the perspective of the film is very far removed from newsreel versions of a Commonwealth that enjoyed continued influence. An early sign of British impotence is the British policy of non-involvement when Africans stage a coup. In line with this policy, the British Colonel (Jack Hawkins) orders his men to stay in barracks and hands over command to the African Captain Abraham (Earl Cameron) until what he calls 'this little spot of bother' blows over.

British impotence and the diminishment of British territory and action are prominent themes. All the action is African as supporters of the coup, led by Lieutenant Boniface (Errol John), take Abraham prisoner and raid an ammunition store to arm themselves. The British, oblivious to these events, are shown indoors in their mess, drinking, chatting and playing billiards. Their passivity is emphasised by the comments of one soldier: 'Bloody marvellous! Two hot chocolate mechanics chuck bricks at each other and the whole British army is immobilised.' Powerlessness is also evoked: when Lauderdale (Richard Attenborough), the Regimental Sergeant Major, gives shelter to Abraham, who has been seriously wounded while escaping capture, Boniface taunts Lauderdale with his power to train guns on the mess, threatening to blow it and all its occupants up if they do not hand over Abraham within an hour: 'For the first time in the history of my country, it is we … who give the order to fire.' Boniface never gives that order – the British are not entirely powerless, taking action against this threat and successfully blowing up the guns. But even though the British break out of confinement, this action involves a movement of a few yards only, still within sight of the mess.

The perspective of the film resembles the views of white-settler communities in African colonies like Kenya and Rhodesia that found some support in Britain: black Africans are getting the upper hand, and British politicians do nothing to stop them. The politician in the film is Miss Barker-Wise (Flora Robeson), an MP on a visit to Africa, who champions Boniface. She knew him in England where she taught him as a student, and describes him on various occasions as 'a very humane man' whose 'principles are very sound' and 'a civilised and cultured man'. When Lauderdale describes her idea of Africa as 'smarmy, silly, bloody half-baked' and reminds her that 'You're not in Parliament now, this isn't England and I know more about these people than you do', he draws on an analysis familiar in white-settler communities: metropolitan administrators and politicians are ignorant of Africa and Africans, knowing nothing at firsthand.

If Miss Barker-Wise champions the new Africa of decolonisation, Lauderdale's values belong to an imperial tradition. He regards Boniface as a mutineer. The film gives his values considerable endorsement in his conflicts with Miss Barker-Wise. Her misjudgment of Boniface is heavily underlined: unlike other educated Africans in British film, Boniface is cruel, untrustworthy and unprincipled. In the final sequences of the film, Miss Barker-Wise admits her error, but also tells Lauderdale that Boniface has been made a Colonel. The coup succeeds and Boniface, not Lauderdale, has the last word, demanding that Lauderdale leave the country. The British Colonel confesses his own impotence as he orders Lauderdale to return to England by the next available plane, at the same time admitting that in Lauderdale's place he would have done exactly the same 'step for step'. The action of the soldier hero in the aftermath of loss of empire is thus shown as more likely to earn punishment than medals. *Guns at Batasi* is imbued with sadness for a lost world, and shows the British Army profoundly affected by decolonisation – its capacity for action eroded to the point of immobility, its authority diminished and its soldiers unhonoured.

The spectacle characteristic of films on Africa was wholly missing from *Guns at Batasi*. It was filmed in black and white, mainly at Pinewood Studios in England. There were no expansive landscapes, magic or romance. The adventure that it offers is limited and the British government repudiates Lauderdale's action. Lauderdale is an unlikely hero – middle-aged, a boring raconteur of army stories and prone to loud snoring when asleep. In so far as imperial adventure survived, *Zulu* (1964) rather than *Guns at Batasi* furnished a model for the future, drawing on the history of empire, unyoked from the contemporary Commonwealth. But it is perhaps significant that *Zulu* and *Khartoum* (1967), both set in the nineteenth century, told stories of the British under siege.

CONCLUSION

In the immediate aftermath of war and through the 1950s, most films on Africa gestured at a liberal perspective, offering a vision of Africa with moral overtones, but one that drew on stock images obscuring African diversity. British cameras neglected urban Africa in favour of the rural and the spectacle of wildlife. Their focus was on the British in Africa – there were few leading roles for Africans. Family served as a symbol of white civilisation, but African family life was rarely portrayed and parts for African women were scarce. With the exception of the new figure of the Western-educated African and the characters in *Cry, the Beloved Country*, Africans were not individuated. They were subordinate figures serving the British as 'houseboys', *askari* and porters or uttering 'mumbo-jumbo' as witch doctors. As extras they contributed to the spectacle through drumming, dancing, chant and song. Modernity was shown as a gift bestowed by the British through modernising and welfare projects on an Africa that was 'still backward'.

In the early 1960s much of this continued but, as decolonisation gathered pace, British cameras were also active in reworking imagery of Africa. Newsreels and travelogues proclaimed a 'new Africa'. A new gift that the British were bestowing was much in evidence in newsreels: Independence. Travelogues produced a vision of Africa as an alluring holiday destination, tamed for the benefit of tourists who could easily photograph wildlife from cars. Urban Africa received more attention but its modernity was associated with whites. Black Africans were happy servicing and entertaining tourists in cities, but belonged in rural Africa where their happiness extended to life under apartheid.

Newsreels and travelogues reworked the idea of Africa as a white man's continent. Newsreels showed the British still influencing if not ruling, remaining at the centre of a global community. Travelogues showed whites as the beneficiaries of African modernity. Both reworkings obscured loss of imperial power, but this emerged in some feature films. *Guns at Batasi* showed the end of empire as diminishment of British power, territory and capacity for action. One common feature united most stories told across the period: they reflected well on the British.

NOTES

1. Tom Fleming (ed.), *Voices out of the Air: The Royal Christmas Broadcasts 1932–1981* (London: Heinemann, 1981), p. 74.
2. Kenneth Cameron, *Africa on Film: Beyond Black and White* (New York: Continuum, 1994), p. 199.
3. But see Anandi Ramamurphy, 'Images of Industrialisation in Empire and Commonwealth during the Shift to Neo-colonialism', in Simon Faulkner and Anandi Ramamurphy (eds), *Visual Culture and Decolonisation in Britain* (Aldershot: Ashgate, 2006), pp. 43–69.

4. *The Times*, 11 September 1946.

5. Letter from Lapido Solanke, 27 July 1943, National Archives (NA), CO 875 17/6.

6. Memorandum from T. K. Lloyd, 20 August 1943, NA, CO 875 17/6.

7. It seems likely that Kisenga was loosely based on Rudolph Dunbar from British Guiana, who had worked in Paris in the 1920s, arriving in Britain in 1931. His wartime activities included conducting the London Philharmonic Orchestra at the Royal Albert Hall – the first black man to do so. According to Stephen Bourne, the film's director had considered casting Dunbar in the role of Kisenga. See Stephen Bourne, *Black in the British Frame: The Black Experience in British Film and Television* (London: Continuum, 2001), p. 74.

8. 'Draft Announcement for Colour Prejudice Discussion', BBC Written Archives Centre, R51/92, Talks, Coloured People 1943–1954.

9. Quoted in Bourne, *Black in the British Frame*, p. 74.

10. *Daily Mail*, 6 November 1951.

11. Donna Haraway, *Simians, Cyborgs and Women: The Reinvention of Nature* (London: Free Association, 1991), p. 223.

12. *Daily Telegraph*, 6 November 1951.

13. *Liverpool Evening Express*, 31 August 1946.

14. 'Assignment Mau Mau', *Pathé News*, 7 May 1953.

15. David Anderson, *Histories of the Hanged: The Dirty War in Kenya and the End of Empire* (London: Weidenfeld and Nicolson, 2005); Caroline Elkins, *Imperial Reckoning: The Untold Story of Britain's Gulag in Kenya* (London: Jonathan Cape, 2005).

16. John Newsinger, 'A Counter-insurgency Tale: Kitson in Kenya', *Race and Class* vol. 31 no. 4, 1990, p. 70.

17. *Daily Express*, 25 and 26 November 1952; *Daily Mail*, 27 November 1952.

18. Cameron, *Africa on Film*, p. 183.

19. Mark Beittel, '"What Sort of Memorial?": *Cry, the Beloved Country* on Film', in Isabel Balseiro and Ntongela Masilela (eds), *To Change Reels: Film and Film Culture in South Africa* (Detroit, MI: Wayne State University Press, 2003), p. 79.

20. David Anderson, 'Mau Mau at the Movies: Contemporary Representations of a Colonial War', *South African Historical Journal* vol. 48, 2003, p. 78.

21. Ania Loomba, *Colonialism/Postcolonialism* (London: Routledge, 1998), p. 173.

22. 'Modern Uganda', *Pathé News*, 21 August 1961.

23. 'Kenya Story', *Pathé News*, 20 February 1961; 'Zanzibar Story', *Pathé News*, 27 March 1961, 'Tanganyika', *Pathé News*, 15 May 1961; 'Uganda', *Pathé News*, 3 July 1961.

24. 'The Royal Tour of Ghana', *British Movietone News*, 16 November 1961; 'The Royal Tour Continues', *British Movietone News*, 20 November 1961; 'Durbar for Queen', *Pathé News*, 23 November 1961; 'Queen in Sierra Leone', *Pathé News*, 30 November 1961; 'Bo Durbar', *Pathé News*, 7 December 1961; 'Drums for a Queen', *Pathé News*, 1961.

25. See, for example, 'Nigerian Independence', *British Movietone News*, 6 October 1960; 'Sierra Leone Independence', *Pathé News*, 4 May 1961; 'Tanganyika Independent', *Pathé News*, 14 December 1961; 'Uganda Wins Independence', *Pathé News*, 15 October 1962; 'Kenya Gains Independence', *Pathé News*, 16 December 1963.

26. 'African Safari', *Pathé*, 27 August 1962.

27. Wendy Webster, *Englishness and Empire 1939–1965* (Oxford: Oxford University Press, 2005), pp. 171–81.

14

Dislocations: Some Reflections on the Colonial Compilation Film

Laura Mulvey

SECTION I

As compilation films are made from pre-existing footage, the form depends on the resources of archives. The film-maker has to approach the material that the archive has preserved, as it were, archaeologically. Out of the excavated, selected and assembled footage, a narrative, an argument or an aesthetic endeavour ultimately emerges. However, the process of sequencing never completely integrates the raw material into a smooth and coherent whole; nor is it intended to do so as the rawness of the raw material is, in many ways, of the essence. The compilation film is thus constructed around a gap or dislocation between the original archival raw material and the new reading offered by its rearrangement.

The gap works on three different levels. First of all, there is the simple, but crucially important, gap in time between the filming of the original material and its compilation. Second, to compile is to quote. It is here that, beyond the question of a gap in time, a more complicated level of dislocation arises. As Jakob Hesler points out

> Filmic quotation as such subverts the original's aura of ontological originality. Bracketed by implicit filmic quotation marks, the contour of the fragment is delineated and thus its fragmentary nature, the fissures of its extraction ... . What the compiled fragment seems to lose in terms of authenticity finds compensation in the productive intellectual and aesthetic potential opened up by this reflexivity, by its natural tendency towards playfulness and dialectical irony.[1]

In quotation, the film become fragment has a double existence: as part of the footage to which it originally and coherently belonged, and as a now-extracted shot or sequence producing new meaning in a new context. On a third level, Hesler's phrase 'intellectual and aesthetic potential' draws attention to the way the completed film will endow the original footage with cultural value bestowed by the very work of the compiler film-maker.

However, the tension that necessarily exists between footage and compilation is in certain circumstances aggravated. The film-maker may well approach the archive material from an ideological distance, a shift in perspective extending to an explicit critique, creating a more pronounced dislocation between the original and its recomposed form.[2] In the case of colonial material, it is almost inevitable that the film-maker looks back at these records of empire and its mentality from a very different historical position. The dislocation created by critique thus extends further: it produces a tension not only between the material and its compiler but also between the concept of the compilation film and the archive that protects and preserves its raw material. While, as Hesler points out, the act of bracketing, fragmenting and the fissure of extraction necessarily undermine the aura of any original footage, the colonial compilation film goes further, often working against and in direct opposition to its nature and its authority. There is something here of the hijacking spirit of the Situationist device 'deceptive detournement' whereby 'an intrinsically significant element derives a different scope from a new context'.[3]

The gap in time between the 'then' of the footage and the 'now' of its excavation might seem, at first glance, to be fortuitous in contrast to the more over-determined dislocations in ideological perspective inherent in the colonial compilation film. The two however are closely connected and the apparently 'simple' gap in time should be reconfigured and understood historically as a more culturally inflected delay. Paul Gilroy emphasises in his essay in this volume that the legacy of empire has historically presented difficulties for the British public sphere, and indeed continues to do so. Repressed rather than worked-through, its marks and traces were either left dormant or emerge in symptomatic eruptions across British politics, society and its mentalities. Not uncoincidentally, the loss of the empire, and subsequent accession to freedom and independent national status of the former colonies, constitute one of those breaks in history in which a 'regime' or 'order' slips rapidly out of public attention and its memory, and thus records and documents left behind decline into a dusty obscurity. In a sense, the energy of 1960s modernity might be seen as collective rejection of British investment in empire, rendering archaic, almost overnight, its authority, voice and attitudes. In this context, colonial film footage raises particular questions. The delay in interest in its archive is not only a matter of politics and ideology: as archived material is hard to evaluate aesthetically, it may well have been neglected also on cinematic grounds. But, while all archived footage might struggle with the question of value, these films, even as finished products, were further contaminated by the voice of colonial propaganda and so became repressed records of empire in action.

The return to this material (represented acutely by this Arts and Humanities Research Council project on Colonial Film) coincides with another sense of an ending era that, paradoxically, might have contributed to bringing visibility back to the other. Once digital technology has swept into the sphere of visual media, its celluloid predecessor comes to be associated more and more clearly with the twentieth century, its culture and its history. As the historical and the material specificity of celluloid lose their immediate currency, connoting the past more than the present, both acquire a special quality, an aura of the kind that Walter Benjamin recognised in painting as it faced the ageing effects of photography. From this perspective, cans of film left for decades unnoticed in archives suddenly assume a new significance and interest that logically leads to a reassessment of their value as documents of twentieth-century history. In a sense, celluloid now exudes a kind of preciousness that even attaches itself to insignificant bits of film. It is here that the specificity of the medium, its indexicality (in semiotic terms) and its inherent aesthetic qualities fuse with history. Any celluloid strip preserves whatever the camera sees, profilmically, at its moment of registration and, as time passes, these records can mature into new historical significance. Paradoxically, perhaps, a turn towards the accumulated stock of twentieth-century celluloid, bringing with it new interest, and new analytic tools, might be instrumental in bringing greater visibility to the traumatic implications of British imperialism and its colonial adventures.

A question, a further paradox even, emerges out of this interesting situation. How can these film documents find a place in the world beyond the safety of the archive that has collected and preserved even scraps of celluloid? The compilation film, not in spite of, but because of its contradictions, makes an exemplary contribution to this process (alongside, in the case of this project, a website that can preserve the integrity of the archival documents). In this sense, the genre allows the archive, as site of preservation of the past, to find a dialectical relation between its present and future. This is a delicate balance in which any simple linear relation between a particular past and its future in compilation is complicated by the temporal complexity of the photographic medium. The persistence of the actual instant of registration, the photographic quality that Roland Barthes evokes as 'this was now' adds extra poignancy to Jacques Derrida's reflection of the temporality of the archive more generally:

> In an enigmatic sense, which will clarify itself *perhaps* (perhaps because nothing should be sure here, for essential reasons), the question of the archive is not, we repeat, a question of the past. It is not a question of a concept dealing with the past that might be already at our disposal, *an archivable concept of the archive*. It is a question of the future, the question of the future itself, the question of a response, a promise and of a responsibility towards tomorrow. The archive: if we want to know what that will have meant, we will only know in times to come. Perhaps. Not tomorrow but in times to come, later on or perhaps never. A spectral messianicity is at work in the concept of the archive and ties it, like religion, like history, like science itself to a very singular experience of the promise. And we are never very far from Freud in saying this.[4]

While I will discuss the colonial compilation film in the light of some aspects of psychoanalysis towards the end of this paper, Derrida's points have a particular relevance to archive film as such, and to the way that colonial film can carry 'in' its material a delayed promise that lies in wait for the future. Of course, any recognition of the promise is partial and inadequate in the light of the history of imperialism and Derrida's emphasis on uncertainty is theoretically important. However, there might '*perhaps*' be a way in which the colonial compilation film might focus and contribute to the question of 'promise'.

To reiterate: this complex imbrication of temporalities that Derrida ascribes to the archive has even greater significance for the film archive, given film's particular temporality. From the point of view of the particular significance of the film archive, Derrida's analysis of Freud's 'archive fever' has poignancy. He argues that Freud, in pursuit of his archaeological desire to make 'stones speak',

> wants to pursue a more archaic *impression*, wants to exhibit a more archaic imprint ... . An imprint that is singular in time, an impression that is almost no longer an archive but almost

confuses itself with the pressure of the footstep that leaves its still living mark on a substrate, a surface, a place of origin.[5]

The idea of footprint produced by the singular pressure of a footstep on a receptive surface conjures up its indexicality and thus easily transfers to that of photosensitive material; the analogy is further enhanced by Derrida's emphasis on the 'still living mark' that evokes in turn the impression of life left on film.

The analogy could lead further, beyond the materiality of the index, to the content of the archive as a doubly 'fossilised' record of imperial power and oppression. The colonial film preserves the colonial symbolic order, and, at the same time, its inability to perceive the dislocation concealed within its own filmic images. In fact, those aspects of documentary footage that have usually been understood as distorting the camera's relation to reality (any individual choices of camera position, angle, etc.) make a key contribution to its inscription of colonial discourse. In the first instance, the colonial archive has impressed on it the authority of its source: the films carry the impression of empire, as it were, like a stamp. On the other hand, the camera sees and film records beyond that authorising source, leaving on the colonial film another impression, perhaps more like the more casual footprint. This impression is derived from imperialism's blind spot, and it is this material residue of a reality unseen (or overlooked) by its perpetrators that dislocates the stamp of colonial discourse. These are the visible signs and traces of the unequal relation between the coloniser and the colonised, the indigenous people and their invaders, that have been caught by the camera and are inscribed and preserved. After decades of invisibility, these actual instances and split seconds recorded can emerge into emotional significance and political recognition through the work of the compilation film. In the last resort, this material, that has waited decades to be analysed and evaluated, carries in the celluloid footprint something (*perhaps* even something of the 'promise') that can be returned to the historical consciousness of the present day. Just as celluloid confuses temporality, so does the concept of promise speak from the past towards a future in which it could be redeemed?

SECTION 2

I would like to discuss these questions further through their visualisation and materialisation in two colonial compilation films. *Mother Dao, The Turtle-like* (*Moeder Dao, de schildpadgelijkende*, Vincent Monnikendam, Netherlands, 1995) records from archive footage the colonisation of the Dutch East Indies, now Indonesia. (I have discussed this film in greater detail, in a previous paper that includes some of this material).[6] And Filipa César's *Black Balance* (2011), compiled for this project, shown in London and Pittsburgh, PA, is available on the project's website.

First, a brief digression: in the long history of the compilation film, unlike in any other cinematic genre, two of its leading exponents are women. From this perspective, it is very satisfying that this AHRC project has enabled another to be added to that list. Compilation film was born as political commentary. Its formal founding moment (although films had been 'compiled', particularly as pseudo newsreels, from the earliest days of cinema) reaches back to Esfir Shub's *Fall of the Romanov Dynasty* (USSR, 1927). As one of the film projects commissioned to celebrate the tenth anniversary of the 1917 Revolution, Shub excavated the archives of pre-revolutionary film to compose a document of life under the Tsars, using their own material to expose dialectically the oppression and exploitation of the Tsarist regime. In post-World War II France, Nicole Védrès made a further crucial contribution to the genre with *Paris 1900* (France, 1947), a critique of *Belle Époque* life, culture and politics constructed from contemporary film footage. Védrès's work with compilation also had a theoretical underpinning: she argued that the rearrangement of pre-existing footage allowed a 'second meaning' to be found within it.[7] Rather as Eisenstein had assisted Shub, so Alain Resnais worked as Védrès's assistant on *Paris 1900*. Needless to say, his later *Night and Fog* (France, 1955) is one of the notable examples of compilation film 'turning' original material into a new reading, using Nazi film of Auschwitz to reveal the horrors of the concentration camp.

Black Balance focuses on colonisation within Africa and Filipa César has selected and rearranged archive material from the Imperial War Museum and the British Film Institute that she filmed off a Steenbeck editing table. Early in the film, she makes visible the gaps and dislocations essential to compilation film that I mentioned earlier, by inserting her own figure, as film-maker, into the screen. Her head intrudes in front of the Steenbeck, ultimately blocking out the image and precipitating a fade to black, that carves out an 'in-between' space. First of all, this image gives a spatial dimension to the double temporality of compilation film, confusing its linearity and drawing attention to process. César's actual presence on the screen also evokes the more abstract figuration of 'film-maker', and with it her personal choices and decisions, her necessary confrontation with and distance from the material itself. At the same time, the filmed figure puts her, in a certain sense, into the film as yet one more ghostly presence alongside all the others who will inhabit the screen. And yet, this essentially 'live' celluloid ghost gives greater poignancy to the phantoms that the film has preserved and will endlessly reanimate.

The original material, out of which Filipa César and Vincent Monnikendam have compiled their films, mostly reflects the complacency of the colonial masters. The recordings reveal a certainty about the rightness of their actions and an unshakeable belief in their ability to bring progress to the indigenous people. This undoubtedly reflects a reality: the way well-meaning high-mindedness fused with cruelty and exploitation in the colonial project. (This personal investment by the colonisers is more vividly portrayed in *Black Balance* and is one of the key themes of the film.) It may well be out of this very certainty and belief that the white protagonists enact and willingly embody for the camera (almost naively it now seems) a power that appears in such a different light to contemporary eyes. In keeping, the colonised people's subordination is not so much enacted as simply recorded, subjects included in the frame of the camera and the subordinating frame of the colonial project. This creates a crucial difference in bodily presence out of which a disjuncture arises within the 'body' of the films themselves. The signs of inequality and its political and economic consequences are spread vividly across the screen, only partially concealed in the original material, waiting to be deciphered, discovered and restored to the centre of the story. This in a basic sense is central to the colonial compilation film. The film-makers make use of the visual, cinematic dislocations to address the power relation that enabled the original material to be shot in the first place: while the original material celebrates one story it also, unwittingly, records another. The dislocations affect the filmed material in various different ways. I would like to discuss how these two films draw attention to the following: the literal content of the shots, the contrast between colonial performance and images of the indigenous people, and also the question of the camera's gaze, and, in the case of *Black Balance*, voice.

Both films include many of the images that are typical of colonial footage in general, with its favoured and recurring tropes, for instance, the destruction of nature, the clearing of forests, the penetration of missionaries. That is, the transformation of nature and the introduction of colonial culture are shown to be forces that detach, almost literally uproot, the indigenous people from their social and cultural traditions. This process represents an initial shock. In *Mother Dao*, raw material is assembled into sequences that show, alongside the evacuation of tradition, the second shock. Colonisation opens a space for capital and the industrialisation of agricultural production; the people are transformed into a labour force and subjected to the inexorable logic of capitalist exploitation. Typically, the colonial economy is concentrated on primary products that will be transformed into commodities for the colonising power.

While both films depict the subjection of large numbers of indigenous people by a few agents of colonial power, this is particularly the case in *Mother Dao*, which pieces together the story of the industrialised production of tobacco, an imported crop not native to the archipelago. The footage shows indigenous people systematically and humiliatingly transformed into a mobilised labour force. They are measured, weighed and their fingerprints recorded before they are collected into large processing camps. Small children wade along water-filled ditches to care for the plants. Other sequences show workers tending the huge machines that prepare the tobacco crop for export. Each phase of the process is shown and filmed clearly with pride: the huge, modern machines dominate the workers while the colonial managers and administrators walk up and down a raised platform in their white suits. Furthermore, recurring shots of the railway, the steamship, the motorcar and the aeroplane demonstrate the power of the colonising force over the primitive conditions of the indigenous people and confirm the integral part that these machines play in imposing a new order. *Mother Dao* shows how tobacco plantations transform the people and landscape, subordinating both to monoculture and the interests of colonial capitalism.

In the Africa shown by *Black Balance*, the colonisation of the land is conveyed by spatial imagery, combining different kinds of material to evoke the process conceptually, allegorically and ultimately dramatically. The film begins with a Colonial Office spokesman summing up the colonial project; then, an enormous arrow crosses a map of Africa, describing the drive 'to master' the continent. This idea is literalised by wide, sweeping shots of the landscape and, ultimately, images of surveyors, enacting the dictum that the mapping of a territory is the first necessary step towards its subordination. The surveyor offers a key figuration of empire, not only signifying abstract, symbolic ownership of the land but also the individual mastery of the coloniser. Footage of Africans working for the coloniser leads on to another of the film's central images: in an extended sequence, Africans are shown going through each stage of building a house, making bricks, constructing walls, windows and doors. The house seems to stand for the colonial project itself, literally 'built' by the labour of the colonised, a monument to the imposition of an alien culture.

Mother Dao, the Turtle-like has no guiding voiceover. Occasionally poems mourning the suffering of the people and the effects of colonisation are read on the soundtrack or specific images are given relevant sounds, trains and factories, for instance. With the absence of verbal commentary, the film avoids any attempt to provide the colonised people with a retroactive, retrospective 'voice'. On the contrary, the absence of speech becomes an eloquent statement that bears witness to loss of control over meaning, or in Lacanian terms, a lost 'Symbolic Order', that characterises colonial conditions. The absence of speech puts further weight on the images themselves, allowing them to 'speak' the past more vividly. In its overall structure, the cultural space that the film offers the indigenous people is the silence of shock, trauma and loss.

Black Balance deals with silence in a different way. First of all, the film draws attention to the particular quality of voice that belongs to the English upper class and so defines its hierarchical relations whether of class or the colonies. We can hear this voice repeatedly in the films gathered together on the project's website in the so-called 'voice of God' that accompanies the colonial documentaries. Filipa César's reversal of the Colonial Office spokesman's opening statement works as a distanciation device, to jumble up and undermine that particular English, authoritative tone of voice. Gradually, the film introduces extracts from a fiction film about Africa, which brings the voice back from time to time, reiterating this accent, tone and mode of speech. Shots of Englishmen exhorting the native people to follow civilisation, and so on, are intercut with tracking shots across the faces of the assembled Africans. The question of address, as that of high to low, is further literalised as the English sit in chairs overlooking the Africans who sit silently, voiceless, on the ground. César introduces fiction footage increasingly towards the end of the film. In the first instance, this suggests that a drama about empire can stand as a document alongside non-fiction film. Although the distinction between fiction and document can never be clear-cut, the overlap is often very noticeable in the colonial archive. But the drama also provides an African sound to counter the dominating 'voice' of the British imperial power: extended sequences show the African people gathering in ritual dance, intercut with shots of the English besieged inside bricks and mortar by the sound of drums. While these sequences are exemplary of what the original drama would have seen as 'savagery', as opposed to the civilising forces of Christianity, they also document, ethnographically, African music and dance.

The assembled footage of these films presents a record of the process of colonisation in which pain and trauma have been preserved on film and now appear on the screen. *Mother Dao, the Turtle-like* and *Black Balance* alike show the shock of colonisation, regimentation, exploitation and the multiple brutalities and humiliations associated with the colonial regime. But, unacknowledged as they are in the raw material, the language of cinema itself contributes to revealing the dislocations of power. Here, a clear division emerges between the colonisers and the colonised. The camera's gaze represents the gaze of power. These films, made to celebrate the achievements in the colonies, not only function as a triumphal record of the process (for both local and Colonial Office consumption) but also inscribe the reality of colonial power into the very moment of filming. The camera's gaze solicits participation from its equals. The white people acknowledge its presence: families stand facing the camera for a traditional portrait, white-suited functionaries and factory managers 'perform' their roles. Towards the end of *Mother Dao*, three functionaries start to ham for the camera. As they move towards it, their gestures become increasingly ridiculous and excessive, and the camera, with characteristic relentlessness, captures and exposes their arrogance and vanity.

The indigenous people, on the other hand, are the objects of the camera's gaze and its very presence asserts the superiority of the colonial regime. The indigenous people can neither return its look nor acknowledge its presence. In *Mother Dao*, the camera sometimes takes up a distant position, celebrating the grandiose dimensions of the factory space. This not only affords a telling visual image of the workers' powerlessness but it also seems to inscribe, through its own mastery of space, the power of ideology and the immaterial forces to which these people are subordinated. In the first instance, the camera's presence, its imposition of power in filming, represents, as a metonymy, the gaze of the regime, that is, a discourse of politics. On the other hand, as the camera subordinates each individual worker to its gaze, its significance shifts towards metaphor. The worker's averted look, visibly inscribed in the process of filming, evokes the camera's easy transformation of the relations of power into the hidden drives of voyeurism and sadism. As the camera asserts its 'will to power', it introduces the discourse of psychoanalysis. In *Mother Dao*, the rare glances that the workers give the camera stand out, almost like moments of defiance.

These rare glances flash out as a sudden instance of a 'Real' (in something like Lacan's sense of it), a moment of truth that evades translation. If the cinema has preserved time and made history palpable, these moments of affect condense time, returning the spectator to their original instant. The films of the colonial archive display an extraordinary network of interwoven threads, not always but frequently producing that flash of wordless intimation of reality that Walter Benjamin associates with the dialects of history. They lead to a consideration of histories rather than history as such, and how these histories are folded within each other, eddying and interacting (even waiting to be unfolded) and mutating and changing meaning across time's literal passing.

SECTION 3

Although the theory of trauma was developed for the individual psyche, the history of colonised people suggests that it should be extended to collective experience. Unspeakable and unassimilable events that take place within the external, social world challenge psychoanalytic theory's primary focus on the personal and the individual. The colonial films demonstrate over and over again the porous nature of the boundary between the individual and the collective psyche. Freud suggests that trauma brings with it a sense of 'helplessness' in the face of conditions that cannot be controlled or internalised by the psyche. Helplessness pervades the images in *Black Balance* and *Mother Dao*, both those of individuals and of the collective. The significance of film as a historical document lies precisely in its inability to generalise. The indexical sign can only record the individual instance. However, as the colonial film reveals its own political construction, it oscillates between the individual and the general. To pause the film image on one person is to see his or her specificity and then the incorporation of a living body and individuality into the gestures and way of life demanded by the colonial system. This pause for thought leads back into the material nature of the film image: the fossilised presence of a nameless worker (an image still attached, like the footprint, to its substrate) whose otherwise unmarked history has been recorded, if only for a fleeting instant. The pause also, of course, leads out of the specific image into a wider reflection on the history of colonialism and its legacy of damage.

The encounter between the raw material of the archive and its later reorganisation and revision in the compilation film enables a possible meeting point between psycho-analytic thought and historical thought through the medium of film. If psychoanalysis has, by and large, been concerned with the study of the individual psyche, history, on the other hand, studies collective, generalised experience. But, clearly, both are absorbed in excavating and questioning the past, in keeping with Freud's archaeologi-cal metaphor, and both search for those 'stones' that can 'speak'. While psychoanalysts actively decipher the subject's unconscious, that is, the individual's personal 'archive' of his or her past history, historians, whatever their interpretation of the legacy of events across time, equally have to decipher archival raw material into a narrative for the present and the future.

A further analogy between the compilation film and psychoanalysis can be found in the dislocations both processes make visible. With the concept of *Nachträglichkeit*, Freud directly addressed the question of psychical temporality, indicating that certain past events are subject to later revision. As defined by Jean Laplanche and Jean-Baptiste Pontalis, 'deferred action' (as Strachey translated the term) implies that

> experiences, impressions and memory traces may be revised at a later date to fit in with fresh experiences or with the attainment of a new stage of development. They may in that event be endowed not only with a new meaning but also with psychical effectiveness.[8]

Laplanche and Pontalis point out that the memory traces are a residue of trauma, the legacy of material that surpassed the subject's understanding at the time of the original event. The indexical persistence of the past into the present, characteristic of photographic time and comparable to the memory trace, as well as the compilation film's revision of the archive's raw material, both suggest an analogy with the structure of trauma. The colonial compilation film vividly inscribes the dislocation between the empire's dominant narrative of progress and civilisation (in fact, the films seem to have been made in response to the need to recount these achievements to the British people) and the lot of the people for whom the experience appears to be primarily one that cannot be incorporated into a meaningful context. Laplanche and Pontalis also point out that the effect of the deferred action concept is to detract from an overly linear pattern to human psychic development. Here, the time of the traumatic event and its later revision are intricately woven together.

With film, the confusion of time is further complicated by its duration, the very 'liveness', the animated nature, of these celluloid inhabitants of history. Although the reordering of found footage offers a revision of past events within the context of an altered consciousness, the new narrative does not completely dissolve the impact of the unassimilable presence of the past. The effect may be compared, perhaps, to an unresolved, incomplete, deferred action. Laplanche expanded his thoughts on *Nachträglichkeit* with a new translation of the word as 'afterwardsness'. He argues that hidden in these kinds of memory traces is 'a message from the other':

> Even if we concentrate all our attention on the retroactive temporal direction, in the sense that someone reinterprets their past, this past cannot be a purely factual one, an unprocessed or raw given. It is impossible therefore to put forward a purely hermeneutic position on this – that is to say, that everyone interprets their past according to their present – because the past already has something deposited within it that demands to be deciphered, which is the message of the other person. But does not modern hermeneutics forget its very beginning, when it was – in the religious interpretation of sacred texts – a hermeneutic of the message?[9]

To adapt Laplanche, the revision of the original archive footage that represented the colonial vision and understanding of the indigenous peoples reveals 'something deposited within it that demands to be deciphered': the traces of the trauma of colonial experience. The colonial compilation film has a unique ability to bear witness to the past, to render the 'message' visible and carry forward its 'demand'. But the reordering and rearticulation of the footage stops short of a coherent narrative, and reaches out, by analogy, to history and psychoanalysis, as though these two disciplines might address the task of decipherment demanded by the 'message'.

●

To conclude:

Derrida's combination of the words 'spectral messianicity' brings together images of a past haunting a future, once again confusing and fusing temporalities. Given that the ghost stands for something that refuses to be laid to rest, that insists on 'returning', colonial film footage returns the 'now' of this conference, book and archival project, to the question of the colonial legacy, very particularly through the haunted nature of the celluloid medium. Here, the idea of Derrida's 'promise' and Laplanche's 'message from the other' may (*perhaps*) be relevant. The 'other', in Laplanche's terms, the ancestral child that leaves its legacy on its progeny, the adult, should be reconfigured around the legacy left by the empire on its descendants, through the decades and into 'now'. The 'promise', on the other hand, relates to the haunted and haunting figures of the colonised preserved on film, in the archive, living traces left by repression and to which the ghost returns. Paul Gilroy associates collective amnesia that clouds the memory of the British empire and its legacies with a failure to mourn; the mourning process represents a recognition that the present owes something to the past, just as the promise comes from the past towards the future. Both confront amnesiac desire. Derrida says towards the end of *Archive Fever* that 'Nothing is thus more troubled and more troubling today than the concept archived in this word archive.'[10] He has suggested throughout that the archival institution is essentially 'authoritative' and may be interpreted in terms of a primal father against whom the sons must rebel.

There are two ways in which this Oedipal drama might be relevant to the colonial compilation film at the present moment. First of all, the digitalisation of archived moving images alters their currency, bringing them out into the world, into a wider consumption that displaces inaccessibility and secrecy. Second, the compilation film engages directly with the complex cinematic nature of colonial film, the way its contradictions and dislocations are 'impressed' on and by the medium. In this sense the compilation film can make a gesture towards an ethical response to the original raw material, implicitly challenging both its authoritative nature as well as that of empire. And (perhaps) its promise, the ghosts' message suspended across time (in its messianicity), might begin to be articulated in history and psychoanalysis and ultimately, the British public sphere.

NOTES

1. Jakob Hesler, 'Reading the World: The Essay as Film Form in Left Bank Non-Fiction Cinema, unpublished doctoral thesis, Birkbeck College, University of London, 2011.
2. This element of critique is not essential to the compilation form. In its rich avant-garde tradition, or in the historical compilation films that have recently been produced by the BBC (for instance, *The Second World War in Colour*, 1999), critique is not central to the process.
3. Guy Debord, Gil J. Wolman, 'A User's Guide to Detournement', 1956. The hijacking strategies of the compilation film may well be too '*bien pensant*' for true Situationist radicalism.
4. Jacques Derrida, *Archive Fever: A Freudian Impression*, trans. Eric Prenowitz (Chicago, IL: University of Chicago Press, 1996), p. 36.
5. Ibid., p. 97.
6. Laura Mulvey, 'The Compilation Film as "Deferred Action": Vincent Monnikendam's *Mother Dao, The Turtle-like*', in Andrea Sabbadini (ed.), *Projected Shadows: Psychoanalytic Reflections on the Representation of Loss in European Cinema* (London: Routledge, 2005).
7. Hesler, 'Reading the World'.
8. J. Laplanche and J. B. Pontalis, *The Language of Psychoanalysis* (London: Institute of Psychoanalysis, Karnac Books, 1988), p. 111.
9. Jacques Laplanche, 'Notes on Afterwardness', in *Essays on Otherness* (London: Routledge, 1999), p. 265.
10. Ibid., p. 91.

AFTERTHOUGHTS
ON COLONIAL
FILM

●

15
Notes on the Making of *Black Balance*:
An Ongoing Film Essay on the Colonial Archive

Filipa César

The title is not a metaphor but the technical mechanism in a video camera. *Black balance* is an operation similar to *white balance*, a calibration of the tone and light level of white in a video camera. As *white balance* gives the camera a reference to 'true white', *black balance* gives a reference to 'true black'.

This function is normally available only in professional cameras. The mechanism *black balance*, as an absent calibration, raises the question that the politics of the development of video equipment integrates decisions on the colour of the subject represented with the technical means of representation. The title, like the sampled images that compose the film essay, is a signifier whose meaning floats for each individual viewer.

I shot the material with a video camera from films playing through a Steenbeck. The Steenbeck allowed me to move back and forth in the film narrative, breaking the order the narrative imposed. I chose a corpus of educational and instructional films because the decisions made in their editing can reveal information about the unspoken colonial assumptions about the psychology of race.

Montage in the corpus: the combination of staged images and documentary footage to construct a storyline. The storyline produces both the problems and their solutions. Montage in *Black Balance* (2010): the subtraction of plot and story to reveal a common grammar and its political motivations. A portrait of the African as the receiver of messages, a kind of double of the film spectator; a portrait of the speech of the white man; the white man speaks, the black man hears. What does the white man say/mean? What does the black man hear/understand? Fear is portrayed in the face of the white man; the black man is portrayed as the producer of this fear.

The films in the corpus use symphonic music. What Straub would call, with his hatred of non-diegetic cues, images submerged in a kind of a soup. The opposition between symphonic Western music and the African drums. The symphonic music accompanies the flow of the narrative; the African drums disrupt the ongoing action.

Black Balance is a work in progress because it is a film that is only finished by its viewers. And because the colonial moving-image machine is a work in process. How do we look at these images? What do they activate in me and in subsequent viewers? Do we have to identify with one side? Must we feel like the victim as we identify with the African grandmother, or do we have to feel like the colonial oppressor as we identify with the European father? How can we relate to these images today? How can these images provoke us to relate to our own system of producing meaning (for example,

Black Balance attracted critiques that its images of the African were always negative, as well as others claiming that these images are the sole property of the victims). The images in the corpus are strongly manipulative and the camera is wielded with enormous power to subdue its African subjects.

But there is always something in these images that resists the film-makers' colonisation, a disobedience which is both rebellion and dignity.

NOTE

Black Balance can be seen at <www.colonialfilm.org.uk/work in progress>.

16
The Repatriation of Jamaican Film Images

Franklyn St. Juste

[P]assionate research ... directed by the secret hope of discovering beyond the misery of today, beyond self contempt, resignation and abjuration some very beautiful and splendid era whose existence rehabilitates us both in regard to ourselves and in regard to others.
(Frantz Fanon)

Taken out of context, these words by Frantz Fanon summarise the need to collect and preserve evidence of our history in whatever form, so that we can discover who we really are: 'not rediscovery', as Stuart Hall – that great communication scholar – puts it, 'but the production of identity. Not an identity grounded in the archaeology, but in the re-telling of the past.' At the moment, several thousand feet of motion-picture film produced by the Jamaican government representing aspects of Jamaican history are held in vaults in London. This should be an indication of how imperative is the need to repatriate this material for the preservation of and access to our history.

A SHORT HISTORY OF THE JAMAICA FILM UNIT

First, it is necessary to deal with some aspects of the history of the development of the film industry in Jamaica. With the establishment of the Jamaica Social Commission as a company of limited liability in the late 1930s it was recognised that the motion picture was vital in community development, particularly in the rural areas, and was an important means of communication. National hero Norman Washington Manley spearheaded this movement. In 1938 a documentary film service was launched with the purpose of producing films and, more importantly, exhibiting films throughout the island to present educational information and promote community development. The Colonial Film Unit (CFU) in England produced most of the films shown and some originated from the United States, even though many of these were considered inapplicable to local conditions and native culture. The films from the CFU were classic examples in the documentary mode, such as *Daybreak in Udi* (1950) about community development in East Africa, *Song of Ceylon* (1934) and the celebrated *Night Mail* (1936) about the train carrying mail from London to Glasgow.

In 1949, recognising the need for more locally produced films in empire domains, the Central Office of Information (COI) embarked upon a programme of establishing film training schools in the British territories. Also on the agenda was the plan to close down the CFU because of the high costs of producing films for these countries. A one-year training programme was established on the campus of the then University College of the West Indies, with representatives invited from Jamaica, Trinidad, Barbados and Guyana. Although the curriculum was advanced and comprehensive, some criticism was levelled at its relevance to the culture of the territories concerned as no attempt was made to examine the possible societal and cultural differences that could be reflected in the structuring of the communicative material. Instead, established filmic techniques for English culture were 'combined with some paternalistic and neo-colonialist approaches' and, as Martin Rennals puts it, 'superimposed as relevant for our audiences' – Caribbean that is. What was most important was the fact that this proved to be a landmark in the development of film-making in the Caribbean region.

The first government-sponsored film production unit was launched in Jamaica in November 1951 and was named the 'Jamaica Film Unit'. It was attached to the Education Department and consisted of a staff of three, with one 16mm film camera and some related editing equipment. Its objective was to produce films in Jamaica, for Jamaica, with Jamaicans and by Jamaicans. It later expanded to include a film library and mobile projection services and became known as the Central Film Organisation. Shortly after, the COI in England began to wind down its film-production arm known as the CFU and the Jamaica Film Unit, which had maintained a close relationship with that organisation, was the beneficiary of some of the used equipment. Realising that most of these newly formed film units around the Commonwealth would need post-production services, a company called Victor M. Gover & Co. Ltd was formed, later to become the Overseas Film and Television Centre, with a COI member on its board of directors in the person of William Sellers. More importantly, the establishment of a film-processing lab was too costly for these countries so Victor M. Gover & Co. Ltd satisfied those needs.

In 1954, a decision was made to switch from 16mm to 35mm because this increased the distribution potential to local cinemas and, from the point of view of quality, reduction prints from 35mm to 16mm maintained better quality than the reverse process. This did not mean the total abandonment of the 16mm gauge as films of a specialised nature, of primary interest to special groups, were still produced on 16mm. The COI gave the Jamaica Film Unit a complete 35mm Newman Sinclair camera outfit to initiate this change. The use of synchronous sound recording in 16mm was still in its infancy and 35mm was well advanced although somewhat cumbersome. All films were sent to England for processing and sometimes editing. If editing was done locally, then the film would be finished in England and a completed production consisting of picture and sound would be returned to Jamaica. In 1955 a new 35mm sound camera as well as sound-recording equipment were purchased to enable synchronous filming.

Television was introduced to Jamaica in 1963 and the Jamaica Film Unit expanded its 16mm capabilities to cope with the increased demand for material. By that time, rapid technological changes in the film industry worldwide resulted in the acquisition of new and, as they say, improved equipment. Smaller, more portable and more sophisticated equipment enabled the coverage of a wider range of subject matter. New types of film stocks enabled the recording of scenes at lower light levels than before and colour photography was just as easy to achieve as black and white.

The year 1968 saw the introduction at the Jamaica Film Unit of a black-and-white lab capable of processing negatives and making prints complete with an optical soundtrack. A dubbing theatre was also built to enable the mixing of soundtracks and create optical tracks for printing. More editing equipment was purchased to meet the demands of television. Soon, approximately a million feet of film was running through the lab annually. These major technical advances ensured a greatly reduced dependence on foreign assistance and granted Jamaican film responsibility for the total completion of black-and-white film productions. Colour film processing still took place in labs in England.

Today the rapid development and digitalisation of the technology of motion-picture production have greatly simplified the creation of visuals. Cameras have become so cheap and small that they can be held in the palm of one's hand and the automatic mode makes it possible for anyone to make pictures at the touch of a button. This has interrupted the ability to be able to tell a story in pictures, which was the hallmark of the efforts of the Jamaica Film Unit.

A DESCRIPTION OF SOME OF THE FILMS HELD OVERSEAS

Approximately 394 film titles featuring Jamaica are being held in London. Of this number roughly 286 are Jamaican productions, the bulk of these from the Jamaica Film Unit and consequently owned by the Jamaican government. Most of these films represent the history of the political and social development of the Jamaican people between the years 1950 and 1980. Examples include *Jamaica Tercentenary Celebrations* (1955), recording the celebration of three hundred years of British rule; *It Can Happen to You* (1955), a film about venereal disease and prevention approaches; *Jamaica's Great Day* (1957), showing the achievement of full internal self-government in November 1957; and *Our Children* (1958), depicting the dangers of leaving the youth in all areas of the society without guidance and supervision. It is interesting to note that most of these films adopted the dramatic narrative format, which it was hoped would enable audiences to identify with the situations presented. In other words, story films. Other films included *Government by the People* (1960), telling the story of Hibbert House on Duke Street with aspects of the history of the time, and to mark the move to Gordon House; *Our New Government* (1962), showing national heroes Manley and Bustamante returning from the historic Independence conference and subsequent elections; *Towards Independence* (1962), with Jamaica seceding from the Federation after a referendum; *A Nation Is Born* (1962), all about the splendour, colour and frenzy of celebrating the achievement of Independence (featuring representatives from all over the world, including Princess Margaret and Lord Snowdon and US Vice President Lyndon Johnson); *Time of Fury* (1965), a docudrama about the Morant Bay rebellion and its consequences.

The preceding list represents a small percentage of the total amount of titles held in England but hopefully gives an idea of the range of material relating to the history of Jamaica. Not mentioned are the newsmagazines that dealt with topical and current events including visits of very important persons. Also not mentioned are the numerous productions devoted to the dissemination of information about government programmes in health, education, agriculture and culture. All of these films represent a rich tapestry of social and developmental endeavours involving the Jamaican people before and after the achievement of Independence.

THE NEED FOR REPATRIATION

Because of the fragility of film stock, proper preservation usually involves storing negatives and prints in climate-controlled facilities. The vast majority of films in Jamaica were not stored in this manner and this resulted in widespread decay of the films held. It was therefore suitable to allow most of the original negatives and sound-tracks to stay in England. With new advances in the technology of storage and the availability of digital techniques it is now possible to address the problems in a more positive manner. The need to repatriate these films has now become imperative and crucial for these reasons:

1   to preserve aspects of the history of Jamaica shown on film made by the Jamaica Film Unit;
2   to allow convenient access for the purposes of research by historians and other interested parties;
3   for use in schools for the teaching of Jamaican history;
4   to generate a source of revenue.

The idea of repatriation is not new. Some years ago efforts to locate the material in England had proved futile so that, despite intentions voiced to 'bring the material home', no action could be taken. The following tasks are necessary if this material is to be returned to Jamaica:

1   Determine intellectual ownership. Some of the material is fifty years' old so could now be in the public domain, although the copyright period applying to film is understood to be sixty years. It is important to note that the material was being stored for the Jamaica Information Service, which paid for this service. However, in the later years, the 1990s to 2000s, it is understood that storage fees ceased to be paid. It is rightly the property of the government of Jamaica.
2   Determine the legal strategy best followed to safely reacquire the material.
3   Conduct an on-the-spot inspection to ascertain the present condition of the material.
4   Decide the best method of repatriation. Most of the material consists of original negative in A & B Rolls, some containing metal sensor clips for printing that might have to be removed. There are also magnetic and optical soundtracks, which will require resynchronisation with the picture. Decisions will have to be made regarding the most appropriate medium on which to repatriate the material e.g. videotape, DVD or in its original form.
5   Create a cataloguing system to enable easy access.

Long ago, film ceased to be only seen in cinemas; as film technology and now video became simpler and more accessible, motion-picture images have entered many areas, in education, industry and documentation. The challenge now is to appreciate the fullness of the variety of these moving images, to locate and consolidate them as representations of our history and to prevent further decay. The result will be more images for ourselves and future generations to study and enjoy.

17
Undoing the Colonial Archive

Isaac Julien

It gave me great pleasure to attend the conference, 'Film and the End of Empire', because my own work has often drawn on archives – *Looking for Langston* in 1989, *Black and White in Colour*, a two-part documentary on race and ethnicity in British television, produced by Colin MacCabe in 1992 and then, perhaps most relevantly for this conference, my film on Frantz Fanon – *Black Skin, White Mask* (1996). *Black Skin, White Mask* has the most direct relevance for the themes of the conference because part of its purpose was to undo and remake the colonial archive. And the comments that I would like to make are the comments of an artist, of a film-maker rather than an academic. It is from the point of view of a practitioner that I want to address the questions of what we want from the archive or what we want to read from it.

As a film-maker, a methodology that I have applied when selecting archive film to reuse in one of my films, is to eliminate the voiceover. This undoing of the voice of authority is very important for me, because it is a way of actually trying to re-look at these images. And there is a related set of deconstructive approaches: slowing the material down, refocusing and rephotographing the imagery. These methods represent a kind of formalist approach to developing what I would like to call a certain 'optical unconscious', an unconscious that is obliterated by a voice of anxiety – the voice of *authority*, which is the soundtrack.

But this voice of anxiety is always cloaking the rather nebulous and ambivalent representations that we see in this colonial archive. Of course, one thinks of this imperial moment, this moment of war and counter-insurgency, as being something like a prophetic reading in today's contemporary world of violence. This violence from the past confronts very directly whoever consults the archive and writes about it. Because to my mind it seems to be very important to try to think about this violence as a continuum that must work its way into our critiques of these representations.

The other thing that the conference has made me reflect on is the role of the film theorist and the role of the artist. I've been thinking back to *Screen* magazine in the period 1985–7 when Kobena Mercer and I edited a special issue entitled 'The Last Special Issue on Race?'. Of course this title was meant to be ironic, but also to indicate that all the different interventions in relation to subjectivity, identity formation, spectatorship, all of these things would be considered alongside our thinking about representation in the present and this would be the way that cinema studies would develop. And we saw it as a continuum of the work that people like Laura Mulvey and Homi Bhabha had done, the work that had been developed in cultural studies, and so we therefore felt that it would be a normal progression if this kind of theorisation of deconstructed images became part of the vocabulary of film studies.

Now of course that didn't happen. What happened was a sort of philosophical turn, a return to the visual let's say, which in a way left behind unfinished business. And what I think was fascinating about this conference and its attempt to look at this archive and the intervention that it might make takes us back to the rereading that Kobena Mercer and I had been advocating. This rereading of war and surveillance, of propaganda, demands that we consider its relevance for today. So, to my mind, most of the films intend to create moral panic, and this moral panic is constructed through the voice and sound – the tonality of the voice, the scripting and the audience address.

And I feel that this whole project – both the papers that we've heard and the films that we have seen – really do constitute an attempt to give voice back to the images. This oppositional voice raises the question of subjectivity. And I thought it was very interesting looking at the amateur footage, for example, say of the Malayan Emergency, with a major describing his own material, and the way in which this sort of footage makes a certain intervention.

I also wonder about the kind of murky question of our attraction to these images – this question of having perhaps a critical nostalgia, the fact that some of these images are in fact quite beautiful, some of them are very disturbing, and this kind of surplus identification that comes about when looking at these images. And I think that slippery question of what constitutes a canon, that was brought up by Tom Gunning, and this indexicality of the ways in which these images are producing this kind of other identification, this surplus pleasure.

It's this area that I find very interesting, this ghosting of the imperial past, and the pleasures and critical knowledges we are forming today in this rereading of them. To my mind, it would seem perhaps that this is in a way a continuation and development of some of the theoretical inventions that we were trying to make in the mid-80s and early 90s around film theory, and which have got lost and then picked up in an art context, which I presently work in.

But when I consider how our questions vanished and how they might now be coming back, I also, more pessimistically, have to wonder about the setting in which we've been viewing these images. I've been thinking about that relationship to looking at images both as someone who makes images, and someone who's interested in which type of ideas get produced. Whenever I'm in a pedagogical scenario, that the attention given to how they should be projected and seen is not made a priority, and I'm wondering about that relationship to the way that we view them, the way that we watch them.

I think about this very ironically, in terms of someone who makes images, and I'm reflecting on this kind of fading out of image that occurred during the course of the couple of days, and how that is an accomplice of the fading out of these questions that have arisen and are reappearing. And so I felt paradoxically that, on the one hand, the deconstructing of the archive and its relevance for the present is at work in the papers that we heard and the films that we saw and I feel that picks up on themes that have been lost over the past two decades and, at the same time, I feel that there is not enough attention to the image as image to really develop these questions for the present as we should. For it is the contemporary that matters in all this and if we do not pay full attention to the image then we will not make our questioning fully contemporary.

The contemporaneous aspect, to me, is what matters. Because as someone who makes images, or has made documentaries using archives, I'm really interested in terms of how those might resonate with a contemporary audience.

18

The Colonial Regime of Knowledge: Film, Archives and Re-Imaging Colonial Power

Anthony Bogues

In many ways colonial power was about ordering the world. Integral to such an ordering was a 'certainty of representation', in which colonial power developed techniques of truth and representation that illustrated a colonial gaze of hierarchical difference, while mapping the world and human population groups into visual spectacles. In the nineteenth century, two forms of these visual spectacles became central to the colonial power's ordering project. The first were the world exhibitions where, as Timothy Mitchell has argued, 'world exhibition here refers not to an exhibition of the world, but to the world conceived and grasped as though it were an exhibition'.[1] Mitchell makes the point that the 'effect of such spectacles was to set the world up as a picture ... to be viewed, investigated and experienced'.[2] For the colonial zone of the world, to be 'viewed, investigated and experienced' was to be 'represented' as the so-called 'authentic' expressions of 'primitive cultures'. It was to make visible the colonial gaze, affirm the domestication of the colonial world and reaffirm colonial power's 'right' to rule. The second form of visual spectacle was the colonial cinema. It was perhaps not accidental that Louis Lumière screened at the Paris World's Fair of 1900, *Indochina: Namo Village, Panorama Taken from a Rickshaw*. Here we have both visual spectacles congealing as the film produced a slice of the colonial zone in ways which showed that the colonial subject was a happy one, one with a smile that welcomed the colonial adventurer. In this sense the colonial everyday, which cinema makes legible, became graspable for the colonial audience while once again reaffirming colonial power. Both the world exhibitions and colonial cinema are instances of colonial regimes of representation and power. The issue this project poses for us is how do we, in the contemporary moment, read the colonial cinema as an archive of representation?

There are, of course, two issues. One is about the archive and the second is about reading critically and what does it mean to read with both an eye to the past and to the present? The collection presented on the project's website is a formidable one, over 6,000 films from the collections of the British Film Institute, the Imperial War Museum and the British Empire and Commonwealth Museum. It therefore constitutes an archive but one which is anti-auratic, in Walter Benjamin's terms since, as Mary Ann Doane tells us, the 'the print is never the original'.[3] But there is something else about an archive which should give us pause. While the archive is about a way of life no longer lived it is often structured around the questions of life in the present, so while the archive 'is a protection against time',[4] it is constructed through a desire of the present. So what animates this contemporary desire?

I have been troubled by the title of the conference this book emerges from, 'Film and the End of Empire'. Initially I thought that my concerns drew in part from the fact that a conference talking about empire being held in America should at least gesture towards the fact that the US is an empire albeit in some sort of difficulty. In other words should there not be some specificity about empire? The end of which empire? Yes, of course the colonial one. But the obvious question that strikes one is this. How did the practices of various technologies of rule, the different regimes of colonial representation create traces which are spectres of our moment? Thus is our desire to construct these archives partly in order to grapple with these traces and spectres or to discern within them forms of historical colonial knowledge? What seems clear is that there is an issue of the meaning and significances of coloniality in the present moment for Britain. This is of course, as Paul Gilroy and others have suggested, a very important matter. But it would also seem to me, that to think about coloniality and British society is also to think about the ways in which empire has constructed various forms of rule today.

In this regard, I am reminded of one of the colonial figures visible here and there in films from the archive, Winston Churchill who, in a 1943 speech at Harvard University a few years before the political independence of India, observed that 'the empires of the future are empires of the mind'. [5] Here I think Churchill meant that, in the future, empires could only rule through desire and fantasy. With regards to cinema we know of the positioning of the spectator to visual representation and how looking and absorbing what one sees creates a 'circularity' of power in which images work at two levels. One level of course is the stereotype and the other is a fantasy which is often not shown but which is drawn upon in this circuitry of imagery, representation, knowledge and power.

Stuart Hall in his work on representation makes a crucial point that images connect language and meaning. When you connect language and meaning, you get categories and in this process, images become the material force in a process of conceptual mapping which in turn establishes correspondences between objects, concepts and signs. Thus to think about this colonial film archive is both to reflect on the spectres and traces of imperial rule in our contemporary moment as well as to think hard not so much about the images and what they represented at any precise historical moment but rather about *the work* these images do in creating knowledge categories which still have currency today.

Let me give an example of what I mean, of how colonial power remains a trace which continues to shape knowledge categories. There was a very robust discussion at the conference about 'witch doctors'. In this discussion, we talked about the feature film made by the British Colonial Office, *Men of Two Worlds* (1946). Our discussion ranged from how the so-called 'witch doctors' are portrayed in Nollywood, to Ousmane Sembene's novel, *Xala*, to the transformation of witches in Western feminist thinking. But there were two things missing from the discussions. In the first place, there was an absence of the genealogy of the word in the colonial regime of knowledge with particular reference to Africa. Second, there was a startling absence of the ways in which the countries of contemporary Africa, for example, South Africa, are confronting these colonial categories in deploying new conceptions of the so-called 'traditional' and the indigenous. In other words there was an overhang of the colonial trace in our categories of knowledge which I would suggest needs to be confronted. I am not making here a pointed criticism of the conference but rather recognising how in subtle ways traces may constrain and shape a debate. So when Gilroy calls upon us to confront the colonial past, I would like to suggest that there is a knowledge regime of colonial power which must also be confronted. Indeed it is this regime which is most insidious in its subtle reproduction of our habits of thinking.

In many of the films on the project's website, Africans are portrayed as diseased and unclean bodies, and Africa a place of untamed nature where locusts often abound. This is of course not new and continued what Stuart Hall tells us is the colonial project expressed in 'imperial advertising – the quality of the fetish – object'.[6] However, to what degree do these images of Africa and Africans prevail today and work to undergird an imperial project of humanitarianism in the twenty-first century? So there is a politics of the present in this archive which I think we must be attentive to.

I now turn to the matter of the re-imaging of colonial power. In reflecting on this question, I am reminded that V. Y. Mudimbe observes that colonial power has three dimensions. He lists these as an economy of extraction and the insertion of the colonised space into the Western economy, creating a new geographic space. Second, he notes that the colonial power is about external political domination and finally, that colonial power was about the control of the native mind, what I want to call the creation of new subjectivities. I wish to pay attention to this third aspect, the creation of new subjectivities as a crucial element of colonial technology of rule, a technology of rule which requires the management of desire and the imagination. I think we can see this technology of rule in a film made in 1945 on the eve of India's political independence. Simply called *District Officer*, the narrative of the film deploys the language of power as one of *caring for* and a certain kind of power which Michel Foucault would call pastoral. It is a film about the perceived success of the British colonial power in India and how it was supposed to have carried out its civilising, caring mission. How can we forget the scene when, after working a long day, and retiring to bed with papers and reports, a telephone call interrupts the District Officer's reading, informing him of new matters he must attend to. He puts on his clothes and moves to take care of the business at hand. This Indian District Officer was a product of the culture of the colonial regime, devoted and self-sacrificing. He exemplifies the so-called nobleness and high-mindedness of colonial power. Of course, in this narrative the conquering dimension of colonial power is obliterated – silenced; and the audience can comfort themselves in the supposed 'civilisation mission' of the colonial project. What I wish to focus on is this creation of a new subject – this Indian District Officer. I want to ask what does this drive of colonial power mean for technologies of rule today? It would seem to me that to think about this aspect of rule might allow us to reconfigure a genealogy of power in which hegemony functions through desire and fantasy becomes the physical glue that maintains order.

There is an argument which many of us may be familiar with, that 'modernity' can be defined as the 'mobility of signs and commodities', the circulation of 'vast new amounts of visual imagery and information'.[7] It is an argument about quantity, about velocity and movement and in many ways, it is accurate. But what if these signs and commodities and I would add bodies are already marked by a certain historicity? What is being circulated? How do these signs and bodies become excessive, creating a knowledge regime which shapes our thinking?

It would seem to me that in the end what this archive on the 'end of empire' pushes us to do is to think about this historicity of those marked bodies alongside technologies of rule which shaped our world and leave traces that haunt our present.

NOTES

1. Timothy Mitchell, 'The World as Exhibition', *Comparative Studies in Society and History* vol. 31 no. 2, April 1989, p. 222.
2. Ibid., p. 220.
3. Mary Ann Doane, *The Emergence of Cinematic Time* (Cambridge, MA: Harvard University Press, 2002), p. 222.
4. Ibid., p. 82.
5. Cited in Robert Aldrich, *The Age of Empires* (London: Thames and Hudson, 2002), p. 302.
6. Stuart Hall, 'The Spectacle of the "Other"', in Stuart Hall (ed.), *Representation, Cultural Representations and Signifying Practices* (London: Sage, 2003), p. 241.
7. Doane, *The Emergence of Cinematic Time*, p. 79.

19

Perennial Empire: Its Ends Provide the Means for National Despotism in Lanka Even Today

Arjuna Parakrama

INTRODUCTION

In this brief essay I shall examine key tropes and themes of British documentary films on Ceylon, using Basil Wright's *The Song of Ceylon* (1934) as my symptomatic example *par excellence*, to demonstrate the core complicities between current postcolonial nationalist discourse and late colonialist imperial discourse on Ceylon/Sri Lanka. I seek to use this documentary to interrogate the following thesis which runs against the grain of both received wisdom and scholarly analysis: Rather than governing via the principle of 'divide and rule' (which may serve to empower minorities *vis à vis* the dominant majority), the British rulers (wittingly and unwittingly) pandered to majority ethnic and class elites, creating a reciprocal relationship which not only made colonial exploitation easier, but laid the foundation for the post-Independence nationalist hegemony of these elites in Sri Lanka. This, in turn, formed the bedrock discourse that is being employed today, sixty years after independence, to justify majoritarian dominance of a plural polity by privileging a single history, culture and religion.

The choice of Wright's documentary needs no justification since it has been seen both as magnificently sensitive to local culture and tradition, as well as unsympathetic to colonial orthodoxy. In fact, of the twenty or so scholarly texts I have read which discuss this film, few are less than adulatory of its cultural depth, and none is critical of its broader political stance. The following is typical:

> One of the finest achievements of the British documentary movement was Basil Wright's *The Song of Ceylon*, which has been called the world's finest example of lyrical documentary. The film's theme, as its producer John Grierson described it, is 'Buddhism and the art of life it has to offer, set upon by a Western metropolitan civilization which, in spite of all our skills, has no art of life to offer'.

> Graham Greene, reviewing the film when it played as the second feature in a London art theatre, described it as having an 'air of absolute certainty in its object and assurance in its method'.[1]

The Song of Ceylon serves as a template here to analyse the central categories that locate and circumscribe the broad overarching themes of history/historiography, religious and cultural values, and political economy.

'Divide and rule' suggests that non-dominant groups within the (Lankan) polity were provided opportunities pro-actively by the empire's modalities of 'governance'. Yet a much more seamless and mutually beneficial relationship seems to exist between the dominant elites and the colonial administrations. The point is that Wright's film charts the terrain of a mono-historical, mono-religious, mono-cultural Ceylon, which maps only the dominant Sinhala Buddhist sites to the exclusion of everything else. In the citation above, for instance, there is a slippage between 'Ceylon' and 'Buddhism', as if they had the same referent. Sinhala Buddhism becomes, in this sense, all that is valuable in Ceylon: endows it worth and pervades its domain. This exclusivist discourse of history, culture and economy is both a derivative of dominant Sinhala nationalism at the time as well as a valorisation of it, which in turn provides the basis of post-Independence domination.

Thus, Wright as sympathetic, sensitive observer of Ceylon participates in the systemic discursive exclusion of diversity, difference and plurality that was a hidden hallmark of British colonialism, and which laid the foundation for postcolonial majoritarianism.[2]

BACKGROUND

- North Indian Parsee theatre and other strands from India made up for the fact that the local traditions did not easily lend themselves to stage or screen. Thus, in the early twentieth century, urban public entertainment in Lanka was influenced, even driven, by non-nationalist ideologies and non-majoritarian worldviews.
- This 'external' and irreverent (non-traditional, non-religious, even countercultural) influence on dominant culture was frowned upon by the elites (ethnic, religious, cultural) and mainly embraced by urban middle- (and under-) class elements.
- Wright and others understood and espoused the fears of dominant elites, rejecting popular culture and public religion in favour of older rural cultural traditions, seen as *the only and uniformly followed traditions of all of Lanka*. It is this move to identify a single uniform strand of culture, history, tradition, religion and economy that constitutes the point of transition from empire to post-empire nationalism.

KEY TROPES AND CONCEPT METAPHORS

The following is a summary of the rhetoric of Wright's film which serves as a bridge and platform for the current *official* identity of Sri Lanka.

History

1. The country was 'covered with darkness' and evil until the arrival of (the Buddha and) Buddhism. The language of Thomas Knox, from his seventeenth-century book on Ceylon, was used to powerful effect here: 'in these days did men prostrate themselves by night to the honour and service of the devil' until the

'coming of the great god whom they call the Buddha', unto whom 'the salvation of souls belongs'. *Buddhism protects Lanka* and Lankans have a responsibility to safeguard the country from other religions, as entreated by the Buddha.

2. 'The Virgin Island' portrays *an idyllic society* with consensual and equitable division of roles and responsibilities that are mapped along occupation and caste lines. There is a romanticised and distorting (inaccurate) description of collective labour and sharing (in the paddy fields), as well as the half-truth of village-level self-sufficiency. Modernisation is then the perceived evil and disrupter of traditional equality and harmony. Caste and class oppression are non-existent in Wright's Ceylon. Traditional dance-teaching is focused upon bringing together continuity and excellence, social cohesion and mutual respect. This fits the 'simple' people model which combines innocence and tradition (the good side of Marx's Asiatic Mode of Production).

3. Hence, the 'Voices of Commerce' section is jarring, non-harmonious, even disruptive, both as text and sound/image. Commerce disrupts the old order and fosters exploitation. The continuous whine and worse of the machines and communication networks interfere with the text and images. Overlapping of word and image here engenders deliberate nonsense and jars on the eye and ear, in sharp contrast to the lyricism of the other three sections. The text here is not from Knox, and contains implicit criticism of language and context. There is a collage of disembodied voices, inappropriate and impersonal, as opposed to the laughing, friendly banter immediately preceding the section.

4. Attributes of modernisation such as upward mobility, widespread communication and technology are shown to be alien and divisive, inappropriate and exploitative. 'Modern' concepts such as democracy, it can be argued in this vein, are also not helpful in traditional contexts.

5. Caught in this trap of commerce, the traditional way of life is valorised and romanticised. The fourth section, 'The Apparel of a God' reverts back to spirituality seen as embodied in Kandyan dancing and drumming, which is driven home by the juxtaposition (even superimposition) of statues of the Buddha (Gal Vihare in Polonnaruwa and Samadhi in Anuradhapura). Traditional skills and crafts are tied to religious belief and become a part of living religion among these simple, contented people, in Wright's paternalistic discourse.

6. The film ends by going back to the beginning, to reiterate the potential doom from commercialisation and exploitation. (Marx's description of Romantic anti-capitalism is still the best analysis of this sort of rhetoric.)

Religion and culture

7. Buddhism itself is portrayed as a monotheistic religion, transforming a non-theistic philosophy into what Obeyesekera describes as 'Protestant Buddhism' with the key metaphors and concepts deriving from the Judaeo-Christian template; hence, the Buddha being described as a 'great god', as engaged in 'the salvation of souls', and 'from whom is derived the food of life'. (These

descriptions appear both at the beginning and towards the end of the documentary).

8. There is no space for any other local religious belief system, which means that either the Hindus, Muslims and Christians don't exist (in 1934, not 1680, even though they did even then) and/or they don't have the same legitimacy.

9. The history, traditions of value, cultural artefacts, sites of veneration, occupations, language and religion are all southern Sinhala-centric. Others, if they exist, are there by sufferance and therefore have no claims to equal ownership or rights.

Economy

10. Note that in all of the other occupational areas, labourers are shown as human beings – faces, smiles, interactions, beliefs, etc. – but in the entire footage on the tea plantation, not a single face is shown. Only backs, baskets, hands, groups and machinery. The Tamil tea-factory workers, unlike their Sinhala counterparts, are faceless, cultureless, history-less, religion- and language-less. The northern and eastern economies and the Muslim trading communities do not exist in Wright's Ceylon.

11. There is no space for education, development, change and no serious assessment of tradition vs modernisation.

Themes and ideologies

12. Sri Lanka is a Buddhist country, and it is Buddhism that created a pre-colonial golden age from the country's dark prehistory, which must be recovered now at all cost (to non-Buddhist outsiders). This Buddhism is made special because it is Sinhala (where Indian origins are acknowledged, but credit is given to the Sinhala culture for single-handedly shaping and nurturing Buddhism against a hostile world) See (1) and (2) above.

13. All that is best in culture and values derives from Buddhist roots and traditions. Thus, even the most exploitative caste and cultural practices are seen to be consensual and an integral part of the greater good. Non-Buddhist traditions and practices have no place in the new Sri Lanka, where there are only two ethnic groups: those who are Sinhala Buddhist and those who are opposed to Sinhala Buddhism. Many may be misguided in their alternative views and therefore need to be persuaded to see the light.

14. The history of Sri Lanka has been and will continue to be a struggle between the forces of good (Sinhala, Buddhist) and the forces of evil (non-Sinhala, non-Buddhist). Some 2,500 years of documented wars between Tamils (read India) and Sinhalas (read Lanka) demonstrate the problems encountered by the Sinhalese, which is the only nation practising the *proper* Buddhism in the world today. The concepts of Dhammadveepa and 'the nation besieged' are both products and justifications of this kind of thinking. Other religions and cultures have other

'homes' to go to, but not so the Sinhalas, the argument goes, so they have more at stake and must assert themselves more.

15. Western-led modernisation has brought with it the degradation of traditional values and practices. Democracy and human rights are Western conspiracies, which are not entirely appropriate for Sri Lanka today, where strong stable leadership is needed, much like during the time of the ancient kings during our pre-colonial golden age. See (4) above.

16. As long as the supremacy and innate superiority of Buddhism and Sinhala are recognised, there is perfect freedom for others to espouse other cultures, religions, languages, etc., but they should not test the tolerance of the infinitely tolerant Buddhists in doing so. See (8) above.

17. The Tamils in the plantations are labourers, aliens to this country, whose identity is tied to their work. They are not really people, and certainly have no say in their future. (The ability to generate conflict is, one should remember, a function of some level of empowerment, and hence they will remain docile for many more years, unlike the Tamils in the north and east of the country. See (10) above.

18. The model for governance in Sri Lanka today is centralised/despotic leadership and family bandyism (described as strong stable leadership with anti-Western rhetoric seen as national courage) as in the time of the ancient kings.

19. The complicities between empire's end and nationalism's beginning are well documented. Thirty years ago, it was fashionable to speak about the transition from colonialism to neocolonialism within the former colonies. Now globalised capital claims to have broken down the boundaries that confine the nation-state. It is paradoxical that the more the state disintegrates economically, the more it is reinforced politically.

20. Thus, documentary films on the last stages of colonial Ceylon provide a crucial record of how this paradigm shift from colony to independence is rhetorical more than real from the point of view of the marginalised and different.

NOTES

1. See <www.filmreference.com/Films-So-St/Song-of-Ceylon.html>.
2. The fact that Tamil and Muslim elites also dined at the Governor's table has been misunderstood to infer that the British 'divided and ruled' in Ceylon. These elites of all three groups were anglicised and even their occasional opposition to British rule was based on Western models and modalities. More importantly, the use of well-looked-after intermediaries from all three groups to govern the country says nothing about the way the country's history, etc. was perceived and reproduced in colonial discourse, which is what I'm seeking to describe in this paper.

20

Missing the End:
Falsehood and Fantasy in Late Colonial Cinema

Francis Gooding

Under a variety of pressures, geopolitical, financial and local, the decade that stretched between Ghana's Independence in 1957 to the loss of Aden ten years later saw the British empire effectively dissolve. By 1968, notwithstanding the status of Ian Smith's post-UDI Rhodesia, the largest and most ambitious imperial venture in human history was reduced to a mere rump, a far-flung global archipelago where just a decade prior there had been a near endless expanse of territory. In fact the period effectively opens with the Suez débâcle in 1956, Britain's final disastrous attempt at a unilateral show of force, but the end in all but name is surely the ignominious, desperate and violent scramble out of Aden in 1967 – a humiliation that brought to a close all major affairs east of Suez with the sole exception of Hong Kong.

The period is not a crisis of empire, a local paroxysm, but the final curtain. How do the British authorities, in the metropole and elsewhere, handle and display this unprecedented circumstance on film? Do films from this period accept the end of empire and represent it accurately? Or is the end of British colonial control registered, like so much else in colonial cinema, through the same distorting lens that habitually looked away when it claimed to look toward, that compulsively substituted bureaucratic fantasies for daily realities, and that sometimes peddled plain untruths?

In some ways the heyday of official colonial film-making continues into this period – the various local film units continue their work, often up to independence, producing films for the usual variety of purposes. Some remain effectively functional in one way or another after Independence – the Malayan Film Unit, for instance, with its high proportion of Malay and Chinese staff, was absorbed into the new government's Department of Information Services. Elsewhere they simply dissipate, mirroring the fate of the political entities that gave them sustenance: this was the case with the Central African Film Unit, which broke up on the demise of the Central African Federation.

But on the matter of what the films actually show and how they show it, we can take two concrete examples of films made in countries on the brink of Independence. First, a picture from Aden, one of the oldest and smallest colonies, not much more than a tiny city state, but of signal strategic importance due to its position at the mouth of the Red Sea. Second, a film made in Nigeria, the most populous country in the empire at this time, and the African colony which was viewed as having the greatest potential.

Aden of course had no official film unit; it was far too small, its polity too limited, its uses and potential too circumscribed to warrant any such thing. The colony features fairly irregularly on film, though during the worst and final years of the insurgency it appears with some regularity on television news programmes, especially Independent Television News's *Roving Report* news magazine. However, in 1965, when the unrest that would eventually force the British out was already very severe in the city's hinterland – the South Arabian Protectorates – it was the backdrop for a very interesting COI/MOD recruitment film, entitled *Routine Adventure* (1965), and it is to this film that I will turn shortly.

Nigeria, on the other hand, saw the continued production of films by the Nigerian Film Unit and related production outfits such as Information Services of Western Nigeria and Northern Nigerian Information Services. It is no surprise that, during the years up to 1960, these frequently deal with issues that bear directly on the extension of administrative responsibilities to Nigerians, convey positive messages about development in the colony or look directly at Independence. In films such as *Nigeria's First Women Police* (1956), *Self Government for Western Nigeria* (1958) and *Giant in the Sun* (1959), the imminent independence of Nigeria is heralded and celebrated through images of Nigerian self-sufficiency and competence. *Giant in the Sun* is of particular interest, as it celebrates the coming of self-governance to northern Nigeria, the last of the Nigerian provinces to gain this measure of self-determination, and thus also depicts the final administrative hurdle before full Nigerian Independence could be granted.

At the respective times that these two films, *Routine Adventure* and *Giant in the Sun*, were made, both Aden and Nigeria were on the cusp of liberation from British rule, and what is more important, both were heading for Independence in diametrically opposed ways. Aden was heading pell-mell for what would be total severance with Britain in circumstances of quite incredible political chaos and amid a violent insurgency so complex that it verged on civil war. By contrast, Nigeria was moving toward Independence as a member of the Commonwealth through what one might call the official channels, those that were sanctioned and overseen by London – even if some in the Colonial Office thought things were moving rather fast, and privately had their doubts.

What are the foci of British film-making in Aden and Nigeria as film-makers attempt to represent these different moments? We must look at what is represented and how, and view it with an eye on historical outcomes, trying to see whether these films are able to tell something resembling the truth, or if instead, as is so often the case, they imagine in detail an alternative world to the real one and present it fully formed, like a cuckoo in history's nest.

Routine Adventure was an RAF recruitment film, aimed primarily at school-age children, probably school leavers familiar with James Bond or *The Avengers* (TV, 1961) – there are numerous veiled references to such programmes in the film, not least that the commentary was voiced by a sometime member of *The Avengers* cast. The theatre chosen to display the exciting life of an RAF airman was the South Arabian Protectorates: the rugged mountainous hinterland of Aden, where successive attempts to impose British control over a variety of highly independent peoples had been continuously failing for decades, and where the military was involved in an unpleasant campaign against nationalist and tribal insurgents who were acting in part as Egyptian proxies. The film portrays this conflict as interminable, an endless struggle against 'rebels'. It is therefore an ideal conflict to indicate the routine, everyday nature of military adventure that awaits a prospective recruit – the daily flights that ferry soldiers and pilots from Aden to the frontlines are even likened to bus journeys into central London. War is like work, but more exciting. In a sense, the South Arabian mountains here take on the mantle of another mountainous Islamic region which existed in a state of more or less continual war under the empire, India's North West Frontier Province (NWFP).

The NWFP was a place where enemy contacts were guaranteed, a permanent conflict zone which was famously used for 'blooding' new recruits, refining counter-insurgency tactics and perfecting the niceties of frontier warfare. The military tactics developed in the NWFP were employed wholesale in the South Arabian Protectorates: road-building, air-dropped propaganda, piqueting and patrols with RAF back-up, and 'air policing'. Most of these tried and tested techniques of long-term attritional frontier conflict can be seen in *Routine Adventure*.

In the barren mountains of the Protectorates, war is presented as the ordinary, permanent state of affairs. Aden colony itself, on the other hand, is portrayed as an air-conditioned, civilised refuge where, at the end of a hard day, the returning soldier or airman might enjoy a cold beer on the beach. It is home, and the civilisation of cool air and alcohol is a world away from the tedious, interminable barbarian warfare of the mountains.

The image presented by the film thus resolves into a neat, durable set of expanding dualisms, epitomised by the title itself: routine/adventure, work/leisure, war/peace, hot/cold, barbarism/civilisation, city/country, and so on. The film's vision of the colony is structured by this binary flickering back and forth, a mental model as familiar and predictable as night and day.

However, in the real Aden of 1965, everything was about to end; there was no 'routine' by this stage, and the city itself was steadily turning into a pressure cooker of random deadly violence. The war in the Protectorates that the film shows as a workaday slog was directionless, unwinnable, and indeed being lost, and would shortly encroach on and engulf the city state. The film's unconscious recollection of the glory days of frontier soldiery in the Raj is the precise sign that what is being shown is not a reflection of reality, but a projection of desire. Colonial control in Aden was as good as finished within months of the film being made – and the approaching shadow of impending loss is dimly registered in a romantic trace memory of the Raj, the ultimate sign of imperial plenitude. The pathetic wish to emphasise the endlessness of the situation is a symptom of the imminent termination of that situation; the film indulges in an exciting fantasy of colonial permanence that is the disavowal – and thus the certain sign – of the coming real collapse.

The dream of permanence is also motivated by a compulsion to return to the colonial trauma of 1947, when the biggest and most vital part of the empire was lost. In Aden in 1965, as in India before it, the movement of events was only flowing one way and, as the city was finally overtaken by violence and chaos, the British scrambled out. In reality there was no endless back and forth from the front to the beach, from war to peace; as in the empire as a whole, there was only entropy. The film invents itself as the missing binary term, trying to restore what had been lost already, and trying to protect the colonial ego against what, inevitably, was going to be lost. As the first post east of Suez, and long the point on the map where the garrisoned Indian Army took control of imperial military matters, the loss of Aden is the event that truly signals the end of the British empire. Britain itself was involved in transitions, from being the possessor of a global empire to being a small European island, moving from world status to increasing irrelevance. *Routine Adventure* is a desperate wish that it was not so.

Turning to *Giant in the Sun*, we might ask what it shows by comparison. Quite unlike *Routine Adventure*, it claims to show and indeed celebrate the imminent end of imperial control, as the last of the Nigerian provinces gains the self-government that would give almost immediately onto full Nigerian Independence. This is a film about a fresh start, a new country that is about to make its way blinking into the sunlight as a fully grown 'giant', but which is still under British tutelage for now – a helping hand from an experienced friend is always welcome when one is just starting out, after all.

But independent Nigeria is just about to stand on her own two feet: there are Nigerian doctors, politicians, vets and scientists depicted here, and agriculture, development, and industry too, as well as the colourful panoply of the old traditional Nigeria that will be happily folded into the new nation. The age-old industries of pottery, fabric and glasswork are smoothly linked with modern mechanised industry and factory work. Political evolution is the mirror of technological improvement. Nigeria is moving out of the past, into a modern future. No doubt the fearsome complexity of the film's relationship with reality could bear sustained analysis in all of its aspects, but here we can look at just one short passage, the very brief reference to heavy industry, and more specifically to the mining industry of the Jos Plateau.

There is but one small sequence of this major heavy industry – significantly, the operator of the digging machine pictured in this sequence is European – and it is qualified by some very brief lines of dialogue, which include the assertion that mined land is reclaimed ('as in British open-cast sites, the soil is put back, and the land returned to agriculture'). As with the rest of the film – and the counterpoint with British mining makes this explicit – the clear implication is that the Nigerian mines will form an integral part of the new Nigerian state, like its doctors and vets. (There were certainly those within the Nigerian nationalist movement that wanted this.) The reality was actually somewhat different, and through looking at the records of one British tin-mining corporation, Bisichi Mining, a quite different picture emerges.

Bisichi specialised in tin mining on the Jos Plateau; at Independence it was one of the larger tin-mining corporations. In 1956–7 Bisichi bought up the Naraguta Tin Mines Company (the first British tin concern to be founded in Nigeria), and the period 1956–64 saw it consolidate its holdings, buying up numerous other companies and leases. In fact, it seems that the coming of Independence did not affect its operations at all. This is borne out by the figures: in 1959, it made a profit of £44,800, paying a shareholder dividend of 20 per cent; in 1960, £45,800 with a dividend of 22.5 per cent; and in 1961, as its new purchases came on stream in the newly independent Nigeria, it recorded a nearly quadruple profit of £193,200, paying a 25 per cent dividend. By 1964, this had increased to £240,000.[1]

This is what Bisichi's historian has to say about Independence for Nigeria:

These were good years for Bisichi; production was generally high, and substantial dividends were paid to reward shareholders for their loyalty … . Independence made little immediate impact on Bisichi's operations, or indeed on the life enjoyed by the Company's expatriate employees. For some years there were no restrictions on the transmission of funds, nor on the employment of expatriates; most of the senior positions in the Civil Service, police, army and the judiciary continued to be held by British citizens, many of whom, together with their families, devoted their working life to administering and developing the country. Ultimately independence had far-reaching consequences for the Company, as for all Plateau tin-mining concerns, leading, in Bisichi's case, to its eventual withdrawal from Nigeria and active mining and its resurrection as a mining finance house. *Yet so little was Bisichi affected at the time that in contemporary board minutes the word independence does not even appear.*[2]

Bisichi continued to do business in Nigeria until 1978, when legislation forced companies to limit foreign ownership to 40 per cent; at this point it effectively withdrew, and changed its business profile to property; however, it presently operates coal mines in South Africa, and is still a UK-registered company. In 2009, it recorded a gross profit of £5 million.[3]

Moving on to the statement that tin-mining land was reclaimed for agriculture, it will suffice to note that local practice appears to have been to store excavated topsoil, subsoil and overburden mixed indiscriminately, rather than separately as is the industry-recommended standard. The open casts were then filled with the mixture, again indiscriminately, making reclamation near impossible; the Jos Plateau was declared a 'disaster area' in 1982 by the state government and much of it remains poisoned, damaged land.[4]

So here again, in this small individual example – and perhaps a detailed analysis might find it repeated in one way or another throughout the film, in relation to industry, education or government – we have what appears to be a straightforward inversion of values; as with Aden, where decay and transience was configured as permanence, here the continuation of colonial era concerns is elided in favour of the narrative of newness, change and Independence. The reality of transnational business arrangements could never be addressed, and this is only a way of saying that the complex structure of the colonial edifice was not fully addressed by Independence in the form that came to Nigeria (at least not immediately). The kernel of dishonesty at the heart of the short sequence on the mines is flagged, unconsciously, by the presence of a white driver operating the vast digger, a fact which at once transforms the scene into a metaphor for the entire colonial enterprise, and also appears as a premonitory signal that seems to change the entire film into a demonstration of the mechanism of transition to post- and neocolonial economic orders. Nigerians will control Nigeria, the films says; but the white digger driver, puppeteer of his mechanised dinosaur, is the stowaway in the film, who indicates that in the boardrooms that control Nigerian wealth, Nigerian freedom is beneath mention.

It could be no other way of course. No film from this period could say to a British audience: our empire is finished, the men from the hills have beaten us and we must run for our lives, no more than any film could address a Nigerian audience with the message: the riches of your country will still belong to UK-registered mining companies, despite your independence. But these things – the Nigerian mines, the war in the Protectorates – could equally have been ignored: it is the compulsion to display them so prominently that is telling of their hidden meaning.

What is the net effect of these elisions, these pathological mis-statements of the case? As the empire dissolves, what function do they perform for film-makers, audiences, officialdom? Paul Gilroy has argued forcefully that the shock of losing the colonies in the decades after World War II was so severe that the celebrated memory of victory over the Nazis has come to function as a screen, shielding the British popular imagination from the pain of acknowledging Britain's decisive and ongoing loss of international prestige and power. The British never came to terms with the end of their empire. They never mourned their loss, preferring instead to take refuge in the heady mythology and endless details of the Battle of Britain, D-Day and other such decisive and rightfully celebrated events of World War II. One way of reading the strange disavowals and half-truths that structure British films from the end of empire is to see them as bedding in the process of repression and denial even before the loss is fully unfolded.

It may be that the process of 'mourning' the empire has not been so easy because, in films like these, we see consciousness of empire being riddled with amnesic blank spots, its outline softened and bruised by a dazzle of half-truths and misprisions. When it finally went to its death, it was already unknown, and the types of effect that burgeon and proliferate systematically in films from the very end of empire, the same phenomena which flare up with such mad dishonest verve in *Giant in the Sun* or *Routine Adventure*, had served to make it unknowable. Even before the empire had formally ended, the sense and direction of the colonial footprint were erased, the trail concealed, the door closed silently on the way out. And who mourns a stranger?

NOTES

1. Robert Mackilligan and Christopher Pick, *The Bisichi Story* (London, Bisichi Mining, 1994).
2. Ibid. Emphasis added.
3. See <www.bisichi.co.uk/>.
4. Michael J. Alexander, 'Reclamation after Tin Mining on the Jos Plateau Nigeria', *Geographical Journal* vol. 156 no. 1, March 1990, pp. 44–50, p. 45.

Index

Page numbers in **bold** denote extended/detailed treatment; those in *italic* refer to illustrations.